Display pop-up menu of parent folders

Close current folder (all open folders)   ⌘-W (⌘-Option-W)

Expand folder in list view (and its   ⌘-→ (⌘-Option-→)
subfolders)

Collapse folder in list view (and its   ⌘-← (⌘-Option-←)
subfolders)

Bring folder window to front   click title bar

Move background folder window   ⌘-drag title bar

Change order of files in list view   click label in window header

Deactivate all folder windows/activate   ⌘-Shift-↑
desktop

DIALOG BOX FUNCTIONS

Activate scrolling list/file name option box   Tab

Display contents of the desktop in   ⌘-D
scrolling list

Display contents of next (previously)   ⌘-→ (⌘-←)
mounted disk

Scroll one screen up (down)   Page Up (Page Down)

Scroll to the top (bottom) of the window   Home (End)

DUPLICATION AND DELETION

Cut selected text or image   ⌘-X

Copy selected text or image   ⌘-C

Copy selected icon at Finder   ⌘-D

Copy icon to new location on same disk   Option-drag

Paste a cut or copied item   ⌘-V

Delete selected text or image   Delete

Delete icon   drag to Trash folder

Delete locked icon   Option-choose Empty Trash

(Continued on inside back cover)

Rave reviews from readers of *Macintosh System 7: Everything You Need to Know*

"Was I lucky (or clever?) enough to buy a copy of *Macintosh System 7: Everything You Need to Know.* Great book! Thanks Deke. It is very well done and makes very enjoyable reading. I couldn't put it down!"

John Cole

"I'm glad you took the time and effort to go beyond the rehash of Apple's documentation that seems to be the standard fare for these System 7 books. I learned a few useful things just thumbing through your book, and I thought I knew just about everything about System 7! Good job!"

Dave Lamkins

"I'd like to take this opportunity to compliment you on your book *Macintosh System 7: Everything You Need to Know.* As a newcomer to the Macintosh, [I've found the book to be] quite helpful. I especially like your comments about various commercial and shareware utilities. It's a jungle out there what with the myriad of programs to choose from, and it has helped to have the guidance of an expert such as yourself."

Len Gilbert

"Your System 7 book is the best I've seen so far, in spite of the fact that it caused me to corrupt the system file for the first time since I've been using System 7. (Of course, it didn't *make* me do it—merely inspired me to start hacking away.) I like the way you use humor without seeming condescending, as too often instructional writers seem to do."

Thomas Rees

"You have made good on your title: your book was everything I needed to know and is now my most useful reference."

Jon Leonard

For a complete catalog of SYBEX publications:

SYBEX Inc.
2021 Challenger Drive, Alameda, CA 94501
Tel: (510) 523-8233/(800) 227-2346 Telex: 336311
Fax: (510) 523-2373

SYBEX®

MACINTOSH SYSTEM 7.1:
Everything You Need to Know

MACINTOSH® SYSTEM 7.1:
Everything You Need To Know
Second Edition

Deke McClelland

SYBEX®

San Francisco
Paris
Düsseldorf
Soest

Acquisitions Editor: Dianne King
Editors: Kenyon Brown, Kathleen Lattinville
Technical Editor: Celia Stevenson
Book Designer: Lisa Jaffe
Production Artist: Claudia Smelser
Screen Graphics: Cuong Le, Aldo Bermudez
Typesetter: Deborah Maizels
Production Editor: Carolina Montilla
Proofreader/Production Assistant: Kristin Amlie
Indexer: Anne Leach
Cover Designer: Ingalls + Associates
Cover Illustration: Max Seabaugh

ACKNOWLEDGMENTS

My heartfelt thanks go out to the following people, without whose help I could not have written this book:

The incomparable Melissa Rogers, for proving a general wealth of information and a pal (and to John Stroud for introducing me to her).

Gifford Calenda, for being talked into writing the foreword to this book.

Other folks at Apple (and Claris), including Ricardo Batista, Pace Bonner, Ian Hendry, Jeff Miller, and Bryan Ressler, for their products and advice.

The wonderful folks at Adobe and UserLand, including LaVon Collins, Terry O'Donnell, Linne Garell, Alice Lankester, and Judi Lowenstein.

Kevin Aitken, Luis Bardi, Don Brown, Steve Christensen, Bill Goodman, David Lamkins, Greg Landweber, Robert Mathews, Robert Polic, Mike Puckett, Melissa Rogers, Chris Sanchez, Jeffery Shulman, Adam Stein, and Marcio Luis Teixeira for contributing products that are included on the disks offered at the back of this book.

Sara and Ken Abbott of Abbott Systems, Rick Barron of Affinity Microsystems, David Schargel of Aladdin Systems, Jim O'Gara and Meaghan Hogan of Altsys, Russ McCann of Ares Software, Jeffery Sauve of Berkeley Systems, Judy Frey of Casady & Greene, Sue Nail and Debbie Hess of Central Point Software, CE Software, Renée Risch of Claris, Debra Young of CompuServe, Greg Hale of Connectix, Stephen Lovett of Dubl-Click Software, Trudy Edelson and Tricia Chan of Farallon Computing, Jerry Saperstein of FontBank, Brian Coleman of Mainstay, Kim Haas of McClaine Public Relations, Chris Walke of Microcom, Fran Knight of Microlytics, Lori Mueller of Microseeds Publishing, Lynn Halloran of Now Software, Kevin McGrath of Software Ventures, Jermaine Ward of Symantec, Jay Bartlet at Tactic Software, Linda Kaplan of Thought I Could, and Bill Monk of ZMac for agreeing to submit their products for inclusion in this book and generally doing their corporate thing.

Craig Danuloff and the PRI, Inc. crowd—R.D., J.G., S.R., J.M., A.E.—whose initials tend to vary from one book to the next. I believe this is number 22.

Ken Brown at SYBEX, for remaining patient and taking my side.

John Duane for loaning me *Inside Mac VI* ("The Weapon") and finally going out and purchasing a new copy for himself.

Elizabeth Pheasant for her unending supply of help and support. Watch for her three-volume autobiography *The Work of the Corporate Slave is Never Done*, *I See Years of Laundry Stretching Out Before Me*, and *I'd Walk a Mile for a Bottle of André's*.

CONTENTS AT A GLANCE

Contents

Chapter 4 Running Software in the New Multitasking Environment   85

Chapter 5 Using TrueType and PostScript Fonts   111

**Chapter 6   Using Desk Accessories and Other
System Utilities   163**

**Chapter 7   Customizing the Finder Desktop—
Aliases and Other Techniques   247**

Chapter 8   Organizing, Categorizing, and Locating Files on Your Hard Drive   285

Chapter 9   Expanding and Managing Application Memory   315

FOREWORD

System 7 is the most significant revision to system software since the development of the original Macintosh operating system. In the first six months, over 1,000,000 Macintosh users upgraded to System 7. Not only that, most of the major applications now take advantage of the full range of System 7's new features.

If you're not yet using System 7, you're missing out on much of the power provided by your Mac. System 7 is the first operating system for any personal computer to offer built-in networking, virtual memory, scalable fonts and a protocol by which different programs can communicate with each other. If you aren't yet using System 7, I strongly encourage you to upgrade.

If you are using System 7, you'll find that this book stands out as an accurate and complete reference. Deke McClelland has taken the time required to get the facts straight.

In fact, *Macintosh System 7.1: Everything You Need to Know* is just that. Deke dishes out an inexhaustible supply of information mixed with common sense, humor, and hundreds of insightful figures. Seldom can you gain such a useful education and enjoy yourself at the same time.

Best of all, Deke has taken the real world into consideration. As a regarded Macintosh expert, he explores not only System 7, but also how it works with other programs and utilities. In the course of reading this book, you'll discover inexpensive, sometimes free programs that will dramatically enhance the already powerful System 7.

Read this book, and you'll fall in love with the Mac all over again.

Gifford Calenda
Director, Macintosh System Software
Distinguished Technologist
Apple Computer, Inc.

INTRODUCTION

I hate introductions. I hate reading them, and I hate writing them. In fact, I've never met anyone who will even admit to having read an introduction. Face it, you've got better things to do with your time than read about why I decided to write this book.

> **In this book, the term "System 7" includes System 7, System 7.01, and System 7.1.**

So let's skip the prose and get to the facts. This book is about the new Macintosh system software, known as System 7. If you're already using System 7, this book will help you become more familiar with both your system software and your Macintosh computer. It's my intention that the book will enable you to work faster and—perhaps more importantly—work less. If you aren't yet using System 7, this book explains why it's about time you switched over and helps to smooth over some of the rough spots that arise during any transition. If you've already purchased a System 7 book, you'll find that my book serves as an ideal companion volume, packed with the kind of details that simply won't fit into an introductory volume. In fact, this book contains every snippet of information I was able to beg, borrow, or steal about System 7. I swear it.

If you find yourself wishing you had some of the freeware and shareware utilities I talk about throughout the following chapters, you can send off for the four-disk collection advertised at the back of the book. I've handpicked each utility based on its capacity to enable you to exploit System 7 more conveniently and efficiently. There's even a few TrueType and PostScript fonts to expand your collection. Note that I've used high-density disks so that I can include as many programs as possible on as few disks as possible. If your computer can't read high-density disks, please include a note with your order requesting 800K disks.

WHAT'S INSIDE

I have organized this book into twelve chapters and four appendices:

- *Chapter 1: The System 7.1 Primer* defines the purpose of any system software and covers how to work in System 7 specifically.

- *Chapter 2: Starting Up System 7.1* explains how to install System 7 onto your computer's hard drive and begin using its new capabilities.

- *Chapter 3: Exploring the Finder—the Macintosh Control Center* explains every single function related to the new Macintosh Finder, the portion of the system software devoted to naming, viewing, and organizing folders and files.

- *Chapter 4: Running Software in the New Multitasking Environment* describes how to use multiple programs at a time to write documents, balance numbers, and organize data simultaneously. Error handling tips are also included.

- *Chapter 5: Using TrueType and PostScript Fonts* takes the fear out of using typefaces by explaining every nuance associated with installing and using both TrueType and Post-Script fonts. PostScript and TrueType fonts are also compared so you can make informed purchasing decisions.

- *Chapter 6: Using Desk Accessories and Other System Utilities* is the longest chapter in the book, covering the use of every system utility included with System 7. Specialty programs such as keyboard layouts, language scripts, and Fkeys are also explained.

- *Chapter 7: Customizing the Finder Desktop—Aliases and Other Techniques* covers the use of aliases, custom icons, desktop patterns, startup screens, and anything else that can be used to customize the appearance and performance of your Macintosh system software.

- *Chapter 8: Organizing, Categorizing, and Locating Files on Your Hard Drive* takes a hard look at your hard drive, the file cabinet of your computer. I examine techniques used to label files, locate files on disk, and protect files from being read or damaged by other users.

- *Chapter 9: Expanding and Managing Application Memory* explains one of the most complicated issues related to personal computing—random access memory. Here you'll learn how to expand your supply of RAM and use it effectively to eliminate out-of-memory errors and provide speedier data processing.

- *Chapter 10: Inside the System 7-Savvy Application* looks at ways in which software manufacturers have and will implement new capabilities provided with System 7. The most prominent discussions revolve around the Edition Manager, which allows you to share portions of a document with other users and change their documents as you change yours.

- *Chapter 11: Inter-Application Communication—the Future of Mac Program Integration* covers Apple events, the protocol employed by System 7-savvy applications to communicate with each other and share functions. I'll also introduce AppleScript and Frontier, two up-and-coming scripting environments that will revolutionize the way software interacts on a Macintosh computer.

- *Chapter 12: Sharing Data over a Network* examines System 7's built-in networking capabilities. Whether you use a LocalTalk, Ethernet, or token ring network, System 7 allows you to swap data with other users more quickly and more efficiently. You can even hook up with different models of computers, including IBM PCs.

- *Appendix A: QuickTime* discusses how to use the QuickTime extension that now comes with System 7.1.

- *Appendix B: At Ease* takes you through this easy-to-learn alternative to the Finder that is included with System 7.1.

- *Appendix C: Application Creator Codes* lists every application registered with Apple Computer according to creator code. This is useful for matching documents with the software that created them.

- *Appendix D: Featured Products and Vendors* lists every vendor whose software is featured in the book complete with address, phone number, and retail price.

A FEW CONVENTIONS

Throughout this book, you will occasionally see a margin icon that highlights special information printed on a gray background. However, to make this convention more meaningful, I employ it sparingly, only when a paragraph of text absolutely *must* be called to your attention. Three icons are used in this book:

> **Tips.** Computer journals are oversaturated with tips, most of them little more than commonsense observations. It is my sincere intention that the tips in this book will actually improve your ability to operate your computer.

> **Warnings.** No computer is foolproof, not even the Macintosh. To help you avoid some of the pitfalls I've encountered, I include warnings.

Notes. This icon calls attention to special notes related to the current topic. Neither tips nor warnings, notes cover additional information that you will want to keep in mind when using System 7.

To the best of my knowledge, the icons make up the only unusual conventions used in this book. I also make a point of duplicating the exact wording and capitalization of the menu commands, options, and dialog boxes you will encounter when using System 7, allowing you to easily compare my explanations to what you see on-screen. And because no thousand of my words can rival a picture, I use figures liberally throughout, accompanied by captions that explain—rather than merely label—what you're looking at.

To the best of my knowledge, every word in this book is accurate. It has been technically reviewed by both novices, Macintosh authorities, and Apple employees alike. But despite my precautions, I'm sure something somewhere was missed. If you have any comments or criticisms you would like to share, please write to me at the following address:

Deke McClelland
1911 11th Street, Suite 210
Boulder, CO 80302

If you subscribe to an online bulletin board service, I can also be reached at the following addresses:

CompuServe: 70640,670
America Online: DekeMc

Thank you for your purchase. I hope you find the book helpful.

The
System 7.1
Primer

THE OTHER DAY I asked a friend of mine
if she were using System 7. She answered
that no, of course she wasn't. Her reasons were simple: Everyone knows
you're not supposed to upgrade your Macintosh system software until at
least three or four months after it's been released. By then, Apple has had
enough time to iron out the worst of the bugs, and third-party developers
have released updates that make their software compatible. In the meantime, there wasn't any System 7 feature that she needed so much as to
risk upsetting the delicate balance she had established on her computer.
She was trying to get work done, not keep up with the latest fad.

There's absolutely nothing wrong with this argument. In fact, it's
probably much safer to wait awhile than to do what I do, which is to jump
head first into the newest junk I can get my hands on, slap it onto my
hard drive, and hope for the best. In the long run, my methods also
work, but they require more attention to detail, versatile work methods,
and an awful lot of screwing around.

Whether you're a mild-mannered user just trying to do your job or
Captain Macintosh, Master of the Computer, the time has come to
upgrade your Macintosh system software.

Macintosh System 7.1: Everything You Need to Know is designed to help
you every step of the way, from installing the System 7 to mastering its
new features. It is, in fact, the first book to address the needs of intermediate and advanced System 7 users, while at the same time offering all
the basic information required to accelerate the skills of beginning users.
In a sense, this book guides you from Kindergarten to your Senior year
at a comfortable pace that should leave you less bewildered and substan-
tially better informed than when you started.

> **Throughout this book, references to System 7 encompass System 7.0, System 7.01, and System 7.1. References to System 7.1 indicate a new feature found only in System 7.1.**

Every chapter is divided into three primary sections:

Getting Started   Few of us like to spend hours reading through a book before we feel like we can begin using a piece of software. System software is no different. Every chapter in this book begins with a series of steps designed to get you up and running with a specific aspect of System 7. If you're a tactile learner, these initial steps will lead you to a point where you can experiment a little and see what happens. If you run into problems, read the next section for additional information.

Learning Fundamental Concepts   This section contains all the basic information you'll need to understand and operate System 7. If you've been reluctant—or even downright scared—to use System 7 because you thought it would be hard to learn, this section will dispel your anxieties. The text is straightforward; the information is clear and sensible.

Exploring Advanced Topics   After you get to know System 7, you may begin to wonder what all the fuss is about. This section will show you just how powerful your Macintosh computer can be. In addition to specific information aimed at intermediate- and advanced-level users, I'll suggest keyboard shortcuts and operating tricks that will allow you to navigate within the system more quickly and efficiently. Also, should you encounter problems using fonts, virtual memory, or system utilities, look to this section for the answers. Many chapters will offer specific advice and discuss late-breaking advances found in updated or upcoming versions of System 7.

If you're anxious to get started using your new system software, skip ahead to Chapter 2 which describes how to install the software. If you want to learn more about System 7, read on.

Touring the Macintosh
▬ Operating System

You turn on your computer and it works. If you want to use a word processor, spreadsheet, or other piece of *application software* (also called an *application* or *program*), copy that software to your hard disk, start it up, and away you go. When you're finished typing a letter or balancing an account, save the file to disk and print it out.

Sound pretty easy? It is from a user standpoint. But none of this would be possible without an *operating system,* also called the *system software.* The Macintosh system software provides an essential link between you, your computer (or CPU—*central processing unit*), the current application, and supplementary hardware including the mouse, keyboard, hard drive, monitor, printer, scanner, memory chips, and so on, as shown in Figure 1.1.

FIGURE 1.1

The system software provides essential links between the user, the CPU, the application software, and accessory hardware devices.

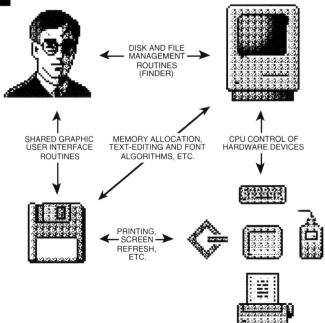

DISK AND FILE
MANAGEMENT
ROUTINES
(FINDER)

SHARED GRAPHIC
USER INTERFACE
ROUTINES

MEMORY ALLOCATION,
TEXT-EDITING AND FONT
ALGORITHMS, ETC.

CPU CONTROL OF
HARDWARE DEVICES

PRINTING,
SCREEN
REFRESH,
ETC.

HOW THE SYSTEM IS ORGANIZED

Some of the Macintosh operating system is stored on your computer's permanent memory chips, called ROM (*read-only memory*). Representing the core of the operating system, this information is vigilantly protected by Apple to prevent other companies from developing true Macintosh clones. It handles the most fundamental operations of the Macintosh computer by managing external hardware devices, screen display, and the manner in which applications and other files are stored in memory and written to disk. A special portion of the ROM-based operating system called the *Toolbox* offers a collection of graphic routines that allow any piece of software—including the system software itself—to quickly draw windows, create dialog boxes, handle fonts, and perform basic text editing functions.

Since ROM-based data may not be manipulated, this portion of the system software can be updated only by physically replacing the ROM chips on your computer's logic board, an expensive and intricate proposition. For this reason, the majority of the system software is distributed on disk and loaded into your computer's variable memory chips, called RAM (*random-access memory*, or more aptly *read/write memory*). This is the portion of the operating system that you will replace when you install System 7.

Note that Apple also periodically updates and fixes portions of the ROM-based operating system by including special *patch routines* with the disk-based system. Patch routines instruct the CPU to bypass specific instructions included in ROM in favor of the updated routine loaded into RAM. For example, System 7 includes patches that allow applications to scale TrueType fonts, access color scroll bars and menu icons, display 24-bit color images, and so on.

WHAT THE SYSTEM INCLUDES

It boggles the mind to think about all the things your system software does. But lucky for you, you don't have to. The system performs its tasks seamlessly and with only a handful of basic instructions from you.

Much of this is due to the *modular* composition of the Macintosh system software. Rather than a single file, the system software comprises an entire folder of files working in tandem. You may customize the performance of your system by adding, deleting, and altering specific files in the aptly named *System Folder.* These files include the following:

- **System.** The *System* file is the first of the two key files that make up the disk-based portion of the Macintosh operating system. It contains the system code and patch routines discussed earlier, as well as two kinds of *resources,* which are files made available to all applications. The first resource is the *font* (typeface) file, which acts as a means of displaying and printing text from any application. The second resource is the *sound* file, which determines the noises produced by the computer in order to alert the user, much like the horn on a car. (Two other varieties of resources, *desk accessories* and *function keys,* were reappraised in System 7. Desk accessories, also called DAs, now run as independent applications. Function keys, or Fkeys, have been abandoned.)

- **Finder.** On its own, the System file communicates with applications and hardware, but it can't communicate with the user. This is the job of the System's mouthpiece, the *Finder,* which is actually an independent piece of application software, just like HyperCard or Microsoft Word. The Finder *desktop* appears immediately after you start up your Mac. It acts as the home base from which you can launch applications, view the contents of disks and hard drives, and rename, organize, duplicate, and delete files.

Both the System and Finder files are essential to using a Macintosh computer. The following files represent optional elements of the system software:

- **System utilities.** This category of software is often called *desk accessories.* But in the context of System 7, I prefer the term *system utilities,* since such software now operates virtually identically to any other *utility* (a variety of application software that performs a few select functions). The most important system utility is the Chooser, which provides access to printer and network drivers (discussed below). Lesser utilities include the Alarm Clock, Calculator, Key Caps, and Scrapbook. Though not technically a desk accessory, the Print-Monitor also qualifies as a system utility, sending files to PostScript and QuickDraw printers while another application runs in the foreground.

- **Drivers.** *Drivers,* also called *Chooser extensions,* act as interpreters that allow your computer to communicate accurately with printers and networking systems, such as AppleTalk and Ethernet. For example, the LaserWriter file is a printer driver that translates instructions from the QuickDraw screen format to the PostScript printer language. All drivers are selected using the Chooser system utility.

- **System extensions.** Previously known as *inits, system extensions* (or just plain *extensions*) expand or modify the performance of the system software. Extensions are loaded into your computer's memory along with other portions of the disk-based system software during the startup procedure. Many extensions provide icons that are displayed along the bottom of your screen as they are loaded.

- **Control panels.** Once called *Control Panel devices* (*cdevs* for short), *control panels* are now independent utilities that expand or modify the performance of the system software or control some aspect of the CPU or a supplemental hardware device. Like system extensions, many control panels are loaded into memory when starting up your Mac. Unlike system extensions, control panels may be opened to display a window of options that govern the performance of a feature or piece of hardware. For example, you may use the General Controls control panel to change the time, date, or desktop pattern.

■ **Support files.** This is a generic term for the files frequently required for the successful operation of system utilities, extensions, and control panels. These files may contain preference settings or essential data. The most common example of a support file is the *Clipboard* file, which offers access to pictures or text transferred to the memory-resident Clipboard using the Cut or Copy command.

Many of the system files listed above are organized into one of several predefined subfolders within the System Folder. Specific descriptions of these folders are the subject of Chapter 6.

USING YOUR MAC

To understand the information covered in this book, you'll need to understand how to interact with your computer and be aware of some basic Macintosh terminology. The following sections provide the briefest of all possible introductions.

THE KEYBOARD

To interact with your computer, you use your keyboard and mouse. By pressing one or more keys on the keyboard, you communicate textual information and automated instructions. If you've used a typewriter, you'll recognize the standard key set, as well as Tab and Return. You press Shift plus a letter or number key to get capitals and special characters—@, $, %, &, and so on. (Press Caps Lock to get capital letters, but not special characters.) Other special characters may be accessed by pressing Option plus a key, or both Shift and Option plus a key.

The Command (⌘), Control, and the Function keys across the top of the keyboard (if any) serve a different purpose. You press Command and/or Control plus a key or press a single Function key to perform a predetermined operation. For example, by pressing ⌘-P—that is, simultaneously pressing Command plus the P key—prints a file. Many keyboard operations are determined by the current software, whether it be the Finder or another application. Other keyboard operations may be as-signed using a *macro* utility such as MacroMaker, QuicKeys, or Tempo.

THE MOUSE

Use your mouse to move items on-screen, perform simple operations, and draw. Moving your mouse moves the arrow-shaped *cursor* on your computer screen. Pressing and releasing the mouse button—also called *clicking*—selects items so they may be manipulated. Clicking twice in rapid succession—*double-clicking*—opens a selected item. Pressing and holding the mouse button while moving the mouse—called *dragging*—moves the selected item to a different part of the screen.

The mouse and keyboard may be used in tandem. For example, pressing the Shift key while clicking allows you to select multiple items. In fact, such actions are so common that key and mouse operations may be joined into a compound verb, as in *Shift-clicking* or *Option-dragging*.

MENUS AND COMMANDS

Each of the words across the top of the screen is a menu. Drag on a menu (press and hold the mouse button on a word and drag downward) to display a list of *commands,* each of which performs a specific function. When the appropriate command becomes *highlighted*—white against a black background—release your mouse button to perform the operation indicated by the command. This procedure is known as *choosing* a command.

Choosing a command followed by a right-pointing arrowhead displays a *submenu* of additional related commands. Drag onto the sub-menu, then drag up or down the menu until the desired command is highlighted. If the entire submenu cannot display on screen, an up-pointing and/or down-pointing arrowhead icon will display; additional commands scroll into view as you drag up or down. If a command ap-pears gray—also called *dimmed*—that command is not applicable to the current situation and may not be chosen.

DIALOG BOXES AND OPTIONS

If a command is followed by an ellipsis (...), such as Page Setup..., choosing the command causes a *dialog box* to appear, as shown in Figure 1.2. The dialog box is the system software's way of requesting additional information before executing the command.

Dialog boxes request information by presenting a variety of options. Your response to each option determines the manner in which the command is eventually executed. Figure 1.2 shows the five kinds of options that may appear:

- **Radio button.** Only one round radio button within a set of radio buttons may be selected at a time. To select a radio button, click on the button or on the option name that follows. A selected radio button is filled with a black dot; a deselected radio button is hollow.

- **Option box.** An option for which you must enter data is called an option box. Double-clicking an option box highlights its contents. When the contents of an option box are highlighted, they may be replaced by entering new values from the keyboard. If a dialog box contains multiple option boxes, press the Tab key to advance from one option box to the next.

- **Check box.** Any number of check boxes within a set of check boxes may be selected at a time. Like a radio button,

FIGURE 1.2

The Page Setup dialog box presents five kinds of options that request additional information.

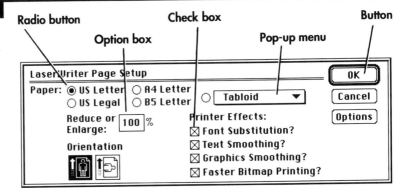

a check box may be selected by clicking on the box or on the option name that follows. Clicking on a selected check box deselects the option. A selected check box is filled with an X; a deselected check box is empty.

- **Pop-up menu.** To conserve space, some multiple-choice options may appear as pop-up menus. Click and hold on the shadowed box to display a menu of option choices. Drag to highlight the desired option and release your mouse button to select it.

- **Button.** Not to be confused with the radio button, the button allows you to close the current dialog box or display others. For example, click the Cancel button to close the dialog box and cancel the current command. Click OK to close the dialog box and execute the command according to the current settings. A button surrounded by a heavy outline will execute when you press the Return or Enter key.

There's more, of course, but this should be enough to get you started. If you want to really get to know your Mac, a variety of good books are available on the subject, including *The Little Mac Book* (Peachpit Press, 1991), *Inside Macintosh* (Simon & Schuster, 1990), and *Encyclopedia Macintosh* by Craig Danuloff and myself (published by SYBEX, 1990).

SYSTEM 7 (INCLUDING 7.1)

The System 7 generation of the Macintosh operating system is arguably the most dramatic enhancement since the debut of the first Mac. If you are familiar with previous versions of the System software, or even if you aren't, you may want to take a moment and read through the features offered by System 7. Each enhancement is described in depth in later portions of this book. For specific information on any feature, consult the index.

- **Balloon Help.** After choosing the Show Balloons command, you may display online help for tools, commands, and other features inside compatible applications simply by pointing to them with your cursor.

- **TrueType fonts.** This new font format competes directly with the popular PostScript format. A single font file is required, providing outlines that may be displayed on screen and printed at any size.

- **File sharing.** Files and folders can be shared between two or more Macs, or even between a Mac and a PC connected with AppleTalk cables, without relying on a dedicated server or communications software.

- **Edition Manager.** One application can *publish* selected material by saving the selection to disk as an *edition* file. A second application can then *subscribe* to it; that is, import the material with a "live" link to the original file. If and when you update the original published data, the document that subscribes to the corresponding edition file will be updated as well.

- **Apple Events.** Applications can share not only files, but also capabilities. For example, using IAC (*Inter-Application Communication*)-compatible software, you might ask the spell checker in a word processor to examine selected text in the current drawing application. The IAC acts as a language of commands—or events—by which different applications can communicate with each other.

- **16-million color display.** System 7 integrates the 32-Bit QuickDraw file shipped with System 6.0.3, allowing you to display over 16 million colors simultaneously when using a 24-bit video card.

- **Virtual memory.** *Virtual memory* allocates space on your hard disk to simulate RAM. Any computer with at least a 68020 processor and a PMMU chip can access 14MB of virtual memory or more.

- **32-bit addressing.** Computers with *32-bit clean ROMs*—including only the Mac IIsi, IIci, and IIfx—can address up to 128MB of RAM (16 times the previous maximum of 8MB) and over 1,000MB of virtual memory.

- **Multitasking.** System 7 eliminates the distinction between Finder and MultiFinder, allowing you to open more than one application at all times. Regardless of the current application, the Finder application runs in the background. System 7 also provides true *multitasking* capabilities, allowing you to copy large files, print multi-page documents, and perform other time-consuming tasks while using another piece of software in the foreground. You may also hide background applications, allowing you to prevent your desktop from becoming too cluttered.

Multitasking is only one major improvement made to the Macintosh Finder. In fact, the improvements made to the Finder are so numerous as to deserve a list of their own:

- **Installing resources.** Sounds may be installed into the System file by drag-copying. Fonts may be installed into the Fonts folder by drag-copying, eliminating the need for Font/DA Mover. Desk accessories now run as independent applications.

- **Control panels.** Control panels are now independent utilities that are opened directly rather than going through the now-defunct Control Panel desk accessory. The Control Panel that you see under the Apple menu is in fact an alias of the Control Panel folder found in the System Folder. For more about aliases, see Chapter 7.

- **Color icons.** Any icon at the Finder level may include up to 256 colors. You may create custom icons by drawing them in a paint program and pasting them into the Info dialog box (accessed by choosing the Get Info command).

- **Get Info.** Comments entered into an Info dialog box may be displayed in any Finder directory window, allowing you to easily convey information about a file to other users or to a service bureau. You may also use the Info dialog box to convert a document to a *stationery pad,* which acts as a master file from which new documents may be created without overwriting the original file.

- **Labels.** The Colors menu has been changed to the Label menu, offering both colors and key-word identifiers. Colors and identifiers may be changed using the Labels control panel.

- **Views.** The Views control panel permits you to alter the way files are displayed at the Finder level. You may change the font and type size used for file names and icon labels. You may also control the display of information such as labels and comments in the Finder window.

- **Windows.** When viewing the contents of a disk or folder by *list view* (by Name, by Size, by Kind, and so on), icons display to the left of each file name. Click the triangle icon that precedes a folder name to display the contents of that folder in hierarchical outline form. You may also click a header name to reorganize files according to size, date, label, and so on. You may drag-copy a file from a background window without bringing it to the foreground. Finally, windows scroll both vertically and horizontally, and dragging a file beyond the boundaries of a window causes it to scroll automatically.

- **Desktop button.** The document selection and document destination dialog boxes (accessed by choosing the Open and Save commands, respectively, from any application software) provide a new Desktop button that displays all files, folders, and disks located on the Finder desktop, making it easier to select between multiple disks or file servers. You may even access the contents of the Trash folder (discussed next).

- **Trash folder.** The Trash icon now acts very much like a standard folder. You may copy files from the Trash and even open them. Files in the Trash will not be deleted until you choose the Empty Trash command, even if you turn off your computer. The Trash icon may also be moved to any location on the desktop.

- **File search.** The Find command searches the contents of any specified disk or file server by name, by size, by comment... even by whether or not its locked. The amazingly swift search operation concludes by opening the specific folder that contains the found file and selecting it. Choose Find Again to continue the search. Alternatively, you may display all files that match the specified criteria at once.

- **Drag-opening.** Drag a document icon onto a compatible application icon to open the document in the specified application, whether or not it was originally created in that application.

- **Aliases.** You may duplicate the icon for an application, document, or folder to create an *alias* that tracks the location of the original file. The alias may be moved to any location, such as the Apple Menu Items folder, but it will never lose track of the original file, even if the original is moved. Multiple aliases may be created for a file, allowing it to act as if it is in several places at once.

- **System Folder subfolders.** If you place an application or its alias in the Startup Items folder inside the System Folder, that application will launch automatically when you start up your computer. Applications placed in the Apple Menu Items folder will display as commands under the Apple menu, as if they were desk accessories.

System 7.1 also offers the QuickTime system extension that allows you to integrate movies into your applications. QuickTime is discussed in Appendix A. Appendix B describes another System 7.1 enhancement— At Ease—an easy-to-use alternative to the Finder.

Just in case you're wondering, many of these features far exceed those provided by MS-DOS—the operating system for IBM-PC and compatible computers. Despite the fact that DOS 5.0 received rave reviews for providing enhanced memory capabilities (breaking the 640K barrier) and increased operating speed, *InfoWorld*—one of the most respected computer industry publications, though often accused of bias in favor of the PC—awarded System 7 a score of 8.2, compared to DOS

5.0's score of 6.8 (on a scale of 1 to 10, 10 being the highest). More than any other single aspect, System 7 has got to make you glad you own a Macintosh computer.

You should read on to find out how you can put the Mac's most powerful operating system to date to work for you.

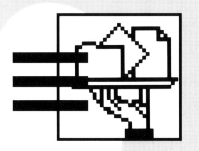

Starting
Up
System 7.1

WHEN YOU REACH for the power switch ▬▬ to turn on your Macintosh computer, you probably don't give it much thought. But what you're really doing when you flip that switch is turning on your Macintosh hardware and loading its system software. For those of you interested in the inside scoop, here's how it works:

The surge of electricity generated by turning on the computer zaps the CPU chip, waking it up like the buzzer on an alarm clock. Immediately, the CPU performs the only function it knows how to perform without consulting other parts of the computer: It grabs a predetermined line of information from ROM—always the same one—reads it, and follows the instructions. Its first instruction is to enact a series of diagnostic tests to make sure that the computer's internal hardware is fully operational, much as if the first thing you were to do in the morning was take your blood pressure and pop a thermometer in your mouth.

The CPU's next instruction is to look for a *startup disk* that contains a System Folder. It first checks the floppy drives. If there's no disk there, it searches for a hard drive. Once a System Folder is found, the happy Mac icon appears, as shown in Figure 2.1. The CPU loads portions of the system software from the System file into RAM, where it can be directly accessed by the CPU during the subsequent operation of the computer. Extensions and control panels are also loaded into RAM, as indicated by the appearance of icons along the bottom of the screen.

Finally, the system instructs the CPU to run its first application of the day, the Finder. The startup process concludes with the display of the Finder desktop, as shown in Figure 2.2. The Finder acts as a base from which you can run other applications, copy files, and perform other disk-management tasks.

FIGURE 2.1

The happy Mac icon appears after the CPU locates the system software.

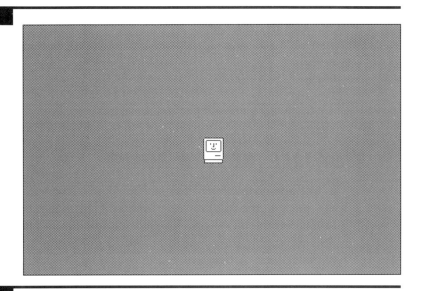

FIGURE 2.2

The Finder desktop is displayed when the Finder is up and running.

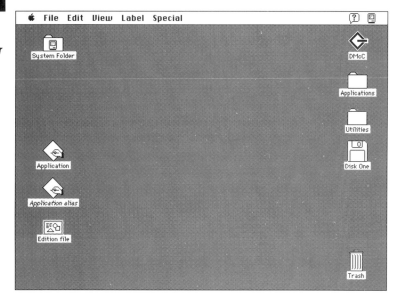

Before you can use System 7.1, you must *install* it on your hard drive so that it gets loaded each time you turn on your Macintosh. A one-time operation, installing System 7.1 removes the existing version of system software from your hard drive, but leaves all of your other inits, cdevs, utilities, and other applications intact.

Getting Started
—

There are two ways to install System 7.1: the quick automatic way, detailed here, and the more laborious method, covered in the *Learning Fundamental Concepts* section. If you're anxious to begin using Sytem 7.1, the following steps will get you there in about 15 minutes.

Why Take the Slow Road?

Before you go any farther, let me spell out a few reasons for bypassing the quick method in favor of the careful approach. While the automatic installation method works fine in the short run, it may cause problems in the long run. Some applications and utilities on which you now rely will require updating before they can be used with System 7.1. Some cdevs and inits may even result in system errors, causing your computer to crash. The result may be lost data and hours of trouble-shooting to prevent future errors.

Also, you may want to know a little more about what you're getting into before you install System 7.1. The steps laid out in the *Learning Fundamental Concepts* section cover not only the installation process itself, but also discuss how System 7.1 works with specific models of Macintosh computers and varieties of application software.

If you already know the score and you feel comfortable with trouble-shooting problems later on, go for it. You can perform the following steps and get up and running immediately. Otherwise, spend the extra hour or so needed to read through the *Learning Fundamental Concepts* section in this chapter and get to know your computer a little better in the process.

The Speedy Path to System 7.1

The following steps assume that you have the five 1.4MB disks or equivalent *disk images* (contents of the disks) required to install System 7.1. These include *Install, Install 2, Fonts, Printing,* and *Tidbits.* (The sixth disk, *Disk Tools,* contains important files, but is not required to complete the installation procedure.) You may also install System 7.1 from CD-ROM.

1. Insert the disk labeled **Install.**

2. Double-click on the Installer icon to open the Installer utility.

3. Once the Welcome to the Apple Installer screen is displayed, as shown in Figure 2.3, read its instructions and press the Return key to continue.

4. The Easy Install dialog box will display, as shown in Figure 2.4. Check that the disk named at the bottom of the dotted rectangle is the hard drive onto which you want to install System 7.1. If it is not, click the Switch Disk button until the correct disk name displays.

5. The Installer utility automatically evaluates the current computer and makes installation decisions based on what devices it finds connected to your Mac. Its decisions are listed inside the dotted rectangle. These decisions are probably correct, but if you want to add or subtract items from the list, click the Customize button and select the

---

FIGURE 2.3

The first screen to appear explains how options in the upcoming Installer utility work.

 Welcome to the Apple Installer

 Your Macintosh needs certain software to start up.

The Installer places this software on your disk in the System Folder.   System Folder

"Easy Install" chooses the software Apple recommends and creates a disk which can be used to start up your Macintosh.

("Customize" if you are sure you want to override those recommendations.)

[OK]

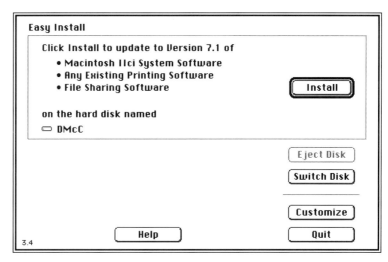

FIGURE 2.4

The Easy Install dialog box allows you to install System 7.1 automatically, or customize the procedure.

desired installation options from the scrolling list in the Customize dialog box. These options are especially useful if your machine is connected to an Ethernet or token ring network.

6. Click the Install button, instructing the Installer utility to begin the installation process. Since essential System 7.1 data is contained on five of the six installation disks, you will have to swap disks several times. Do so when prompted.

7. When the installation procedure is complete, click the Restart button to restart your computer and begin using System 7.1. It's a whole new world!

You may now skip ahead to the next chapter to begin using System 7.1, or read on to see what you missed.

LEARNING FUNDAMENTAL CONCEPTS

The following pages describe the kinds of computer on which you can use System 7.1 and how to install System 7.1 onto your computer's hard drive. To perform the installation, you will need the floppy disks or CD-ROM provided with the System 7.1 upgrade kit, which may be purchased from your local Macintosh dealer, user group, or perhaps borrowed from a fellow Macintosh enthusiast. If you have access to the CompuServe Information Service or AppleLink (each a popular BBS—short for *bulletin board service*—that may be accessed using a modem), you may download the installation files. On CompuServe, System 7 disk images may be found in Library 8, "Apple System Files," of the Macintosh Developers forum (GO MACDEV). On AppleLink, the disk images are located in the Software folder which is inside the System 7 Information folder. However, because the files take over four hours to download using a 2400-baud modem and must then be decompressed using StuffIt Deluxe or the AppleLink decompression utility, you may want to use this option as a last resort only (for example, to replace the contents of a single bad disk).

*R*EQUIREMENTS

As of this writing, Apple distributes fourteen major models of Macintosh computers. At least twelve previously distributed models have been discontinued. Including the countless variations in which each model may be or may have been configured—different ROMs, different amounts of RAM, different hard drives—there are a heck of a lot of unique kinds of Macs out there.

Some of them *cannot* run System 7, at least not without first being upgraded. To run System 7, your computer must live up to the following criteria:

- 20MB hard drive
- 2MB RAM (3MB RAM if you'll be using the 8-bit internal video port supplied with the Mac IIsi and IIci)

Most Macs have a hard drive. (If yours does not, consult your local Macintosh dealer.) Many Macs, however, lack sufficient memory. The early model Macs—128, 512, 512E—provided less than a quarter of the memory necessary to run System 7.1 (and, in fact, will not run System 7 without first upgrading both the ROM chips and logic board, for the price of which you could purchase a used Mac Plus). While these models are rarely used anymore, many 1MB-RAM machines still flourish, such as standard-equipment Mac Pluses and SEs, and these must be upgraded before installing System 7. I recommend upgrading to at least 4MB to leave room for running two moderate-size applications. Additional RAM may be purchased quite inexpensively through your local Macintosh dealer or by calling a mail-order company such as the Chip Merchant 1-800-426-6375. The latter is the least expensive alternative, but you will have to install the RAM yourself, which means taking apart your machine.

To take advantage of System 7's improved memory handling, you must own even more sophisticated machinery. The *virtual memory* feature, which allows you to augment the amount of RAM available to your computer by borrowing some from disk (as covered in Chapter 9), requires that your computer offer a 68020 CPU chip or better with an optional PMMU (*Paged Memory Management Unit*), such as the Motorola 68851. To use *32-bit addressing*, which allows you to access more than the previous maximum of 8MB of RAM (also covered in Chapter 9), your computer must offer compatible ROMs, preferably combined with a 68030 CPU chip.

Table 2.1 shows how 26 currently available models of System 7-compatible Macs shape up in terms of support for virtual memory and 32-bit addressing.

TABLE 2.1   *System 7-Compatible Macintosh Computers, from Slowest to Fastest*

MODEL	CPU	PMMU	VIRTUAL MEMORY	32-BIT ADDRESSING
Plus	68000 (8-MHz)	no	no	no
SE	68000 (8-MHz)	no	no	no
Classic	68000 (8-MHz)	no	no	no
Portable	68000 (16-MHz)	no	no	no

| TABLE 2.1 | *S*ystem 7-Compatible Macintosh Computers, from Slowest to Fastest (continued) |

MODEL	CPU	PMMU	VIRTUAL MEMORY	32-BIT ADDRESSING
PowerBook 100	68000 (16-MHz)	no	no	no
II	68020 (16-MHz)	can be added	yes (w/ PMMU)	no
LC	68020 (16-MHz)	can be added	yes (w/ PMMU)	yes (up to 10MB)
SE/30	68030 (16-MHz)	yes	yes	no
Classic II/ Performa 200	68030 (16-MHz)	yes	yes	yes (up to 10MB)
IIx	68030 (16-MHz)	yes	yes	no
IIcx	68030 (16-MHz)	yes	yes	no
PowerBook 140	68030 (16-MHz)	yes	yes	yes (up to 8MB)
LC II/ Performa 400	68030 (16-MHz)	yes	yes	yes (up to 10MB)
IIsi	68030 (20-MHz)	yes	yes	yes (up to 65MB)
PowerBook 145	68030 (25-MHz)	yes	yes	yes (up to 8MB)
PowerBook 170	68030 (25-MHz)	yes	yes	yes (up to 8MB)

| TABLE 2.1 | *S*ystem 7-Compatible Macintosh Computers, from Slowest to Fastest (continued) |

MODEL	CPU	PMMU	VIRTUAL MEMORY	32-BIT ADDRESSING
PowerBook 160	68030 (25-MHz)	yes	yes	yes (up to 14MB)
Duo Dock 210	68030 (25-MHz)	yes	yes	yes (up to 24MB)
IIci	68030 (25-MHz)	yes	yes	yes (up to 128MB)
Performa 600	68030 (32-MHz)	yes	yes	yes (up to 68MB)
IIvx	68030 (32-MHz)	yes	yes	yes (up to 68MB)
PowerBook 180	68030 (33-MHz)	yes	yes	yes (up to 14MB)
Duo Dock 230	68030 (33-MHz)	yes	yes	yes (up to 24MB)
Quadra 700	68040 (25-MHz)	yes	yes	yes (up to 68MB)
Quadra 900	68040 (25-MHz)	yes	yes	yes (up to 128MB)
Quadra 950	68040 (33-MHz)	yes	yes	yes (up to 128MB)

> **Mode32, an init from Connectix Corporation, included on the disk that you can order with the coupon found at the back of this book, allows any 68020 or 68030 machine—including the Mac II, SE/30, IIx, and IIcx—to access 32-bit addressing.**

PREPARING TO INSTALL

To help software developers create programs that are compatible with both current and future versions of the Macintosh system software, Apple releases programming guidelines. In most cases, developers of Macintosh applications follow these guidelines, but occasionally a programmer will break one or more of Apple's rules in order to make some feature work in a way, or at a speed, that would otherwise be impossible. For example, in order to achieve arcade-style speed and graphics, a game such as Dark Castle will address certain ROM-based code directly, rather than relying on slower disk-based system software routines. In the short run, such an infraction will work perfectly. However, when a new system software release appears, problems may occur. The software may even be rendered completely incompatible.

This means that most of your applications, cdevs, and inits will work with System 7, but some will not. Before installing System 7, you may find out which documents pose potential problems by running the Compatibility Checker, included on the *Before You Install* disk that came with your System 7 upgrade kit. This step is not absolutely necessary—I didn't do it myself—but it will help avoid confusion by eliminating incompatibilities before you encounter them.

1. Copy the Compatibility Checker 1.0 stack from the *Before You Install* disk to your hard drive.

2. Double-click the Compatibility Checker on your hard disk to inspect every hard drive connected to your Mac.

3. If any files in the current System Folder are considered possibly to be incompatible with System 7.1, the screen shown in Figure 2.5 will display. A scrolling list features the suspect cdevs and inits. You may move these files to a separate folder, thus preventing them from interfering with the new system software, by clicking the Move button.

FIGURE 2.5

The Compatibility Checker allows you to move cdevs and inits that may cause problems when loaded with System 7.1 into a new folder.

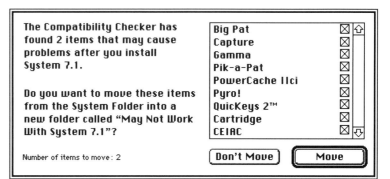

4. Next, a Compatibility Report screen will display, listing every software application found on the one or more inspected hard drives. Each application is judged regarding compatibility. Upgrade information, vendors, and phone numbers are provided for many products. You may print the results or save them to disk.

5. Click the Quit button to return to the Finder.

I P

> **If you use an init manager to specify the inits that are loaded during the startup process, you may want to turn on all inits before installing System 7. Many init managers— including Aask, Inix, and Startup Manager—disable cdevs and inits by changing their file type so that the system software will not recognize them. Unfortunately, this means that the System 7 Installer program will not recognize them either, and thus will not convert disabled cdevs and inits to System 7-compatible control panels and extensions. (This is not an issue if you use Microseeds' INIT Picker.)**

INSTALLATION

Before installing System 7.1 (or any other major piece of software), you should first *back up* all important files on your hard drive by copying them to floppy disks or to some other medium such as tape or removable cartridge. Be very careful to back up all system software documents, including the System and Finder files, as well as fonts, desk accessories, cdevs, inits, and so on. Also, you may want to run the new version of the Disk First Aid utility that's included on the *Disk Tools* disk to verify the condition of your hard drive. If any errors are discovered, you will have to restart your computer and boot from the *Disk Tools* disk to perform repairs.

To install System 7.1, run the Installer utility as outlined in the *Getting Started* section earlier in this chapter. Intermediate and advanced users may want to consider the following options when installing:

- If you own a SyQuest, Bernoulli, or Ricoh removable hard drive, you may want to install System 7.1 on a newly formatted cartridge. This allows you to experiment with the new system before altering the contents of your primary hard drive.

- Before installing System 7.1 on a hard drive that already
  contains an earlier version of the system software, move the
  current Finder out of the System Folder, preferably into a
  new folder named Old Finder or the like. Then change the
  name of the System Folder to Old System. This prevents the
  installer from converting your existing fonts and desk accessories and automatically installing third-party inits and
  cdevs into the proper folders. This means you will have to
  move fonts, desk accessories, inits, and cdevs manually from
  the Old System folder to the new System Folder, affording
  yourself greater control over the installation procedure.
  You need to keep in mind, however, that System 7.1 requires about 5MB of free space on disk.

Having two systems on the same hard drive may sound
dangerous. But with System 7.1, it actually affords you a
greater degree of versatility, allowing you to switch back and
forth between System 7.1 and an earlier version such as
System 6.0.8 . The Mac will boot from any folder—whether
or not it is named System Folder—that contains both a
System file and a Finder file. The recognized system folder
is identified by a computer icon, as shown in Figure 2.6. To
switch back to the old system, you should move the Finder 6
file from the Old Finder folder into the Old System folder,
then move the Finder 7 file from the active System Folder to
the Old Finder folder (renaming it New Finder to keep
things straight). To *bless* the Old System folder so that your
Mac knows this is the folder that contains the current system
software, open the folder and double-click the Finder icon.
Then reboot your computer.

*F*olders containing the
active system software
before (top) and after
(bottom) moving the
Finder out of one folder
and into another.

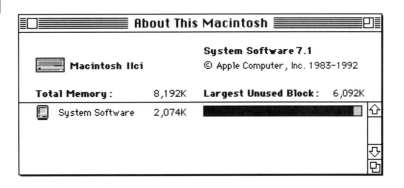

Note that the blessing procedure may be automated using the Folder Blesser, a free utility created by Dave McGary. On CompuServe, the Folder Blesser may be found in Library 2, "Using System/Finder," of the Macintosh Systems forum (GO MACSYS). Other utilities include SystemSwitcher by Keisuke Hard and System Picker by Kevin Aitken (System Picker is included on the disks which you can order with the coupon found at the back of this book).

If System 7.1 installs successfully, your Mac will start up as described at the beginning of this chapter. To make sure you are using System 7.1, choose the About This Macintosh command from the Apple menu. The dialog box shown in Figure 2.7 will appear, displaying the version number of the current system software in its upper right corner. If it reads "System Software 7.1," you're ready to proceed to the next section to learn how to use the System 7.1 Finder.

*T*he About This Macintosh
dialog box lists the
version of the current
system software.

About This Macintosh

System Software 7.1
Macintosh IIci   © Apple Computer, Inc. 1983–1992

Total Memory :   8,192K   **Largest Unused Block :**   6,092K

System Software   2,074K

You should note that the Macintosh system software is never set in stone. At any time, you may change the system by adding or deleting control panels, extensions, drivers, and resources such as fonts and desk accessories. You may also customize the system using various commands, control panel options, and other features. If you're interested in enhancing your system immediately, skip ahead to the *Getting Started* sections of Chapters 4, 5, and 7. To install additional utilities and make last-minute adjustments to your newly installed System 7, read the *Exploring Advanced Topics* section of this chapter.

INSTALLATION FAILURE

If the installation process fails, it may be because your Mac does not provide adequate memory or a hard disk. If you are sure your computer is compatible with System 7, then something is wrong with the manner in which the information is being copied from floppy disk to hard drive. This may be because 1) one of the six installation disks is corrupt, 2) your floppy disk drive needs to be serviced, or 3) your hard drive has one or more bad sectors to which files cannot be copied.

If the installation procedure fails, I recommend that you reattempt the installation at least twice more. If the installation consistently fails when copying a specific floppy disk, the disk is probably to blame. You should return the System 7 installation disks to the store from which they were purchased and trade them in for new disks. Then reattempt the installation procedure.

If the procedure continues to fail despite new installation disks, your hardware is very likely to blame. You should take your computer to an authorized Apple service center and have the floppy disk drive and hard drive examined.

EXPLORING ADVANCED TOPICS

The automatic system installation process installs all the files you absolutely need to use System 7. However, a few applications may have been omitted that you may want to manually copy to your hard drive. These include the following:

- **Apple File Exchange.** If you use Apple File Exchange to transfer files from the IBM-PC to the Mac or from one format to another, upgrade the Apple File Exchange utility only—be careful not to delete the conversion format files—with the one included on the *Install 2* disk.

- **TeachText.** Few people use this utility as a word processor, but just about every major software vendor includes a version of TeachText in its installation scheme to allow you to open its ReadMe file. The result is 50 TeachText utilities scattered all over your hard disk! To avoid this problem, copy the TeachText 7 utility included on the *Install 3* disk to a Utilities folder on your hard drive. Then locate all other versions of TeachText on your hard drive using the Find command (as described in Chapter 8), and throw them in the Trash.

- **Disk First Aid.** A new version of Disk First Aid is included with System 7.1. In addition to performing the standard task of verifying and repairing floppy and hard disks, it also tackles the job of repairing damage caused by bugs—a problem that plagued many users: disappearing files and folders. Under the previous System 7.0, occasionally a file or folder would disappear from the Finder level. The data would remain intact, but it was hidden from view. To correct it, users had to backup and reinitialize their drives and reinstall everything. Originally, Apple denied that the problem existed, but they eventually came around and provided an easier way to solve the dilemma. Now when you install System 7.1, you are protecting yourself from this problem, just as you would if you used System 7 Tune-Up on an older version of System 7. This should prevent the bug from rearing its ugly head, but if it does occur, use your Disk First Aid to recover the use of your files or folders.

- **LaserWriter Font Utility.** If you intend to print to a PostScript-equipped output device, you will want to copy the

LaserWriter Font Utility program from the *More Tidbits* disk. This utility allows you to download TrueType and PostScript fonts to a printer's memory or hard drive, print font samples, and enable or disable the startup page.

- **Font/DA Mover.** Sure, System 7 renders the Font/DA Mover unnecessary, a relic from the past. However, there are some functions—such as creating new suitcase files— that cannot be performed without the Font/DA Mover. The Font/DA Mover must be upgraded to version 4.1 to be used with System 7. Since the upgrade is not included on the System 7 disks, I have licensed the program from Apple and included it on the disk which you can order with the coupon found at the back of this book.

More information about each of these utilities will be presented in later chapters.

Exploring the Finder—
the Macintosh
Control Center

AFTER COMPLETING THE installation
▬ process, you're ready to begin using
System 7. Any introduction to a Macintosh operating system must
include a discussion of the *Finder*, which displays immediately after you
start up your computer. The Finder acts as the control center for the system software, and as such, it is undoubtedly the most important application on the Mac.

That's right: The Finder is an *application*, just like a word processor,
spreadsheet, or graphics program. It's the first application that you use
and, under System 7, it's the only application that is *always* running.

ONCE UPON A FINDER

To understand the Finder's relationship to the system software, you
might think of your Mac as a book or a movie that tells a story. For example, a good narrative begins with an introductory scene that estab-
lishes the plot, acquaints you with the main characters, and sets the tone
used throughout the remainder of the story. Future scenes further the
plot, but rely on familiar characters and conform to the introductory tone.

As the introductory Macintosh application, the Finder embodies
the plot, characters, and tone that is sustained throughout future applications. The plot is computing via the *graphical user interface* (GUI—
pronounced *gooey*), in which familiar images are displayed by the
computer to convey information to the user, and are in turn manipulated by the user to convey information to the computer. For example, to
move a file in the Finder, you simply drag it to a new location. If you were
using an operating device that lacks a graphical user interface, such as

MS-DOS on the IBM PC, you would have to enter movement commands from the keyboard, requiring prior knowledge of the command structure and perfect syntax (no misspellings).

The familiar images that make up the GUI constitute the characters in the Macintosh story. These include the document icons, the menu bar, the directory window, and many others, as shown in Figure 3.1.

FIGURE 3.1

The Finder desktop contains familiar images that may be manipulated to convey information to the computer.

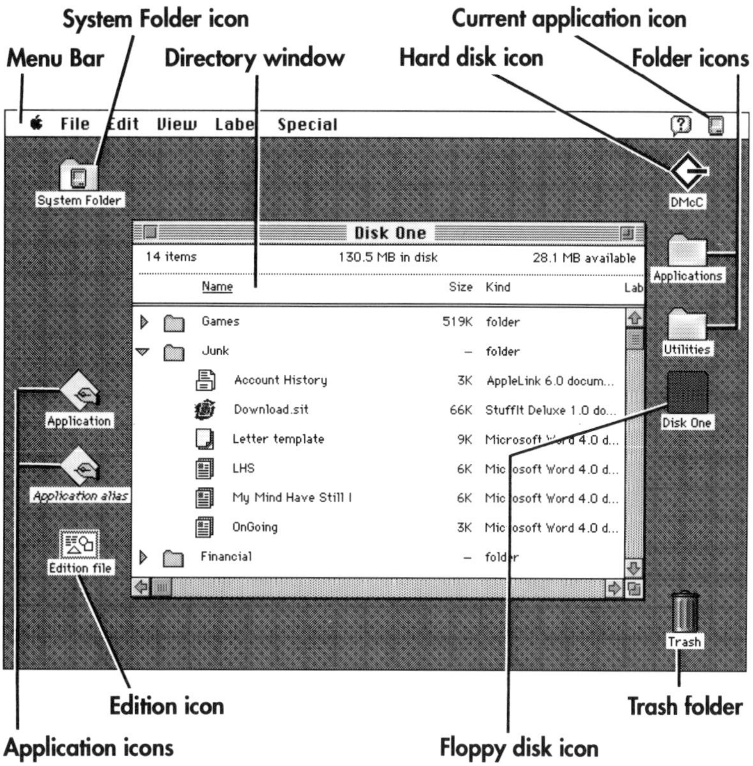

Finally, the Finder *desktop* sets the tone, acting as a constant backdrop throughout all Macintosh applications. Other applications offer their own desktops, complete with unique icons, menu bars, and windows. When running multiple applications, changing from one to another is as simple as clicking an element belonging to its desktop.

Understanding the Finder application is therefore key to understanding the Mac, as well as to understanding other Macintosh application software. The following section introduces parts of the Finder desktop and describes their function. Later sections explain how to use the Finder to organize the contents of disks and hard drives.

GETTING STARTED

The primary function of the Finder is to display and organize the contents of *disks*—whether they're floppy disks, hard drives, cartridges, or volumes shared over a network. The Finder desktop facilitates this function by providing the following items:

- **Cursor.** The *cursor* follows the movements of your mouse with respect to the desktop. Though it generally appears as an arrow, the cursor may change to reflect the current operation. For example, the cursor looks like an I-beam when editing file names.

- **Icons.** At least two *icons* will display on your Finder desktop: The icon in the upper-right corner of the screen represents the hard drive that contains the current system software. The icon in the lower-right corner represents the Trash folder, which is used to delete documents from a disk. Folders, applications, and other files may be located anywhere on the desktop, as determined by the user. Icons for additional disks display in a column below the first hard drive icon.

- **Menu bar.** A single *menu bar* appears along the top of the desktop, a trait shared with all other Macintosh applications. Each word in the menu bar represents a menu, which contains a list of commands that may be used to manipulate selected files, manipulate windows, and initiate other disk-management operations.

- **Directory windows.** Double-click a disk or folder icon to display the contents of the disk or folder in the form of a *directory window.* The manner and order in which files are displayed in a window is determined using commands from the View menu.

The Window

The window is an especially important part of the Macintosh interface. At the Finder level, a window serves to display the contents of an open disk or folder. In other applications, a window displays the contents of a file. Whether displayed at the Finder desktop or in some other application, a window includes the following basic elements (shown labeled in Figure 3.2):

- **Title bar.** The *title bar* along the top of a window lists the name of the disk, folder, or file to which the window belongs, called the *window title*. Drag the title bar to move the window.

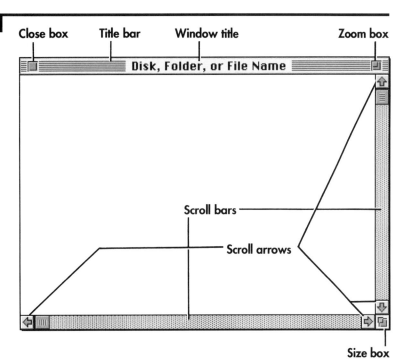

FIGURE 3.2

Virtually any window, whether displayed at the Finder level or in some other application, offers a title bar and two scroll bars.

> **Press the Command key and drag the title bar to move a background window without making it active.**

- **Close box.** Click the *close box* in the upper-left corner of the title bar to close the current window.

> **Press the Option key and click the close box to close *all* windows on the desktop.**

- **Zoom box.** Click the *zoom box* in the upper-right corner of the title bar to resize the current window to display as much of its contents as will fit on screen. Click the zoom box a second time to return the window to its previous size.

> **Option-click the zoom box to enlarge the window to full screen size, regardless of its contents.**

- **Size box.** Drag the *size box* in the lower-right corner of the window to resize the window manually.
- **Scroll bars.** Use the *scroll bars* along the right and bottom sides of a window to display hidden contents of a disk, folder, or file. If you click a *scroll arrow,* the window is nudged slightly in that direction. Click in the gray area of a scroll bar to scroll the window more dramatically. Drag a

scroll box to manually determine the distance scrolled. If all contents of a window are displayed, the scroll bars will appear empty.

Using an *extended keyboard*—one which includes function keys along the top row—you may scroll the active window from the keyboard. Press the Page Down key to scroll down one screen, as if you had clicked the gray area in the vertical scroll bar below the scroll box. Press Page Up to scroll up one screen. Press the End key to scroll all the way to the bottom of the active window. Press Home to scroll all the way to the top.

Only one window is *active* at any one time. Generally the foremost window, the active window is distinguished by the appearance of horizontal lines across the title bar. If you select an icon outside this window (or, often, if you simply click on an empty portion of the desktop), you will *deactivate* it. The scroll bars, close box, zoom box, and size box of a deactivated window are invisible.

THE FINDER MENUS

Finder 7 includes eight menus, as shown in Figure 3.3. Among these, the Help and Application menus—located on the right side of the menu bar—were new as of Finder 7. Also, the old Color menu which allowed you to colorize files, changed to the Label menu in Finder 7. This menu allows you to both colorize and label files, even if you own a black-and-white monitor.

The following lists provide a brief synopsis of every command shown in Figure 3.3. More complete explanations of many of these commands are featured in later sections of this chapter, organized according to function. Other commands are covered in later chapters (consult the index for specific locations).

FIGURE 3.3

Finder 7 includes eight menus featuring several commands each.

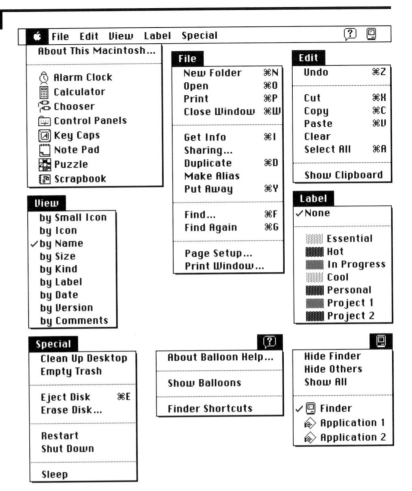

The Apple Menu

In previous versions of the Macintosh system software, the Apple menu contained a list of all desk accessories loaded into the current System file, followed by a list of the currently running applications. In addition, applications other than the Finder sometimes offered Help commands under this menu. Often, the result was an enormously long menu whose contents could not be displayed simultaneously on screen. To alleviate this problem, the applications list and help features have been spun off into their own menus.

The Apple menu includes the following:

- **About This Macintosh…** Displays the About This Macintosh dialog box, which lists all running applications followed by the amount of RAM used by each, the amount of free RAM available for use, and the current version of Macintosh computer and system software.
- The names of all desk accessories and other utilities located in the Apple Menu Items folder inside the System folder.

The Apple menu is common to all Macintosh applications. Only the About This Macintosh command changes to reflect the identity of the current application. Note also that some third-party control panels and extensions, such as CE Toolbox and QuicKeys (neither of which are included with System 7), will add their own commands to the Apple menu without being located in the Apple Menu Items folder.

The File Menu

The commands under the File menu allow you to manipulate and print a selected file. In Finder 7, you may also search one or more disks for file names and share disks and folders across a network.

The new File menu includes the following:

- **New Folder (⌘-N).** Creates a new folder icon in the active directory window.

I P

> **If no directory window is active, choose New Folder to create a new folder icon on the desktop.**

- **Open (⌘-O).** Opens a selected disk, folder, or file (just like double-clicking an icon). If a disk or folder is selected, choosing Open displays a directory window. If a document is selected, choose Open to launch the application software in which the document was created. The Open command may also be initiated by pressing ⌘-↓.

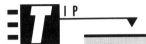

Press Option when choosing the Open command to open the selected folder or file and close the active window (just like Option-double-clicking an icon).

- **Print (⌘-P).** Launches the application in which the currently selected document was created, prints the document, quits the application, and returns to the Finder. This command is dimmed if a disk or folder is selected.

- **Close Window (⌘-W).** Closes the active window (just like clicking the close box).

Press Option when displaying the File menu to access the Close All command, which closes all open windows (just like the Option-clicking close box).

- **Get Info (⌘-I).** Displays the Info dialog box, which lists specific information about the selected icon, including its size and location. You may annotate an icon by entering text into the "Comments" option box at the bottom of the Info dialog box. Select the icon in the upper-left corner and paste a graphic from the Clipboard to assign a new icon to the current file, folder, or disk.

- **Sharing**... Shares a folder or disk with other users over an AppleTalk network. No communications software is required, and you may even share data with IBM PCs and Macintoshes running System 6. If you choose this command

before activating the file-sharing feature using the Sharing
Setup control panel, choosing the Sharing command will
activate the control panel for you.

> **If you choose this command for the first time while a
> cartridge or disk is mounted on the desktop, the Finder will
> not allow you to dismount that disk without first disabling
> the file-sharing feature. Therefore, you will generally want to
> enable file sharing when no extra disks are mounted.**

- **Duplicate (⌘-D).** Makes an exact copy of the selected file or
  folder in the same directory as the original. The word "copy"
  will be appended to the name of the duplicate file to distinguish it from the original.

> **To create a duplicate of a file or folder in a different
> directory, press Option and drag the file outside the active
> window, or into a folder if the original file is on the desktop.
> (You can copy files by Option-dragging from, but not to, the
> Trash folder.) The duplicate file will not have the word
> "copy" appended to it.**

- **Make Alias.** Clones a file's icon but ignores its contents to
  create an *alias* that takes up very little room on disk. In the
  future, double-clicking or otherwise opening the alias will
  open the original file or folder, allowing a file to occupy
  multiple locations simultaneously. The name of an alias is
  italicized to distinguish it from the original file.

> You may also create aliases for disks. If you double-click the alias of a disk or networked volume that is not currently mounted, a message will display requesting you to insert the disk or locate the volume.

- **Put Away (⌘-Y).** Returns a selected file or folder icon from the desktop to its original folder. Select a disk and choose the Put Away command to *dismount* the disk (just like dragging the disk to the Trash folder).

- **Find... (⌘-F).** Displays the Find dialog box, which allows you to search file names for a string of characters entered from the keyboard. Click the More Choices button to search by size, date, comments, or some other parameter.

- **Find Again (⌘-G).** Repeats the Find command using the previously entered parameters.

- **Page Setup.** Displays the Page Setup dialog box for the currently selected output device. Use this dialog box to determine the paper size, the orientation of the page (horizontal or vertical), and the scale at which an image is printed.

- **Print Window/Desktop.** Prints a list of the files contained in the active directory window, complete with size, kind, label, and so on, depending on how the window is displayed. If no window is active, choose Print Desktop to print all icons located on the desktop.

The Edit Menu

The Edit menu is one of the few menus that has remained unchanged since the early days of Macintosh system software. Its only function in Finder 7 is to provide access to the Macintosh Clipboard.

For the record, the Edit menu includes the following:

- **Undo (⌘-Z).** Negates the last immediate operation performed in the Finder. Most Finder operations—such as moving, duplicating, and deleting a file—cannot be undone. This command is most useful for restoring altered file names, icons pasted into the Info dialog box, and contents of the Scrapbook (a popular desk accessory). The Undo command may also be initiated by pressing the F1 key on an extended keyboard.

- **Cut (⌘-X).** Deletes the highlighted portion of a file name, a selected icon in the Info dialog box, or an image in the Scrapbook and stores it in the Clipboard, replacing the Clipboard's previous contents. The Cut command may also be initiated by pressing the F2 key on an extended keyboard.

- **Copy (⌘-C).** Makes a copy of the highlighted portion of a file name, a selected icon in the Info dialog box, or an image in the Scrapbook and stores it in the Clipboard, replacing the Clipboard's previous contents. The Copy command may also be initiated by pressing the F3 key on an extended keyboard.

- **Paste (⌘-V).** Makes a copy of the contents of the Clipboard and places them in the active portion of the Finder, whether it's a highlighted file name, a selected icon in the Info dialog box, or a page in the Scrapbook. The contents of the Clipboard are unaffected. The Paste command may also be initiated by pressing the F4 key on an extended keyboard.

- **Clear.** Deletes the highlighted portion of a file name without storing it in the Clipboard or disturbing the contents of the Clipboard (just like pressing the Delete, Backspace, or Clear key).

- **Select All (⌘-A).** Selects all icons in the active window, all icons on the desktop if no window is active, or all text in the highlighted file name.

■ **Show Clipboard.** Displays the Clipboard window which lists the current contents of the Clipboard (just like double-clicking the Clipboard icon in the System Folder).

The commands in the Edit menu may not be used to cut, copy, paste, or delete files, folders, or disks.

The View Menu

The commands under the View menu determine the manner in which icons are displayed in the active window. If no window is active, the entire menu is dimmed. (The desktop is always viewed by a full-sized icon.)
The View menu includes the following:

■ **by Small Icon.** Displays quarter-sized icons in the current window, each measuring 16 by 16 *screen pixels* (individual dots on the screen).

■ **by Icon.** Displays full-sized icons in the current window, each measuring 32 by 32 screen pixels.

■ **by Name.** This view and all those that follow are known as *list views,* since they display file names in consecutive lines. When viewed by name, files are listed alphabetically.

■ **by Size.** Lists files and folders with respect to the amount of space they consume on disk, from largest at the top to smallest at the bottom.

■ **by Kind.** Lists each file alphabetically according to the application that created it, followed by folders and special system software files (if any).

■ **by Label.** Lists files and folders according to their labels, in the same order that they appear in the Label menu.

■ **by Date.** Lists files and folders with respect to the date on which they were last modified, from the most recent at the top to the most ancient at the bottom.

■ **by Version.** Lists files according to version number. This is generally most useful for listing application files, since document files and folders offer no version numbers, and are simply listed at the end in alphabetical order.

- **by Comments.** Lists files and folders according to their comments entered into the Info dialog box.

Some of the commands listed above may be missing from your View menu. This is because a property such as labels or comments may not be displayed in the current window. To control the displayed properties, use the Views control panel, as discussed in Chapter 7.

The Label Menu

The old Color menu from System 6 was upgraded in System 7 to the Label menu, which allows you to assign both a color and a short label to any selected file or folder. While this labeling scheme may at first seem like little more than the newest gimmick, labels are in fact useful disk-management tools, providing a means to organize files in the active window and search for files via the Find command.

The Label menu includes the following:

- **None.** Assigns no label or color to the selected file or folder.

- Seven color-and-label commands are displayed below the None command, each of which may be used to colorize an icon—or shade an icon that contains multiple colors—and assign a label that may be displayed in any of the list views.

You may edit the colors and text displayed in the Label menu using the Labels control panel, as discussed in Chapter 6.

The Special Menu

Like the Edit menu, the Special menu contains the same commands found in previous versions of the Macintosh Finder. But while the commands look the same, two commands—Clean Up and Empty Trash—operate slightly differently as of System 7.

The Special menu includes the following:

- **Clean Up Window/Desktop.** Aligns icons in the active directory window to the nearest grid increment. If no window is active, choose Clean Up Desktop to align icons located on the desktop. This command is dimmed if files in the active window are displayed in list view.

> **Press Option when displaying the Special menu to access the Clean Up by Name command, which aligns icons in the active window in alphabetical order, or the Clean Up All command, which aligns all icons on the desktop in columns along the right side of the screen in alphabetical order from top to bottom and right to left.**

- **Empty Trash.** Deletes the contents of the Trash folder from a disk, hard drive, or networked volume. The Trash no longer empties on its own, so this command must be chosen to delete files and folders. To skip the trash warning—"Are you sure you want to permanently remove these items"—press Option when choosing the Empty Trash command.

> **You may also press Option when choosing Empty Trash to delete locked files.**

- **Eject Disk (⌘-E).** Ejects the selected disk or cartridge without dismounting it (as does the Put Away command in the File menu). The disk icon remains on the desktop, allowing you to access it later. If no disk is selected, the Eject Disk command ejects the first disk it finds. Similar effects can be accomplished by pressing Shift-⌘-1, Shift-⌘-2, or Shift-⌘-0, each of which ejects the floppy disk in drive 1, drive 2, or an external disk drive, respectively.

- **Erase Disk**... Formats the selected floppy disk, cartridge, or hard drive. This command cannot be used to format the disk containing the current System Folder. All information on the current disk will be erased, so use this command with care!

- **Restart.** Reboots your Macintosh computer. All floppy disks, cartridges, and networked volumes will be dismounted.

- **Shut Down.** Closes down the computer. When using a Macintosh II series machine, choosing Shut Down both closes down the computer and turns off the power. You must turn off Mac Pluses, SEs, and Classics manually, but only after being instructed to do so. To avoid system-related problems, never turn off your computer without first choosing the Shut Down command.

- **Sleep.** Activates the default screen-saver utility that is built into the PowerBook series computer. Sleep dims the screen so the PowerBook saves power. If you are using a third-party screen-saver utility such as Pyro or After Dark on your standard model Mac, you will also have the Sleep command, but it is not a default command.

The Help Menu

The first of two new menus on the right side of the screen is the Help menu, which looks like a cartoon balloon with an inset question mark. This menu allows you to access on-line help for using the Finder and other applications.

The Help menu includes the following:

- **About Balloon Help**... Displays a dialog box that briefly explains the *balloon help* feature.

- **Show/Hide Balloons.** Activates the balloon help feature. Once activated, a cartoon balloon will display any time you move your cursor over an item for which there is on-line help. The balloon will contain specific information about the current item. To turn the balloon feature off, choose the Hide Balloons command.

- **Finder Shortcuts.** Displays a window of keyboard and mouse operations that can be used to quickly perform various Finder operations.

The Help menu is common to all Macintosh applications. Only the Finder Shortcuts command changes or is deleted to reflect the identity of the current application.

The Applications Menu

When multitasking became a permanent fixture in System 7, Apple added an independent Applications menu, accessed by clicking the icon on the extreme right of the menu bar. This menu allows you to switch between running applications and hiding open application windows without closing them.

The Applications menu includes the following:

- **Hide (Current Application).** Hides all windows associated with the current application and switches to the next running application. The windows are not closed; they are merely hidden from view to present a less cluttered desktop. If no application other than the Finder is currently running, this command is dimmed.

- **Hide Others.** Hides all windows *except* those associated with the current application. If no application other than the Finder is currently running, this command is dimmed.

- **Show All.** Displays any and all hidden windows. If no application other than the Finder is currently running or if no window is hidden, this command is dimmed.

- The names of all applications that are currently running, including the Finder and any open desk accessories, listed in alphabetical order.

The Applications menu is common to all Macintosh applications.

LEARNING FUNDAMENTAL CONCEPTS

When I first started using computers, I remember buying a box of five disks and thinking that it was going to last me an inordinately long time. Counting the occasional term paper and the database of my tape collection (or some other equally simple-minded waste of time), I couldn't imagine filling a single disk, much less five. However, that was back when a typical application consumed less than 200K and a typical document was about a tenth of that size.

Nowadays, the system software is shipped on CD-ROM, an application takes up four disks, and a document may be any size imaginable. Hard drives have evolved from a convenient luxury to an absolute necessity.

Even so, the Finder can seem like a big to-do over nothing, especially when you're just starting out. After all, like a corporate trader, the Finder doesn't *create* anything. It juggles, it disperses, and it oversees.

Unlike a corporate trader, however, whose contribution to society some might judge to be dispensable, the Finder is absolutely essential to the operation of a Macintosh. Once you've had time to create the collection of documents contingent upon a full transition from pen, typewriter, calculator, and paste-up board to computer, the Finder provides the balance between harmonious order and unmitigated anarchy.

THE HIERARCHICAL FILING SYSTEM

Rather than requiring you to learn an abstract labyrinth of organizational techniques, the Finder was designed to conform to your world. Documents are placed into folders, which may be labeled and relabeled as desired. Some documents and folders may be laid out on the desktop for easy access. Others may be positioned inside other folders, or inside folders within folders, up to 32 folders deep.

The blueprint for this vast arrangement of files and folders is known as the *hierarchical filing system,* or HFS. It embodies three simple rules:

- Any file or folder may be placed inside another folder.
- Folder boundaries are recognized by all software.

- Two files or folders with the same name can exist on a single disk, as long as they are relegated to different folders.

For example, suppose you have created several files, each with the name "Balance Sheet." The *path* of the first file—that is, the route of disks and folders through which you must travel to arrive at that file—is *Corporate Finance:Accounting:Department One:Balance Sheet,* meaning that the Balance Sheet document is inside the Department One folder which is in turn inside the Accounting folder on the Corporate Finance disk, as shown in Figure 3.4. The path to a second Balance Sheet file may be *Corporate Finance:Accounting:Balance Sheet,* or *Corporate Finance:Accounting: Department Two:Balance Sheet,* or *Corporate Finance:Accounting:Department One:Fiscal 1990:Balance Sheet,* and so on, just so long as it isn't the same as that of the first file. Files that have identical names may contain different data and have been created in different applications.

FIGURE 3.4

Identically named files may exist on the same drive provided they are placed in different folders.

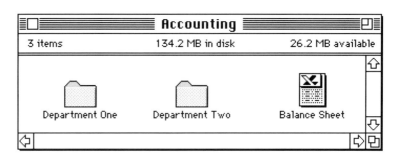

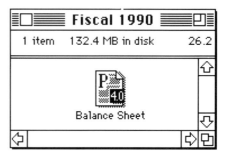

CREATING A NEW FOLDER

The only kind of icon that may be created at the Finder level is the folder. Creating a folder is a two-step process:

1. Open the folder or disk inside which you want to locate the new folder. If you want to position the folder on the desktop, click any icon currently located on the desktop to deactivate all windows. (A folder created on the desktop belongs to the hard drive containing the current System Folder.)

2. Choose the New Folder command from the File menu (⌘-N).

A new folder named *untitled folder* will appear in the current directory window or on the desktop.

SELECTING ICONS

Any existing file, folder, or disk icon may be renamed, moved, or copied. Before you can manipulate an icon, however, you must *select* it by clicking on it with the arrow cursor. You should note that the upper-left corner of the arrow cursor represents its *hot spot,* which is the specific point that must touch an icon to produce any effect. Figure 3.5 shows the locations of hot spots for various cursors.

FIGURE 3.5

The highlighted hot spot in each cursor is the only pixel in that cursor that produces any effect.

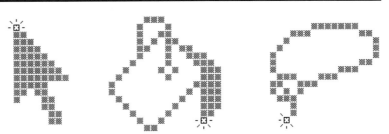

Clicking on an icon not only selects that icon, it also deselects all previously selected icons. To select multiple icons, you can click on the first icon that you want to select, then press the Shift key and click on each additional icon.

Another way to select multiple icons is to *marquee* them. You can drag on an empty portion of the desktop or inside the active window to create a rectangular marquee with a dotted outline, as shown in Figure 3.6. One corner of the marquee is positioned at the point at which you begin to drag; the opposite corner follows the movement of your cursor as you drag. All icons partially surrounded by the marquee become selected.

FIGURE 3.6

Drag on an empty portion of a window to marquee multiple icons (top). In System 7, you may also marquee icons in list views (bottom).

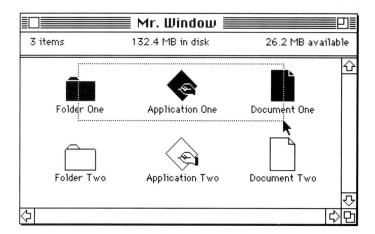

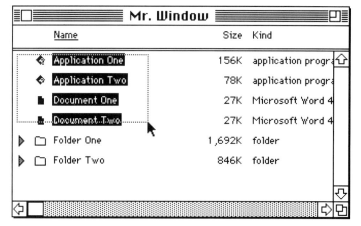

Marqueeing can be combined with Shift-clicking to select multiple icons. You may also press Shift as you marquee, thereby adding the marqueed icons to an existing set of selected icons.

You may only select multiple icons if all icons reside in a single directory window or on the desktop.

SELECTING FROM THE KEYBOARD

Finder 7 provides several additional ways to select icons in the active window or on the desktop, all of which are easily made by pressing a few keys:

- **Tab to next icon.** Press Tab to select the next icon in alphabetical order after the currently selected icon. If no icon is selected, press Tab to select the very first icon in alphabetical order in the active window or on the desktop.

- **Shift-Tab to previous icon.** Press Shift-Tab to select the previous icon in alphabetical order before the currently selected icon. If no icon is selected, press Shift-Tab to select the very last icon in alphabetical order.

- **Arrow to the left, to the right, up, or down.** Press any of the four arrow keys to select the icon to the left, right, above, or below the currently selected icon. If no icon is selected, press the ↑ or ← key to select the icon in the upper-left corner of the window; press the ↓ or → key to select the icon in the lower-right corner.

- **Select by key entry.** Type the first few letters of an icon name to select that icon. If only one file name begins with the letter *A*, for example, press the A key to select that file. If there are two *A* files, one named *abacus* and another named *apple*, you'd need to type *A-B* or *A-P* to distinguish between the two.

DESELECTING ICONS

Sometimes you will want to *deselect* icons to prevent them from being affected by a command or mouse operation. To deselect all icons, you can simply click with the arrow cursor on an empty portion of a directory window or the desktop, or press the Escape key. All currently selected icons can also be deselected when you perform any of the following operations:

- Select an icon that was not previously selected by clicking on it.
- Activate any directory window that does *not* contain selected icons.
- Close the active window.
- Duplicate, copy, or make aliases of the selected icons.

To deselect a single selected icon, you can Shift-click on it with the arrow cursor. Furthermore, any selected icons that are surrounded by a marquee will be deselected when you press the Shift key, as shown in the second example of Figure 3.7.

Naming Icons

The first operation that you may perform on a selected icon is to re-name it. Unlike other operations, the Finder allows you to rename only one icon at a time. Also, you may not rename an icon if multiple icons are selected.

To change the name of a selected icon, click on the text portion of the icon and move your cursor away from the icon immediately. (If you allow your cursor to linger over the icon name, it will take longer to high-light.) In either case, the name will become *highlighted*—that is, it will be surrounded by a black outline, as shown in Figure 3.8.

You may also highlight an icon name by selecting the icon and pressing the Return or Enter key.

After highlighting an icon name, simply enter new text from the keyboard. The previous icon name will be replaced entirely. If you prefer

If you Shift-marquee icons, selected icons become deselected and vice versa (top). This technique is also available in list views (bottom).

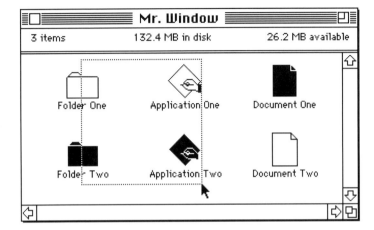

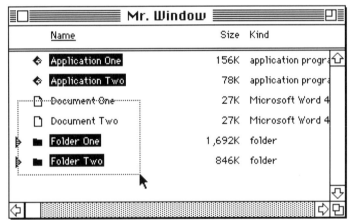

to insert one or more characters in an icon name, position your cursor over the highlighted text. The arrow cursor will change to an I-beam. Click between any two characters in the icon name to specify the position of the blinking *insertion marker*. Text entered from the keyboard will begin at this point.

Use the arrow keys to move the insertion marker inside the icon name. Press the ← or → key to move the insertion marker left or right one character. Press the ↑ key to move the insertion marker to the beginning of the icon name; press ↓ to move it to the end.

FIGURE 3.8

Click the icon name and immediately withdraw your cursor to highlight the icon name (top). Drag across the icon name to highlight a portion of it (bottom).

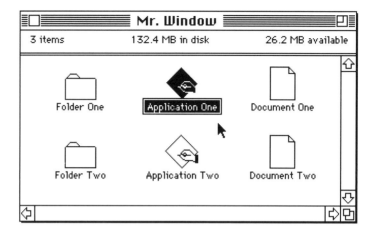

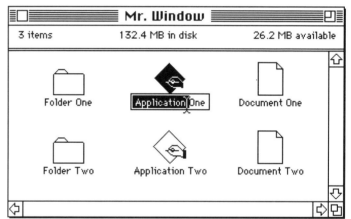

You may also change specific characters in an icon name while leaving other characters intact. To highlight one or more characters, you can do the following:

- Drag over the characters that you want to highlight, as shown in the second example of Figure 3.8.

- Double-click on a word to select that word only. Hold down the mouse button on the second click and drag to highlight additional words.

- Click to set the insertion marker at one end of the characters you want to select, then Shift-click at the opposite end of the desired text. All characters in between the first and second clicks will become highlighted.

- Click anywhere inside the icon name and choose the Select All command from the Edit menu (⌘-A) to highlight all characters in the name.

Highlighted characters may be replaced by entering new characters from the keyboard. They may also be deleted by pressing the Backspace, Delete, or Clear key, or choosing the Clear command from the Edit menu.

To copy highlighted characters to the Macintosh Clipboard, you can choose the Copy command from the Edit menu (⌘-C). You may also delete the highlighted text and, at the same time send a copy to the Clipboard by choosing Cut from the Edit menu (⌘-X). Finally, you may replace highlighted characters with type that you copied earlier by choosing the Paste command (⌘-V).

To restore an original icon name immediately after entering new text from the keyboard, choose the Undo command from the Edit menu (⌘-Z).

An icon name may be up to 32 characters long. The only illegal character is the colon (:); if you type a colon character from the keyboard, it will be replaced by a hyphen (-). Figure 3.9 shows the order in which various characters will display when viewed in alphabetical order.

MOVING ICONS

To move an icon to a different folder on the same disk, simply drag the icon using the arrow cursor. You may drag an icon either into an open folder window or onto a folder icon to move it into an existing folder. If you drag onto a folder icon, wait to release the mouse button until the stationary folder icon becomes reversed. To move an icon onto the desktop, drag it to an empty portion of the desktop and release.

FIGURE 3.9

This listing, read vertically, shows the alphabetization of special characters and the key combinations used to produce them.

(Option-Spacebar)	0 (Zero)	[(Bracket)	≤ (Option-,)
(Spacebar)	1 (One)	\ (Backslash)	≥ (Option-.)
! (Shift-1)	9 (Nine)	] (Bracket)	¥ (Option-Y)
" (Option-[)	; (Semicolon)	^ (Shift-6)	µ (Option-M)
« (Option-\)	< (Shift-,)	_ (Shift--)	∂ (Option-D)
" (Shift-')	= (Equal)	` (Grave)	∑ (Option-W)
" (Shift-Option-[)	> (Shift-.)	{ (Shift-[)	∏ (Shift-Option-P)
» (Shift-Option-\)	? (Shift-/)	| (Shift-\)	π (Option-P)
# (Shift-3)	@ (Shift-2)	} (Shift-])	∫ (Option-B)
$ (Shift-4)	A	~ (Shift-`)	º (Option-9)
% (Shift-5)	Å (Shift-Option-A)	† (Option-T)	º (Option-0)
& (Shift-7)	Æ (Option-')	° (Shift-Option-8)	Ω (Option-Z)
' (Option-])	B	¢ (Option-4)	¿ (Shift-Option-/)
' (Quote)	C	£ (Option-3)	i (Option-1)
' (Shift-Option-])	Ç (Option-C)	§ (Option-6)	¬ (Option-L)
((Shift-9)	D	• (Option-8)	√ (Option-V)
) (Shift-0)	O	¶ (Option-7)	ƒ (Option-F)
* (Shift-8)	Ø (Option-O)	® (Option-R)	≈ (Option-X)
+ (Shift-=)	Œ (Option-Q)	© (Option-G)	∆ (Option-J)
, (Comma)	P	™ (Option-2)	… (Option-;)
- (Hyphen)	ß (Option-S)	¨ (Shift-Option-U)	- (Option--)
. (Period)	Z	≠ (Option-=)	— (Shift-Option--)
/ (Slash)		∞ (Option-5)	÷ (Option-/)
		± (Shift-Option-=)	◊ (Shift-Option-V)

ARNING

Avoid dragging a document icon onto an application icon. This will launch the application software, as described in the next chapter.

In System 7, you may move an icon from an inactive window into an active window without activating the former. To do so, merely drag the icon without delay from the inactive window to the active window. If you delay after selecting the icon, or attempt to select more than one icon, the rear window will become active.

COPYING ICONS

If you drag one or more icons from a folder on one disk to a folder on a different disk, you will copy—rather than move— the dragged icons from the first disk to the second. A message box will appear as shown in Figure 3.10, complete with a status bar and an item listing the number of icons that remain to be copied. To interrupt the copy process, click the Stop button.

FIGURE 3.10

The Copy message box lists the number of icons that remain to be copied.

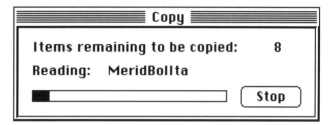

You may also copy icons from one folder to another on a single disk by Option-dragging the icon.

You can drag a disk icon into a folder on a second disk or directly onto the second disk's icon to copy the entire contents of the first disk onto the second. The Finder will automatically deposit the copied contents into a folder on the second disk which bears the name of the first disk. You should note that this technique works only if the second disk contains enough free space to accept the entire first disk. For example, when copying an 800K disk onto a hard drive, the hard drive must offer 800K of free space, even if the copied files only add up to 45K.

DELETING ICONS

The Trash icon in the lower-left corner of the Finder desktop serves as a depository for files and folders that you want to delete. When using Finder 6, files and folders dragged to the Trash were deleted from disk the moment the Finder became inactive, whether caused by launching an application (except when using MultiFinder) or restarting the computer. Starting with Finder 7, the Trash has been elevated in status to a folder. Icons are preserved on disk in the Trash folder until you specifically request their deletion by choosing the Empty Trash... command from the Special menu. Also, you may view the contents of the Trash folder from within dialog boxes, just as you may view the contents of other folders.

You may delete one or more selected icons from disk as follows:

1. Drag the icons to the Trash icon. Wait until the Trash icon becomes reversed, as shown in Figure 3.11, before releasing the mouse button. The Trash icon will change to a bulging can.

After selecting the icons that you want to delete (left), drag them onto the Trash icon (middle). When icons reside in the Trash folder, the Trash icon

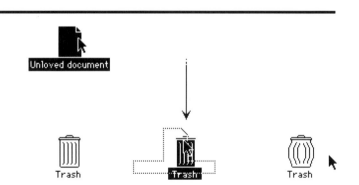

2. Choose the Empty Trash... command from the Special menu. The message shown in Figure 3.12 will appear, telling you how many icons are in the Trash folder and asking you to confirm your request.

FIGURE 3.12

After you choose Empty Trash..., a message will appear asking you to confirm the deletion of all icons in the Trash folder.

⚠️ The Trash contains 471 items, which use 14.8 MB of disk space. Are you sure you want to permanently remove these items?

[Cancel]   [OK]

3. If you click OK, the icons will be deleted. Depending on the number of files and the amount of room they consume on disk, a message box with a status bar will display, listing the number of icons that remain to be deleted, as shown in Figure 3.13.

FIGURE 3.13

The Trash message box lists the number of icons that remain to be deleted.

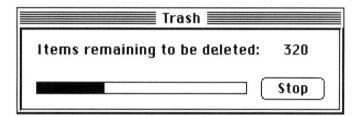

Trash

Items remaining to be deleted: 320

[Stop]

TIP

While deleting the contents of the Trash folder, a message may appear telling you that some items are locked, as shown in Figure 3.14. This means that at least one of the enclosed files has been protected from being renamed or deleted using the "Locked" check box in the file's Info dialog box (as described in Chapter 8). If you click the Continue button, only those files that are not locked and folders that contain no locked files will be deleted. Others will remain in the Trash folder. To delete all icons, locked or not, press Option when choosing the Empty Trash command.

FIGURE 3.14

This message box alerts you that some files in the Trash folder are locked.

> ⚠ **Some items could not be deleted because they are locked. Do you want to delete the other items?**
>
> [Stop]   [[Continue]]

The Trash warning shown in Figure 3.12 can be useful if you're a new user. It warns you that the following action will result in the permanent deletion of certain files. However, if you're an experienced user, this warning can be equally irritating. You know that emptying the Trash deletes files and you don't need some stupid dialog box to display every time you choose the Empty Trash... command.

To temporarily bypass the Trash warning, you can press the Option key when choosing the Empty Trash command. (The ellipsis will disappear to indicate that no dialog box will display.)

To permanently bypass the Trash warning, you can select the Trash icon, then choose the Get Info command from the File menu (⌘-I). The Trash Info dialog box shown in Figure 3.15 will display. This dialog box lists the location of the Trash icon (always "On the desktop"), the contents of the Trash folder, and the time at which the last contents were entered or the Trash was last emptied. Deselect the "Warn before emptying" check box to turn off the Trash warning.

To reactivate the Trash warning, you have only to select the "Warn before emptying" check box. Close the Trash Info dialog box by choosing the Close command from the File menu (⌘-W) or click the close box.

FIGURE 3.15

*T*he Trash info dialog box—shown as it appears when the Trash folder is empty (top) and filled (bottom)—allows you to permanently deactivate the Trash warning.

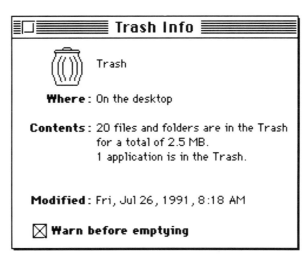

> If you are not the only person who uses your machine
> and the hard drive contains sensitive data that you don't
> want others to delete, you may want to leave the Trash
> warning enabled. Rather than turning off the warning, use a
> macro utility such as QuicKeys from CE Software to create a
> key combination that will simultaneously press Option and
> choose the Empty Trash command. This way, you may
> personally avoid the Trash warning, but display it for others.
> As a further protective measure, lock those files that you
> decide are particularly important. For more information on
> locking files, see Chapter 8.

RESCUING ICONS FROM THE TRASH FOLDER

Theoretically, a file is gone for good once you choose the Empty Trash...
command from the File menu. (For an exception, see the next section.)
Before you empty the Trash folder, however, you may rescue any file as
follows:

1. Open the Trash folder by double-clicking the Trash icon.
The Trash window shown in Figure 3.16 will appear.

2. Select the file or files that you you want to rescue.

3. Drag them back to their original folders or disks, or better
yet, choose the Put Away command from the File menu (⌘-Y).

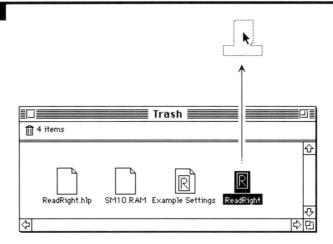

FIGURE 3.16

To rescue an icon from the Trash folder, open the folder and drag the icon to a safe place.

EXPLORING ADVANCED CONCEPTS

The Trash folder discussion is by no means over. But from here on out, things get a little thorny and beyond the scope of the Macintosh system software alone. So for this reason, I'll continue to describe file deletion in the context of a technical discussion, and afterward pursue additional advanced information.

RESCUING FILES FROM BEYOND THE GRAVE

Disks may contain hundreds, even thousands of files. To keep track of these files, your computer writes a *file directory* to the disk, which lists all file names and their location on the disk. When you choose the Empty Trash... command, the file name and its location are deleted from the file directory. However, the file itself is *not* deleted. In other words, the file data remains on disk, but your computer is no longer aware of its existence. In fact, the data remains intact until new data is written over it, a process that may take place any time after the directory location is deleted.

This means that there is a protracted chance of recovering a deleted file, although that chance becomes slimmer and slimmer with every new file that you create. To bring a file back from the dead, you need the help of a special reanimator utility such as the SUM Disk Clinic from Symantec or MacTools Deluxe from Central Point Software. Both programs allow you to install special recovery utilities—Guardian in the case of SUM, Mirror in the case of MacTools—that track the locations of documents and applications long after they have been deleted from your hard drive. Even if the recovery files have not been installed, you can generally restore deleted files by searching a disk for data, selecting files that remain entirely or partially intact, and copying these files to a different disk. Both utilities work remarkably well; one or the other should be considered an essential utility for the experienced Macintosh user.

PERMANENT FILE DELETION

If you have security concerns, you may find it unsettling that a file thrown away can be recovered days or even weeks later using relatively inexpensive technology. But just as there are recovery programs, there are programs that prohibit recovery by completely erasing a file from disk. One such program is File Zero, a shareware utility available on CompuServe in Library 9, "Disks/Storage," of the Macintosh Systems forum (GO MACSYS). Although this product hasn't been updated since 1987 and, judging by several attempted phone calls, the vendor seems to have completely disappeared, the product works fine with System 7. You simply launch the utility, select a file, and zap, it's gone forever. The file is deleted both from the file directory and from its original location on disk. The data may *never* be recovered.

AUTOMATIC TRASH EMPTYING

Finally, if you hate having to choose the Empty Trash command every time you want to delete a file, you may want to try out Trash Chute 2.0. Designed especially to work with System 7, Trash Chute is a 6K application whose sole purpose is to empty the trash. If you double-click the utility, it will run, empty the Trash folder, and automatically quit, a process that takes about the same amount of time as choosing the Empty Trash command. The Trash warning will be bypassed, even if the "Warn before emptying" option is turned on in the Trash Info dialog box.

If you copy the Trash Chute application to the Startup Items folder (as discussed in Chapter 6), it will run every time you start up your Mac, deleting Trash files automatically, much as was the case in System 6. But best yet, position the utility on the desktop, then drag one or more selected files that you wish to delete onto the Trash Chute icon and release, just as if you were dragging a file to the Trash folder. The utility will launch, delete the selected files automatically, and quit. You may even move the Trash folder to a new location on the desktop and position the Trash Chute icon where the Trash folder used to be.

Another automated trash utility is TrashMan 2.1. When placed in the Startup Items folder, this program will automatically empty files that have been in the Trash folder for a specified period of time. For example, suppose you drag one file to the Trash on Monday, and a second on Tuesday. Assuming that you have instructed TrashMan to empty files that have been in the Trash folder at least two days, TrashMan will delete the first file on Wednesday but leave the second file intact until Thursday. You may also specify how often the program searches the Trash folder and whether or not application files are deleted.

A third utility called Basura is a system extension that allows you to delete a selected file from the keyboard. After loading the extension, pressing ⌘-Delete moves all selected files to the Trash folder; press ⌘-Option-Delete to move the file to the Trash and empty the Trash folder.

Trash Chute 2.0 is included on the disk which you can order with the coupon found at the back of this book. TrashMan and Basura are available from CompuServe and other bulletin board services.

VIEWING DIRECTORY WINDOWS

When viewing the contents of the Trash folder or any other open directory window, you may change the way files are listed by choosing a command from the View menu. Several commands appear under the View menu, each of which fit into one of two main categories: *icon views* and *list views.* The two icon views are accessed by choosing the by Small Icon and by Icon commands from the View menu. The results of both commands are shown in Figure 3.17.

The appearance of an icon is determined by a resource included in the file itself. Applications that take advantage of System 7's capabilities—known as *System 7-savvy* applications—offer two sizes of icons: 16-by-16-pixel icons that display in the small icon view and 32-by-32-pixel icons that display in the standard icon view. An older application may lack the 16-by-16-pixel icons. If an application does not provide the smaller icons, then the program and the documents created in that program are assigned reduced versions of their 32-by-32-pixel icons, which tend to look

FIGURE 3.17

Viewing the contents of a folder by small icon and by icon.

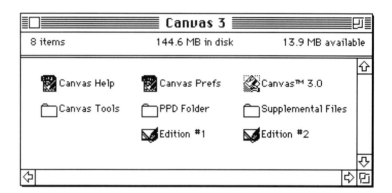

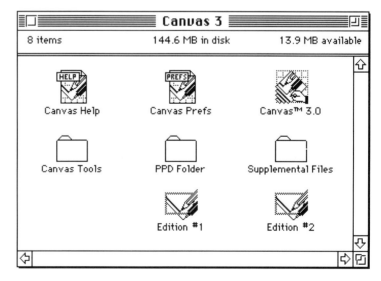

pretty awful. If this bothers you, you may create your own 16-by-16-pixel icons, as described in Chapter 7.

All the other commands in the View menu produce list views, two of which are shown in Figure 3.18. List views display icon names in rows. Columns intersect the list rows. The name of each column is listed in the *header bar,* just below the title bar. Each column imparts the following information:

- **Icon.** The first column in a list view displays a tiny 8-by-8-pixel version of each icon to show whether the listed name represents a document, an application, or a folder.

*V*iewing the contents of a folder by name and by size.

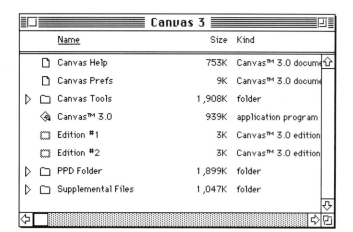

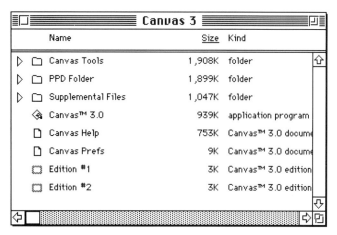

- **Name.** The next column tells the name of each icon.

- **Size.** The third column lists the amount of room each icon consumes on disk in *kilobytes* (1000 bytes; 1K is equal to the approximate size of a long paragraph of unformatted text).

- **Kind.** The fourth column lists the kind of file each icon represents—that is, a folder, an application, or a document. If the file is a document, the Kind column tells what application was used to create it.

- **Label.** The fifth column lists the label, if any, that has been assigned to the icon using a command from the Label menu.

- **Last Modified.** The sixth column lists the exact time at which the icon was last modified, allowing you to compare files with identical names to see which is the more recent version.

- **Version.** The next column lists the version number of an application icon. Folders and documents may not be assigned version numbers.

- **Comments.** The last column shows any comments entered into the Info dialog box for each icon.

Unlike in System 6, you may now scroll a directory window horizontally when displayed in a list view. This allows you to see additional information, such as modification dates and comments, which are generally so far to the right that they extend beyond the width of a directory window. Incidentally, don't worry if one or more of the list view columns—such as Labels or Comments—are missing from your directory window display. You may add or subtract column categories using the Views control panel, as described in Chapter 7.

> In addition to using View menu commands to change
> the order in which icons are displayed on screen, you may
> click a column name in the header to change the order in
> which icons are displayed. For example, if you click the word
> *Size* in the header bar, the icons will be listed in order of
> their size, from largest to smallest, just as if you had chosen
> the by Size command from the View menu. The word Size
> will become underlined to show that it is the active view.

CLEANING UP ICONS

Certain unique organizational features are available depending on
whether the current directory window is shown in icon view or list view.
For example, when you view a window by icon, you may rearrange icons
using a grid that measures 56 pixels high by 72 pixels wide. The grid for
small icons measures 24 pixels high by 106 pixels wide. You may align
icons to either of these grids using the Clean Up command from the
Special menu.

The Clean Up command is available in five forms, each of which
allows you to align icons according to a unique criterion:

- **Clean Up Window.** When a directory window is active,
  choose the Clean Up Window command to align every icon
  in the window—whether in plain view or hidden—to the
  nearest grid point, as demonstrated in Figure 3.19.

- **Clean Up by Name, Size, Kind, etc.** When a window is
  active, press Option when displaying the Special menu to
  access the Clean Up by [Attribute] command, where [*Attribute*]
  represents the most recent list view used in this window. For
  example, if you choose the by Name command from the
  View menu and then choose by Icon, pressing Option when
  choosing from the Special menu will display the Clean Up

FIGURE 3.19

A directory window before (left) and after (right) choosing the Clean Up Window command

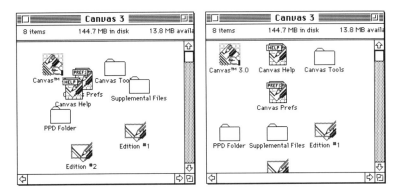

by Name command. Icons will be aligned to the grid in alphabetical order according to icon name—from left to right then top to bottom—as shown in the first example of Figure 3.20.

FIGURE 3.20

A directory window after choosing Clean Up by Name (left) and Clean Up by Size (right)

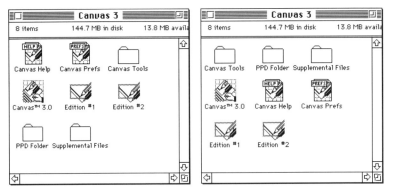

- **Clean Up Desktop.** When *no* directory window is active, choose the Clean Up Desktop command to align every icon on the Finder desktop to the nearest grid point, as shown in Figure 3.21.

- **Clean Up All.** When *no* window is active, you can press Option when displaying the Special menu to choose Clean Up All, which rearranges all files and folder on the desktop—except the Trash folder—in alphabetical order according to

FIGURE 3.21

The desktop after
aligning all icons to the
56-by-72-pixel grid

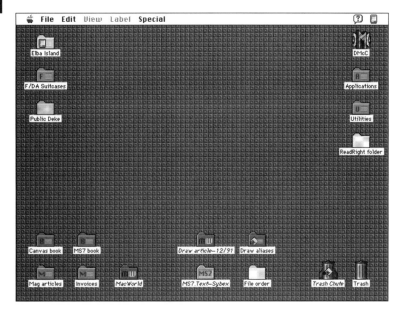

icon name from top to bottom then right to left, as shown
in Figure 3.22. The hard drive containing the active System
Folder is moved to the upper-right corner of the desktop.
All additional disks are arranged below the active hard
drive in order of device ID number. The Trash folder is
moved to the lower-right corner of the desktop.

- **Clean Up Selection.** Press Shift when displaying the Special
menu to choose the Clean Up Selection command, which
aligns all selected icons to the nearest grid points. This command is dimmed if no icon is selected.

NAVIGATING IN LIST VIEWS

List views offer no arrangement options except those contained in the
View menu. However, they do offer specific navigational functions that
surpass those associated with icon views. In the first column of a list view,
one of various icons precedes each file name; a tiny folder icon precedes

FIGURE 3.22

Use the Clean Up All command to list files and folders in alphabetical order. If icon names are so long they may overlap, a grid point is skipped as shown to the left of the "Draw article" and "F/DA Suitcases" folders.

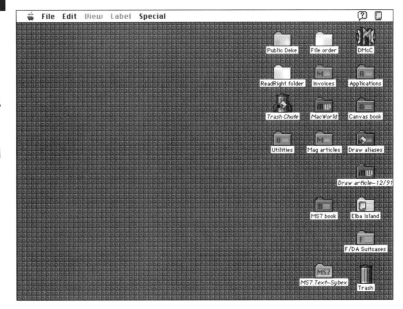

each folder name. To the left of the folder icon is a small triangle, which may point either toward the folder or downward. You can click the triangle to toggle its orientation. When a triangle is pointed toward its folder, the contents of the folder are not displayed in the current window. In the vernacular of the realm, such a folder is said to be *collapsed*. When the triangle is pointed downward, the folder is *expanded*. The contents of an expanded folder appear slightly indented in a list directly below the folder name, as shown in Figure 3.23. In this way, you may glean the hierarchical structure of an open folder by viewing not only its contents, but also the contents of the folders within the opened folder, folders within those folders, and so on, several folders deep. Folders within folders are called *nested folders*, or *subfolders*.

Additionally, Finder 7 provides the following ways to expand and collapse listed folders from the keyboard:

- ⌘-**Arrow.** To expand a selected folder from the keyboard, simultaneously press ⌘ and →. To collapse a selected folder, press ⌘←.

FIGURE 3.23

To view the contents of a folder in a list view, click the small triangle that precedes the folder icon (top). The contents of the folder will then display in an indented list below the folder name (bottom).

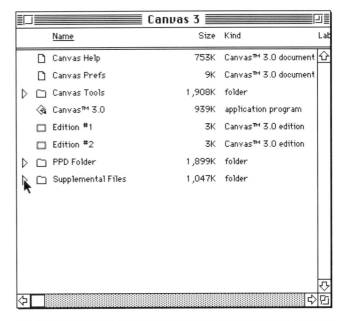

- ⌘-**Option-Arrow.** To expand the selected folder as well as
  all nested folders inside the selected folder, press ⌘-Option-→.
  To collapse a selected folder as well as all folders inside it,
  press ⌘-Option-←.

Finder 7's hierarchical folder display allows you to simultaneously
select files from different folders. For example, if the contents of three
folder levels are displayed—that is, 1) the contents of the open folder,
2) the contents of a subfolder within that folder, and 3) the contents
of a subfolder within the previous subfolder—you may select files from
all three folder levels by clicking on the first file name and then Shift-
clicking on each additional file name, as shown in Figure 3.24. This allows you to move or copy icons from various folder levels at once, rather
than digging through folders and moving or copying files one at a time.

FIGURE 3.24

To view the contents of a folder in a list view, click the small triangle that precedes the folder icon (top). The contents of the folder will then display in an indented list below the folder name (bottom).

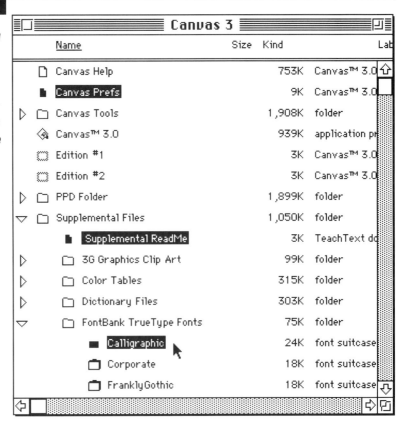

In a list view, you may use keyboard techniques to select any icon displayed in the current directory window, including icons in an expanded folder. In Figure 3.23, for example, pressing the D key will select the Dictionary Files icon inside the expanded Supplemental Files folder. Pressing the Tab key will then select Edition #1, the next displayed icon in alphabetical order, even though that icon exists in a separate folder from the Dictionary Files icon. Jumping around inside a window in this way can prove confusing at first, but with a little practice, this technique becomes familiar and useful.

GENERAL NAVIGATION TECHNIQUES

Other navigation techniques may be used within any directory window, whether displayed in icon or list view. For example, all directory windows provide *autoscrolling* capabilities. If you drag an icon beyond one of the edges of the window, the window will scroll in that direction (provided, of course, the window *can* scroll in that direction). To scroll upward, you can drag the file into the header bar, as shown in Figure 3.25. To scroll downward, you just drag into the horizontal scroll bar. To scroll to the right, you drag into the vertical scroll bar. To scroll leftward, you may drag within about ⅛ inch of the left side of the window.

Another Finder feature is the directory window *folder bar.* Just like the folder bar long found in the standard document selection dialog box, the folder bar in the directory window allows you to bring a parent folder to the front of the desktop. To access the folder bar, press the Command key and drag from the title bar of the active window, as shown in Figure 3.26. The name of the current folder will display first, followed by the name of the folder that contains the current folder, and so on. Choose the desired folder as you would a command, and that folder will become the active directory window.

FIGURE 3.25

Drag an icon to the edge of the directory window to autoscroll the window in that direction.

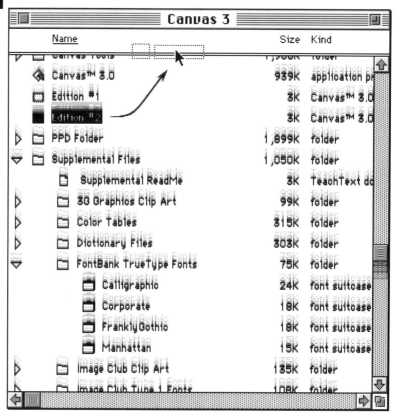

Several other navigation techniques can be accessed from the keyboard. These include the following:

- **Opening folders.** To open one or more selected folders, double-click a selected folder name or press ⌘-↓. To open a selected folder and simultaneously close the current directory window, you can press Option while double-clicking a folder name or press ⌘-Option-↓.

- **Opening parent folders.** To activate the directory window for the folder that contains the current folder, press ⌘-↑. To close the current window when activating its parent folder, you can press ⌘-Option-↑ or press ⌘ and Option and choose the desired folder name from the folder bar pop-up menu.

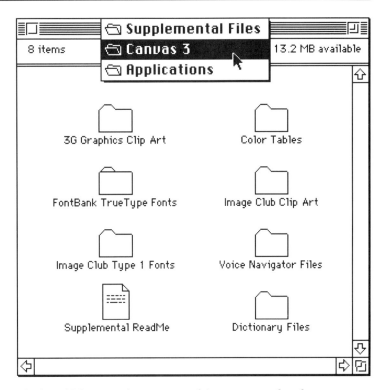

FIGURE 3.26

*P*ress Command and drag from the title bar to access the folder bar pop-up menu, which lists the path to the current folder.

Congratulations! Now you know everything you need to know to use the Finder. In the following chapter, I'll explain how to launch applications and open files. However, if you're interested in bigger and better Finder knowledge, skip to Chapter 7 for complete information on customizing the Finder, including how to use the Views control panel, create icon aliases, and design custom color icons.

Running Software in the New Multitasking Environment

YOU CAN SAY goodbye to the Multi-
▬ Finder and hello to the new improved
multitasking environment at work in System 7. Well, to be honest, the
term *multitasking* can be applied only loosely in the context of System 7.
Contrary to the occasional rumor, the Macintosh computer cannot chew
gum and walk at the same time. However, it can do one or the other in
such rapid-fire alternation—chew, then walk, then chew, then walk—that
it *appears* to be doing both simultaneously.

WHAT IS MULTITASKING?

The old MultiFinder was integrated into System 7 and improved. First,
you can run two applications at the same time. For example, every time you
start up, or *launch,* an application, the Finder application continues to
run in the background. You may think you're running only one program;
perhaps Microsoft Excel, MacWrite, or Aldus PageMaker, but you're actually running two—Excel *and* the Finder, MacWrite *and* the Finder, or
PageMaker *and* the Finder. Provided that sufficient memory is available,
you may even run Excel, MacWrite, PageMaker, and the Finder all at the
same time.

Even when running two or more programs, your computer frequently has to contend with instructions from one application only. The
foreground application—that is, the program at the front of your screen—
is typically the program in control of your computer. Meanwhile, *background applications*—programs that are running but are *not* at the front of
the screen—lie dormant, waiting patiently for the moment you again
wish to call on their capabilities. There are no overlapping operations
and no applications competing for attention.

But what happens when you want to perform two or more operations at once? After all, the real power of a computer is that it automates certain jobs, completing them faster so you can go home earlier. You might be writing a letter in the foreground application while the background application prints a 100-page report. Or you could perform spreadsheet calculations in the foreground while both decompressing a newsletter file and E-mailing a 750K photographic scan in the background.

To keep up with your many instructions, System 7 relies on *cooperative multitasking,* in which programs are on their honor to amicably share the computer's processing time. If two programs are trying to perform tasks at the same time, the system switches control between the two programs in equal increments. This works fine if all programs can complete their respective operations in the allocated time segments. But if one application doesn't feel like playing nicely, it can refuse to relinquish sufficient control to other applications. Some uncooperative programs will simply refuse to perform tasks in the background. Others will slow down foreground operations, prevent your cursor from moving smoothly, and so on.

For the meantime, you'll have to grin and bear it. The only solution is to upgrade your applications to System 7-friendly versions that are theoretically better at completing tasks during small, interrupted windows of time. If you've an eye toward the future, System 8 will reportedly offer *preemptive multitasking,* in which application and system software work together to arrive at realistic time-sharing scenarios. System 8 will act as a hands-on manager, actively controlling the amount of time available to each running program. For example, a typical conversation between a preemptive multitasking system and a running application might go something like this:

System: "I've got a 5-second time slot coming up. Do you want it?"

Application: "Ah, man, 5 seconds? What the heck am I going to do with 5 seconds?"

System: "Okay, okay. What do you need?"

Application: "At least 14 seconds!"

System: "You must *like* making my life miserable. Look, I've got a 12-second time slot coming within the next minute. But that's it. You go over 12 seconds and I'll pull the plug on you."

Application: "Yeah, man. You just get me the time and let me worry about using it."

And you thought software was all harmony and brotherly love. It's a jungle in there!

MAKING THE BEST OF IT

System 7's application-handling may not be perfect, but most users will hardly notice the difference between the cooperative multitasking that's available today and the preemptive multitasking that you'll find in the future. In this chapter, I'll explain how to launch applications, switch from one running program to the another, use the Applications menu, copy files in the background, and perform a variety of other background tasks. In short, you and I will branch out from the Finder into the wide world of application software, allowing you to put your computer to work on time-saving or perhaps money-making projects.

GETTING STARTED

When you start up your computer, the system software instructs the CPU to automatically launch the Finder application. In System 7, the Finder remains running as long as you use your Mac. One or more additional applications may be launched from the Finder in any of the following ways:

- **Open each application directly.** Double-click the application icon or select the icon and choose the Open command from the File menu (⌘-O).

- **Open a document belonging to an application.** Double-click the document icon or select the document and choose Open from the File menu (⌘-O). The system software locates the application in which a file was last saved, launches that application, and opens the selected document.

- **Drag the document icon onto an application icon.** Say that you've located an old piece of bitmapped clip art. It's saved as a MacPaint file, but you want to open it in Photoshop where you can colorize the image and apply special effects. You may either 1) launch Photoshop, then open the Mac-Paint file or 2) eliminate the middle man by dragging the

MacPaint file icon onto the Photoshop application icon, as shown in Figure 4.1. If the application supports the format of the file being dragged onto it, the application icon will become highlighted, as shown in the figure. If the format is not selected, the icon will not become highlighted, nor will the application launch.

FIGURE 4.1

Drag a document icon onto an application icon to open the selected document in the selected application.

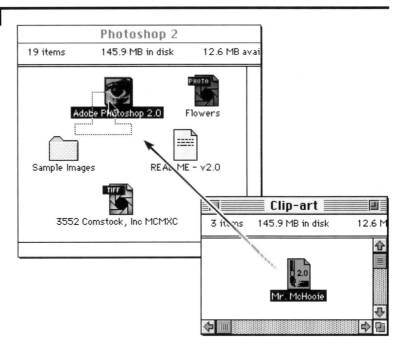

Other methods for launching an application involve the use of macro programs, aliases, and the Apple Menu Items and Startup Items folders inside the System Folder. These techniques are described in the *Exploring Advanced Topics* section near the end of this chapter.

SWITCHING BETWEEN RUNNING APPLICATIONS

There are two primary methods for *switching* between applications; that is, bringing one application to the foreground and sending the previous foreground application to the background.

- **Choose the application from the Applications menu.** The Applications menu, represented by the far-right icon in the menu bar, provides access to every running application, including the Finder. Choose the desired application from the menu to bring that application to the foreground.

- **Click a background window.** Like the Finder, every application offers its own desktop, including a menu bar, windows for open documents, and other items that vary from application to application—including toolboxes, palettes, and floating rulers. Clicking on an open window or other item will bring the application to which the item belongs to the foreground. For example, when working in Microsoft Word, you may click a Finder window, a desktop icon, or the desktop pattern itself to bring the Finder to the fore-ground, as shown in Figure 4.2; then click the open Word document to again bring Microsoft Word to the foreground, as shown in Figure 4.3.

FIGURE 4.2

Clicking an open directory window brings the Finder to the foreground.

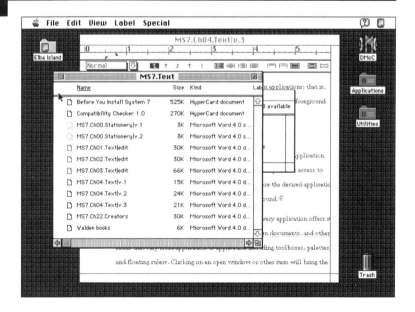

TIP

Under System 6, you used to be able to cycle through running applications by clicking the application icon on the far right side of the menu bar. Now that the application icon has been upgraded to the Applications menu, this technique is no longer possible. If you miss this function, several utilities are available that allow you to reinstate the real thing or a reasonable facsimile. Included on the disks you can order with the coupon at the back of this book, Just Click from Tactic Software is available both as a system extension and as an Fkey. The system extension allows you to click the Applications menu icon to switch applications; the Fkey cycles when you press ⌘-Shift-6. QuicKeys 2.1 provides two System 7.1 extensions that cycle to the next or previous running application. But my favorite is a system extension by Jeff Bock, called Switch—available on CompuServe in Library 3, "Assembly Language," of the Macintosh Developers forum (GO MACDEV)—which cycles through programs when you press the power-up switch in the upper-right corner of a newer-model keyboard. A similar extension, PwrSwitcher by David Lamkins, is included on the disks which you can order with the coupon found at the back of this book.

HIDING AND SHOWING RUNNING APPLICATIONS

Normally, I'm one of those people who live comfortably in a cluttered environment. But clutter on my computer screen is another matter entirely. Forget that it's unattractive; the problem is that GUI clutter prevents you from being able to access important files, folders, disks, and data. For example, how do you access a folder on the desktop when a huge Microsoft Word window is in your way?

The answer: Hide the Word application from view. Hiding an application does not close its windows; it merely makes them temporarily

FIGURE 4.3

Clicking an open document window brings the document and the application to which the document belongs to the foreground

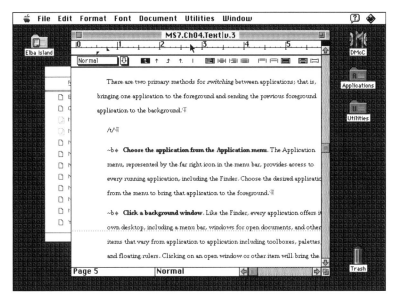

invisible. One or more applications may be hidden and redisplayed at any time using commands under the Applications menu.

- **Hide the current application.** Choose the first command from the Applications menu to hide the current application. All windows and other items associated with the current application will disappear. The application running immediately behind the hidden application will move to the foreground.

Press Option and choose a program name from the Applications menu to bring that program to the foreground and hide the previous foreground application. The current foreground application may also be hidden by Option-clicking on a window or other item belonging to another running application.

- **Hide all background applications.** Choose the Hide Others command to hide all applications except the current foreground application. This command is especially useful when working at the Finder level, wherein windows from other applications can prove especially distracting.

- **Show a single application.** Icons shown in the Applications menu appear dimmed if they belong to hidden programs. To redisplay a running application with a dimmed icon, choose its name from the Applications menu. The application will simultaneously display and move to the foreground.

- **Show all applications.** Choose the Show All command to redisplay all hidden applications without bringing them to the foreground. This command is dimmed if all open windows are already displayed.

OPENING A DOCUMENT IN A RUNNING APPLICATION

Once a desired application has been launched, you may open a document in one of two ways:

- **Open from inside the application.** Choose the Open… command from the the application's File menu (⌘-O). With remarkably few exceptions, virtually every Macintosh application offers such a command. Select the document that you want to open from the resulting dialog box and press Return. For more information about using this and other standard Macintosh dialog boxes, see Chapter 10.

- **Open from the Finder.** In System 7.1, you may open a document from the Finder desktop, even if its application is already running. Simply double-click the document icon or select the icon and choose the Open command from the Finder File menu (⌘-O). The corresponding application will be brought to the foreground and the document will be opened in a new window.

Quitting an Application

There are all kinds of reasons to quit an application. Your day's work may be done or you may simply want to take a break. Perhaps most commonly, no one has an inexhaustible supply of memory, which means that you must occasionally quit one application to make room in your computer's RAM to launch another application.

To quit the foreground application, choose Quit, the last command in the File menu (⌘-Q). The application next in line behind the quit application will be moved to the foreground.

Learning Fundamental Concepts

Remember that old Crewcuts song, *Sh-Boom?* Four or five guys with hair like freshly mowed grass gleefully croon, "Life could be a dream, sh-boom, if you would take me up to paradise above, sh-boom, and tell me I'm the only one you love, life could be a dream sweetheart," followed by some more sh-booming. Having never set foot in the 1950's myself, I can only guess that such giddiness was the result of a world-wide proliferation of prescription drugs, or perhaps too much ozone. But from the previous section, you might think I was under a similar spell, having described the running of programs as if it was all sweetness and cream. In fact, as you may already be aware, juggling applications can be a real nightmare.

Where Did This File Come From?

Much as I would love to report otherwise, an application may not always open as desired. One of two problems commonly occur. If you are trying to launch an application by double-clicking a document icon, the message shown in Figure 4.4 may appear, indicating that the application in which the document was last saved cannot be located on any mounted disk. For example, suppose you want to update a newsletter created a couple of years ago in PageMaker 3.0. Being the on-the-ball kind of person you are, you've long since upgraded to PageMaker 4.01 (or maybe an even higher version). When you double-click the newsletter file, the

Finder goes from application to application saying, "I've got a Page-Maker 3.0 file here. Who does it belong to?" Not being smart enough to recognize the offspring of its ancestors, PageMaker 4.01 ignores the inquiry. The Finder can't launch what it can't find, so it displays the message shown in Figure 4.4.

This message will display if the application in which a document was last saved cannot be found.

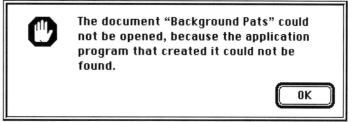

> The document "Background Pats" could not be opened, because the application program that created it could not be found.
>
> [OK]

The solution? You may launch the application and then open the document or drag the document icon onto the application icon, as I describe in the previous section. However, both of these techniques assume that you know of an application that will open the desired document. Sadly, this is often not the case. I wish I had a nickel—make that $100—for every time I've run across a document of entirely unknown origin. When I do, I can't remember what the heck the document is, much less what application was used to create it. The easiest way to remedy this problem is to look at the document's icon, either by displaying the active window in the icon view or by selecting the document and choosing the Get Info command from the File menu (⌘-I). Often, the icon will appear familiar enough to help jog your memory, or at least point the way toward a program that will open the document.

This solution is flawed, however, since 1) you may not recognize the icon or 2) the icon may be the generic document icon, which looks like a blank page with a folded upper-right corner. The generic icon displays if no specific icon was applied to the file when it was created or if the original icon has become lost (a common occurrence, generally the result of rebuilding the desktop file on a disk when the application in which the file was last saved is not present). The generic document icon is no help in finding the parent application.

But thanks to the foresight of the Mac's early developers, every Macintosh application is required to offer a four-character *creator code,* which is registered with Apple to ensure that no two codes are alike. The application transfers its unique creator code to every document during the saving process. PageMaker 4.01, for example, recognizes its files because it has marked them with the creator code *ALD4*, but it doesn't recognize files created in PageMaker 3.0 which contain the creator code *ALD3*.

Creator codes may be displayed using a variety of third-party utilities, including Symantec Tools, CE Software's DiskTop, Apple's ResEdit, and several others. To determine which application created a document, display the creator code for that document as shown in Figure 4.5. Then compare the document's creator code to those contained in Appendix C, which represents the most up-to-date list of creator codes registered with Apple, along with the applications to which they belong.

FIGURE 4.5

The Disktop desk accessory from CE Software allows you to view documents in technical mode, showing type and creator codes.

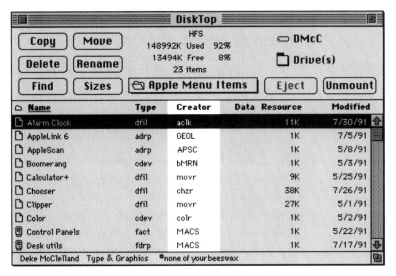

OUT OF MEMORY

The second error message, shown in Figure 4.6, will appear if your computer does not have a sufficiently large uninterrupted block of RAM available to open an application. The only solution is to quit one or more of the applications that are currently running—this will free up some memory.

FIGURE 4.6

This message will display if there is not enough memory available to launch a program.

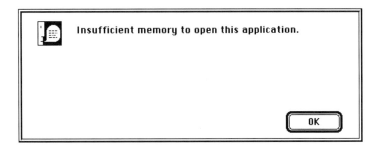

Insufficient memory to open this application.

OK

I'll discuss memory in detail in Chapter 9. But, in the meantime, there are two things you should know. First, the system software can occupy anywhere between 1MB and 2MB of RAM, depending on the number of fonts and sounds loaded into the System file and the number of currently running control panels and system extensions. This means that if your machine is equipped with the minimum 2MB of RAM required to run System 7.1, you'll have at most 1MB of free RAM for launching applications—enough room for a basic program such as Microsoft Word or MacPaint to run independently. With such a small amount of RAM, you'll likely never be able to run two applications (other than the Finder) simultaneously, and you'll never be able to run moderately sophisticated number-crunching and desktop-publishing programs.

Simply put, no matter what machine you use, everything from a Mac Plus on up should be equipped with at least 4MB of RAM. If your computer is RAM poor, now is a great time to upgrade. As of this writing, RAM is cheap, about $35 to $40 per 1MB SIMM (*single-in-line memory module*, the small circuit board on which RAM chips are distributed). As is the case in the oil industry, American computer manufacturers depend on foreign markets for microchips. For this reason, RAM chips are unlikely to go down in price in the near future and there is forever speculation that their prices will increase.

Second, memory can become *fragmented*—that is, subdivided into blocks too small to launch other applications. For example, suppose that no application other than the Finder is running on a machine equipped with 8MB of RAM. The system software is small, leaving 7MB of RAM free to run additional application software. You first launch Microsoft Word, which consumes 1MB; then MacPaint, which consumes another 1MB; then Adobe Photoshop, which eats up 4MB. Only 1MB of RAM remains free, as shown in Figure 4.7. Now suppose that you want to launch Aldus

PageMaker, a program that requires 2MB to run. But before you can launch PageMaker, you must quit one or more applications to free up enough RAM space. Since 1MB of RAM is currently free, you reason that you need to free up only 1MB more, so you quit MacPaint. But when you try to launch PageMaker, an out-of-memory error message appears. Although you have 2MB of free RAM available, the memory is fragmented in 1MB chunks, as shown in Figure 4.7. PageMaker requires 2MB of uninterrupted RAM.

FIGURE 4.7

*T*he horizontal bars represent RAM available to your computer. As shown in the five steps above, launching and quitting software may result in memory fragmentation.

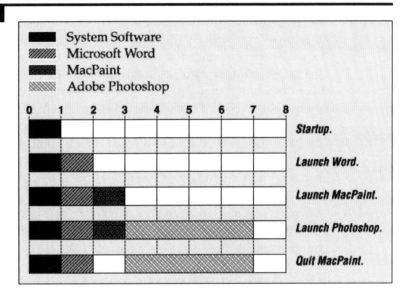

The only sure-fire way to avoid memory fragmentation is to quit applications in the *opposite* order that you launch them. But since few of us work that systematically, you may find that sometimes, before you can launch a new application, you must completely free up your RAM by quitting *all* applications and relaunching the desired software.

THE BOMB

Sometimes you don't get to decide when to quit an application; the computer decides for you. The complex threads of communication that flow between the current application, the system software, background applications, control panels, extensions, and various other components of your computer sometimes go haywire, resulting in a *system error.*

If you're lucky, a *bomb message* like the one shown in Figure 4.8 will appear. Click the Continue button to quit the current application and return to the Finder or other running application; click Restart to reboot the computer. In either case, you will most likely lose all the data created in the current application since you last saved. Some applications—including many file management and accounting packages—store data in temporary files as you work, helping to prevent the loss of time and effort. But most applications require you to save and update files manually. If you lose a great deal of data due to a system error, try to learn from your mistake. Like it or not, system errors are a fact of life; saving regularly can make it less painful.

FIGURE 4.8

The bomb message alerts you that the current application has become snagged in a system error.

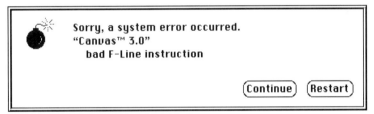

Sometimes, the Continue button is dimmed and your only option is to restart your computer, which results in the loss of all data created in *all* applications since you last saved. However, if the Continue button is available, I recommend the following course of action:

1. Click the Continue button to exit the current application without saving your data.

2. Go to each running application in turn, save your work, and quit the application.

3. After all data has been saved and all applications have been quit, reboot your computer by choosing the Restart command from the Special menu in the Finder.

A system error always disables the current application. It may also pose subtle problems for other applications, even if you're allowed to continue to work. Rebooting allows the system software to recollect itself and erases all illegal information from RAM, lessening the risk of encountering a future system error that may pose a more serious threat.

THE FREEZE

The bomb message appears when the system software manages to correctly identify a system error. When the system software fails to identify an error, your computer may *freeze* or *lock up*—synonymous expressions for what happens when your computer stops responding to input from the keyboard, mouse, or any other device. The cursor freezes in place and all operations cease.

There are two ways to deal with this problem. The first, less elegant solution is to restart your computer by turning it off for about ten seconds and then turning it back on. The second, more graceful solution is to interrupt the power supply by pressing the reset button on the *programmer's switch*—that little plastic gizmo that attaches to the lower-left side of a Plus or other single-unit Mac or to one of several other locations on LCs and series II computers (see Figure 4.9). For reasons that defy understanding, programmers' switches are included with every Macintosh computer ever sold, but they are not installed, nor is their installation

FIGURE 4.9

*T*he programmer's switch included with the Macintosh Plus, SE, and Classic

explained in the manual that accompanies your computer. So I'm afraid you're on your own. Hint: Call your local Macintosh users group. Every Macintosh nerd… er… excuse me… Macintosh *guru* knows how to install one of these suckers.

> System 7 introduces a possible third way to exit a frozen program called the *forced quit.* You may be able to exit the current application only and rescue data included in other applications by pressing ⌘-Option-Escape. This forces an application to quit without saving changes and may be applied any time when using your Mac. The alert message shown in Figure 4.10 will request that you confirm the operation. This technique will not necessarily work when a program is frozen, but when it does, the system software exits the current application and unfreezes other applications, allowing you to save changes and quit back to the Finder in a normal fashion. As when exiting from a bomb message, you should restart your computer as soon as possible to clear the memory and rebuild the system.

FIGURE 4.10

*T*his message appears when you press ⌘-Option-Escape.

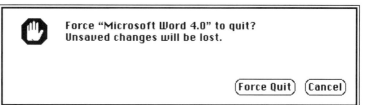

EXPLORING ADVANCED TOPICS

There's nothing particularly advanced about launching an application. And while dealing with an error can prove a little tricky, everyone who uses a Mac—regardless of their skill level—must quickly come to terms with errors. So what the heck can you learn about running software from an advanced section?

The answer is *speed*.

Have you ever seen a couple of master chess players at work? One player moves, slaps the timer, the opponent moves, slaps the timer, back and forth, back and forth, all in the time it takes a normal person to remember how that one horse piece moves. An expert chess player moves quickly because 1) the expert knows the pieces intimately, 2) the expert is well versed in the strategy of the game, and 3) the expert recognizes the tricks of the game. For that person, chess has become second nature.

Similarly, a Macintosh master works at a speed generally associated with dialing your home phone number. A master is a user for whom managing files, launching applications, and organizing data have become second nature.

Granted, Mac masters don't get out enough. And they eat, drink, and breathe electromagnetic emissions. So maybe these people shouldn't be your role models. But you have to admire their speed. Imagine the things you could do if you could cut the time you spend on your computer by 25%, or even more. You could go fishing, spend some quality time with the kids, get a part-time job at McDonalds. The possibilities are endless.

So how do you gain speed without experience? Getting to know your software intimately requires experience. Becoming well versed in Macintosh strategy requires experience. But recognizing the tricks of the game requires only that you read the following pages.

AUTOMATED APPLICATION LAUNCHING

Anyone with more than ten pieces of software should invest in one more, a *macro* program. In case you don't already know, macros are user-defined shortcuts that allow you to record one or more operations— choosing a command, launching an application, clicking your mouse at a specific point on screen—and assign those operations to a keystroke. By far and away the best are QuicKeys 2.1 from CE Software, and Tempo II

Plus from the local Boulder-boys at Affinity (about six blocks from my office). Of the two, I must admit to preferring QuicKeys for launching applications (Figure 4.11). Its design is more straightforward than Tempo's nested-dialog-box approach. Also, QuicKeys provides a dedicated application-launching feature, which simplifies the process admirably. But Tempo excels at high-end macro-making. It allows you to record virtually any series of actions that you can perform using a Macintosh computer. And from experience, I can tell you that *no* program performs hour after hour of repetitive tasks without supervision better than Tempo does.

FIGURE 4.11

QuicKeys is the ideal utility for launching applications from the keyboard.

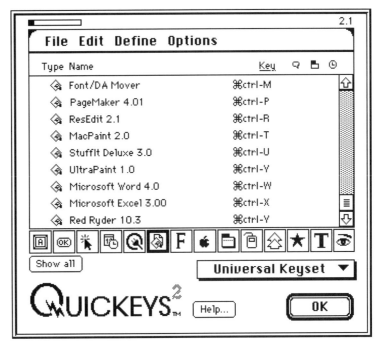

When using a macro program, I recommend sticking to a regular keystroke strategy. For example, I use ⌘-Control key combinations to launch applications exclusively: ⌘-Control-W launches Microsoft Word, ⌘-Control-X launches Excel, ⌘-Control-P launches PageMaker, and so on. Some might knock my strategy because it involves the use of both hands—one to press ⌘-Control and the other to press the character key—but including the keypad, it allows you to launch up to 62 applications from the keyboard. And there's no overlap with keyboard equivalents provided in running applications; almost no application provides built-in ⌘-Control key combinations.

> Under System 7, any macro that will launch a piece of software will also bring it to the foreground if the application is already running. So rather than having to create a separate macro that chooses a program name from the Applications menu, you can use a single macro to access an application regardless of whether it is running or not.

As long as I'm on the subject of application switching, I'll mention one more item of possible interest. If you ever used System 6 with Multi-Finder, you might remember that clicking on the application icon on the far right end of the menu bar would switch to the next running application. To the dismay of some users, this functionality has been lost with the creation of the Applications menu under System 7. If you miss this feature, QuicKeys 2.1 provides an extension called System 7 Specials which allows you to bring the next or previous running application to the foreground by way of a keystroke. The dialog box provided to create such a macro is shown in Figure 4.12.

FIGURE 4.12

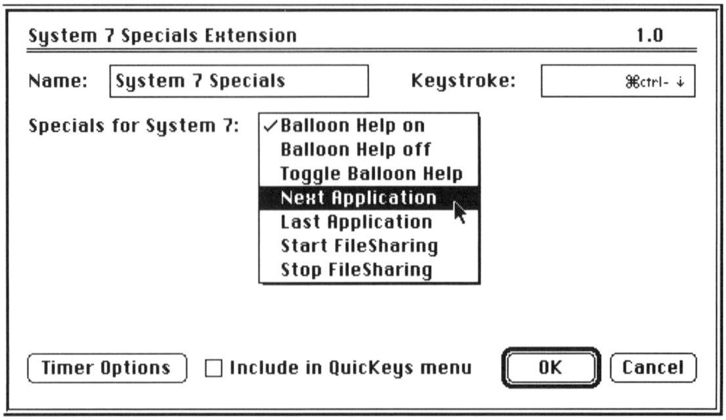

The System 7 Specials extension provided with QuicKeys 2.1 allows you to switch to a different application, toggle the balloon help on and off, and control file sharing.

System 7 Specials Extension	1.0

Name: [System 7 Specials]   Keystroke: [⌘ctrl-↓]

Specials for System 7:
- ✓Balloon Help on
- Balloon Help off
- Toggle Balloon Help
- **Next Application**
- Last Application
- Start FileSharing
- Stop FileSharing

[Timer Options]   ☐ Include in QuicKeys menu   [OK]   [Cancel]

In addition to macros, you may automate the application-launching process using features provided as an integral part of Finder 7. Use the Make Alias command from the File menu to create 3K icon *aliases* that track the location of an original application or document. Aliases can be located in any folder or on any disk, making it possible to quickly and easily launch an application from various locations in the desktop hierarchy. For complete information about aliases, refer to Chapter 7.

Icons or aliases placed inside the Apple Menu Items folder inside the System Folder will appear under the Apple menu on the far left side of the menu bar. You may then launch the corresponding application as easily as choosing a command from the Apple menu. If you use an application on a daily basis, as a writer might use Microsoft Word or Mac-Write Pro, place an alias of the icon in the Startup Items folder inside the System Folder. Any application represented in the Startup Items folder is automatically launched along with the Finder application immediately after you start up your computer. For more information about the Apple Menu Items folder, the Startup Items folder, and other specialized folders inside the System Folder, read Chapter 6.

BACKGROUND PROCESSING

Imagine if you were a housewife in the 1960s. Your dream of dreams—I mean, *besides* that of divorcing your husband and escaping your meaningless bourgeois existence—was to be able to set your oven to clean itself automatically while you performed some more important task. Herein lie the roots of *background processing,* the capability to perform one or more tasks automatically in the background while performing a more demanding task manually in the foreground.

System 7's cooperative multitasking environment allows you to perform a variety of background tasks. For example, as I compose this text in Microsoft Word, my computer is simultaneously engaged in printing a large, full-color image from Adobe Photoshop. But perhaps the most notable example of background processing in System 7 is file copying. Try this: Launch an application—say, MacWrite. Then bring the Finder to the foreground. Drag-copy a large file—about 500K, from your hard drive to a floppy disk. Once the copying process begins, bring MacWrite to the foreground again. As you enter text into the word processor, the file will continue to copy in the background without any supervision from you, freeing you to complete other essential duties unhampered.

The following is a list of additional tasks that will run in the background using various applications. Experimenting with these and other background tasks will increase your speed dramatically.

Compressing and Decompressing

A *compression utility* is a program that reduces the size of a file on disk, allowing you to archive a large amount of data to relatively few backup disks. Various compression utilities—including StuffIt Deluxe from Aladdin Systems, DiskDoubler from Salient Software, and Compact Pro from Bill Goodman—will compress and decompress files in the background.

Uploading and Downloading

There's nothing more irritating than tying up your computer as you *upload* (send) or *download* (receive) a file over the modem. When using a telecommunications program such as CompuServe Information Manager, Red Ryder or White Knight (both from FreeSoft), or Microphone II (Software Ventures), you can send or receive a file over the phone lines in the background without noticeably affecting the speed of a foreground application.

Converting Fonts

In the following chapter, I discuss how to use PostScript and TrueType fonts with your Mac. I also discuss two utilities—Metamorphosis Professional from Altsys and FontMonger from Ares Software—which can be used to convert fonts from one format to the other. Because font conversion is time consuming, both will convert fonts in the background.

Printing

When printing to various kinds of laser printers and high-end PostScript devices, you can print files in the background using the PrintMonitor utility. Included with System 7, the PrintMonitor resides in the Extensions folder inside the System Folder. This self-launching utility may be set into operation in the following way:

1. Choose the Chooser desk accessory from the Apple menu. The Chooser dialog box shown in Figure 4.13 will display.

2. Select the desired *printer driver* from the scrolling list of icons on the left side of the dialog box. The printer driver

FIGURE 4.13

The Chooser desk accessory allows you to select a printer driver and activate background printing.

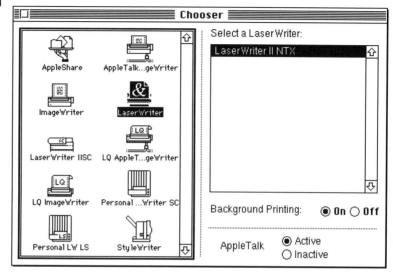

controls the manner in which information is translated from your Mac to the output device. The LaserWriter, Laser-Writer II SC, Personal LaserWriter SC, and Personal LW LS driver each offers a "Background Printing" option. Select this option to instruct the system software to automatically launch the PrintMonitor during the printing process.

3. Close the Chooser dialog box.

4. Print one or more pages from one or more desired applications. Each document is quickly *spooled* to your computer's memory, allowing you to continue to work in an application without waiting for each page to print. The PrintMonitor then launches and monitors the printing process in the background. You may spool as many pages as you like and initiate as many printing operations as you like, assuming sufficient memory is available.

The PrintMonitor utility allows you to control the time at which documents print. When printing, you may choose the PrintMonitor from the Applications menu to display the PrintMonitor window, as shown in Figure 4.14. The document that is currently printing displays in the "Printing" box at the top of the window; other spooled documents

FIGURE 4.14

The PrintMonitor window allows you to control the time at which spooled documents print.

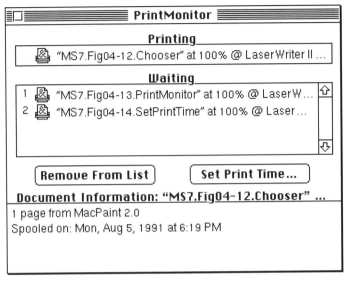

appear in the scrolling list labeled "Waiting." To cancel the current print job, click the Cancel Printing button. To cancel a spooled document that is waiting to print, select the document from the scrolling list and click the Remove From List button.

To set the time at which a waiting document should print, select the document from the scrolling list and click the Set Print Time... button. The Set Print Time dialog box will display, as shown in Figure 4.15. Enter a time and date at which you would like the PrintMonitor to print the document, or select the "Postpone indefinitely" option to save the spooled document to disk so that the printing process may be restored at some later time.

FIGURE 4.15

Enter the time at which you want to print a spooled document in the Set Print Time dialog box.

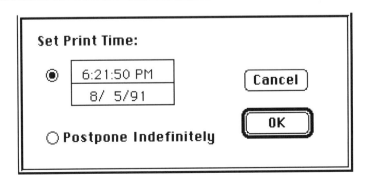

After specifying times for one or more documents to print, the scrolling list in the PrintMonitor window will change. As shown in Figure 4.16, a timed document is preceded by a clock icon, a postponed document is preceded by a dash. The PrintMonitor will retain its settings, even after restarting the computer.

FIGURE 4.16

In the scrolling list, a clock displays in front of a timed document; a dash appears in front of one that has been postponed indefinitely.

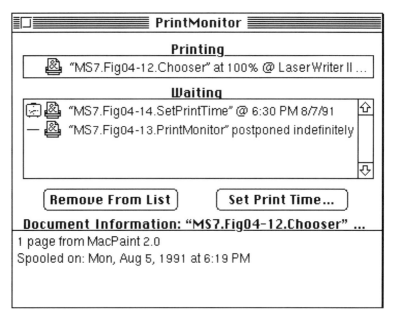

Compressing, downloading, and printing are but a few possible background tasks. Generally speaking, any lengthy operation that continues without your supervision—a mathematical calculation, a database sort, a HyperCard script—can be performed in the background.

For the time being, I don't recommend running more than one operation in the background at a time. For example, if you try to download a file over the modem as you copy a large file in the background and use a spreadsheet in the foreground, you run a high risk of encountering transmission errors during the download.

Also note that any background task will sometimes require your supervision. When a background application needs instructions from the user—as when it runs into a problem or completes a task—the Applications menu will blink, alternating between the icon of the foreground application and the icon of the application that requires attention. Choose the application whose icon is being interchanged to attend to the problem.

Using
TrueType and
PostScript Fonts

P ERHAPS THE MOST confusing aspect of ■ System 7 is *fonts,* which are electronic descriptions of typefaces such as Helvetica, Times, and Courier. Fonts enable you to generate distinctive letterforms and text effects. As with the very first version of the Macintosh system software, fonts in System 7 may be accessed inside any and every application running on your computer. With the advent of PostScript printing technology shortly after the introduction of the Mac itself, fonts that offered mathematical character-by-character outline definitions could be printed to high-resolution output devices, including professional-quality typesetters. At the time, pockets of professional type designers ridiculed PostScript's reliance on outline fonts, charging that digital type lacked the potential for delicate serifs and typographical nuances associated with metal type and film stencils. A scant six years later, outline type technology has become the accepted standard among typesetters, designers, and publishers.

I say "outline font technology" because, although Adobe introduced outline technology in the form of its PostScript language, PostScript is no more than a brand name. In the years to come, competing brands will no doubt emerge. In fact, one substantial competitor first appeared with the introduction of System 7 in the form of Apple's TrueType fonts.

Two brands of outline type—PostScript and TrueType—provide freedom of choice. But with choice sometimes comes confusion, especially when you're trying to evaluate items as complex as computer languages.

Many users feel like they need to choose between the two. But, in fact, this is far from the case. Just as Kleenex and Puffs can live together in the same bathroom cupboard, PostScript and TrueType fonts can coexist harmoniously on your hard drive.

 **ARNING**

If you currently use a LaserWriter, Adobe Type Manager, or otherwise rely on PostScript fonts, do *not* purge your fonts or go on a rampage converting them to TrueType. Rest assured, PostScript technology is perfectly compatible with System 7, and PostScript fonts will remain a standard— if not *the* standard—for several years to come.

GETTING STARTED

The first and most important question regarding fonts is how do you use them with System 7, regardless of format. In this section, I will quickly explain how to install both PostScript-format fonts and TrueType-format fonts. If you already know how to do this, you may want to skip ahead to the *Learning Fundamental Concepts* section, in which I'll explain the differences between the two formats and examine which fonts are best installed in which format. Incidentally, while bitmapped fonts such as Geneva, New York, Monaco, and hundreds of other fonts named after cities are compatible with System 7, you will likely want to scrap them in favor of their TrueType equivalents—if available—as described later in this section.

INSTALLING POSTSCRIPT SCREEN FONTS

Every PostScript font includes two parts: a bitmapped *screen font* (also called a *fixed-size font*) and a mathematically-defined *printer font*. Technically, the screen font is designed to display characters on your monitor; the printer font contains the mathematical character-by-character outline defini-tions employed by the printer. However, if you use Adobe Type Manager, the printer font works with the screen font to display text on screen.

A screen font defines a single type style—plain, bold, italic, or other—when displayed at a single type size, measured in *points* ($1/72$ inch)—generally 9, 10, 12, 14, 18, or 24. Multiple screen fonts are pack-aged in a special file called a *suitcase*, as shown in Figure 5.1. To access a PostScript font in an application, its screen font must be transferred to the Fonts folder in the System folder. Prior to System 7, screen fonts were transferred using Apple's Font/DA Mover utility. As shown in Figure 5.2,

---

FIGURE 5.1

Multiple screen fonts are packaged into a single suitcase file (top). Printer fonts files are available individually (bottom).

Helvetica Screen Fonts

Helve   HelveBol   HelveObl   HelveBolObl

FIGURE 5.2

Before System 7, you had to use the Font/DA Mover to install screen fonts in the System file.

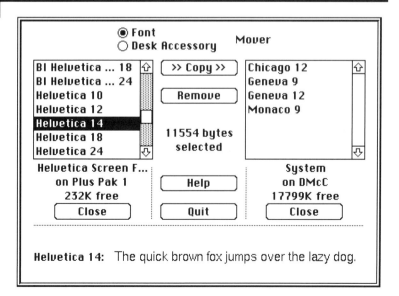

the Font/DA Mover allowed you to open suitcase files and the System file. You then copied the desired screen fonts from one file to another.

In System 7, the Font/DA Mover is not required to copy fonts. (In fact, Font/DA Mover 3.8 is incompatible with System 7.) Now, you may open a suitcase at the Finder level merely by double-clicking the suitcase icon as if it were a folder icon. A directory window will appear, displaying the contents of the suitcase, as shown in Figure 5.3. You may even change the view using commands from the View menu.

FIGURE 5.3

PostScript screen fonts shown as they appear when viewed by icon

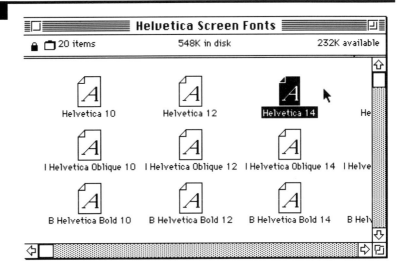

A screen font icon looks like a folded page with a single letter *A* on it. If you double-click a screen font icon, a window like that shown in Figure 5.4 will appear, displaying a simple sentence set in the current type style and size.

To install a screen font in System 7.1, drag the screen font or screen font suitcase onto the System Folder icon. A message will appear, informing you that the system software wants to place the font in the Fonts folder, located in the System Folder, as shown in Figure 5.5. The Fonts folder, new with System 7.1, is designed for storing PostScript screen fonts—as well as PostScript printer fonts and TrueType fonts as mentioned later in this chapter. Before in System 7.0, you installed screen fonts by placing them into the System file. The System file did not accept font suitcases, but instead stored

FIGURE 5.4

A window showing a sentence set in 14-point Helvetica plain.

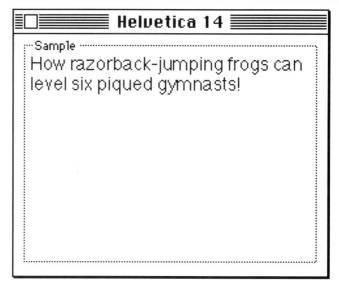

fonts loose. The Fonts folder accepts font suitcases and allows you to use the fonts within the suitcases. The Fonts folder can only accommodate 128 suitcases and loose screen fonts. If you have more than 128, you will have to combine suitcases by removing the contents of one suitcase and placing them into another. Try to combine suitcases that contain only a few fonts.

FIGURE 5.5

System 7.1 tries to automatically place fonts in the Fonts folder.

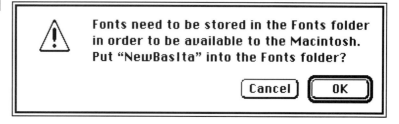

Note that if you add fonts to the Fonts folder while you are running any application, you will not be able to use the font until you quit and restart the application.

For more information about the Fonts folder and other special directories in the System Folder, see Chapter 6.

INSTALLING POSTSCRIPT PRINTER FONTS

Every PostScript-equipped printer contains at least four font families, meaning that the printer fonts for these typefaces are built into the ROM chips in the printer. The four families include Courier, Helvetica, Times, and Symbol, as shown in Figure 5.6. More recent PostScript printers, such as the LaserWriter IINTX, include the six additional families shown in Figure 5.7: Palatino, Bookman, Avant Garde Gothic, New Century Schoolbook, Zapf Chancery, and Zapf Dingbats.

FIGURE 5.6

The four font families included with every PostScript printer and the styles applicable to each

Courier
Courier Oblique
Courier Bold
Courier Bold-Oblique

Helvetica
Helvetica Oblique
Helvetica Bold
Helvetica Bold-Oblique

Times Roman
Times Italic
Times Bold
Times Bold-Italic

ΣΘξ∇⇑π×⊗Υ (Symbol)

FIGURE 5.7

Six additional font families included with the LaserWriter Plus, IINTX, and other enhanced PostScript printers

Palatino Roman

Palatino Italic

Palatino Bold

Palatino Bold-Italic

Bookman Light

Bookman Light-Italic

Bookman Demibold

Bookman Demibold-Italic

Avant Garde Book

Avant Garde Book-Oblique

Avant Garde Demibold

Avant Garde Demi-Oblique

Schoolbook Roman

Schoolbook Italic

Schoolbook Bold

Schoolbook Bold-Italic

Zapf Chancery Medium-Italic

 (Zapf Dingbats)

To print any PostScript typeface that is *not* built into your printer, the printer font for that typeface must be either 1) installed on a hard drive connected to the SCSI port of the output device or 2) placed in the Fonts folder—as opposed to inside the System file—so that the printer font file may be automatically downloaded to the printer's RAM during the printing process.

Many users with PostScript printers rely on Adobe Type Manager (ATM) to display typefaces smoothly on screen, as shown in Figure 5.8. When using ATM, printer fonts for *all* typefaces that you want to display smoothly—including those already installed in your printer—must be placed in the System Folder. ATM uses outline information from the printer font to display PostScript typefaces on screen. In System 7.0, PostScript printer fonts were identified as system extensions and, subsequently, were designed to be placed in the Extensions folder. Now with System 7.1, you drag the printer fonts onto the System Folder icon. The message in Figure 5.5 will appear, notifying you that the system software wants to place the fonts in the Fonts folder. The only problem is that the older versions of ATM will not function with fonts in the Fonts folder. So the way you respond to the query of Figure 5.5 depends on what version of ATM you are using:

- **ATM 2.0.** Versions of ATM prior to 2.0 will not run under System 7.1 (or System 7.0 for that matter). Version 2.0 will look inside the *root directory* only (that is, not inside any folder inside the System Folder). Therefore, click the Cancel button to hide the message shown in Figure 5.5. Then open the System Folder and drag the desired printer fonts into the System Folder directory window.

FIGURE 5.8

Adobe Type Manager displays type smoothly on screen by borrowing outline information from the printer font.

Large type without ATM

Large type with ATM

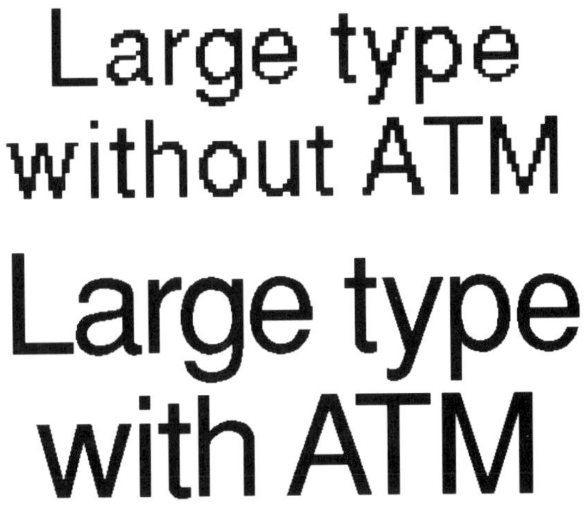

- **ATM 2.0.2 or 2.0.3.** Version 2.0.2 or 2.0.3 of ATM will look both inside the Extensions folder and inside the System Folder *root directory* (that is, not inside any other folder, including the Fonts folder). Thus, click the Cancel button to hide the message in Figure 5.5. Then open the System Folder and drag the printer fonts into the System Folder directory window.

- **ATM 3.0.** Version 3.0 of ATM will look inside the Fonts folder for the printer fonts, so go ahead and click the OK button or press Return.

In this book, I will assume that you are operating with ATM 3.0, and all references to printer fonts will be in terms of the Fonts folder. If you are using ATM 2.0.2 or 2.0.3, then simply replace any Fonts folder references with Extension folder. Adobe, the maker of ATM, is offering ATM 3.0, along with four styles of the Garamond font, for $7.50. To get a copy, contact Adobe at 1-800-521-1976 ext. 4400.

By the way, if you're having problems installing Adobe Type Manager in System 7, here's how it works: Copy the ~ATM™ control panel file to the Control Panels folder inside the System Folder. Then copy one of the ATM drivers—either ~ATM 68000 or ~ATM 68020/030, depending on your computer—to the System Folder root directory. Incidentally, this is exactly where Finder 7.1 wants to place them, so you can copy both control panel and driver directly to the System Folder and let the Finder automatically place the files. If you do this, then you will see the message shown in Figure 5.9. Simply click OK to copy ~ATM to the Control Panel folder.

FIGURE 5.9

*S*ystem 7 tries to
automatically place
~ATM™ control panel
files to the Control Panels
folder.

Control panels need to be stored in the Control Panels folder or they may not work properly. Put "~ATM™" into the Control Panels folder?

Cancel   OK

*I*NSTALLING TRUETYPE FONTS

A TrueType font is made up of a single *variable-size font* file, which is used to both display the font on screen at any size and describe the font to the output device. Like PostScript screen fonts, multiple TrueType fonts are generally packaged in a suitcase file, sometimes along with screen fonts (further confusing the issue). A TrueType font must be placed in your Fonts folder in order to access the typeface in an application.

After opening its suitcase file, a variable-size font icon may be viewed, looking like a folded page with the letter *A* on it, as shown in Figure 5.10. Each variable-size font describes a single type style. If you

FIGURE 5.10

*T*rueType fonts shown as
they appear when viewed
by icon

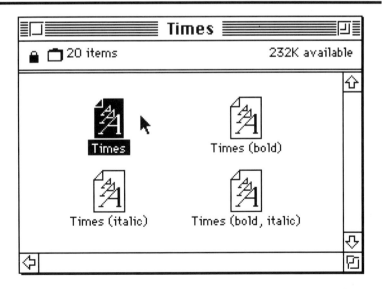

Times

20 items   232K available

Times   Times (bold)

Times (italic)   Times (bold, italic)

double-click a variable-size font icon, a window like that shown in Figure 5.11 will appear, displaying a simple sentence set in 9-point, 12-point, and 18-point type sizes.

A variable-size font window showing a sentence set in three sizes of Times Roman

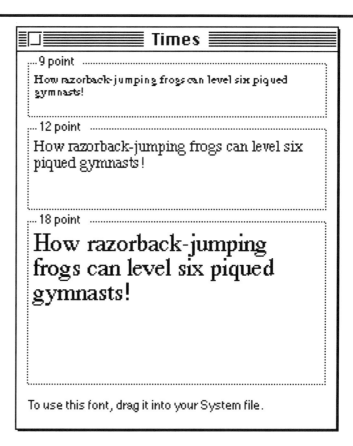

To install a TrueType font, drag the variable-size font icon or variable-sized font suitcase onto the System Folder. The message shown in Figure 5.5 will appear, informing you that the system software wants to place the TrueType fonts in the Fonts folder.

DELETING FONTS

To delete any font—fixed-size or variable-size—from the Fonts folder, simply drag it from the System directory window into the Trash folder, just as if it were a standard file.

LEARNING FUNDAMENTAL CONCEPTS

It's easy enough to learn *how* to install a font in System 7. However, it's not so easy to learn *when* to install a font and *which* font format to use. Some might speculate that Apple wants you to toss all of your PostScript screen and printer fonts and rely exclusively on their TrueType counterparts, where they exist. After all, Apple's long term goal is to gain more control over the output experience, the major component of which is type. But what's good for Apple isn't necessarily good for you, which leaves you with two additional options: Use both TrueType and PostScript fonts, or rely exclusively on PostScript fonts as you very likely have in the past.

Your choice is made more complicated by the following facts:

- **Font overlap.** During the installation process, both fixed-size (screen font) and variable-size (TrueType) versions of Chicago, Courier, Geneva, Helvetica, Monaco, New York, Symbol, and Times are installed in the Fonts folder. Only plain screen fonts are installed; the italic, bold, and bold-italic screen fonts for Courier, Helvetica, and Times—distributed exclusively by Adobe—are not included.

- **Font metrics.** Variable-size fonts include slightly different *font metrics* than fixed-size fonts. Font metrics determine the default amount of vertical space that appears between lines of type (called *leading*) and the amount of horizontal space that separates individual characters (*letter spacing*). If you create a document using fixed-size fonts and then open it using TrueType fonts, lines and letters will shift, changing how text fits on a page. Text that was meant for two pages can shrink to one; text that was meant for one page can expand to two. It's a potential nightmare for desktop publishers and others who rely on a service bureau for output.

- **System fonts.** Four screen fonts are included in your System file, instead of your Fonts folder. These are fonts that the system software uses to display text on the screen. The menus, for example, utilize Chicago 12-point. The other three screen fonts are: Geneva 9-point, Geneva 12-point, and Monaco 9-point. None of these four screen fonts seem to appear in the System file. They are in fact invisible so that they cannot be easily deleted.

- **Differing characters.** Fixed-size and variable-size versions of Chicago, Geneva, Monaco, and New York offer different character sets, so that characters available at one type size may disappear when viewed at another type size.

In an effort to expedite the transition from PostScript to TrueType, Apple has introduced a few flies to the Macintosh ointment, as demonstrated by the previous items. But who's going to notice? If you rely on your Mac primarily for word processing and number-crunching, you might never know the difference. Who cares if a line breaks differently, or if some text shifts from page 45 to page 46? Such problems are cosmetic and certainly not worth worrying about.

But if you're a desktop publisher or graphic artist—ironically, the very people TrueType and PostScript font technologies are designed to help—these stumbling blocks qualify as a major impasse. Identifying a font format to use throughout a series of jobs can be a crucial decision. Understandably, if you're going to switch font formats, you'll want to be sure you're making the correct decision.

TRUETYPE VERSUS POSTSCRIPT

Before I get started, let me warn you: There's no *quick* way to explain the range of differences between TrueType and PostScript font technology. If your interests begin and end with the bottom line, you may want to skip ahead to the *Which Format to Use* section, in which I'll offer specific

advice for choosing the proper font format. But if you want to understand more about outline font technology—and you have a few minutes
to kill—this section comprises what I consider to be the most critical issues surrounding the TrueType/PostScript dispute.

Experience and Support

Having been introduced in 1985, PostScript fonts certainly offer the advantage of time. I would wager that every graphic artist working on the
Mac has at some time used a PostScript typeface and, in most cases, has
met with favorable results.

Over the years, PostScript technology has pervaded other computer
operating systems, including MS-DOS, Windows, OS/2, NeXT, UNIX,
and various mainframe environments. In addition, Adobe has developed a sound support program for font users and PostScript typeface
developers. Adobe provides specific training and implementation
guidelines to ensure uniform quality from a wide variety of developers
across multiple platforms.

Apple, however, is new to the font game. So far, the company offers
basic implementation guidelines for typeface developers, but no specific
support for TrueType users (although installation information and the
like are provided via Apple's System 7 support program). And while True-
Type fonts are now supported by Microsoft Windows 3.1 on the IBM PC
platform, PC support is handled by Apple's TrueType partner, Microsoft.
Owing to the fact that IBM is Apple's most substantial competitor,
Apple's only motive to support the PC is to offer wider compatibility to
Macintosh users and build its own marketshare.

In this light, TrueType is a ship with two captains: Apple governing
its course on the Macintosh and Microsoft steering its way on the PC.
And now that Microsoft's TrueImage printer language—encouraged by
Apple to compete directly with PostScript—has been officially redirected
away from the Mac, you have to wonder whether Apple is truly serious
about its commitment to TrueType or whether the company will settle
for the leverage it has gained in determining the future course of
PostScript technology.

So in terms of experience and support, PostScript wins out over
TrueType, largely by default.

Ease of Installation

If all aspects of using the Mac were as simple as point and click, writers like me would be out of business. What would we have to explain? For this reason, PostScript fonts are a perennial favorite of mine. They seem to get harder to use with the passing of time. In the old days, you had to install a screen font in the System file and a printer font in the System Folder. The fonts looked jagged on screen at large sizes and illegible at small sizes, and documents were always printing in the wrong font because there weren't enough font ID numbers to go around, but it was a relatively simple procedure. When Apple introduced the NFNT resource (*new font number table*) to expand the quantity of screen font ID numbers, Adobe was so far into the font game that it took 16 disks to distribute revamped versions of its 85 screen font families. Then came Adobe Type Manager, the best thing to happen to fonts up to—and conceivably including—System 7. But to use ATM, you had to install two ATM files—a control panel and a driver—along with a whole horde of printer fonts, including those already installed in your printer. In all fairness, the PostScript font structure works great and requires little maintenance once correctly installed, but arriving at that stage requires a little work. During my two years working for a service bureau, the majority of my time interacting with walk-in customers was spent explaining how to use fonts.

One of TrueType's most widely touted advantages over PostScript was its relative ease of use. In this respect, I think Apple has delivered. A single TrueType font replaces the PostScript printer font, multiple screen fonts, and ATM. Installing a font is as easy as copying the font to the System file. What could be easier?

Even Adobe would be hard pressed to deny that TrueType fonts are easier to install than PostScript fonts.

Efficiency

Judging by the fact that a PostScript font comprises several screen fonts plus a printer font and a TrueType font includes only a single variable-size font, you might expect the TrueType font to be smaller. Wrong. Take Times, for example. The TrueType version of Times Roman (plain version) consumes 67K of disk space. Assuming that you're using the 10- and 12-point screen fonts recommended for use with ATM, PostScript Times Roman consumes only 44K—30K for the printer font and 7K apiece for the screen fonts Times 10 and Times 12. If a font takes up more space on disk, it will also consume more space when downloaded to the printer's memory. In fact, because the printer font is the only element of the Post-Script font that needs to be sent to the printer, PostScript fonts typically consume less than half the space required by a TrueType font—30K versus 69K in the case of Times Roman— leaving more room to download additional fonts and process complex graphics.

(Incidentally, I use the example of Times Roman since the True-Type version of Times is designed to closely match the PostScript version of the font. But as you may well note, you don't have to download Times to a PostScript output device since the printer font is already included in the printer's ROM.)

We owe the difference in font size to the difference between the PostScript and TrueType font-construction models. PostScript font outlines are defined using *Bézier curves,* like those used to create images in Adobe Illustrator and Aldus FreeHand. Points anchor the outline, control handles determine the manner in which a line segment curves out from one point and into a neighboring point, as demonstrated in Figure 5.12. The TrueType font-construction model relies on *quadratic curves,* which are made up of anchor points and control handles, like a Bézier curve, but rather than floating independently, a control handle in a quadratic curve is shared by two anchor points, as shown in Figure 5.13. While the number of control handles required to define a

FIGURE 5.12

A Bézier curve includes two control handles for every one anchor point.

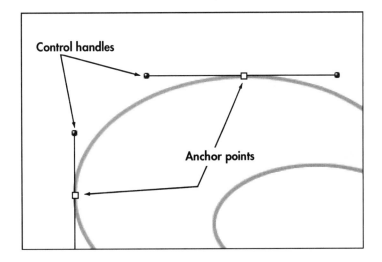

curve theoretically remains the same, the number of anchor points doubles, making the character definition approximately 50% more complex. The result: larger TrueType font files.

FIGURE 5.13

A quadratic curve requires one anchor point for every control handle, doubling the number of anchor points needed to define a curve.

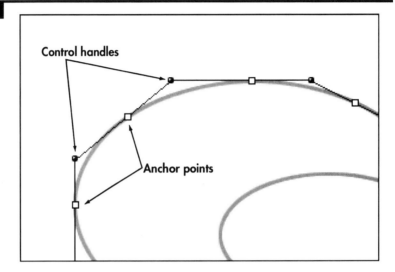

PostScript fonts pack more information into smaller files than their TrueType counterparts, without any loss of quality, making PostScript the more efficient format.

Print Quality and Speed

But wait a second. How is it that TrueType outlines are 50% more complex than PostScript outlines, but TrueType font files can be over 100% larger than their PostScript counterparts? Where's that extra 50% coming from? The answer lies in the way the two font formats convey information to the printer.

Printing a character in either the PostScript or TrueType format is a three-step process, as demonstrated in Figure 5.14. The character outline is set against a grid (left). The printer then applies hinting instructions, slightly altering the outline to better fit the grid (middle), and rasterizes the character to printable pixels (right).

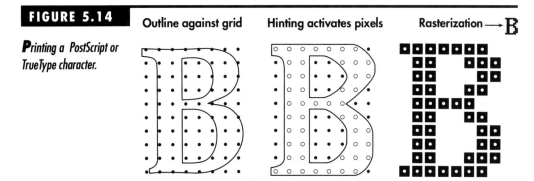

FIGURE 5.14

Printing a PostScript or TrueType character.

Outline against grid   Hinting activates pixels   Rasterization ⟶ B

1. The mathematical outline of the character is scaled against a grid which represents the locations of printable pixels.

2. Special *hinting* instructions govern the adjustment of the character outline to improve the appearance of the type at low resolutions.

3. Once all hinting adjustments are complete, the output device *rasterizes* each character—that is, transforms the mathematical outline to a printable bitmap.

PostScript and TrueType fonts differ in the amount of hinting each font format offers. PostScript fonts typically contain only *declarative hints,* which offer coordinates for key features of a character. For example, consider the letter *O.* The mathematical definition of the letter might describe its top loop as slightly shallower than its bottom loop. When printed from a high-resolution typesetter, this slight asymmetry prevents the letter from appearing top-heavy, giving it the subtle advantage of solid footing. But when printed from a low-resolution laser printer, the bottom loop appears obviously thicker than the top loop, making the letter appear lopsided, as shown in Figure 5.15.

A declarative hint included with the font explains that the top and bottom loops should err toward equal thickness. The PostScript interpreter inside the printer then determines whether or not to implement the hint, and how it should be implemented. In simplest terms, the font is dumb, the printer is smart.

FIGURE 5.15

Both of these characters offer bottom loops that are heavier than their top loops, but while the effect appears elegant at a high resolution (left), it diminishes the appearance of the letter at a low resolution (right).

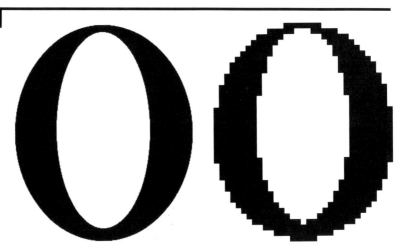

By contrast, TrueType fonts are smart fonts, which prepares them to work with dumb and smart printers alike. The font itself contains both declarative hints and the procedural routines that determine when and how to implement the hints. The grunt work is done by the TrueType *font scaler*—included as part of System 7—but the font is the real brains behind the operation. This necessarily makes the font larger.

Smart fonts are better than dumb fonts, right? Unfortunately, it's not that simple. In fact, when printing to a PostScript output device, the intelligence of a TrueType font is largely repetitive, since the same information could be processed more quickly and more efficiently by the printer's PostScript interpreter. This is not to say that the intelligence of the TrueType font is wasted or that it impairs the printing process, but it does force the font to consume excess space in the printer's RAM that could be better used to process additional fonts and graphics. And then there's the font scaler to consider. Although built into the ROM chips of some newer-model laser printers, such as the LaserWriter IIf and IIg, the font scaler must be downloaded to strictly PostScript devices, such as the LaserWriter IINTX and Linotronic 300, consuming additional space in the printer's RAM. Ultimately, the combined TrueType font and font scaler do more harm than good, slowing down the printing process without producing any beneficial effects.

If you own a LaserWriter Plus or other old-model printer with less than 2MB of RAM (or any RISC-based PostScript printer lacking a C-Exec operator), things get worse. There frequently isn't enough room in the printer's RAM for a TrueType font to coexist with the font scaler. To avoid possible out-of-memory errors, your computer generates an unhinted PostScript version of the TrueType font, which is then downloaded and rasterized by the printer's built-in PostScript interpreter. Because the font lacks hinting, it may look pretty crummy when printed. In other words, when printing TrueType fonts to a LaserWriter Plus, you get the worst of both worlds—no hinting and slow printing time. (TrueType fonts won't even work with the original LaserWriter.)

On the up side, TrueType fonts are just the thing when printing to a dot-matrix or QuickDraw printer such as the ImageWriter II or Laser-Writer SC, respectively. A dot-matrix or QuickDraw device offers no built-in hint interpreter or type scaler. By comparison to a PostScript output device, such printers are less than stupid; they don't have a brain at all. When printing to such a printer, all interpretive work is performed by your Macintosh computer. The Mac implements the hinting and rasterization, and then says to the printer, "Print this."

Needless to say, the declarative hints provided with PostScript fonts are entirely ignored when printing to a dot-matrix or QuickDraw printer. In fact, when using a PostScript font, it is ATM that determines the appearance of your text, just as ATM governs the on-screen display. But since a TrueType font is entirely self-contained, your Mac can read the hinting, interpret it, and rasterize the font.

Conclusion? TrueType fonts provide the best possible output for moderate users and non-DTP-types who rely primarily on dot-matrix and QuickDraw printers. On the other hand, while not necessarily better in quality, PostScript fonts offer the advantage of speed to desktop publishing professionals and graphic artists who use PostScript output devices and frequently find themselves typesetting their finished documents. Keep in mind, there is *no* such thing as a QuickDraw imagesetter; the PostScript language currently enjoys a monopoly at the high end.

Other Benefits

What does the future hold in store for these rival technologies? Frankly, the majority of TrueType's future will probably be spent playing catch-up. Though the typeface giants Linotype, Monotype, Agfa Compugraphic, Letraset, Bitstream, and Kingsley/ATF are starting to make good on their promises to release substantial libraries in the TrueType format, it will undoubtedly be a few years before the number of TrueType fonts equals or surpasses the number available in the PostScript format. TrueType will also need to continue to bolster its standing across non-Mac platforms. Though TrueType fonts are now compatible with Windows 3.1, there is still the arena of UNIX and NeXT in which TrueType has yet to challenge PostScript's monopoly.

Largely due to Adobe's substantial head start in the market, PostScript is better positioned to move in new directions. PostScript's most recent and perhaps most exciting enhancement is a new font technology that Adobe calls *multiple masters,* in which a variety of custom typefaces can be generated from a single font file.

A standard PostScript printer font defines a single outline for each of 256 alphanumeric characters. Each character in the font is consistent in weight (light, plain, bold, black), style (sans serif, serif, oblique, italic), and width (condensed, regular, expanded). Additional weights, styles, and widths are available as separate printer fonts.

A multiple master font will contain several character definitions, called *master designs.* Each master design represents an extreme in weight, style, and width. As shown in Figure 5.16, one master design might define all 256 characters in a light, sans-serif, condensed typeface. Another master design might be light, oblique, and regular width. Using a special utility, a user will be able to interpolate between these master designs to create a custom typeface whose weight, style, and width exactly meet specific criteria.

These fonts will no doubt prove a boon to the design industry. Graphic artists can use multiple master technology to create logo designs. Desktop publishers can generate custom typefaces to facilitate copyfitting without diminishing the quality or legibility of the text. Designers can create special display characters—bulldogs, drop caps, and so

FIGURE 5.16

*F*our master designs
(corners) with 42
interpolated characters,
each unique in weight,
style, and width, all
generated from a single
multiple master font.

Light condensed   Light oblique

Heavy condensed   Heavy oblique

on—whose weight matches that of smaller paragraph copy. Once multiple master features are introduced to page-layout and word-processing applications, moderate users may find ways to apply them as well. Imagine being able to shorten a letter by slightly tweaking a typeface on the fly. It's the perfect way to save paper, fax time, and transmission fees without cutting a single word.

For the typographic aficionado, Adobe's new technology goes one step farther. In addition to weight, style, and width, multiple master fonts will introduce a fourth design attribute, *visual scale,* which will allow you to enhance the appearance and legibility of a typeface at a specific size. Back in the days of metal type, fonts could not be scaled to different type sizes. This meant that a unique font had to be created for each size; say, one for Times 6-point and another for Times 12-point. To make the characters more legible, the type design was altered slightly from one size to another. Small characters tended to be heavier and more angular to thicken serifs and accentuate the white areas inside and between letters. Large characters favored slender stems and rounded curves, enhancing the elegance of the type.

The distinction between small and large type design was lost with the conversion to electronic publishing. Much of the legibility issues were addressed on low-resolution printers through the implementation of hinting. But since hinting is not applicable to high-resolution output, typesetters have had to sacrifice a degree of control enjoyed by the previous generation.

Visual scale addresses this deficiency. One master design might be created especially for 6-point type; another might be best displayed at 24-point. By interpolating between the two, you can create separate typefaces that are most readable at, say, 9-, 12-, and 14-point. Professional users can do no better.

Adobe has recently released two such multiple master fonts: *Myriad* and *Minion*. Both allow for control over weight and width, while Minion additionally offers control over visual scale. Neither offer style as of yet.

WHICH FORMAT TO USE

Personally, I must admit to preferring PostScript fonts. I've gotten used to the installation procedure, I own a PostScript-equipped LaserWriter myself, and I rely heavily on high-resolution output. Likewise, I expect that most graphic artists and desktop publishers will want to stick with PostScript for the time being. PostScript fonts are entirely compatible with System 7.1 and what they lack in convenience, they make up in speed, efficiency, and compatibility when printing to a PostScript output device from any of a wide range of personal computers.

However, if you use a QuickDraw or dot-matrix printer, you will probably want to switch over to TrueType. Because of their built-in hinting routines, TrueType fonts rasterize more reliably to non-PostScript printers. However, keep in mind that TrueType fonts may be problematic if you regularly take your work to be printed at a service bureau.

Changing Your System to PostScript

By default, the Fonts folder contains the following fonts:

- **Chicago.** A TrueType version of the plain type style;
  a screen font version of the 12-point type size (hidden).

- **Courier.** TrueType versions of the plain and bold type styles; screen font versions of the 9-, 10-, 12-, 14-, 18-, and 24-point type sizes.

- **Geneva.** A TrueType version of the plain type style; screen font versions of the 9-, 10-, 12-, 14-, 18-, and 24-point type sizes in the plain style and a 9-point type size in the italic style. The 12-point and 9-point plain screen fonts are hidden.

- **Helvetica.** TrueType versions of the plain and bold type styles; screen font versions of the 9-, 10-, 12-, 14-, 18-, and 24-point type sizes.

- **Monaco.** A TrueType version of the plain type style; screen font versions of the 9- and 12-point type sizes. The 9-point screen font is hidden.

- **New York.** A TrueType version of the plain type style; screen font versions of the 9-, 10-, 12-, 14-, 18-, and 24-point type sizes.

- **Palatino.** No TrueType version; screen font versions of the 10-, 12-, 14-, 18-, and 24-point type sizes.

- **Symbol.** A TrueType version of the plain type style; screen font versions of the 9-, 10-, 12-, 14-, 18-, and 24-point type sizes.

- **Times.** TrueType versions of the plain, italic, bold, and bold-italic type styles; screen font versions of the 9-, 10-, 12-, 14-, 18-, and 24-point type sizes.

If you want to switch over to PostScript, the first thing you'll want to do is open the Fonts folder and delete the TrueType font files labeled *Courier, Courier (bold), Helvetica, Helvetica (bold), Symbol, Times, Times (bold), Times (bold, italic),* and *Times (italic),* all of which are duplicates of printer fonts supplied with any PostScript printer. Do *not* delete the TrueType versions of Chicago, Geneva, Monaco, or New York. These may prove useful, since no PostScript versions of these fonts exist.

WARNING

> For right now, do not remove any other TrueType fonts that may appear in your Fonts folder. Many applications load special fonts that they need, and these fonts are not meant for you to use (although you can use these fonts) and are definitely not designed to be discarded. For example, if you use Microsoft Word or Excel, then you may notice that your Fonts folder contains the MT Extra TrueType font inside the MT Extra suitcase. This font is a necessary part of the applications and would have to be reinstalled if it were deleted.

The screen fonts installed in the Fonts folder are Apple screen fonts. The font metrics included with Apple screen fonts differ slightly from Adobe versions of the same screen fonts. As you might expect, Adobe's screen fonts are closer to the mark. Also, Adobe provides stylized screen fonts, such as *B Times Bold, BI Times BoldItalic,* and *I Times Italic* that correct font metric problems that frequently occur when you stylize a font using a program command. Adobe screen fonts for Courier, Helvetica, Symbol, and Times are included on your Adobe Type Manager 2.0 disk. If you have access to this disk and you use ATM, do the following:

1. Delete all screen font versions of Courier, Helvetica, Symbol, and Times from your System file. (Exception: You may want to keep the 9-point versions of these fonts since they increase the legibility of small type on screen, and are not available from Adobe.)

2. Copy *all* screen fonts included in the Courier, Helvetica, Symbol, and Times suitcase files on the ATM 2.0 disk to your System file.

If you have access to the Adobe version of Palatino (available from most service bureaus), you will also want to delete the Apple versions of the Palatino screen fonts installed into your Fonts folder and replace them with the Adobe versions. Then install any other fonts you wish to use. For best results, copy the 10- and 12-point screen fonts of all styles in the font family. For example, in the case of Palatino, you will want to copy the font files *B Palatino Bold 10, B Palatino Bold 12, BI Palatino Bold-Italic 10, BI Palatino BoldItalic 12, I Palatino Italic 10, I Palatino Italic 12, Palatino 10,* and *Palatino 12.*

Note that if you have been using Apple screen fonts in the past, the leading and letter spacing in some documents will change when you open them using Adobe screen fonts. This means some documents may have to be reformatted.

Avoid Adobe screen fonts that were created earlier than October of 1988. Older screen fonts generally lack NFNT resources, which means that they may cause font identification errors when used in System 7.

If you're short on space, you may also delete all visible screen font versions of Geneva (10, 14, 18, 24), Monaco (12), and New York (9, 10, 12, 14, 18, 24).

Changing Your System to TrueType

The System file is ready to be used for TrueType printing as installed. However, it may benefit from some fine-tuning. As I mentioned in the previous discussion, the Fonts folder contains both screen font and True-Type versions of many typefaces. Since TrueType fonts are capable of generating their own screen display, the screen fonts are largely unnecessary. In fact, the only reason Apple provides these fonts is to protect your old documents. Apple screen fonts provide slightly different font metrics than TrueType fonts. By deleting the screen fonts from your System file, the leading and letter spacing in some documents will change when you open them using TrueType fonts only. This means some documents will have to be reformatted.

Nevertheless, I recommend that you do just that: Delete *all* screen fonts from your Fonts folder. You will probably find the transition troublesome in the short run, but the work that you do now will help to avoid problems in the future. After all, it is the TrueType font that determines the manner in which a typeface prints to a dot-matrix or Quick-Draw device. It therefore follows that for the most accurate screen display, you should rely exclusively on TrueType fonts as well. Only after you delete your screen fonts can you be sure that what you see is what you get.

EXPLORING ADVANCED TOPICS

Just in case you were thinking that I've explained just about every possible aspect of fonts in System 7, let me assure you that I've only scratched the surface. Well, to be honest, I've scratched it up pretty good, but there's a world of issues I haven't even begun to deal with. I have yet to mention font utilities like Font/DA Mover, Suitcase, or Metamorphosis, I haven't described the purpose of font caching, I haven't shown you any new True-Type fonts—in short, I've been *very* delinquent.

The following is a piece-meal attempt to make it all up to you. Sure, there's a lot of stuff I'm going to have to skip—I could write the proverbial book about fonts alone—but hopefully, this section will familiarize you with the range of advanced issues associated with using type in System 7. You might even walk away from this experience being the smartest font user on your block. (Get real!)

ATTACHING FONTS TO THE FONTS FOLDER

In the old days, you had to install fonts into the System file using the Font/DA Mover. Now you can install and delete fonts by dragging them in and out of the Fonts folder at the Finder. But neither of these solutions is as elegant or convenient as using a utility that lets you activate and deactivate fonts, such as Suitcase II 1.2.10 from Fifth Generation Systems and MasterJuggler 1.57 from ALSoft, both of which are now compatible with System 7.

Each utility is a system extension that provides access by inserting a command into the Apple menu. Of the two, I prefer MasterJuggler because it offers a cleaner interface. Suitcase II typically requires the user to plow through two or three dialog boxes to perform a single task. In MasterJuggler, most options are available from a single window.

But in terms of performance, both utilities are remarkably similar. They offer the following advantages over copying fonts into the System file:

- **TrueType support.** Both Suitcase II and MasterJuggler allow you to open any suitcase file, whether it contains screen fonts, TrueType fonts, or both.

- **Combining families.** In addition to their other functions, Font Harmony and Font/DA Utility allow you to combine fonts into single families. In other words, all stylized versions of Times will disappear from an application's Font menu. To access Times italic, you simply apply the Times font and then apply the italic style. (For a different and, I think, better option, see my discussions of Adobe Type Reunion and WYSIWYG Menus in the *Organizing PostScript Screen Fonts* section.)

- **Convenience in turning on and off fonts.** You may find that you have too many fonts on your hands and many of the fonts you have, you use only occasionally. This can be a problem when scrolling through your font listing becomes a time-wasting chore. Both Suitcase II and MasterJuggler can remedy this situation by allowing you to create separate fonts folders (not to be confused with the Fonts folder in the System Folder) where you can place all the lesser-used fonts. You can then open and close these fonts independently for the fonts in the Fonts folder, which always remain open.

*O*RGANIZING *POSTSCRIPT SCREEN FONTS*

One of the things I truly hate about Adobe screen fonts is the way they're named. Since typefaces appear in application Font menus in alphabetical order, the stylized fonts I Times Italic and plain old Times are separated by fonts beginning with J through S, despite the fact that both styles are members of the Times family. The result is that fonts end up being organized by style name rather than family title.

A moment ago, I mentioned how Font Harmony and Font/DA Utility—bundled with Suitcase II and MasterJuggler, respectively—may be used to combine related styles into single font families. What I particularly dislike about this solution, however, is the font confusion that can result when trading documents back and forth between differently equipped machines. For example, suppose you create a document on a Macintosh system in which font families are *not* combined. Portions of the document are created using the screen font I Times Italic. You then take the document to be typeset at a service bureau that relies on combined font families. When fonts are combined, Times italic is accessed by applying the italic style to the Times screen font. Since the font I Times Italic has been eliminated from all Font menus, the application used to print your document will not be able to locate the I Times Italic font, and thus will most likely substitute Courier.

The better solution is to organize screen fonts by family using a utility such as WYSIWYG Menus (part of Now Utilities) or Adobe Type Reunion. WYSIWYG Menus organizes fonts into families and displays them in the actual font—rather than in the standard Chicago menu font—thus allowing you to view the font before applying it. Type Reunion shortens menus by relegating styles into separate submenus, as shown in Figure 5.17. Of the two, I prefer Type Reunion, since it reduces the length of menus, eliminating much of the scrolling associated with enormous font collections. However, Type Reunion 1.0.1 is not entirely compatible with TrueType fonts, sometimes relegating them to the wrong family. For example, when using both Adobe and TrueType versions of Times, Type Reunion presented me with five styles of Times, two of which were Roman.

FIGURE 5.17

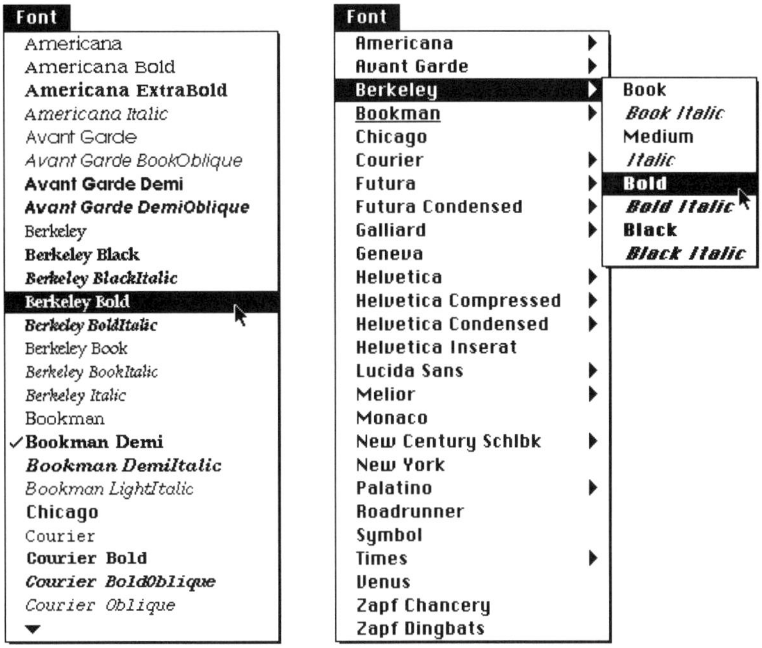

Typical Font menus shown when using WYSIWYG Menus (left) and Adobe Type Reunion (right)

Font
Americana
Americana Bold
Americana ExtraBold
Americana Italic
Avant Garde
Avant Garde BookOblique
Avant Garde Demi
Avant Garde DemiOblique
Berkeley
Berkeley Black
Berkeley BlackItalic
~~**Berkeley Bold**~~
Berkeley BoldItalic
Berkeley Book
Berkeley BookItalic
Berkeley Italic
Bookman
✓**Bookman Demi**
Bookman DemiItalic
Bookman LightItalic
Chicago
Courier
Courier Bold
Courier BoldOblique
Courier Oblique
▼

Font	
Americana	▶
Avant Garde	▶
Berkeley	▶
Bookman	▶
Chicago	
Courier	▶
Futura	▶
Futura Condensed	▶
Galliard	▶
Geneva	
Helvetica	▶
Helvetica Compressed	▶
Helvetica Condensed	▶
Helvetica Inserat	
Lucida Sans	▶
Melior	▶
Monaco	
New Century Schlbk	▶
New York	
Palatino	▶
Roadrunner	
Symbol	
Times	▶
Venus	
Zapf Chancery	
Zapf Dingbats	

Berkeley submenu:
Book
Book Italic
Medium
Italic
Bold
Bold Italic
Black
Black Italic

Reevaluating an Old Standby

The Font/DA Mover is no longer necessary to the process of loading and unloading fonts in System 7. However, this doesn't mean the utility is no longer useful. In fact, there are still a few tricks this old dog can perform that no other utility can.

For example, the Finder offers no way to create new suitcase files, which are particularly useful if you rely on a font-loading utility such as Suitcase II or MasterJuggler. Also, you may install fonts and desk accessories into specific applications. For example, you might want to access an Adobe screen font version of a typeface in one application and a True-Type version of the font in another.

> To open any file except a suitcase file in the Font/DA Mover—including the System file itself—press Option when clicking the Open... button. In Figure 5.18, I've opened HyperCard 2.0. Note that it already contains a screen font called *12* which contains a variety of special characters. Using the Font/DA Mover, I have added several additional screen fonts to HyperCard to prevent the program from complaining every time it launches.

Note that Font/DA Mover 3.8 is not compatible with System 7. You should upgrade to version 4.1—included on the disk which you can order with the coupon found at the back of this book—before attempting to use this utility. Even then, the Font/DA Mover is way behind the times. The utility cannot be sent to the background nor can you add or delete fonts in the current System file.

FIGURE 5.18

*T*o open the System file or any application, Option-click the Open... button.

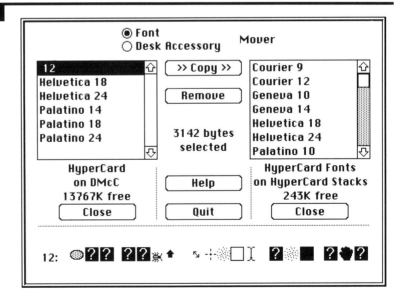

DIFFERING CHARACTER SETS

These detriments aside, the Font/DA Mover provides one additional advantage. It displays all screen fonts, including the fonts that are hidden at the Finder level—Chicago 12, Geneva 9, Geneva 12, and Monaco 9—thus allowing you to delete these fonts from the System file.

Why the heck would you want to do that? Well, the most notable reason is that the screen font versions of Chicago, Geneva, and Monaco provide different character sets than those provided by their TrueType equivalents. To demonstrate this fact, Figure 5.19 shows two versions of the Key Caps desk accessory, which displays the characters available to a selected font in the 12-point type size. When the Geneva 12 screen font is loaded, pressing the Shift and Option keys yields the character set shown in the top example. The rectangles indicate non-existent characters. After Geneva 12 has been deleted, pressing Shift and Option displays the full TrueType character set shown in the bottom example.

FIGURE 5.19

The Key Caps desk accessory shows the characters available when the Geneva 12 screen font is loaded into the System file (top) and when deleted (bottom).

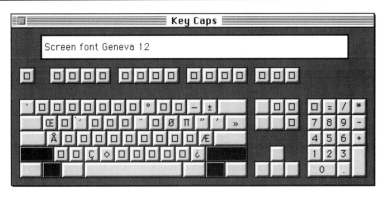

If you plan to use Chicago, Geneva, or Monaco on a regular basis, you may want to remove the screen fonts and rely exclusively on the TrueType versions of these fonts. The advantage is that you'll be able to view all 256 characters available to the font at any type size or magnification level. The downside is that text will appear less legible on screen. Chicago, Geneva, and Monaco are used for screen display as follows:

- **Chicago 12.** Used in all menus, title bars, and dialog boxes.
- **Geneva 9.** Used at the Finder level to display file, folder, and disk names.
- **Geneva (italic) 9.** Used at the Finder level to display alias names. The Geneva (italic) 9 font file is not hidden.
- **Geneva 12.** Used in some dialog boxes.
- **Monaco 9.** Used in special cases that require a *monospaced* font (each character is equal in width).

I do *not* recommend deleting the Chicago 12 screen font since it is used so prominently throughout all applications. However, the three Genevas and Monaco can be removed without adversely affecting few applications but the Finder. The solution: Remove the Geneva and Monaco screen fonts from the System file and transfer them to the Finder as follows:

1. Start up your computer from a floppy disk-based system (such as the one provided on the Disk Tools disk).

2. Launch the Font/DA Mover 4.1. The current System file will open automatically. Click the Close button to close it.

3. Option-click the left Open... button, locate the System 7 file on your hard drive, and open it.

4. Option-click the right Open... button, locate the Finder 7 file, and open it.

5. Select both the roman and italicized Geneva 9 fonts, Geneva 12, and Monaco 9, as shown in Figure 5.20. (Press Shift when selecting more than one font.) Then click the Copy button to copy these fonts from the System file to the Finder.

FIGURE 5.20

Copy the Geneva and Monaco screen fonts from the System file to the Finder to maintain a legible screen display at the Finder level and view all characters at all sizes when using the Geneva and Monaco fonts in other applications.

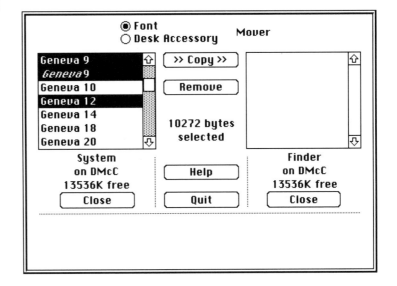

6. The copied fonts will remain selected in the System file. Click the Remove button to delete them. A message will appear asking you to confirm the deletion.

7. Quit the Font/DA Mover utility and reboot your computer.

Now the Finder will use the screen font versions of Geneva and Monaco to display its information, and other applications will rely exclusively on the TrueType versions of the fonts.

T I P

If removing fonts with the Font/DA Mover is too much work, you might want to check out FreeGeneva, a freeware utility by Bryan Ressler that is included on the disk that you can order with the coupon found at the back of this book. This utility unhides Geneva 9, Geneva 12, and Monaco 9 so they may be viewed and deleted at the Finder level. (The Chicago 12 screen font remains invisible.)

SPECIAL CHARACTERS

With the demise of bitmapped fonts goes some of the kitsch associated with the early Mac. By pressing Shift-Option-Tilde (~), you used to be able to access special nonsense characters in Geneva, Monaco, and New York, ranging from rabbits to robots, depending on the font and type size. Alas, the TrueType versions of the fonts supplied with System 7 lack these characters. Pressing Shift-Option-Tilde produces the orthodox grave accent (`). Ho hum. (Actually, you can still access the special character—see Key Caps in Chapter 6.)

But while most fonts have been standardized, Chicago has blossomed into an amalgamation of standard text characters and special symbols. If you're familiar with the Mac, you may recall that the old bitmapped Chicago 12 font provided the Command key cloverleaf symbol (⌘). While it was intended primarily for screen display, users could access the cloverleaf by pressing Control-Q. Not only has this character been upgraded in the TrueType version of Chicago, but several other keyboard characters have been added as well. These include symbols for the Shift, Option, Enter, and Control keys, as shown in Figure 5.21. Even the elusive Apple logo is included, having been deleted from most PostScript printer fonts some four or five years ago.

FIGURE 5.21

The 21 special keyboard characters provided with TrueType Chicago. An asterisk (*) indicates a character that is also included in the 12-point screen font.

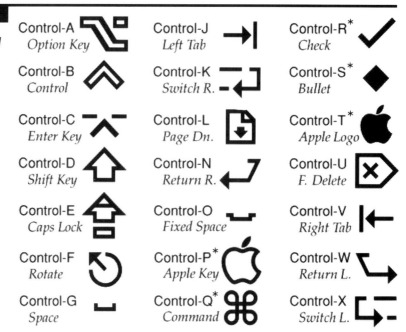

Unfortunately, again Apple has been a little sloppy. The screen font version of Chicago is missing all but five of the special characters. My only recommendation here: Don't view the font at the 12-point type size. (Incidentally, a character's absence from the screen font does *not* in any way impair its ability to print.)

Also, the Enter key character is almost impossible to access. This is because many Control key combinations produce the same effect as pressing a noncharacter key. For example, pressing Control-I advances your cursor just as if you had pressed the Tab key; Control-M creates a carriage return, as if you had pressed Return; Control-H is the same as pressing Delete or Backspace. Pressing Control-C is the same as pressing the *actual* Enter key, thus making it impossible to access the Enter key character provided in the Chicago font.

Well, not *entirely* impossible. There are a few workarounds, the easiest of which is to use the Key Caps desk accessory:

1. Choose Key Caps from the Apple menu. A window containing a representation of your keyboard will appear.

2. Press Control-C. A rectangle will display in the text-entry area above the keyboard representation.

3. Double-click inside the text-entry area to select the Control-C character. Choose the Cut command from the Edit menu (⌘-X).

4. Close the desk accessory. Paste the character into the foreground application.

5. Select the pasted character and change it to the Chicago font. If the character still appears as a rectangle, change the type size.

FONT SUBSTITUTION

Once you access these nifty characters, how do you get them to print? Printing a TrueType font to an ImageWriter or QuickDraw device is never a problem. But because of some odd conventions Apple has implemented over the years, printing TrueType fonts to a PostScript device can provide some unexpected results.

First of all—and this is extremely important—if you want to print Geneva, Monaco, or New York, you must deactivate Apple's automatic *font substitution* function. In the old days, before the advent of PostScript, most Mac users worked with dot-matrix printers. All Macintosh fonts were also bitmapped. The most popular were the serifed New York, the sans serif Geneva, and the monospaced Monaco. Then came the PostScript LaserWriter with its own serifed, sans serif, and monospaced typefaces—Times, Helvetica, and Courier, respectively. To help users make the transition from bitmapped fonts to PostScript fonts, Apple introduced font substitution. Type formatted in New York was printed in Times, Geneva was substituted with Helvetica, and Monaco was replaced with Courier. Never mind the fact that the font metrics were hopelessly incompatible and documents would repaginate on the fly, Apple made it possible for users to bridge the gap without learning any new tricks.

Now that Apple supplies TrueType versions of Geneva, Monaco, and New York, you would think they would have abolished the font substitution function. In fact, it is alive and well and continues to be the default setting in the Page Setup dialog box, which determines how documents print from almost every application on the Mac.

If you want to print TrueType versions of Geneva, Monaco, or New York to a PostScript printer, do the following:

1. Choose the Page Setup... command from the current application's File menu. The LaserWriter Page Setup dialog box will display.

2. Deselect the "Font Substitution?" option from the list of "Printer Effects" check boxes.

3. Press Return to exit the dialog box and implement your change.

Applications that do not rely on the System 7 Laser Prep file, most notably Aldus PageMaker, typically do not support font substitution as a default setting and will therefore print Geneva, Monaco, and New York without prompting. Also, note that font substitution does not affect the Chicago font.

FONT PRIORITIES

Second, when printing any TrueType font to a PostScript device, it is useful to know the order in which your computer searches for and implements fonts. This information will better prepare you for events in which the TrueType version of a font displays on screen but the PostScript version emerges from your printer, or vice versa. Suppose, for example, that your System software contains both the screen font and TrueType versions of a single typeface, say, Bitstream Charter. You've also copied the Charter printer font and installed ATM. What will you see displayed on screen and what can you expect to print?

(By now, I hope that you recognize that this combining of PostScript and TrueType versions of a single font isn't a good idea. Theoretically, you should try to stick with one or the other. However, if you absolutely *need* to be able to access both versions of a font, see the next section for information about providing a means to distinguish between the two.)

When displaying a typeface on screen, your system software searches for font information in the following order:

1. Screen font. The system first searches for a fixed-size screen font. For example, if you've created a document in 12-point Bitstream Charter, and the Charter 12 screen font is loaded into your System file, the screen font takes precedence.

2. TrueType. If no fixed-size font can be located, the system then searches for a variable-size TrueType font. This step also occurs under System 6 if the TrueType init is loaded.

3. ATM. Last, the system software turns control over to third-party extensions or control panels. The most notable of these is Adobe Type Manager, which searches for a PostScript printer font in the Fonts folder or the root level of the System Folder.

So when displaying a font on screen, TrueType takes precedence over the PostScript printer font. But when printing to a PostScript printer, the Macintosh system software favors PostScript:

1. **ROM-resident.** When printing, the system first looks to the printer's ROM to see if the current font is built into the output device.

2. **RAM-resident.** Like your computer, your printer stores data in its RAM temporarily when processing information. Left up to the computer, fonts are automatically downloaded into the RAM and flushed back out when the print cycle has completed. Using a utility such as the LaserWriter Font Utility supplied with System 7, you may manually download fonts to your printer's RAM. These fonts will remain stored until the printer's power supply is interrupted. Thus, the RAM is the next place the system software searches for fonts.

3. **Printer hard drive.** Some newer model PostScript devices, such as the LaserWriter IINTX, provide SCSI ports. If an optional hard drive is connected to this port, the system software will search the hard drive for printer fonts.

4. **Everywhere else for PostScript.** Having so far failed, the system software sets about searching various parts of your hard drive and other mounted disks for a PostScript printer font. After searching the Fonts folder and root level of the System Folder, the system checks out the root directory of the start-up disk. The PostScript search concludes by searching the Extensions folder, Fonts folder, System Folder, and root directory of all mounted disks.

5. **The TrueType search begins.** Only after no PostScript printer font can be located will the system stoop to searching for a TrueType font. Once again, the system searches the Fonts folder and the System Folder. Once the TrueType font is found, the computer generates an unhinted PostScript version of the TrueType font and downloads this along with

the original TrueType definition and the font scaler to the printer. If the printer is short on RAM, the TrueType font and font scaler are flushed and the printer relies exclusively on the unhinted PostScript font. If the printer provides 2MB of RAM or more, the unhinted PostScript font is abandoned and the font scaler sets about interpreting the TrueType font instructions.

6. Substituting Courier. By now, your system software is pretty near exhausted. Rather than prompting you to give it the correct font, a message will typically display in the printer status bar telling you that the font Courier is being substituted in place of the unknown font. If you see this message, your best course of action is to cancel the printing process and place the PostScript or TrueType font in a location where the system can find it, or download the font to the printer's RAM.

WHEN ONE FONT FORMAT IS NOT ENOUGH

Wouldn't it be great if you could access both the PostScript *and* True-Type versions of a font? Rather than displaying the TrueType version of, say, Times on screen but being forced to print with PostScript Times, you could elect to print with either the TrueType or PostScript version, even to a PostScript printer. Well, you can, but it involves some not-altogether-safe hacking.

For those inspired few who are willing to endure trial and effort to customize their systems, the following steps describe how to change the name of a TrueType font, an operation that cannot be accomplished from the Finder. You must own ResEdit 2.1 or later to perform these steps.

ARNING

> As I will no doubt say more than once throughout the course of this book, ResEdit is a powerful utility that can not only customize files, but also damage them irreparably. For the best results, follow my steps carefully and protect yourself from any stupid mistakes *I* may have made by working from copies only. Any file that you manipulate with ResEdit should be backed up!

The following steps describe how to rename the TrueType font Times to TTTms:

1. Use the Font/DA Mover 4.1 to create a suitcase containing all styles belonging to a specific TrueType font. (To create a new suitcase, click the Open… button and then click the New button in the ensuing dialog box.) Name the suitcase file TTTms. Then copy the four TrueType fonts associated with the Times family, one each for the styles roman, italic, bold, and bold-italic.

2. After quitting the Font/DA Mover 4.1, launch ResEdit and open the suitcase you just created. Two *resource* icons will display in a TTTms window—FOND and sfnt—as shown in Figure 5.22.

3. Double-click the FOND resource icon to open it, displaying a second window. A single resource called "Times" appears in this window.

4. Select the "Times" resource and choose the Get Resource Info command from the Resource menu (⌘-I). The Info dialog box will appear. Enter the name *TTTms* into the "Name" option box, as shown in Figure 5.23. You may use another name if you prefer, but it must be 1) consistent throughout and 2) the same number of characters as the original font name.

FIGURE 5.22

When opened with ResEdit, a TrueType suitcase contains two resource icons.

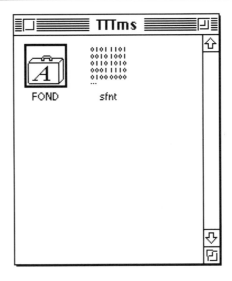

FIGURE 5.23

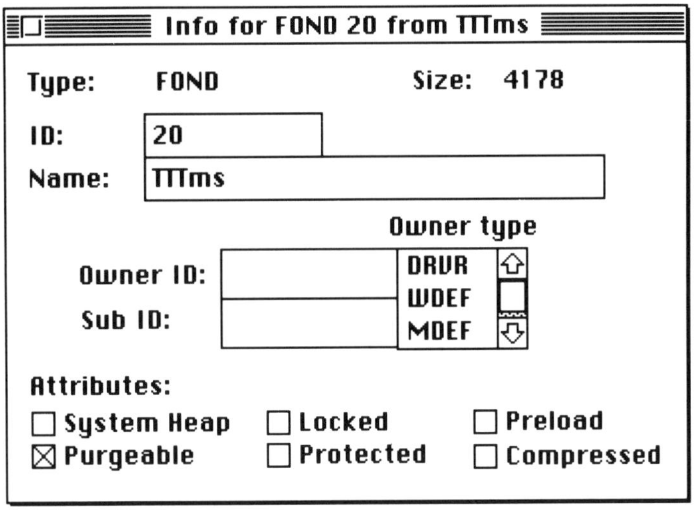

Change the name of the FOND resource using the Get Resource Info command.

5. Close the Info dialog box to return to the FONDs window. With the "TTTms" resource still selected, choose the Open Using Hex Editor command from the Resource menu. The imposing window shown in Figure 5.24 will appear.

FIGURE 5.24

*O*pen the FOND resource as a hex file to locate coded versions of the font name.

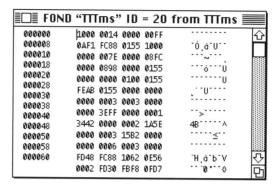

6. Choose the Find ASCII... command from the Find menu
(⌘-G) to display the Change ASCII dialog box. Enter *Times*
into the "Find ASCII" option box and *TTTms* (or your own
five-letter name) into the "Change To" option box, as
demonstrated in Figure 5.25. Then click the Change All button. A message will warn you that your changes cannot be
undone. Press the Return key to continue.

FIGURE 5.25

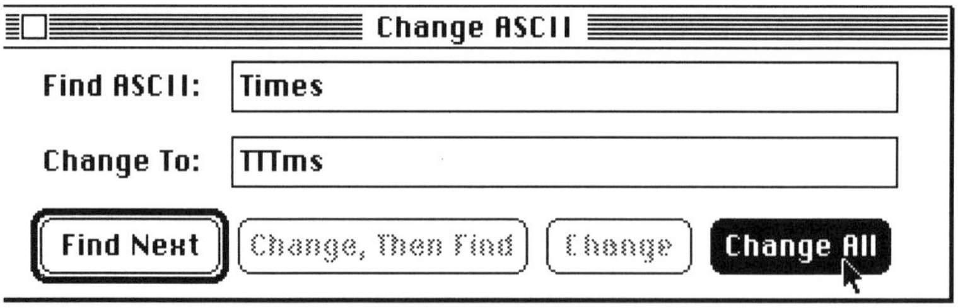

*U*se the Find ASCII...
command to search for
coded names and replace
them with a new name.

```
▤☐▤▤▤▤▤▤▤▤▤▤▤  Change ASCII  ▤▤▤▤▤▤▤▤▤▤
Find ASCII:    │Times                              │
Change To:     │TTTms                              │
  ╔═══════════╗ ┌───────────────┐ ┌──────────┐ ┏━━━━━━━━━━━┓
  ║ Find Next ║ │Change, Then Find│ │ Change │ ┃ Change All ┃
  ╚═══════════╝ └───────────────┘ └──────────┘ ┗━━━━━━━━━━━┛
```

7. Close the Change ASCII dialog box, the scary code window,
and the FONDs window to return to the original TTTms
window. Then double-click the sfnt resource icon. The
sfnts windows shown in Figure 5.26 will appear, displaying
one resource for each type style.

FIGURE 5.26

The sfnts window lists the names of every type style in the current suitcase.

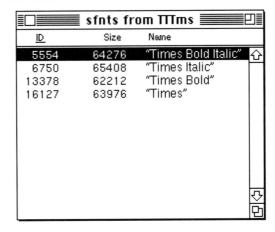

8. Perform the following on each of the four style resources:

   - Choose the Get Resource Info command from the Resource menu (⌘-I). Replace the word *Times* with *TTTms* (or your own name) in the "Name" option box. Close the Info dialog box.
   - Double-click the resource to display the code window.
   - Choose Find ASCII... from the Find menu (⌘-G) to display the Change ASCII dialog box. Enter *Times* into the "Find ASCII" option box and *TTTms* (or your own name) into the "Change To" option box. Click the Change All button then press the Return key to continue after the warning appears.
   - Close the Change ASCII dialog box and the code window to return to the sfnts window.

9. Choose the Save command from the File menu (⌘-S) to save your changes. Then quit ResEdit. Also quit all other open applications except the Finder.

10. Double-click the TTTms suitcase file to open it. The suit-case window will appear as shown in Figure 5.27. Copy the four TrueType files to the System file to install them.

The finished suitcase window viewed at the Finder level.

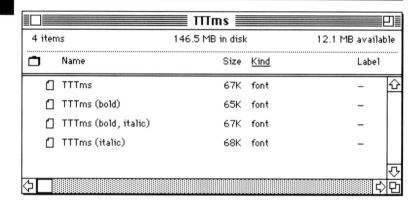

Name	Size	Kind	Label
TTTms	67K	font	—
TTTms (bold)	65K	font	—
TTTms (bold, italic)	67K	font	—
TTTms (italic)	68K	font	—

TTTms — 4 items — 146.5 MB in disk — 12.1 MB available

Once you distinguish between the two formats of Courier, Helvetica, and Times, you may change from PostScript to TrueType versions simply by selecting the text that you wish to change and choosing the altered font name from the current application's Font menu. You may even combine different formats of the same font in a single document, as shown in Figure 5.28. While the different versions of Helvetica and Times are very similar, you may notice that the TrueType characters tend to be slightly heavier and more squarish than their PostScript counterparts. The only font that differs dramatically between the two formats is Courier. The Courier built into most PostScript printers is a *stroked font*; that is, it is defined as a series of open-ended lines with rounded terminals. The primary difference between the plain and bold styles of PostScript Courier is in the thickness of these lines. The TrueType version of Courier is composed of filled shapes, as is every other TrueType and PostScript font in existence. This outline scheme provides the font

FIGURE 5.28

PostScript and TrueType versions of Courier, Helvetica, and Times. Note that Times is the only family of the three TrueType fonts that provides italic styles. Most software will not let you slant TrueType Courier or Helvetica, even if the font appears slanted on screen.

PostScript Courier

AaBbCc123!&¢
AaBbCc123!&¢

TrueType Courier

AaBbCc123!&¢
AaBbCc123!&¢

PostScript Helvetica

AaBbCc123!&¢
AaBbCc123!&¢

TrueType Helvetica

AaBbCc123!&¢
AaBbCc123!&¢

PostScript Times

AaBbCc123!&¢ *AaBbCc*
AaBbCc123!&¢ *AaBbCc*

TrueType Times

AaBbCc123!&¢ *AaBbCc*
AaBbCc123!&¢ *AaBbCc*

developer with more control, accounting for the more studied, consistent appearance of the TrueType font. (Interestingly enough, the Courier printer fonts included with ATM are also outline fonts. Therefore, the Courier you see on screen always differs to some extent from the PostScript output.)

I P

If you have more money than patience, you may want to pick up a copy of FontStudio, the font-creation software from Letraset. It allows you to open a TrueType font and rename it without going through all the rigmarole associated with using ResEdit. Also, FontStudio will let you use any name, regardless of length. And because its primary function is font editing, you may manipulate characters in a font, and even create your own, as demonstrated in Figure 5.29.

CONVERTING FONTS BETWEEN FORMATS

If you rely primarily on a dot-matrix or QuickDraw printer, or you're simply a TrueType font enthusiast, you can quickly bolster your TrueType font

FIGURE 5.29

FontStudio allows you to open, edit, and rename any PostScript or TrueType font. Here, I've opened the TrueType version of Courier and renamed it TrueTypeCourier.

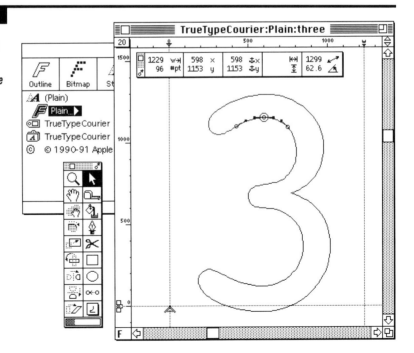

collection by converting fonts presently available in the PostScript format. Three programs currently allow you to convert PostScript fonts to the TrueType (or vice versa). As mentioned in the previous discussion, FontStudio allows you to open any font, regardless of format, edit it, and save it under any name to any format. In this respect, FontStudio is probably the ultimate font-creation/editing/conversion program.

Two other programs, Metamorphosis Professional from the font technology wizards at Altsys and FontMonger from Ares Software, are dedicated font-conversion programs. Metamorphosis Professional offers straight conversion capabilities only, allowing you to convert specific characters or an entire font from any format to PostScript, TrueType, the graphic format PICT or Encapsulated PostScript, or to a database file for use with the Fontographer font design utility, the rough equivalent of FontStudio from Altsys. FontMonger allows you to both convert and slightly alter entire fonts only. Typically, you would use this utility to create small caps, fractions, and other composite characters. Both programs are shown in Figure 5.30.

As far as the legality of converting a font from one format to another is concerned, the technology has yet to be legally tested, so you'll have to rely primarily on common sense. The vendors I've talked to dislike the idea of font conversion, but they generally reason that this is because the process reduces the quality of the typeface. If you own the font, and you're converting it for private use, then there's little chance that anyone is going to begrudge your altering the font for compatibility reasons. However, I would advise against including the electronic definition of a converted font—or even a font in its original form—as part of a HyperCard stack or other multimedia demonstration without the font vendor's written permission. And, obviously, converting a font and distributing or selling it as an original product is entirely illegal.

THE TWO POSTSCRIPT CAMPS

This is pretty much unrelated to everything else I've been rambling on about, but I thought I'd throw in one last bit of font information for extra credit. This information has to do with the fine distinction between the two varieties of PostScript fonts known as Type 1 and Type 3, both of which remain fully compatible with System 7.

FIGURE 5.30

Metamorphosis Professional (above) is a versatile font-conversion program. FontMonger (below) offers fewer font-conversion capabilities, but adds features for creating composite characters such as fractions.

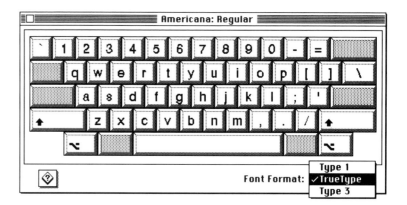

Type 1 fonts are the high-end PostScript fonts sold by Adobe and other international vendors. They provide declarative hints to maximize the beauty and legibility of text printed to low-resolution devices, as explained earlier in this chapter. However, they are limited to the extent that no stroking or filling instructions may be provided with the font. This means that by default, all outlines in a Type 1 font are filled with black. You may later assign strokes and fills to a character using an application such as Illustrator or FreeHand, but these attributes must be applied uniformly. For example, a Type 1 font doesn't allow for one shape in a character to be colored blue and another shape in that same character to be colored orange.

There are times, however, when this is exactly what you need. For example, suppose you want to create a font of logotypes. Call it American-Soda, the font needs to offer a Pepsi character, which contains both blue and red semicircles, a Mountain Dew character, with its big goofy green and red letters, and so on. This is the domain of the Type 3 format. Less restrictive than Type 1, a Type 3 font can contain any image that may be stored as an Encapsulated PostScript (EPS) file. However, Type 3 offers no hinting, presumably because hints would unduly complicate the output of free-form images.

Fontographer from Altsys and FontStudio from Letraset are both typeface creation programs that allow you to construct whole fonts in either the Type 1 or Type 3 format. A third utility, Art Importer (recently discontinued), will import images created and saved in the EPS format. Because it allows you to use your favorite drawing package—be it Illustrator, FreeHand, or Canvas—to create original character designs, Art Importer provides an extremely versatile working environment. Fontographer and FontStudio create Type 1 fonts, which are automatically hinted according to algorithms provided with the software. Art Importer creates Type 3 fonts only.

So if Type 1 is hinted and restricted and Type 3 is unhinted and free-form, what the heck is Type 2? According to Adobe, Type 2 was an early model that didn't work. It was bagged several months before the first Type 1 fonts were released in 1985.

If you ask me, there's something more to it than that. I mean, is it just a coincidence that switching around Type 2 gets you TwoType?

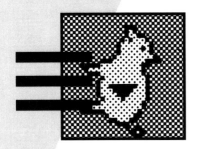

Using Desk Accessories
and Other
System Utilities

C OMPUTERS CAN BE very confusing.
■ Even the Mac, with its friendly interface,
is no exception. Much of the confusion inherent in using a Macintosh
computer is that so much of the way it works today is based on the way it
used to work. The current interface may appear thoroughly modern on
the surface, but it is riddled with leftover conventions that haven't been
removed because their absence might confuse old users. Thus, to understand the Mac, you have to occasionally take a ride down memory lane.

Take *desk accessories,* for example, which are those mini-utilities—
Alarm Clock, Chooser, Scrapbook—that appear under the Apple menu.
Also known as *DAs,* these utilities were provided with the first Macintosh
system software as a way of accessing specific system functions while running an application other than the Finder. You couldn't run two applications at the same time, as you can under System 7, so DAs provided
the next best thing: You could perform a function outside the range of the
current application without quitting and launching a new application.

The advent of the MultiFinder, which allowed you to run more than
one application at a time, and System 7's multitasking-only environment
have rendered DAs largely obsolete. But because so many DAs remain in
existence, and so many users and vendors have made financial and be-
havioral investments in this brand of utility, Apple has chosen to enhance
their performance rather than wipe them out entirely. Under System 7,
DAs may perform like standard utilities, and standard utilities may be
accessed under the Apple menu.

For this reason, I'll discuss DAs in the larger context of *system
utilities,* which are any programs that augment or enhance the performance of your Macintosh system software. These include *control panels*
(previously called control panel devices, or cdevs) and *system extensions*

(previously called inits) which load into RAM as part of the system software during the computer's startup routine. I'll also discuss how to access and edit *sound files,* which allow your computer to make some noise; *keyboard layouts,* which change the way in which characters are accessed from the keyboard; and the largely vanishing breed of *Fkeys,* the most ancient and ignored of all system software holdovers.

Getting Started

Before you can use system utilities, you have to install them. To make a long story short, you copy desk accessories to the Apple Menu Items folder, control panels to the Control Panels folder, system extensions to the Extensions folder, and sound files and keyboard layouts to the System file as described for fonts in the previous chapter. If that all went by a little too fast, read the rest of this section for the long story. If the short story was enough for you, skip ahead to the *Learning Fundamental Concepts* section.

Installing Desk Accessories

Back in the dim days of System 6, you had to install DAs into the System file just as you installed fonts; that is, by using the Font/DA Mover. Now, DAs may run independently of the system software. In fact, you can launch a DA from anywhere on your hard drive or floppy disk, just like a standard application.

Like fonts, DAs may be packaged in a suitcase file or they may be supplied loose inside a folder or on disk. To access a DA inside a suitcase file, you double-click the suitcase icon. A directory window will appear. If the DA includes an icon, that icon will appear inside the window, as shown in the first window of Figure 6.1. If no icon exists, as is true of DAs created prior to the release of System 7, a generic application icon will display, as shown in the second window of Figure 6.1.

To install a desk accessory so it shows up in the Apple menu, drag the DA icon from the open directory window onto the System Folder icon. The message shown in Figure 6.2 will appear, informing you that the system software wants to place the desk accessory in the Apple Menu Items folder. To confirm, you click the OK button or press Enter. The DA will now be available as a command from within any application.

FIGURE 6.1

*D*esk accessories supplied
with System 7 offer
specialized icons (top).
Older DAs that lack icons
are assigned generic
application icons (bottom).

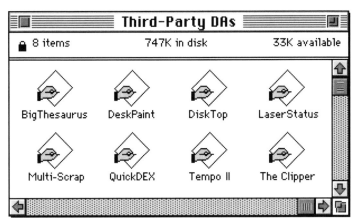

FIGURE 6.2

*S*ystem 7 tries to
automatically place desk
accessories in the Apple
menu Items folder.

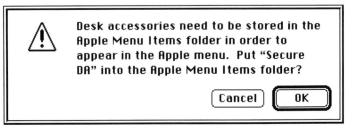

INSTALLING CONTROL PANELS

Previous versions of the Macintosh system software offered a Control Panel desk accessory that provided access to special utilities called cdevs. These utilities generally controlled the operation of peripheral hardware devices, such as monitors and tablets, as well as the operation of various—sometimes augmented—system software functions.

Like just about everything in System 7, cdevs are now self-running programs. The Control Panel DA has been replaced by the Control Panels folder. Though a Control Panels command still appears under the Apple menu, choosing this command does no more than open the directory window belonging to the Control Panels folder (the result of an alias of the Control Panels folder having automatically been installed in the Apple Menu Items folder). You then double-click the desired cdev, now called a control panel, to display a window containing preference options that guide the operation of the corresponding hardware device or system function. Figure 6.3 shows how the General cdev appeared under System 6 compared with the updated General Controls control panel included with System 7.

In order to run properly, most control panels must be loaded into RAM along with the system software during the startup procedure. System 7 will load a control panel as long as it is in one of three locations: 1) the Control Panels folder inside the System Folder, 2) the Extensions folder inside the System Folder, or 3) the root directory of the System Folder.

FIGURE 6.3

The General control panel as it appears under System 6 (left) and System 7 (right). Most options remain the same, except that the "RAM Cache" and "Speaker Volume" options have been moved to their own control panels.

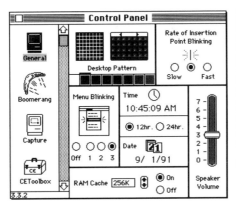
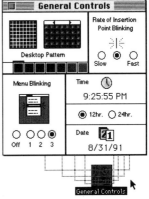

If you want the control panel to appear inside a directory window when you choose the Control Panels command from the Apple menu, the program must be placed in the Control Panels folder as follows: Drag it onto the System Folder icon. The message shown in Figure 6.4 will appear, informing you that the system software wants to place the desk accessory in the Control Panels folder. Click the OK button or press Return.

To use an installed control panel, first reboot your computer so that the control panel can load into RAM. Then choose the Control Panels command from the Apple menu and double-click the control panel icon when it appears in the Control Panels directory window.

FIGURE 6.4

System 7 tries to automatically place control panels in the Control Panels folder.

> Control panels need to be stored in the Control Panels folder or they may not work properly. Put "Capture" into the Control Panels folder?
>
> [Cancel]   [[OK]]

INSTALLING SYSTEM EXTENSIONS

System extensions, once called inits, are like control panels except that they seldom provide preference options. In fact, there is no way to alter the operation of many system extensions; they simply load and work. Examples of system extensions include the File Sharing and Network Extensions, both provided with System 7. Hardware drivers, such as those for removable hard drive cartridges and scanners, are commonly supplied as system extensions as well. PostScript printer fonts are also considered to be extension files, as described in the previous chapter.

If a system extension *does* allow you to adjust its preference settings, it may provide access via the Apple menu, as in the case of CE Toolbox and MasterJuggler, both sold separately. Such extension commands are generally displayed at the top of the Apple menu, as shown in the first example of Figure 6.5. Other extensions, such as DiskDoubler and Tempo II, add commands to the right side of the menu bar at the Finder level.

Like control panels, system extensions must be loaded into RAM along with the system software during the startup procedure if they are to operate correctly. Also like control panels, System 7 will load an extension as long as it is in either the Control Panels folder, the Extensions folder, or the root directory of the System Folder. To install a system extension, drag it onto the System Folder icon. The message shown in Figure 6.6 will appear, informing you that the system software wants to place the desk accessory in the Extensions folder. Click the OK button or press Return.

FIGURE 6.5

When loaded, the CE Toolbox system extension displays a Toolbox command near the top of the Apple menu (top). DiskDoubler appends a DD menu to the Finder menu bar (bottom).

```
 File  Edit  View  Label  Special  DD                    (?) 🖥
 About This Macintosh...
─────────────────────────
 Tools                 ▶   QuicKeys 2      ▶
  🕐 Alarm Clock           Super Boomerang
  🖩 Calculator         ─────────────────────
  📖 Chooser               CEToolbox
  📰 Control Panels                          ↖
  🄰 Key Caps
  🗒 Note Pad
  🔳 Puzzle
  📖 Scrapbook
```

```
 File  Edit  View  Label  Special  DD              (?) 🖥
                                 Compress
                                 Expand
                                 Combine
                                 Split
                                 File Info
                               ─────────────
                                 Help...
                                 Settings...  ↖
                                 About DD™...
```

FIGURE 6.6

System 7 tries to automatically place system extensions in the Extensions folder.

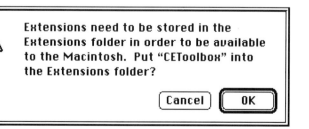

⚠ Extensions need to be stored in the Extensions folder in order to be available to the Macintosh. Put "CEToolbox" into the Extensions folder?

(Cancel)   (OK)

To use an installed system extension, reboot your computer so that the extension can load into RAM. If you're unsure whether an extension offers preference options, check to see if a command has been added to the Apple menu or if a menu has been appended to the Finder menu bar.

INSTALLING SOUNDS AND KEYBOARD LAYOUTS

In its simplest sense, a sound file controls the sound of the beep made by your computer when an application warns or alerts you to a finished operation or error. Sounds are accessed via the Sound control panel, as discussed later in this chapter.

A keyboard layout file controls the location of characters accessed from the keyboard. It is generally designed to facilitate international systems, which require different character arrangements but use the same physical keyboard. For example, using the U.S. layout, the c-cedilla (ç) character is accessed by pressing Option-C. If you change to the France layout (not included with system software purchased in the U.S.), this character is produced by pressing the 9 key. Press the slash (/) key when using the Español layout; press the semicolon (;) key in Português; press 5 in Italiano; press B in Turkish. Not all characters vary this drastically from one layout to the next. But all offer at least slightly different character arrangements than the one presented on a U.S. keyboard. The current keyboard layout is selected using the Keyboard control panel. Foreign key layouts and the Keyboard control panel are discussed in greater depth later in this chapter.

To install either a sound file or a keyboard layout, drag the icon onto the System Folder icon. A message will appear, informing you that the system software wants to place the dragged file in the System file. Press Return to install the file.

You may also transfer sounds into and out of the System file via the Clipboard. To try out this technique, do the following:

1. Choose the Scrapbook command from the Apple menu to display the Scrapbook file.

2 Use the scroll bar to advance to the third card in the Scrapbook, as shown in Figure 6.7. Assuming you haven't altered the contents of the original Scrapbook file, the third card includes a special sound file which is not installed in your

FIGURE 6.7

The third card of the Scrapbook contains a sound file that makes a cricket noise.

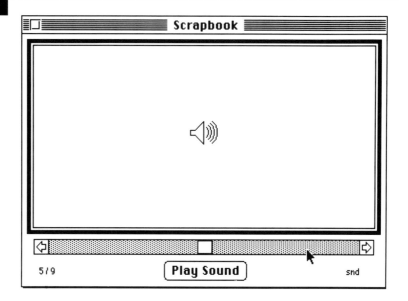

System file. Click the Play Sound button to listen to it. The sound of a cricket will emerge from your computer.

3. Choose the Copy command from the Edit menu (⌘-C) to copy the cricket sound to the Clipboard. Then close the Scrapbook.

4. Now choose the Control Panels command from the Apple menu to display the Control Panels directory window. Scroll to the Sound control panel and double-click it to open it.

5. Choose the Paste command from the Edit menu (⌘-V). A message will display asking you to name the new sound, as shown in Figure 6.8. Enter the name *Cricket* (or whatever you prefer) and press Return. The new sound will appear in alphabetical order in the scrolling list in the control panel. A pasted sound automatically becomes active.

FIGURE 6.8

When you paste a sound into the Sound control panel, you will be prompted to name it.

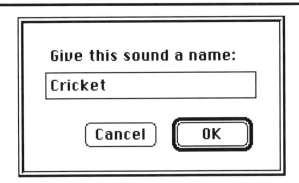

LEARNING FUNDAMENTAL CONCEPTS

In this section, I'll examine the composition of the new System Folder and explain the use of the many system utilities included with your System 7 software.

THE SYSTEM FOLDER

I don't know about you, but under System 6, my System Folder was extraordinarily cluttered. I was constantly adding new cdevs and inits and deleting old ones. I was also adding and deleting applications and other files from various portions of my hard drive, many of which create preference files in the System Folder. The result was a melting pot of cdevs, inits, preference files, drivers, printer preps files, and printer fonts, many of which I no longer used or which belonged to programs I had long since thrown away. Separating the excessive from the necessary was a chore I could never find the time nor the heart to face.

Under System 7, my System Folder remains cluttered, but the loose files number in the 50s rather than the 300s. More importantly, the files that I need to occasionally access are separated from the junk that I don't want to pilfer. This miraculous transformation is the result of the way in which Apple has restructured the System Folder.

The System Folder now contains eight primary components, shown in Figure 6.9. Except for the Finder, each component acts as a reservoir for specific file types, as illustrated in Figure 6.10.

FIGURE 6.9

*T*he System Folder is subdivided into the System file, the Finder file, and seven essential folders.

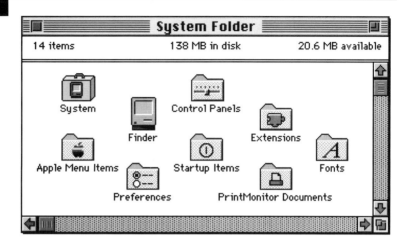

FIGURE 6.10

*T*he System Folder subfolders and the System file itself contain specific kinds of documents.

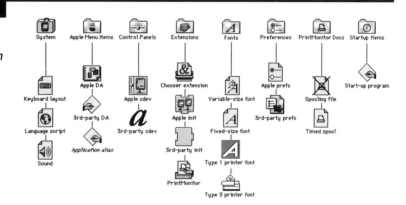

The following sections describe each of the System Folder components shown in Figure 6.10.

The System File   The System file holds *resource files*. These include screen fonts, sound files, keyboard layouts, and *language scripts,* the last of which allow your computer to use the linguistic rules of a foreign language. Language scripts are generally reserved for languages that rely on non-Roman alphabets, such as Arabic, Chinese, Hebrew, and Japanese.

All this copying files in and out of the System file may lead you to view the System as no more than a glorified folder. But aside from the fact that it may be opened at the Finder level and icons may be moved into and out of it, it shares very little in common with folders. For example, while the contents of a folder may be accessed from within any application, the System file is closed to all but a handful of specialized programs, including the Finder, Font/DA Mover, and ResEdit. The System file is a special kind of program and the Finder is an application that can be used to manipulate some—but not all—of the System's contents. This relationship between System and Finder is important to keep in mind because altering the System actually changes the manner in which the program operates.

ARNING

> **Making too many changes can corrupt the System file, rendering it inoperable. (I've done it several times.) Generally, this corruption is a function of corrupt font files, but it can also be due to file fragmentation. As a rule of thumb, you should allow a maximum of 200 to 250 resource files to reside in the System file. Also, be sure to back up your System file before adding or subtracting resources. If your System does become corrupt—as indicated by commands missing from the Apple menu, repeated crashing at the Finder level, the inability to start up your computer, or other strange startup activity—restart your Mac using floppy-based system software, such as that provided on the *Disk Tools* disk, then replace the corrupt System file with the backed up version.**

The Apple Menu Items Folder

Up to 51 icons placed in the Apple Menu Items folder will appear under the Apple menu. Typically, you will want to put your desk accessories in this folder, although a DA will run equally well if you launch it by double-clicking its icon at the Finder level, as you would when launching a standard application.

The Apple Menu Items folder is also a good place to position aliases for applications and folders (discussed in Chapter 7) you use often. As you do so, however, keep in mind that placing additional icons in the Apple Menu Items folder lengthens the Apple menu and slows its display.

The Control Panels Folder   Both system extensions and control panels can be placed in the Control Panels folder. However, because the Control Panels folder is accessible via the Apple menu and because you'll need to be able to directly manipulate control panels—whereas you won't need to regularly access system extensions—you will most likely want to position all control panels, and *only* control panels, in this folder. (For an exception, refer to the tip in the following section.)

The Extensions Folder   This folder is used to store a variety of file types, including printer drivers (also called *Chooser extensions*), and system extensions. The PrintMonitor utility also resides in this folder, permitting it to be launched automatically when printing in the background to a PostScript-equipped output device.

> During the startup procedure, items placed in the Extensions folder load before items inside the Control Panels folder. Thus, placing a control panel in the Extensions folder has the added effect of making it load before other control panels. You may then place an alias of the control panel in the Control Panels folder to make it accessible when you choose the Control Panels command from the Apple menu.

The Fonts Folder   This folder stores all bitmapped, PostScript, and TrueType fonts. System 7.1 will try to store all fonts dragged onto the System Folder in the Fonts folder. This makes it much easier to install and delete fonts overall, since you add fonts directly to the Fonts folder from the Finder without needing to use the Font/DA Mover. Fonts that are added to the Fonts folder while an application is running will not be recognized by that application until you quit and restart the application. You may organize the fonts into suitcases or leave them loose inside the Fonts folder. System 7.1 can handle up to 128 suitcases; any more than that, and you have to combine suitcases.

   If you are using an earlier version than ATM 3.0, then you will have to place your printer fonts in either the Extension folder or loosely in the System Folder. If you are using Suitcase II or MasterJuggler, then you may have voluntarily placed some fonts in a separate folder. Refer to Chapter 5 for more information on either of these topics.

The Preferences Folder   The Preferences folder is designed to hold the hundreds of preference files that are created by the various applications running on your Mac. But while Apple may encourage this convention, it is the job of individual applications to conform. Most applications continue to deposit preference files randomly in the root directory of the System Folder. If you've ever used Microsoft Word 4.0 or earlier, for example, you may have witnessed its peculiar tendency to fill a System Folder with Word Temp files. But an increasing number of applications organize their preferences in the Preferences folders or, in the best of cases, within subfolders inside the Preferences folder, as is currently the case for Microsoft Excel 3.0 and QuicKeys.

ARNING

> Do *not* move preference files from the System Folder root directory to the Preferences directory. In almost all cases, an application that creates a preference file in the System Folder will not be able to locate it if it is moved. Instead, you will lose your previous preference settings and the application will create a new preference file.

The PrintMonitor Documents Folder   Unless you engage in a tremendous amount of printing, you will usually find this folder empty. It is used by the PrintMonitor utility to store temporary files that are in the process of being spooled to a PostScript printer. Crosshairs cover the icon of a spooling file to show that it cannot be manipulated and will soon be deleted automatically. If you have instructed the PrintMonitor to save back a spooled document and print it at a later time or date, the icon will appear without a crosshairs. Such a file may be copied to disk and downloaded using the PrintMonitor on another computer, as when using a service bureau. (Note that the PrintMonitor works only with applications that rely on the Laser-Prep file built into System 7. Applications that use separate prep files, such as PageMaker, cannot take advantage of the PrintMonitor utility.)

The Startup Items Folder   Any icon placed in the Startup Items folder will launch or open automatically when you start up your computer. For example, if you use Microsoft Excel every day, you might create an alias for Excel and position the alias in the Startup Items folder. That way, every time you turn on your computer, Microsoft Excel will load automatically, allowing you to get to work that much more quickly.

If more than one icon resides in the Startup Items folder, System 7 launches the respective programs in two passes, each in alphabetical order (memory permitting). In the first pass, the system launches all applications represented by aliases or documents inside the Startup Items folder. During the second pass, System 7 opens control panels, desk accessories, and folders.

For example, suppose the Startup Items folder contains the following icons (in alphabetical order):

- Color, a control panel alias

- Document 1, a PageMaker file

- Key Caps, a desk accessory alias

- Microsoft Word, an application alias

- Trash, an alias of the Trash folder

- Views, another control panel alias

Immediately after the computer starts up, the PageMaker application launches and displays an open window filled with the contents of Document 1. Next, Microsoft Word launches, since "Microsoft Word" follows "Document 1" in alphabetical order. Now that the applications have launched, the second pass begins. The Color control panel opens first, followed by the Key Caps desk accessory, the Trash folder, and the Views control panel. (Note that while folders represented inside the Startup Items folder are opened, the contents of those folders remain closed.)

This launching order is designed to efficiently subdivide RAM. As explained in Chapter 4, computer memory can become fragmented when launching and quitting programs. By loading DAs and control panels in the second pass—both of which require little RAM and typically remain open for only short periods of time—System 7 prevents very small bits of free RAM from becoming isolated.

> When placing application aliases in the Startup Items
> folder, name a program that you intend to leave open for a
> long period of time so that it precedes one that you will
> likely quit soon after startup. For instance, in the previous
> example, if you were using Microsoft Word longer than
> PageMaker, then you would rename the PageMaker
> document so it followed Microsoft Word. If no document is
> present, and you intend to use PageMaker longer than
> Microsoft Word, rename the word processor *Word* so that it
> follows PageMaker in alphabetical order.

DESK ACCESSORIES

Now that you know how the System Folder works, it's time to introduce
you to the desk accessories and—in the next section— the control panels
that you will be using. Each desk accessory that is provided with System 7
is described in alphabetical order throughout the following pages. At the
end, I mention a couple of DAs from other vendors that take up where
System 7 leaves off.

Alarm Clock

The Alarm Clock DA may be used to set and display the time and date, as
shown in Figure 6.11. Even if you never display this information on
screen, it is important to maintain accurate time and date since both are
assigned to any file when it is saved to disk. You may also turn on an
alarm feature which will cause the computer to beep at a specified time.

When you first display the Alarm Clock window, it displays the time
only. You click the lever icon on the far right side of the Clock window to
display the setting options. You select the clock icon to set the time, the
calendar icon to set the date, and the alarm icon to set the alarm.

To change a time or date, you select the appropriate icon, and then
select the hour, minute, second, month, date, or year that you want to
change. Click the arrow options to adjust the selection incrementally or

To use the Alarm Clock DA, click the lever to display the setting options. The item set depends on which icon is selected.

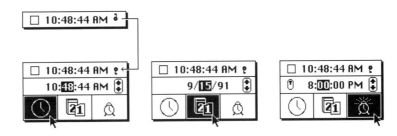

enter new values from the keyboard. You turn on and off the alarm using the switch below the close box. Your changes will take effect when you select a different icon (clock, calendar, or alarm).

TIP

You may also set the time and date using the General Controls control panel, as described later in this chapter. However, if you are trying to set your Mac's internal clock to some exact time—say, accurate to within a second—then the Alarm Clock is a more reliable choice. The reason? When you set the clock option contained in the General Controls control panel, the Mac clock temporarily stops until your change is completed. Thus if you select a time option and wait 10 seconds before selecting a different option, the internal clock will be slowed by 10 seconds even though you made no change. When using the Alarm Clock DA, the time updates continuously regardless of your selection and manipulation of options. For example, if you are setting the clock to jive with the National Institute of Standards Universal Time phone service, you would set the Alarm Clock time to the upcoming minute, 00 seconds, and then click the calendar or alarm icon when you hear the beep, all without interrupting the internal clock in the meantime.

Battery

The Battery desk accessory can be used on the battery-powered Power-Book series computers only. If you try to run the Battery DA on a stand-ard model Mac, the message shown in Figure 6.12 will display, preventing you from going any further. So, if the System 7.1 Installer automatically installed the Battery DA on your Mac (as it did on mine), then go ahead and throw it away.

If you own a PowerBook, you may use the Battery DA, as shown in Figure 6.13, to check how much charge is left in your battery. The in-dicator reads like a gas gauge and you must recharge your battery when the indicator nears empty. When the level of charge in your battery reaches the critical mark, you will hear a beep and your PowerBook will display a warning that it is operating on reserve battery power. Con-tinued use of your PowerBook past this point is not advisable since it could crash at any time due to lack of power. So you should immediately plug in your PowerBook, at which time the Battery DA power indicator will read full.

FIGURE 6.12

*M*ost users will be greeted by this alert message when trying to run the Battery DA.

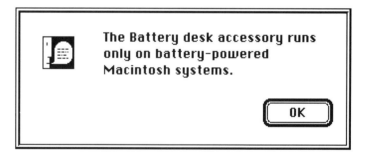

FIGURE 6.13

*T*he position of the flag icon determines whether the PowerBook is on or off.

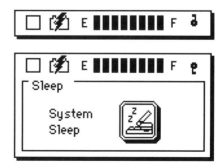

Click the flag icon, at the far right of the Battery DA dialog box, and click on the sleep button to put your PowerBook to sleep (or in *rest mode*). Rather than turning off your PowerBook to save power, sleep allows you to save power and deactivates the screen display and the hard drive while maintaining the contents of RAM. To wake the PowerBook press any key or move the mouse or trackball.

The Battery DA is small, so you can have it on screen with the foreground application that you are running. This allows you the convenience of putting your PowerBook to sleep quickly, without having to exit to the Finder level first and choose the sleep command from the Special menu. Since the battery on the PowerBook only lasts for about two hours before it needs charging, this is an ideal way to save power. As one PowerBook user to another, I strongly recommend that you use this to your advantage, and send your PowerBook to sleep anytime you take a hiatus from your work, no matter how short.

One last comment: If you are adding any peripherals to your Power-Book, you must shut down your PowerBook, not merely send it to sleep.

Calculator

Shown in Figure 6.14, the Calculator DA is a handy little ten key calculator. Enter numbers and arithmetic operations by clicking buttons or by pressing keys on the keypad. (Notice that the keys on the calculator

FIGURE 6.14

The Calculator buttons are laid out identically to the keys on the keypad.

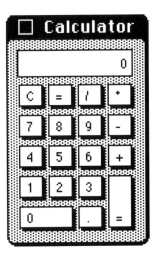

are laid out exactly like the keys on your keypad.) The number keys along the top of the keyboard may also be used, as may the *C* key, which activates the Clear button.

You may paste arithmetic equations into the Calculator and then cut their answers. For example, try this experiment:

1. Inside any word processor, enter the equation *C6+4*3/2–1*. (*C* stands for Clear to ensure that the previous calculation is deleted.) Copy this text.

2. Choose the Calculator command from the Apple menu to display the Calculator DA.

3. Choose the Paste command from the Edit menu (⌘-V). The buttons on the Calculator will highlight in the order entered in your text.

4. Choose the Copy command (⌘-C) to copy the answer, *14*.

5. Return to your word processor and paste the answer to the equation.

If you're looking for a better calculator, my favorite is Calc+ from Abbott Systems, which is demonstrated in Figure 6.15. While it doesn't offer a much wider range of math functions than the standard Calculator DA, it provides a number of unique properties that make it ideal for quick calculations. Most notably, Calc+ offers both a decimal calculator and a graphics calculator, which is used to add measurements such as inches, centimeters, and picas and make automatic conversions between the two. Calc+ allows you to set the number of decimal places, make percentage calculations, scroll through previous calculations, and print your results in a specified font. Calc+ also remembers calculations made between different sessions.

Chooser

The Chooser is used primarily to select an output device and determine the manner in which a document is printed. The Chooser is also used by AppleShare and other network products to select file-server volumes and network zones. To use the Chooser, select the desired *printer driver* (also called a *Chooser extension*) from the scrolling list of icons on the left side

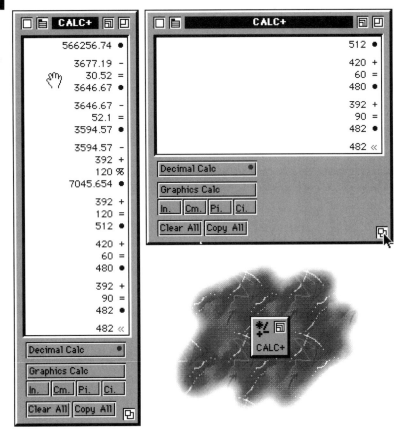

FIGURE 6.15

The Calc+ DA can be scrolled using a hand icon (left), resized (right), and temporarily shrunken to icon size to avoid screen clutter (bottom).

of the dialog box. The scrolling list displays all printer drivers contained in the Extensions folder inside your System Folder.

The driver you select determines the options available on the right side of the Chooser window. If you select the ImageWriter icon, as shown in Figure 6.16, the Chooser will offer two port options. You can select the top icon if the printer is cabled to your printer port on the back of the computer; select the lower icon if the printer is connected to the serial port (also called the modem port).

Other icons—such as the LaserWriter, AppleTalk ImageWriter, and AppleShare drivers—assume that you are using the printer port. In place of the port options, these drivers offer a list of matching printers cabled to the current network.

FIGURE 6.16

The Chooser allows you to select an output device.

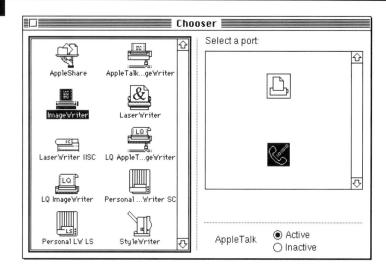

The "AppleTalk" option is offered by every printer driver. You must select the "Active" radio button when AppleTalk cabling is connected to your Mac, or if you will be using any network devices or communicating via an AppleTalk network. You select "Inactive" when no AppleTalk cabling is connected to your Mac. If your AppleTalk network offers multiple zones, you should select the desired zone from the scrolling list below the printer drivers, as shown in Figure 6.17.

The LaserWriter, LaserWriter II SC, Personal LaserWriter SC, and Personal LW LS drivers offer "Background Printing" options. You select this option to instruct the system software to automatically launch the PrintMonitor during the printing process.

One last note: You used to be able to name your computer in the Chooser window using the "User Name" option box. This option has been moved to the Sharing Setup control panel and renamed "Owner Name."

Key Caps

This underrated desk accessory performs two much-needed functions. First, it allows you to find characters that you know exist, but can't remember for the life of you where they are. The popular font Zapf Dingbats, for example, offers over 200 characters. Offhand, can you

FIGURE 6.17

If your AppleTalk network offers multiple zones, a scrolling list of zone names will appear below the printer drivers.

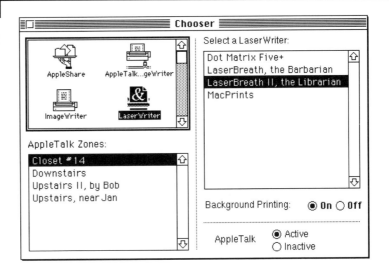

remember the keyboard location of even *one* of them? The same is true for Symbol, Carta, and the bitmapped fonts Cairo and Mobile. Even standard fonts, like Helvetica and Times, offer characters that are not displayed on the keyboard, including ¢, ©, and ¿. These are accessed by pressing Option or both Shift and Option in tandem with a letter or number key.

Any character may be located using Key Caps. You can choose the desired font from the Key Caps menu; press Shift, Option, or both Shift and Option to view special characters. Depending on the font, characters may even display on function keys, cursor arrow keys, and the keypad.

The second purpose of the Key Caps DA is that it allows you to acquire special characters that cannot be created in the current application. As you can see in Figure 6.18, the Adobe font Lucinda Sans offers *ligatures*—in which two characters are joined together, as in æ—and other special characters that are accessed by pressing function keys or Control key combinations. Some applications, including the Finder, block the use of the Control key. Others reserve the Control key and function keys for use as keyboard equivalents for commands and other options. In Key Caps, Control key combinations and function keys create characters. You can enter the breakaway characters into the text entry area at the top of the window; then you can highlight the text by dragging over it, copy it, and paste it into the desired application.

FIGURE 6.18

*T*he Lucinda Sans character set shown when no modifier key is pressed (top) and when Control is pressed (bottom).

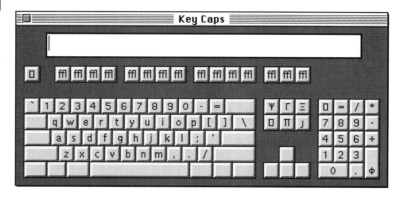

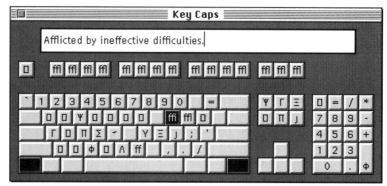

The Key Caps DA provided with System 7 has been enhanced to display two-part characters; that is, characters that are created by entering two separate keystrokes. Most are accented letters, such as *à, ñ,* and *ö.* For example, suppose you want to create the e-acute (´) character. Within Key Caps, you press Option-E. In most fonts, Option-E on its own produces nothing. It is the first step in creating an accented character. Thus, after you press Option-E, Key Caps highlights the characters that are affected by the Option-E accent (`) by surrounding them with heavy outlines, as shown in the second example of Figure 6.19. Among these is *é* which is now made available by simply pressing the E key. Two-part keystrokes may also be used in specialty fonts to create completely different characters, as illustrated by Figure 6.20.

FIGURE 6.19

After you press Option-E (top), Key Caps highlights characters that are affected by the acute accent (bottom).

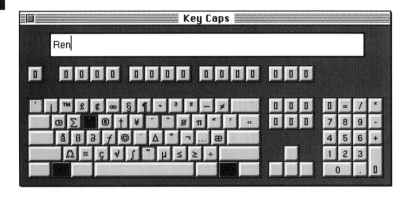

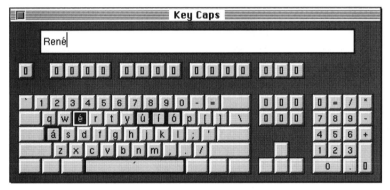

Note Pad

The Note Pad, as shown in Figure 6.21, was originally included with the first Macintosh system software. It required only 2K of memory to run and offered eight pages, each of which held up to 256 characters. It allowed you to jot down notes that you could refer to or edit later, or copy and paste small passages of text to swap between programs.

With the exception of its new color icon, the Note Pad is no different today than it was back then. It is still limited to eight pages and 256 characters per page. It still operates within 2K of RAM. I can't think of one reason to use it. My only recommendation is to throw it in the Trash and free up 9K of disk space.

FIGURE 6.20

In Zapf Dingbats, pressing Shift-U results in a star (top). However, if you first press Option-E, then Shift-U yields an entirely different character in the form of an arrow (bottom).

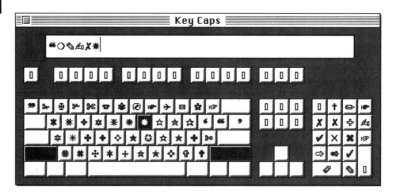

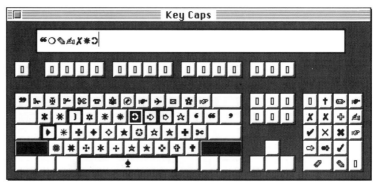

FIGURE 6.21

The Note Pad is one of those rare system utilities that is entirely void of meaning or utility.

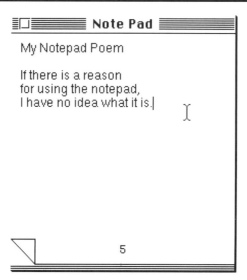

Puzzle

Ah, another impressive DA. As far as I can tell, the Puzzle is designed for people who want to waste time, but haven't discovered a good solitaire game like Shanghai or Ishido.

Actually, it's not all that bad. Unlike the Note Pad, there are a couple of unusual tricks you can perform with the Puzzle DA, as shown in Figure 6.22. For example, when the Puzzle window originally appears, it displays a big Apple logo with the pieces all mixed up. Choose the Clear command from the Edit menu and the Apple logo disappears, leaving tiles numbered 1 through 15 in its place. Choose Clear again, and the Apple logo reappears.

Whew, let me catch my breath. Now, if you really want to have fun, you can copy a bitmapped image, black-and-white or color, and paste it into the Puzzle window using the Paste command (⌘-V). The image is automatically resized to fit inside the 79-by-79-pixel puzzle window and dithered to fit the 256-color system palette.

If you complete a puzzle successfully, you are congratulated with the sound "Ta-da!" Frankly, this is the best part of the puzzle. If you want

Three phases of the Puzzle window, shown when mixed up (top) and when the puzzles are completed (bottom). The puzzle on the far right was created by pasting a bitmapped image into the Puzzle window.

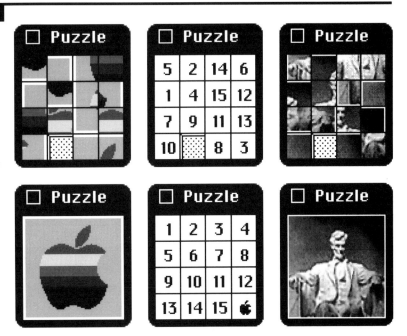

to add this sound to your current sound library, do the following. (This project requires the Apple utility ResEdit 2.1 or later, not included with System 7.)

1. Launch ResEdit and open the Puzzle file. The window shown in Figure 6.23 will appear.

2. Double-click the "snd" resource. A second window will appear, displaying a single sound resource file.

3. Select the sound resource (ID #-16000) and choose the Copy command from the Edit menu (⌘-C).

4. Now open the Sound control panel (discussed later in this chapter) and choose the Paste command (⌘-V).

5. Name the sound *Ta-da* and press Return. You can now hear this marvelous sound any time you like.

FIGURE 6.23

The Puzzle DA opened using the ResEdit utility

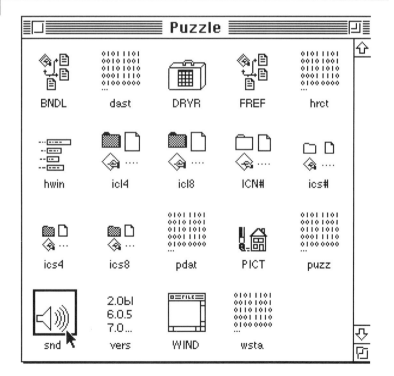

Scrapbook

The Scrapbook is used to hold text, graphics, and sound files copied from one application for eventual use in another. To add items to the Scrapbook, you copy the desired item from the current application, choose the Scrapbook command from the Apple menu, and paste. A new card is created to accommodate the pasted item. To retrieve an item, you scroll to the card on which the item is displayed, and then choose Cut (⌘-X) or Copy (⌘-C) from the Edit menu.

Note that the Scrapbook is not needed when copying from one open application and pasting into another. Nor is it required when copying from an application, quitting that application, launching another application, and pasting. Both of these operations can be handled without help by the Clipboard. The Scrapbook is only necessary when you want to put an item on hold for later use, or when you plan on restarting your computer before pasting an item into a desired application.

Each card in the Scrapbook displays information about its contents. For example, the card shown in Figure 6.24 indicates that the graphic it contains is stored in the PICT format. In fact, all graphics copied to the Scrapbook—bitmapped images and object-oriented drawings alike—are

FIGURE 6.24

The Scrapbook window lists information about the contents of the current card in its lower right-hand corner.

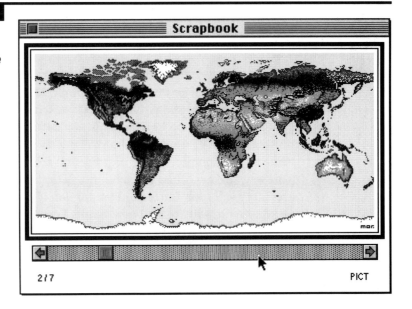

stored in the PICT format. The only time this might prove a problem is when swapping PostScript graphics created in an illustration program such as Adobe Illustrator or Aldus FreeHand, due to inherent differences between PICT and the PostScript language. To avoid this problem, you press the Option key when choosing the Cut or Copy command inside Illustrator or FreeHand. This appends a PostScript definition of the graphic to the PICT screen image, thus allowing the graphic to be pasted into the Scrapbook and other programs without any loss of detail or resolution.

Text is stored as a text only file accompanied by additional code to retain type size, style, and other formatting information. The syntax of this code depends on the application from which the text originates. For example, text copied from Microsoft Word is coded in RTF (the *Rich Text Format*). Other programs, notably PageMaker, also make use of RTF. If you use MacWrite II, formatting is coded in the STYL format. Typically, a program will not retain formatting when importing text via the Scrapbook unless it exports to the Clipboard in that same format. Therefore, text cannot be traded via the Scrapbook between, say, Microsoft Word and MacWrite II or vice versa.

Sound files are stored in the SND format. They may be traded between the Scrapbook, the Sound control panel, ResEdit, Farallon's SoundEdit, and virtually all other sound capturing and editing programs.

As an item is pasted, the Scrapbook DA automatically saves it to the Scrapbook File on disk, which resides in the System Folder. If you have assembled a sufficient collection of items in the current Scrapbook File, you may change the name of the Scrapbook File to prevent it from being altered. This way, the next time you open the Scrapbook, the desk accessory will look for the old Scrapbook File and, upon not finding it, will create a new, empty Scrapbook File. When you want to reuse the old file, rename the current Scrapbook File, restore the name of the old file to *Scrapbook File*, and again open the Scrapbook DA.

Since cards may be accessed in sequential order only, the Scrapbook tends to be an unwieldy program for storing libraries of text, graphics, and sounds. If you plan to use the Scrapbook on a regular basis, you may want to invest in a good Scrapbook substitute, such as Multi-Scrap from Olduvai or SmartScrap from Solutions International, both of which allow you to save Scrapbook files under different names and open them at will. SmartScrap offers the added advantage of letting you name specific items and later search for items by name. You may also print items from SmartScrap and resize the SmartScrap window.

Third-Party DAs

No doubt about it, desk accessories are a dying breed. But while you await the final rattle, you may as well consider picking up a few last minute bargains that will help you manage your new system software more effectively. As I see it, there are only four DAs that absolutely every experienced System 7 user should own: CanOpener from Abbott Systems, DiskTop from CE Software, the recently upgraded QuickDEX II from Casady & Greene, and Virus Detective from Shulman Software.

CanOpener   CanOpener is one of those remarkable save-your-butt-when-nothing-else-will-work utilities. The DA will open *any* file that contains data. It then extracts text and PICT images, allowing you to view them and save them to disk. This can be particularly useful when trying to retrieve data from a corrupted file. CanOpener can also be used to search for a string of text, as shown in Figure 6.25, either within the current file or inside any of several files on disk. While this capability is not as sophisticated as the content-searching feature provided by dedicated search utilities such as Microlytics' GOfer, CanOpener can search through files that other programs can't.

Incidentally, GOfer is bundled with DiskTop 4.01, which is described next. As long as you purchase both CanOpener and DiskTop, you'll have all the file-searching tools you'll ever need to use under System 7.

DiskTop   DiskTop 4.01 isn't entirely compatible with System 7—for example, it does not properly recognize aliases—but it does work with System 7 and can be used to organize files and launch applications much as you can at the Finder level. More importantly, however, it provides

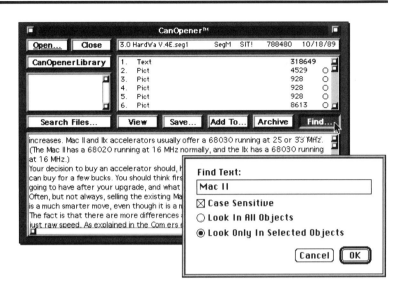

FIGURE 6.25

CanOpener allows you to open any document, regardless of format, and search through its contents.

easy access to technical file information, such as Type and Creator codes. You may also set a file to be invisible, or make an already invisible file—such as Desktop DB or Desktop DF, both introduced in the next chapter—visible. As an extra plus, you may use DiskTop to determine the sum-total size of multiple selected files, whether they reside in the same folder or not, as shown in Figure 6.26. This can be useful when you're considering throwing a few files away or copying them to a floppy disk, only if they add up to less than 760K, for example. On its own, the Finder application does not provide equivalent capabilities.

QuickDEX II   QuickDEX II is a free-form personal-management DA, designed specifically for creating phone number and address lists, much like an on-screen Rolodex file. Although the newest version offers control over fonts and type sizes and allows you to create cards as large as 16K (16,000 characters), the product contains remarkably few bells and whistles. Cards contain no fields for names, phone numbers, comments, and so on, nor may you structure the program by adding fields. But it provides a lightning-fast search feature, so that while on the phone, for example, you can switch back and forth between cards without suffering a single pregnant pause in the conversation. It's as if you could actually

remember everybody's name! QuickDEX will also dial your phone automatically, as demonstrated in Figure 6.27, or produce tones that can be
understood by your phone if you hold the receiver up to your computer's
speaker.

FIGURE 6.26

*DiskTop allows you to
determine the size of
multiple selected files.*

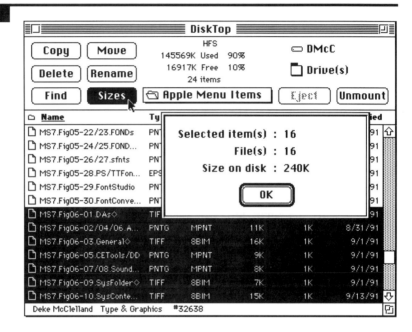

FIGURE 6.27

*QuickDEX II acts like a
Rolodex file that dials
your phone automatically.*

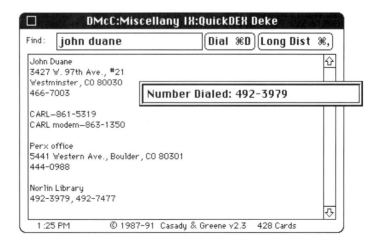

A slightly more expensive version of the product, called Super QuickDEX, provides additional utilities that can be used to print labels and envelopes.

VirusDetective   Everyone worries about computer viruses. But like any other dire threat you might expect to see probed by Geraldo, viruses are more the stuff of Al Capone's vault than Tutankhamen's treasure trove. In seven years of messing around with the Mac, uploading and downloading files over modems, and using disks that I find washed up on beaches, I have to my certain knowledge encountered only one virus.

Just the same, computer viruses do exist, so there's no sense in pushing your luck. The best virus detection and elimination utility I've encountered is VirusDetective, a shareware product by Jeff Shulman, which is shown in Figure 6.28 and is included on the disks that you can order with the coupon found at the back of the book. This DA searches selected disks or files, removes infected resources or deletes infected files, and creates operational logs in any of five common word-processing formats. VirusDetective was also one of the first utilities to allow you to modify the list of strings and resources for which the DA checks. Shulman even notifies registered users of when a new virus hits the streets, enabling you to keep up with the ever-growing world of HTDs ("hexually" transmitted diseases). For both beginners and experienced

FIGURE 6.28

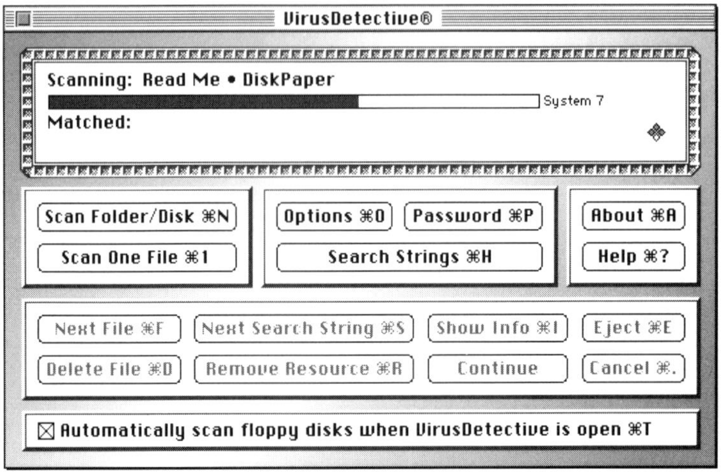

VirusDetective 5.0 searches specified disks, folders, and files for any of 15 HTDs.

users alike, VirusDetective provides unbeatable virus detection and elimination capabilities.

VirusDetective can be registered on its own or in combination with a control panel called VirusBlockade II, also by Shulman. VirusBlockade automates the virus detection process, instructing VirusDetective to scan files as they are created and modified. Since the process is instantaneous, VirusBlockade serves as a viral prevention program. The second a virus sets foot on your hard drive, it is recognized and eliminated.

CONTROL PANELS

The other group of system utilities included with System 7 is control panels. In this section, I'll describe the 21 control panels provided with System 7.1, all of which are displayed in Figure 6.29, as well as a few control panels from other vendors that'll make your life a little easier.

Brightness

The Brightness control panel allows you to adjust the brightness setting of your monitor. To use the control panel, you drag the slider, as shown in Figure 6.30, or use arrow keys. You may also change the brightness by entering a number from 0 to 9.

FIGURE 6.29

The 21 control panels included with System 7.1. (System 7 has two fewer control panels—Numbers and Date & Time.)

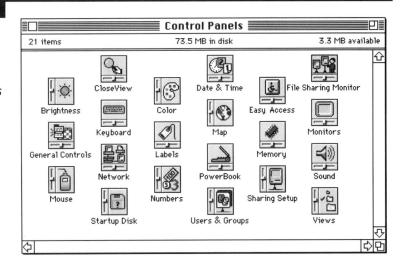

FIGURE 6.30

*D*rag the slider to adjust
the brightness level of a
monitor that lacks an
external brightness knob.

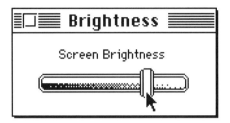

Note that this control panel can only be used with monitors that
offer no brightness knob, such as the monitor included with the Macintosh Portable. If you have somehow managed to install the Brightness
control panel on a computer that offers a knob, throw the control
panel away.

Any computer with a built-in monitor—including the Plus, SE,
and Classic—provides a knob just beneath the overhanging "chin" of the
computer on the left-hand side. An Apple 12-inch or 13-inch stand-alone
monitor provides a knob on its right-hand side toward the top. (As you
feel around the edge of the monitor, you'll find two knobs. The top knob
is the brightness knob; the knob below that controls the contrast.)
Monitors from other vendors provide knobs in various locations.

CloseView

Of the 21 control panels provided with System 7.1 (19 in System 7),
CloseView is the only one that is not installed automatically under any
circumstances. If you want to use this control panel, you'll have to install
it manually from the *Install 3* disk included with your System 7 package.
Then restart your computer to allow the control panel to take effect.

As you can see in Figure 6.31, the CloseView control panel is
designed to help visually impaired users by enlarging the size of screen
pixels, which in turn enlarges images on the screen. Most monitors offer
a default resolution of 72 pixels per inch. Using this control panel, you
may magnify the screen from 2 to 16 times normal size, in effect reducing screen resolution from 36 to 4.5 pixels per inch.

Figures 6.32 and 6.33 demonstrate how the control panel works.
After activating CloseView by selecting the "On" radio button at the top
of the control panel window (⌘-Option-O), a heavy rectangle displays
on screen, as shown in Figure 6.32. This rectangle represents the area

FIGURE 6.31

If you have problems reading characters on your monitor, use the CloseView control panel to enlarge a portion of the screen.

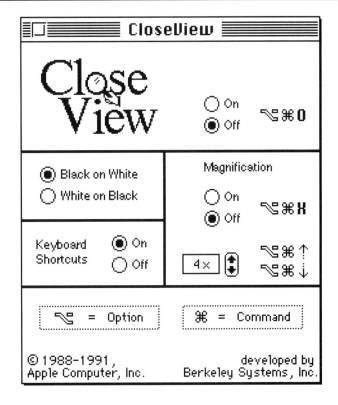

that will be magnified at the current level of magnification set in the CloseView control panel. For the sake of this example, suppose the magnification level is set to "4x." Select the "On" radio button from the "Magnification" options (⌘-Option-X) to initiate the magnification feature. The area surrounded by the heavy outline will quadruple in size, as shown in Figure 6.33. Notice that every pixel grows, including those associated with your cursor. To return the screen to normal magnification, again press ⌘-Option-X.

Note that the CloseView control panel consumes an amount of space in RAM sufficiently large to store the entire screen image—22K on a built-in black-and-white monitor, over 300K on an 8-bit gray-scale or color monitor, and roughly 1MB when running a 24-bit color display device.

FIGURE 6.32

After you turn on CloseView, a heavy outline surrounds and follows your cursor.

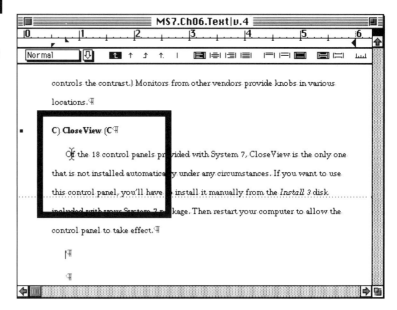

FIGURE 6.33

You can press ⌘–Option-X to magnify the surrounded image on the screen.

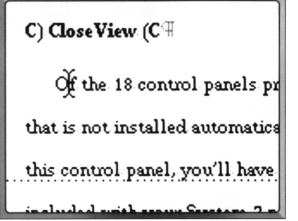

Color

The Color control panel allows you to determine the colors used to display scroll bars and highlighted text. As shown in Figure 6.34, you choose an option from the "Window color" pop-up menu to determine the colors of scroll bars and title bars. You choose an option from "Highlight color" to determine the color used to highlight text at the Finder level and when editing text in word processors and other applications. You can also choose the "Other…" option to display the Apple Color Picker dialog box, which allows you to select a custom color.

Options in the Color control panel can be applied only when using a gray-scale or color monitor set to display 16 colors or more.

*U*se the Color control panel to specify the color of title bars and highlighted text.

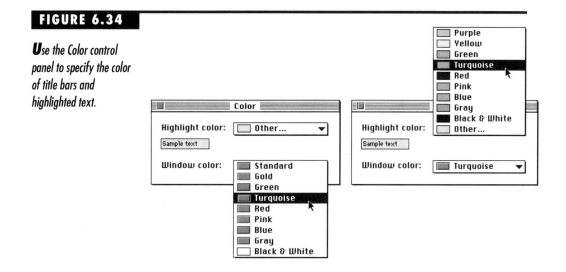

Date & Time

The Date & Time control panel (Figure 6.35), included with System 7.1, lets you change the date and time in the same way described for the Alarm Clock earlier in this chapter. More importantly, it also allows you to choose the format in which the date and time appears.

Click the Date Formats… button to bring up a dialog box for choosing the manner in which the date appears, as shown in Figure 6.36. Under the Long date heading you can choose which date elements—weekday, month, day, year—are used, the order in which they appear,

FIGURE 6.35

*The Date & Time
control panel*

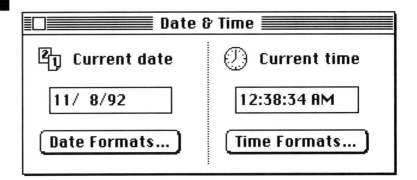

FIGURE 6.36

*The Date Formats
dialog box*

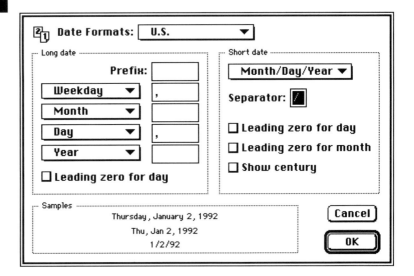

and any notation for separating them. The date displayed presently is in
the U.S. format—the standard for the United States. Each of the boxes
below Prefix is a pop-up menu containing all the date element choices,
as well as the choice of none. Thus, you can change the order of the date
elements. If you prefer the date to read month, day, year, for example,
then you would drag down the menu in the first box, presently indicating weekday, and choose month and continue to affect changes to the
rest of the boxes. The smaller boxes are the prefix boxes that allow you
to enter punctuation (or any character, for that matter) that you want

displayed with the date elements. Select the Leading zero for day check box to insert a zero as a tens digit place holder for single digit days. All changes made are reflected under the Samples heading. Also, any changes made to the original U.S. format are reflected in the fact that the Date Format will no longer read U.S., but instead will read custom since you have created a customized date format. To restore the U.S. format, drag down the menu in the Date Format and select U.S.

The Short date heading contains options for displaying the abbreviated form of the date, as shown in the third line under *Samples*. The large box is a pop-up menu that contains four choices for the short date display. Directly below that is the Separator box in which you enter the symbol you wish to appear between the short date elements. As with any changes to the long date, any made to the short date are reflected in the samples and changes the Date Format to Custom. Click OK to close the dialog box.

Click the Time Formats… button to bring up a dialog box for making changes to the way that the time is displayed, as shown in Figure 6.37. In the upper left-hand part of the window, you can choose between a 24-hour (also known as military time, in which midnight is represented as 00:00:00 and one second before midnight is represented as 23:59:59) or a 12-hour clock display. If you choose a 12-hour display, then you can also choose how you want noon and midnight to display.

FIGURE 6.37

The Time Formats dialog box

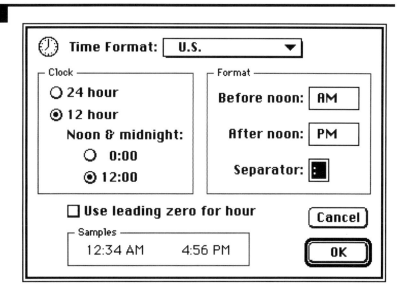

In the upper right-hand part of the window, you enter symbols for indicating before and after noon for the 12-hour display (usually AM and PM). You can choose the symbol for separating hours, minutes, and seconds. Also, as with the date format, any changes are reflected under the Samples heading, and you can restore the original format by choosing U.S. from the Time Formats pop-up menu. Then, click OK to close the Formats dialog box and click the close box to close the Date & Time control panel.

Easy Access

Shown in Figure 6.38, the Easy Access control panel provides three distinct functions. The *mouse keys* function allows you to move your cursor, select objects, highlight text, and so on using the keypad rather than the mouse. The *slow keys* function filters and communicates the acceptance of keystrokes. The *sticky keys* function locks a key in place so that keyboard equivalents may be initiated by pressing one at a time rather than several keys simultaneously.

FIGURE 6.38

The Easy Access control panel enhances the performance of your keyboard.

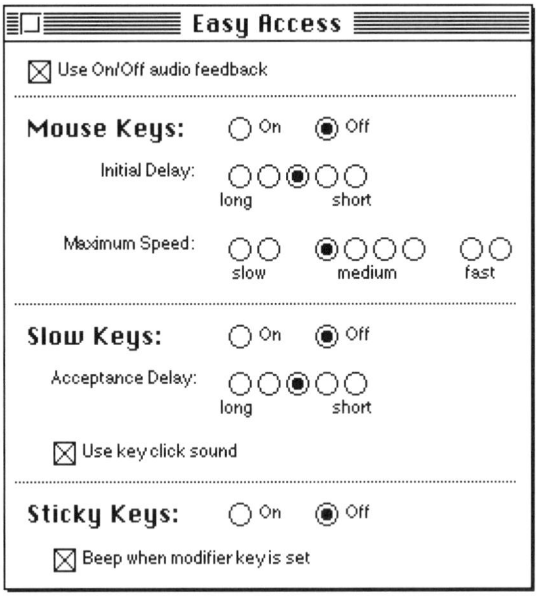

Sticky Keys   Sticky keys and slow keys were designed to help the Mac better conform to the capabilities of physically disabled persons who have difficulty using one or both hands and must therefore rely on a single hand or on a mouth-held device. To activate the sticky keys function from the keyboard, you press the Shift key five times in a row. A tone will sound to let you know that the function is active, and a small icon will appear on the far right side of the menu bar (see Figure 6.39). To use the activated sticky keys, you press a modifier key, such as ⌘, Shift, Option, or Control. The sticky keys icon in the menu bar will change to display a down-pointing arrow. You should continue pressing keys until the keyboard equivalent is complete. For example, suppose you have selected some text in Microsoft Word that you want to make bold. The keyboard equivalent for the Bold command is ⌘-Shift-B. To initiate this command using sticky keys, you would press and release ⌘, then press and release Shift, then press and release B. Easy Access recognizes that B is not a modifier key, and therefore completes the sticky key series and chooses the command.

To lock down a modifier key, you press the key twice. For example, suppose you want to select all the text between one click location and another in Word. You click at the location where you want the selection to begin, press the Shift key twice to lock it in place, then click at the location where the selection should end. Now all text between the two click points is highlighted.

The four settings available when using sticky keys

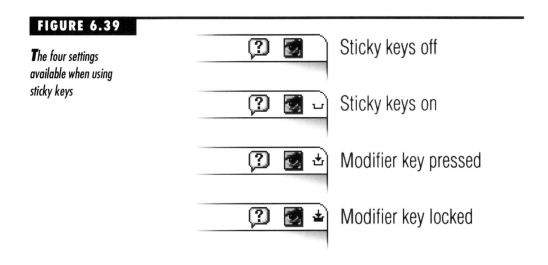

Sticky keys off

Sticky keys on

Modifier key pressed

Modifier key locked

To unlock a key, you press any key on the keyboard. Note, however, that the arrow icon remains displayed in the menu bar, indicating that the previously locked key will act as the first key in a sticky keys series. To turn off sticky keys, you press the Shift key five times in a row, or press any two modifier keys simultaneously.

Slow Keys   If you have problems making discrete keystrokes, slow keys can help. When slow keys is active, your computer will accept a keystroke only if the key is held down for a prescribed amount of time, which is set using the "Acceptance Delay" option in the Easy Access control panel. To keep you abreast of what's going on, the slow keys function beeps when you press a key and then beeps again to let you know that you may release it.

To turn on slow keys, you press and hold the Return key for approximately eight seconds. After four seconds, a warning beep will sound to let you know that the function is *about* to be turned on. *Keep holding the key.* After the full eight seconds, you'll hear a tone which tells you that the slow keys function is now active. To turn off slow keys, press the Return key another eight seconds.

> While using a word processor, have you ever tried pressing the Return key for eight seconds? You'll create a string of carriage returns. To avoid this, bring the Finder to the front when activating or deactivating slow keys.

Mouse Keys   Whether you have problems using a mouse or you're simply looking for a means to move a selection by a precise number of screen pixels, you can put mouse keys to work. For example, suppose you're using MacPaint. You have selected an image and now you need to move it slightly into place. Dragging the image with your mouse proves too clumsy. If only you could nudge it from the keyboard, as you can in more sophisticated applications.

This is a job for mouse keys. To turn on the mouse keys function, you press ⌘-Shift-Clear (the Clear key is located on the keypad). Then you use the keypad to click, hold down the mouse button, and move the cursor, as shown in Figure 6.40. All number keys except 0 and 5 move the cursor in different directions. You Press a number key to move the cursor one pixel; press and hold to move the cursor several pixels. The "Initial Delay" option in the Easy Access control panel determines the amount of time between when a number key is held down and the cursor begins to move—anywhere between 1.9 (the "long" radio button) and 0.9 ("short") seconds. If you hold the key down longer than the initial delay, the cursor will begin moving and accelerate to the speed specified using the "Maximum Speed" option, anywhere between 15 ("slow") and 900 ("fast") pixels per second. The "medium" radio button is generally the most desirable setting, clocking in at about 75 pixels per second.

You may also use the keypad to click and drag. Press the 5 key to click the mouse button; press 5 twice in a row to double-click. To drag the cursor—whether to move a selected object, create a marquee, high-light text, or whatever—you press the 0 key to fix down the mouse button, press a number key (other than 5) to move the cursor, and press the Period key to release the mouse button.

FIGURE 6.40

*U*se the keyboard to perform mouse operations when the mouse keys function is active.

> **If you like to maintain a tidy desktop (hey, no value judgments here), you can use the mouse keys function to move icons at the Finder level. Move your cursor over the icon. Then you press 5 to select the icon, press 0 followed by a number key to nudge the icon to a different position, and press the Period key to release. If the Finder grid is active (as discussed in the following chapter) and you are trying to move an icon independently of the grid, you press ⌘-Period to release the icon and prevent the icon from aligning to the grid.**

Note that when the mouse keys function is active, you may not access numbers from the keyboard. When working in an application that requires the use of the keypad, such as the Calculator DA, you press Clear to turn off mouse keys and access the keypad normally.

File Sharing Monitor

File Sharing Monitor—which has nothing to do with your display monitor or the Monitor control panel—is the first of four control panels that affects file sharing over a Macintosh network. Others include Network, Sharing Setup, and Users & Groups. Although I'll briefly explain each of these control panels in this chapter, you'll want to read Chapter 12 for complete information.

As you can see in Figure 6.41, the File Sharing Monitor control panel allows you to view the folders and disks that are being shared and to see all users that are currently connected to your computer. (Before you can use this control panel, the File Sharing Extension and Network Extension files must be present in the Extensions folder, and you must have started the "File Sharing" option in the Sharing Setup control panel.)

Aside from viewing network activity, the only function you can perform with the File Sharing Monitor control panel is to disconnect users. Perhaps your machine is being slowed by too much network activity, perhaps a user forgot to disconnect before leaving for the evening, perhaps you're just in a foul mood. In any case, you may disconnect any user by

The File Sharing Monitor control panel displays lists of shared items and the users that are currently accessing them.

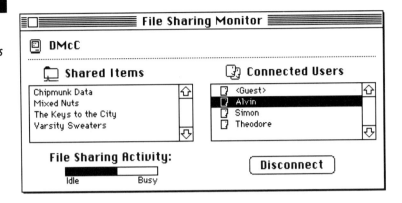

selecting a name from the "Connected Users" list and clicking the Disconnect button. A message will display requesting a number of minutes before the poor soul is disconnected. To ditch the user immediately, you enter 0 and press Return.

General Controls

Shown in Figure 6.42, the General Controls control panel serves a variety of functions. First, it allows you to change the date and time assigned to saved files, in the same way described for the Alarm Clock earlier in this chapter. You may also set the time to conform to a 12-hour or 24-hour standard.

The two "Blinking" options fall into the who-gives-a-darn category. The "Menu Blinking" option determines the number of times, if any, a chosen command flashes on and off. "Rate of Insertion Point Blinking" determines how fast an insertion marker blinks when editing text. Both options are cosmetic and have next to no effect on the speed or performance of your computer.

The most interesting option provided by the General Controls window is the "Desktop Pattern" option, which determines the appearance of the desktop that appears behind windows, icons, and other screen elements. This option is made up of three items: a magnified 8-by-8-pixel pattern display on the left, a miniature desktop on the right that shows

FIGURE 6.42

The General Controls control panel provides options for changing the time, the date, and the appearance of the desktop.

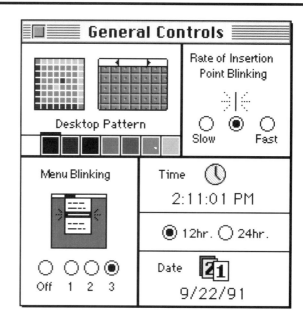

the pattern at actual size, and a series of eight color slots along the bottom (not available when using a black-and-white monitor). To use the options, follow these directions:

1. Select a precreated pattern by clicking the left- and right-pointing arrowheads above the miniature desktop.

2. If you're using a color monitor and you desire to edit the colors in the pattern, double-click a color slot and select a new color using the Apple Color Picker dialog box.

3. To edit the pattern, select one of the eight available colors (if using a color monitor) and click inside the magnified pattern display to change a pixel to that color. When using a black-and-white monitor, clicking a pixel changes it from black to white or from white to black.

4. Click inside the miniature desktop to fill the real desktop with the current pattern. (To cancel the creation of a pattern, close the General Controls window without clicking inside the normal-sized pattern display.)

To change a pattern permanently, you edit the pattern and double-click the miniature desktop. Double-clicking stores the pattern in the System, in place of the old pattern. The custom pattern will now display when you scroll through the patterns in the future.

Note that the General Controls control panel stores 12 color patterns and 12 black-and-white patterns in the current System file. No more, no less. If you apply a custom pattern to the desktop without storing the pattern, the pattern is saved to a temporary disk buffer, in effect, becoming a 13th pattern. This 13th pattern is stored in a separate resource file from the original 12 and the two may *never* mix. Thus, if you edit the 13th pattern in the future, you will not be able to store it with the original 12; double-clicking the miniature desktop for the 13th pattern will produce a beep. The moral of the story: If you want to store a pattern or if you think you'll *ever* want to store it in the future, double-click the pattern the first time you edit it.

Keyboard

The Keyboard control panel allows you determine how frequently characters repeat when pressing a key, as shown in Figure 6.43. For example, when you press a letter or number key, you create a single character on screen. If you press and hold the key, a string of characters will be created. The "Delay Until Repeat" option determines the length of time between when you press a key and when the second character displays—anywhere between 0.9 second (the "long" radio button) and almost instantaneously ("short"). Select the "Off" radio button if you don't want characters to repeat regardless of how long you press a key.

If you hold the key down longer than the initial delay, new characters will appear at the speed specified using the "Key Repeat Rate" option, anywhere from 1 character every other second ("slow") to 24 characters per second ("fast").

FIGURE 6.43

The Keyboard control panel determines the speed at which letters repeat and provides access to keyboard layout files.

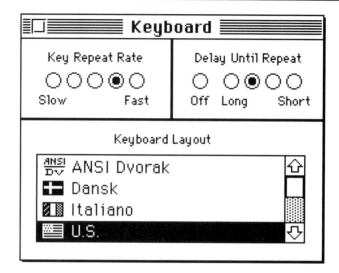

The "Keyboard Layout" list displays all keyboard layout files installed in the current System. Select the desired layout to change the manner in which characters are accessed from the keyboard.

System 7.1 includes the U.S.-System 6 keyboard layout file. It allows you to access all the characters that were available under System 6 that are no longer in the same position on the System 7.1 default. As mentioned under Special Characters in Chapter 5, pressing Shift-Option-Tilde produces the standard grave accent (`) when the U.S. keyboard layout is selected. If U.S.-System 6 layout is activated, then pressing Shift-Option-Tilde produces a special character, such as the running bunny in Geneva.

The number of differences between the keyboard layouts depends on the particular font that you are using. For the Chicago screen font, the differences are minimal. On the other hand, there are about ten differences for the Courier screen font. To illustrate this, choose Key Caps from the Apple menu and choose Courier from the Key Caps menu. Without closing Key Caps, bring up the Control Panels folder from the Apple menu and Option-double-click on the Keyboards control panel. Option-double-clicking launches the Keyboard control panel while closing the Control Panels folder. Position the Keyboard control panel so that you can readily see Key Caps. Watch the Key Caps keys while pressing the Shift and Option keys—notice that Key Caps responds even though it is not in the foreground—and click on U.S.-System 6 in the "Keyboard Layout" list. You will notice that the Shift-Option-T and the Shift-Option-I produce very different characters under the different layouts. This is also the case with other fonts.

T I P

> If you are using more than one keyboard layout, you may select the next layout alphabetically in your System file by pressing ⌘-Option-Spacebar, even if the Keyboard control panel is not displayed.

Labels

The Labels control panel determines the color and names that appear in the Label menu at the Finder level, as shown in Figure 6.44. Click on a color to display the Apple Color Picker dialog box, which allows you to select a custom color. To change a name, you highlight the name and enter a new one from the keyboard. For complete information on this control panel, you should see Chapter 8.

FIGURE 6.44

Use the Label control panel to change the colors and names displayed in the Finder Label menu.

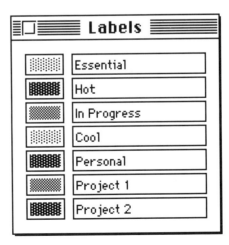

Map

Shown in Figure 6.45, the Map control panel is one of those utilities that doesn't look like much until you get to know it better. Much of its functionality is hidden. Its primary purpose is clear enough: to locate cities around the globe, add new cities, and discover the current time in another portion of the world. To locate a city, you enter the city name in the option box and click the Find button or press Enter. A sparkle on the map shows the city's general location. Latitude and longitude coordinates will display below the city name. If the city is north of the equator, the "N" option is checked. If east of the prime meridian, the "E" option is checked. The time zone is also listed. If the time is later than Greenwich mean time, the "+" option is checked.

FIGURE 6.45

The Map control panel is designed to determine distances and time differences.

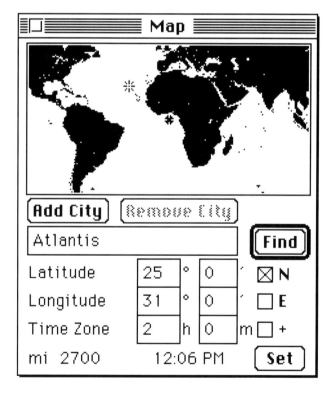

> You press Option and click the Find button (or press Option-Return) to cycle alphabetically through all cities stored in the Map control panel. If a city name has been entered into the option box and searched for, the cycling will follow that city alphabetically. (After Denver, for example, comes Detroit, Djakarta, Djibouti, and so on.) If you haven't searched for a city since opening Map, the cycling begins at the first alphabetical entry, Abu Dhabi, which as we all know is the largest sheikdom in the United Arab Emirates.

Note that some names are not included in the alphabetical loop. You should try entering *Zürich* and pressing Return. Then press Option-Return to see a second list of alphabetical entries starting with Antananarivo (capital of Madagascar) and ending with Yangon (the local name for Rangoon, Burma). Following Yangon are all cities you've added, in the order added.

Adding a City   One of the Map control panel's problems is that it knows the locations of most major cities in the United States, but when it comes to international cities, it knows little more than capitals. Milan, Italy; Alexandria, Egypt; and Yokohama, Japan are all missing. If a city cannot be located, you may add it to the Map database. After entering the name of the unknown city, you drag the sparkle to the approximate location on the map or, better yet, enter the city's exact coordinates in the "Latitude" and "Longitude" option boxes. When the city has been correctly positioned, click the Add City button.

Setting up Home Port   Interesting as all of this may seem, you could locate more cities using a standard atlas. The disguised and more utilitarian purpose of the Map control panel is to determine relative information about a location; specifically, how far is a city like Abu Dhabi from your home town, and what is the time difference. To discover this, you must first set up home base. You search for the city in which your

Macintosh resides, or add it to the Map database. Then you click the Set button to move the cross-shaped marker to this location. Distance and time measurements may now be made relative to this location.

ARNING

> **The Map control panel assumes that the current home port jives with the time set in the General Controls control panel. Therefore, if you change the home port using the Set button, Map will automatically update the time. For example, if it is currently 7:00 PM when the home port is set to 0° latitude, 0° longitude (the original default setting), and you change home port to Boulder, Colorado, your Mac's clock will automatically revert to 12 o'clock noon. Thus, after using the Set button, you will generally have to reset the time using Alarm Clock or General Controls.**

The up side of this is that when you take your Mac on the plane with you to Abu Dhabi, all you have to do is search for your new home port, click Set, and you're back in business.

Once you have set up home port, the relative distance between you and a searched city will be listed at the bottom right corner of the Map window. The default unit of measurement is miles. You click the word "mi" to convert the distance to kilometers. You click again to display the distance in degrees. The time in the searched city is listed at the bottom of the control panel. To gauge the difference between your time and that of the other city, you click the words "Time Zone" to change the option to "Time Differ." If the "+" option is checked, it is later in the selected city than in your home port.

Making a Better Map   If you use a color monitor, you can put together your own improved Map control panel. Rather than seeing a silhouette globe where land masses are black and oceans are white, you can

view a color relief map that shows better detail. Interested? Then you should do the following:

1. Choose the Scrapbook command from the Apple menu to display the Scrapbook file.

2. Use the scroll bar to advance to the second card in the Scrapbook. Assuming you haven't altered the contents of the original Scrapbook file, this card shows a color map of the world.

3. Choose the Copy command from the Edit menu (⌘-C) to copy the color map. Then close the Scrapbook.

4. Now open the Map control panel and choose the Paste command from the Edit menu (⌘-V). A message will display alerting you that the previous black-and-white map will be deleted. Click the Replace button. The new map will appear in the Map window, as shown in Figure 6.46.

In fact, you may paste any image into the Map control panel. It will automatically be scaled to 360 pixels wide by 178 pixels tall.

To display the map image at 200% magnification, as shown in the second example of Figure 6.46, you press Option when opening the Map control panel.

FIGURE 6.46

The color map shown at normal size (left) and when magnified to 200% (right).

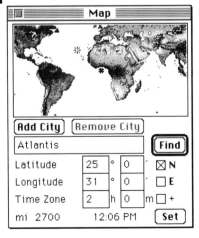
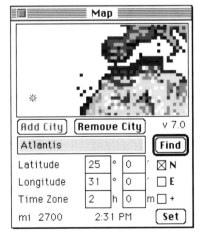

Memory

The Memory control panel is discussed in detail in Chapter 9, but I'll give it a quick treatment here. As shown in Figure 6.47, this control panel permits you to adjust the Disk Cache, activate and adjust virtual memory, and activate 32-bit addressing. To change the *disk cache,* which is the area in RAM to which frequently used data is stored from disk, you click the arrows to the right of the "Cache Size" option. (You cannot turn off the cache as in System 6, but you can set it as low as 32K.) After turning on *virtual memory,* which expands the size of your RAM by setting aside space on your hard disk, you choose the hard disk you wish to use from the "Select Hard Disk" pop-up menu and set the size of the virtual memory partition using the arrows to the right of the "After restart" option. You use the radio buttons at the bottom of the control panel to turn on *32-bit addressing,* which increases the amount of RAM that can be used by your computer.

All changes made inside the Memory control panel will take effect after you restart your computer. If one or more of the options shown in Figure 6.47 is missing from your Memory control panel, your computer

---

*U*se the Memory control panel to manage your computer's RAM.

Memory
Disk Cache Always On   Cache Size   256K
Select Hard Disk: Virtual Memory   ◆ DMcC   ▼ ● On   Available on disk: 13M ○ Off   Total memory : 8M   After restart   11M
32-Bit Addressing ○ On ● Off
Use Defaults

is not able to take advantage of these functions. You should see Chapter 9 for more information.

Monitors

The Monitors control panel affects the colors and elements displayed on one or more monitors. Depending on your video card, you may change the *screen depth*—that is, the number of colors that may be displayed simultaneously on screen—by selecting a value from the scrolling list (see Figure 6.48). You use the "Grays" or "Colors" radio button to determine whether gray values or colors are displayed. Colors are always displayed if you select the "Thousands" or "Millions" value from the scrolling list, since the Mac is not capable of creating more than 256 gray values. Black and white are always available, regardless of which value you select.

If you use a color monitor, there will be times when you'll find it useful to switch back and forth between screen depth settings. One reason is speed. Lowering the number of colors displayed on screen increases the speed at which various applications operate. For example, on a Mac IIsi, Microsoft Word scrolls slowly when viewed in millions of colors, but

---

FIGURE 6.48

The Monitors control panel controls screen colors and elements. Press Option to display the miniature happy Mac icon.

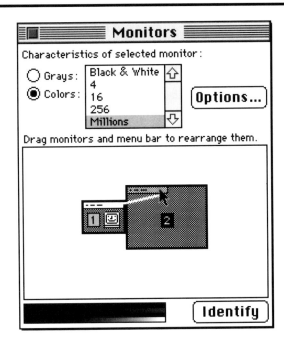

almost instantaneously when displayed in black and white. A second reason is compatibility. Some programs will not launch when too many colors are displayed on screen. (This second problem is generally limited to owners of 24-bit monitors set to display millions of colors.)

I P

Various third-party utilities allow you to change screen depth automatically. The simplest of these is Switch-A-Roo, an Fkey created by Bill Steinberg and sold through Microseeds Publishing as part of Screen Gems, and PixelFlipper, a control panel by Chris Sanchez. Switch-A-Roo allows you to toggle between two specified screen depths simply by pressing a key combination. PixelFlipper pops up a menu of screen depth options when you press a specified key combination. If you're looking for something a little more versatile, QuicKeys 2.1 includes a Screen Ease extension which may be used to set up a screen swapping macro. As shown in Figure 6.49, you may select a number of colors, determine the monitor(s) to be affected, and instruct the program to make depth changes temporary or permanent.

All attached monitors are represented relative to their sizes in the lower portion of the Monitors window. If you are using only one monitor, don't worry about these options. If you are using two or more monitors, drag the monitor in relation to each other to determine how your cursor exits one window and enters the other. For example, if you were using the configuration shown in Figure 6.49, you would have to move your cursor off the right side of the smaller monitor to enter the area displayed in the larger monitor.

You may also drag screen items between monitors. For example, the tiny menu bar icon (shown being dragged in Figure 6.48) represents the main monitor on which the real menu bar will be displayed. If you press the Option key, a happy Mac icon will display. You can move this icon to change the monitor on which startup images display.

The numbers are used to distinguish one monitor from another. If you are using so many monitors that you can't remember, say, which monitor is the third from the right, click the Identify button. A number will display. Without releasing, drag your cursor from one screen to the next. The number will update to show each time your cursor enters a new monitor.

You click the Options... button to determine the type of video card used by a selected monitor. If you press the Option key while clicking the Options... button, you may adjust the *color calibration* for the selected monitor, as shown in Figure 6.50. The job of color calibration is to match screen colors to corresponding colors in the real world. You select the "Use Special Gamma" check box, and then select the desired option from the scrolling list. Generally, there are only two options: a default

---

FIGURE 6.49

The Screen Ease extension provided with QuicKeys 2.1 allows you to change screen depth via a macro.

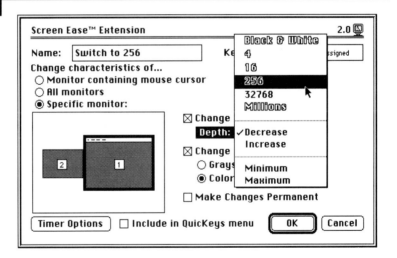

FIGURE 6.50

You can click the optional Options... button to change the color calibration.

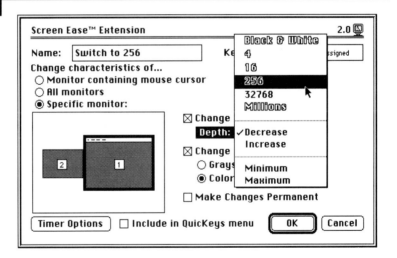

setting, which matches colors according to predetermined routines included with the display card and an "uncorrected" setting, which displays colors with no regard to their real world counterparts.

All changes made inside the Monitors control panel will take effect after you restart your computer.

Mouse

The Mouse control panel allows you determine the speed at which the cursor moves and the manner in which the system interprets double-clicks, as shown in Figure 6.51. The "Mouse Tracking" option determines the relationship between the distance you move your mouse and the distance your cursor moves on screen, called the *tracking ratio*. When set to "Very Slow," the tracking ratio is about 1 to 1; that is, if you drag your mouse an inch, your cursor will move roughly 72 pixels (equal to an inch on most monitors). This speed is intended primarily for tablets, so that the image displayed on screen is equal in size to the image you draw or trace. When using a mouse, however, you'll probably want faster tracking, since a typical mouse pad is smaller than a typical monitor. When set to "Slow," moving your mouse an inch moves the cursor about an inch and a half. When set to "Fast," the cursor moves almost twice as fast.

The "Double-Click Speed" option answers the age-old question: When do two clicks equal one double-click? When you double-click, you

---

FIGURE 6.51

*T*he Mouse control panel
determines the speed of
the cursor and the interval
of a double-click.

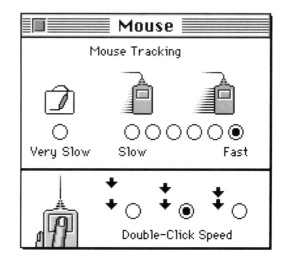

press the mouse button twice within an interval of time. That interval may be as long as 2 seconds (the left radio button) or as short as 1 second (the right radio button). Thus, if you find yourself double-clicking too often, as when selecting an icon and then clicking again to move it, you should select the shortest double-click interval. If you're new to the mouse and you haven't yet mastered the art of the double-click, you can select a longer interval.

Network

Like File Sharing Monitor, the Network control panel affects file sharing over a Macintosh network. For complete information on this and other file sharing options, you should read Chapter 12.

As you can see in Figure 6.52, the Network control panel allows you to switch between multiple network connections. This is useful only if you are connected to an EtherTalk or TokenTalk network. To use this control panel, you select the desired network connection icon and click the close box.

FIGURE 6.52

You use the Network control panel to select between the built-in LocalTalk and EtherTalk or TokenTalk networks.

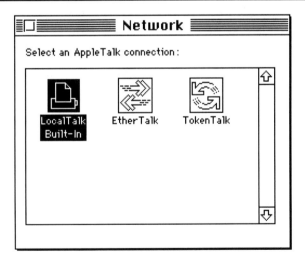

Numbers

The Numbers control panel, as shown in Figure 6.53, allows you to change the manner in which numbers appear. This control panel is

FIGURE 6.53

The Numbers control panel

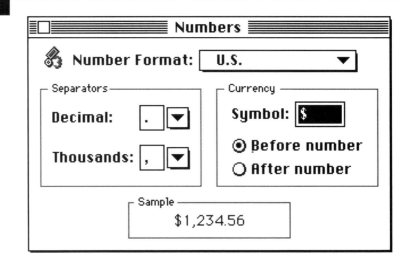

available only in System 7.1. For example, within any directory window, the default view shows the size of all contained files. If the size of one of the files is greater than one thousand kilobytes then the size display will contain one comma separating the thousands digit from the hundreds digit. With the Numbers control panel, you can change the comma to a different symbol.

In the upper left-hand side of the Numbers control panel, you can choose a symbol for the separators for the decimal and thousands place by entering a symbol directly into the respective box, or choose one of the ones from the pop-up menus to the right of the boxes. Any changes are reflected in the sample display at the bottom of the control panel. The number format pop-up menu at the top of the control panel will change from U.S. (the default format) to Custom when changes are implemented.

In the upper right-hand side of the control panel, you can change the symbol for indicating currency (e.g., ¢, ¥, or £) and indicate whether the chosen symbol should precede or follow the number. As before, any changes are reflected in the sample display and the Number Format changes from U.S. to Custom.

PowerBook

The PowerBook control panel can only be used on the battery-powered Macintosh PowerBook series, and replaces the Portable control panel included under System 7.0 and System 7.0.1. If the PowerBook control panel was installed on your standard model Mac, throw it away.

As shown in Figure 6.54, the PowerBook control panel is concerned with battery conservation and SCSI disk mode. The PowerBook control panel has one slider bar for controlling the rate at which your PowerBook's system and hard disk go to sleep. Its predecessor, the Portable control panel, had two independent slider bars: one to set the amount of time before the System (or, effectively, the screen) went to sleep, and the other to set the amount of time before the hard disk went to sleep. Apple felt that two sliders bars caused confusion and thus they implemented the single slider bar on the PowerBook control panel. Now, instead of setting the specific amount of time with the slider bar, you choose between the Maximum Performance and Maximum Conservation extremes. The closer the slider bar is set to Maximum Performance, the longer your PowerBook will continue normal operation without your input before going to sleep. The closer the slider is to Maximum Conservation, the faster your PowerBook will go a dozing. The single bar design will, of course, work fine, but it does lack some of the versatility of the old Portable control panel.

Click the Options… button under Battery Conservation to display the Battery Conservation Options, as shown in Figure 6.55. Here you can choose whether it is possible for your PowerBook to sleep while it is plugged in, and you can select standard or reduced sleep under Processor Speed.

The PowerBook control panel offers options that affect the operation of the Macintosh Portable.

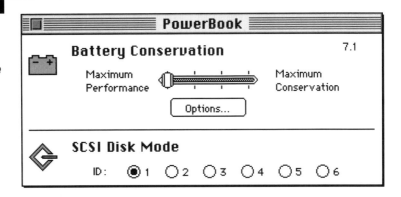

FIGURE 6.55

The Battery Conservation options

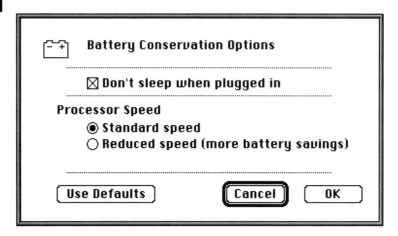

The rest of the PowerBook control panel (see Figure 6.54) deals with the SCSI port number that your PowerBook is assigned. Originally, the PowerBook 100 was designed to be the low end of the PowerBook series. Though it basically lived up to this decree, it offered one feature that the other original PowerBooks—the PowerBook 140 and Power-Book 170—did not. The PowerBook 100 allowed you to directly link it to a standard model Mac as an external hard drive. Apple realized that they had made a mistake in not including this convenience in the other two original PowerBooks, and incorporated it into the newer PowerBook 145 and PowerBook 180. To use your PowerBook with a standard model Mac, you must connect the PowerBook to the SCSI port matching the ID number you have chosen under the SCSI Disk Mode.

Sharing Setup

Like File Sharing Monitor and Network, the Sharing Setup control panel affects file sharing over a Macintosh network. For complete information on this and other file sharing options, you should read Chapter 12.

You use the Sharing Setup control panel to set owner information and initiate file sharing and program linking features. You enter your name as owner or primary user of the current computer into the "Owner Name" option, as shown in Figure 6.56. If you want to prevent network

The Sharing Setup control panel allows you to start and stop file sharing and program linking functions.

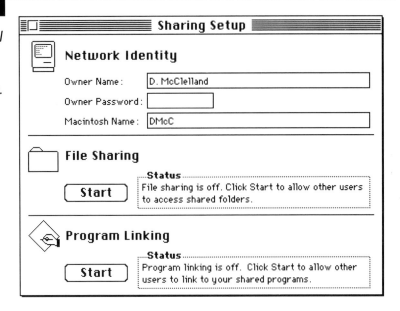

users from accessing sensitive data, you enter up to eight characters into the "Owner Password" option box. The characters will change to bullets when you advance to the next option. Finally, you enter the name of your Mac—which by default assumes the name of your startup disk—into the "Macintosh Name" option.

To initiate *file sharing,* you click the upper Start button. (The button will toggle to a Stop button.) This allows users over a network to access the contents of shared folders and disks specified using the Sharing... command under the File menu. To discontinue file sharing, you click the upper Stop button.

To initiate *program linking,* you click the lower Start button. (Again, the button toggles to Stop.) This allows applications to communicate with each other over a network, a function that takes place automatically between programs on your own Mac. To discontinue program linking, you click the lower Stop button.

Changes made to file sharing and program linking functions will take effect after restarting your computer.

Sound

The features provided by the Sound control panel depend on the brand of Macintosh computer you are using. Generally, the Sound window will appear as shown in the first example of Figure 6.57, offering a volume control and a scrolling list of all sound files contained in the current System file. If you use a Macintosh LC, IIsi, or any forthcoming model that offers an audio input jack, the Sound window will include options for recording digitized sounds, as shown in the second example of the figure. This window may also display if you use a third-party audio input device such as Farallon's MacRecorder.

Regardless of what model of Mac you use, you may set the loudness of alert sounds using the "Speaker Volume" slider. Sounds produced by applications may depend on this volume setting as well.

You can set the "Speaker Volume" slider to 0 to produce no sound and instead flash the menu bar to alert the user. This feature may prove useful to deaf users as well as those who merely get tired of hearing annoying beep noises.

FIGURE 6.57

The Sound control panel as it appears when opened on a standard Mac (left) and on a Mac with an audio input jack (right).

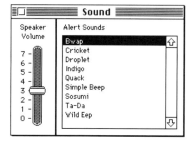

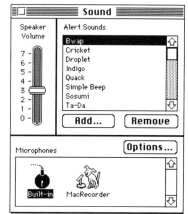

You select a sound file from the scrolling list to serve as a warning sound to alert you of errors, operation completions, and other pertinent events. Remember that you may cut, copy, and paste sound files in the Sound control panel. You may also delete a selected sound by choosing the Clear command from the Edit menu, pressing the Delete key, or pressing the Remove button (if available).

To record a sound, you first select the input device that you wish to use from the scrolling list of "Microphone" options; then you click the Add... button to display the Record dialog box, shown in Figure 6.58, which allows you to digitize a sound up to 10 seconds long. You click the "Record" icon to begin recording. First, you make your sound. Next, you click the "Stop" icon to stop recording. You click "Play" to listen to the sound. Finally, you click the Save button or press Enter to save it as a sound file inside the current System file. A dialog box will display, requesting that you name the sound file.

If the selected input device offers further control settings, you click the Options... button to display a dialog box of additional options. If no options are available for the current microphone, the Options... button will be dimmed (as it is in the case of the built-in microphone provided with the LC and IIsi).

FIGURE 6.58

The Record dialog box is used to capture digitized sounds from an external microphone.

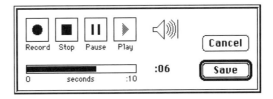

Startup Disk

If more than one mounted hard drive offers valid system software, you may use the Startup Disk control panel to specify which drive acts as the startup disk. You select the desired disk, as shown in Figure 6.59, and click the close box. If you try to select a disk that offers no System Folder, your Mac will search the selected disk during startup and then, finding no system, revert to the previous startup disk (if available).

FIGURE 6.59

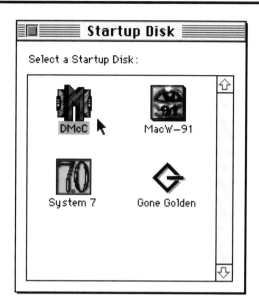

*S*elect the desired startup disk from the Startup Disk control panel.

Users & Groups

Like File Sharing Monitor, Network, and Sharing Setup, the Users & Groups control panel affects file sharing over a Macintosh network. For complete information on this and other file sharing options, you should read Chapter 12.

You open the Users & Groups control panel to display the Users & Groups window shown in Figure 6.60. Here you may specify whether shared data contained on your hard drive may be accessed by individual users or groups of users. You may even assign the user a password. To set the options for a user, you double-click the user icon. To add a new user, you choose the New User command from the File menu (⌘-N). To create a new group, you choose the New Group command from the File menu. To add an existing user to a group, you drag the desired user icon onto the group icon. To view the contents of a group, you double-click the group icon. To change a name of a group or user, you select its icon, press the Enter key, and enter a new name from the keyboard.

FIGURE 6.60

The Users & Groups window allows you to control user access to networked data.

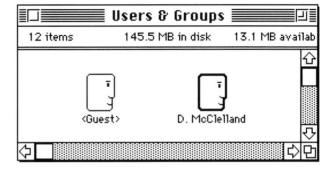

Views

Are you sick of control panels? Ha ha, me too, but we're almost done! The final control panel, alphabet-wise, is Views. Since this control panel is discussed in detail in the following chapter, I'll cover it here very briefly.

As you can see in Figure 6.61, this control panel determines the appearance of icon names at the Finder level. You can choose the desired font and type size used for all icon names from the pop-up menus at the

FIGURE 6.61

Use the Views control panel to adjust the appearance of icons and icon names at the Finder level.

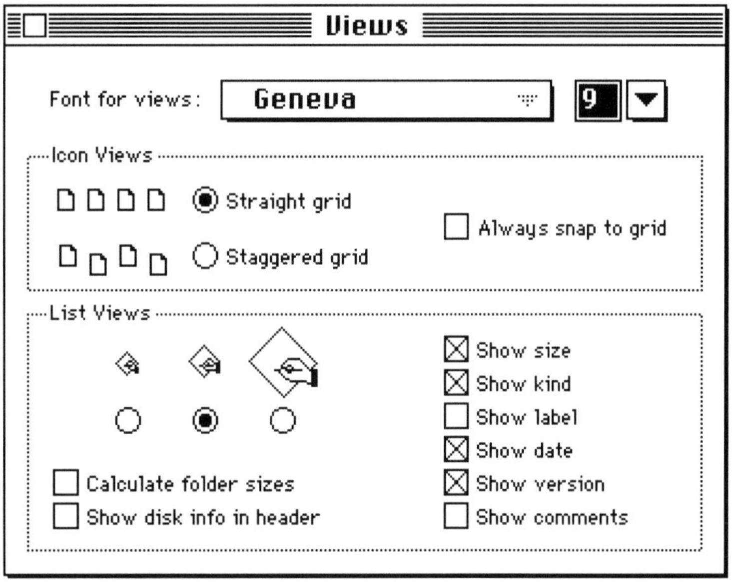

top of the Views window. To establish a grid for files displayed in an icon view, you select either the "Straight grid" or "Staggered grid" radio button. You select the "Always snap to grid" check box to move icons in strict relation to the grid (except when Command-dragging), thus ensuring perfect alignment from one icon to the next.

In the lower half of the window, you select a radio button to specify the size of icons displayed in a list view. You select the "Calculate folder sizes" check box to display the size of all folders in the "Size" column. You select "Show disk info in header" to display the number of items in a directory window and the amount of space being used on disk when in list view. You use the column of check boxes in the lower left portion of the window to control the display of individual file characteristics.

Third-Party Control Panels

Control panels are alive and well under System 7, so it's no surprise that hundreds are available from a wide variety of vendors. Most are unessential, but the following should be considered the staple diet of any Macintosh user.

Access PC   This control panel from Insignia Solutions allows you to mount DOS disks, examine their contents, and copy DOS files using a high-density Macintosh disk drive. You may also link files with certain extensions to Mac programs. For example, you might link .TXT and .DOC files to Microsoft Word or .XLS and .WK1 files to Excel. If you own an IBM PC-compatible computer or occasionally swap files with PC users, this control panel is an absolute must. Version 2.0 is fully compatible with System 7.

Adobe Type Manager   Wow, talk about an essential utility. The Adobe Type Manager permits PostScript Type 1 fonts to be displayed on screen at full resolution, assuming printer fonts are available. Version 3.0 is fully compatible with System 7.

Capture   The Capture utility allows you to take screen shots—black-and-white or in color—as simply as pressing a key and marqueeing the on-screen image that you want to capture. You may run Capture when choosing a menu command, dragging an object, or performing just about any other operation. Generally speaking, marqueed images are stored in memory or, if you press the Option key while marqueeing, stored in the Scrapbook. You may also opt to capture the cursor. Version 4.0 is fully compatible with System 7.

DiskExpress II   Let me put it this way: There is simply no better hard disk defragmenting utility than DiskExpress II from ALSoft. You'll want to start it running before you go to lunch because it takes so long to work, but it performs better than anything else I've used, including similar utilities from Symantec and the Peter Norton Group. Every file is moved to a new location on disk and, in almost all cases, your hard drive will be 100% defragmented. Version 2.07 is fully compatible with System 7.

HAM   Microseeds' HAM stands for Hierarchical Apple Menus. Its primary function is to display the contents of subfolders inside the Apple Menu Items folder as submenus under the Apple menu. HAM will also keep a record of recently used documents, applications, folders, and shared volumes. You control how many items are remembered; HAM automatically maintains the requested number of aliases in a subfolder named *Recent* which resides inside the Apple Menu Items folder. More information about HAM is included in the *Exporting Advanced Topics* section later in this chapter.

Pyro   There went a hunk of the alphabet! Oh well, for those who don't know, Pyro from Fifth Generation Systems is a screen saving utility that dims the screen or displays an animated pattern when the Macintosh is idle. Thus, images are prevented from displaying for an extended period of time and becoming etched on screen, an effect known as *burn-in*. When Pyro is active, your computer is said to be asleep. Pyro can be set to sleep when printing, uploading or downloading information via a modem, and so on, all without interrupting or interfering with the background operation. Version 4.0.1 is fully compatible with System 7.

"But wait," you ask, "What about the *other* screen saver, Berkeley Systems' After Dark?" It's true that After Dark includes far more animated modules than Pyro. Not only that, they're *way* cooler, comprising everything from tropical fish—in which you select the specific fish to be displayed, the speed at which they swim, and the noise they make—to flying toasters—in which you may set the darkness of the toast. If those aren't enough, you can purchase a second package of modules called More After Dark. The two software products combine to perform dazzling screen displays that are sure to make your friends drool with envy. However—and here's where I'm bound to anger the many fans of this product—After Dark has the tendency to interrupt printing and cause telecommunication errors far more regularly than Pyro (which has *never* crashed my Mac since version 4.0 was released). Much of this may be due to the fact that many of After Dark's modules are written by programmers who had nothing to do with the original product. All I can say is that if you're looking for entertainment, After Dark is worth every penny, as shown in Figure 6.62. If you want to get some work done, however, Pyro is the more reliable, albeit conservative, choice.

FIGURE 6.62

When using After Dark, your screen doesn't go to sleep; it comes to life.

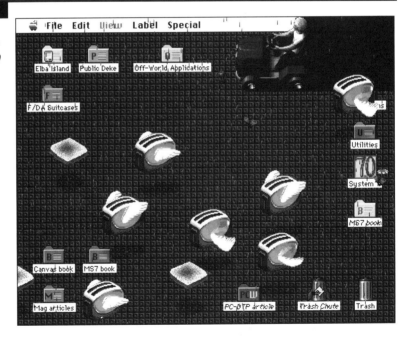

QuicKeys 2   So far, I've made more references to this utility than any other. In fact, if I had to choose only one utility, this would be it. It allows you to launch applications, choose menu commands, and run a variety of custom macros that allow you to instantaneously perform common control panels and system-oriented tasks. Although Tempo II is the more powerful macro program, QuicKeys 2.1.3 is the one more users are likely to find they can't live without. Version 2.1 is fully compatible with System 7, even offering System 7-specific functions.

SCSI Probe   SCSI Probe by Robert Polic allows you to mount SCSI devices such as external and internal hard drives, scanners, CD-ROM players, and so on. You may also view connected devices by ID number. If you own multiple SCSI devices, this is the perfect SCSI management tool. It may even save your butt. Version 3.5, which is compatible with System 7, is included on the disks that you can order with the coupon found at the back of this book.

Super Boomerang   Part of the Now Utilities collection, Super Boomerang is a navigation utility that enhances the performance of any document selection (open) or document destination (save) dialog box by adding a menu bar of options. You may return to a specific disk, folder, or file by choosing a command or pressing a keystroke. The utility also remembers the last file opened in a folder, so you don't have to scroll down immense file lists every time you open a document. For complete information about this control panel, you should see Chapter 10. Version 4.01 is fully compatible with System 7.

SuperClock   SuperClock by Steve Christensen displays the time on the right side of the menu bar, just to the left of the Help menu. You click the time display to temporarily display the date; you double-click to display a timer. You may also set an alarm. That's about all it does, but I wouldn't make a deadline without it. Best of all, it's free. Version 4.0.2, which is compatible with System 7, is included on the disks that you can order with the coupon found at the back of this book.

EXPLORING ADVANCED TOPICS

Now you know how to install system utilities and how to use them. To become a true master of the System 7 arts, however, you need to be able to organize your system utilities in a way that affords control over your system software environment. In this section, I'll explain how to supervise the loading of system extensions and control panels. I'll also show you a few techniques that will make your Apple menu a little less cumbersome and a lot more functional. Finally, I'll describe how to plug desk accessories into applications. Before any of that, let's talk about two little known categories of system utilities available for the Mac, Fkeys and language scripts.

ALL ABOUT FKEYS

Since its inception, a typical IBM PC keyboard has offered a row of function keys and a handful of special keyboard options such as PrtSc and NumLock. Still around today, these keys are used to access functions that are not made available in any menu. In DOS, for example, you may repeat the last command entered from the keyboard by pressing the F3 key, and only by pressing the F3 key. Although virtually every PC user knows this fact, it is learned information. There is no way for a first-time user to implicitly figure it out.

Function keys and option keys are now available to users of the Macintosh extended keyboard as well, but in the early days of the Mac, such key-based features were considered limiting and downright regressive in light of new mouse and menu-based technology that allowed users to produce diverse and predictable results without prior computer knowledge. No matter how you felt about mice and menus, however, you had to acknowledge that *some* operations were made more convenient if they could be accessed directly from the keyboard. Fkeys, short for function keys, were Apple's solution. By pressing ⌘, Shift, and a number key, you were able to invoke a common operation from the keyboard without so much as looking at a menu or moving a mouse. Like a PC function key, there was no menu equivalent and no way to just figure it out.

Ever since the introduction of cdevs, inits, and macro programs, Fkeys have been a dying breed. However, they still exist, even if enthusiasm for these system utilities has all but entirely evaporated. In fact, all but one of the five original Fkeys are integrated into your current system software:

- ⌘-**Shift-1.** This Fkey ejects a floppy disk from the main internal disk drive, but does not dismount it. Because this technique forces the main drive's eject mechanism to operate without regard to ongoing system and application functions, it frequently works when other techniques will not; for example, when your system has crashed. This Fkey may also be used to eject a disk that will not mount and thus does not appear on the Finder desktop. For all practical purposes, pressing ⌘-Shift-1 is the same as sticking a straightened paper clip into that tiny hole to the right of the main disk drive.

- ⌘-**Shift-2.** This Fkey ejects a floppy disk from the secondary disk drive. Otherwise, it works the same as ⌘-Shift-1.

- ⌘-**Shift-0.** If you use an external floppy drive with a Mac that offers two internal floppy drives, this Fkey ejects a floppy disk from the external drive. Otherwise, it works the same as ⌘-Shift-1.

- ⌘-**Shift-3.** Although the previous Fkeys work with System 7, ⌘-Shift-3 is the only Fkey that has been enhanced for use with System 7. This Fkey creates a PICT file on disk that contains a *screen shot* (also called a *screen dump*) of the current screen display. All screen information is saved, just as if you had taken a picture of it with a camera, to a file named *Picture #,* where # is a digit assigned sequentially from 1 to 9. This picture file may be opened in TeachText and printed or opened in a color painting program and edited. Unlike screen dumps created in previous versions of the Mac system software, System 7 screen dumps save the entire screen area and may *not* be opened using MacPaint.

The only Fkey missing from System 7 is ⌘-Shift-4, which printed the screen. This must now be accomplished by first saving the screen using ⌘-Shift-3 and then printing the file from TeachText or some other compatible application.

TIP

> **Suppose that you want to to take a screen shot of a single icon displayed on screen. If you press ⌘-Shift-3, you'll get the entire screen. You'll then have to edit the screen down to a more reasonable size. If you want to be able to specify a portion of the screen to capture, you'll need to purchase a screen shot utility, such as Capture from Mainstay or Snipper, part of the QuickTools package from Advanced Software. Of the two, I prefer Capture. It allows you to store captured areas to the Clipboard or to disk in the MacPaint, PICT, or TIFF format. You may also enlarge or reduce a screen shot, assign a delay before taking the picture, and capture the cursor. However, Snipper is the better bargain. For little more than half the price of the Capture control panel alone, QuickTools includes a total of eight System 7-compatible utilities.**

INSTALLING FKEYS

Though they're rare, commercial Fkeys are still available. A notable example is Switch-A-Roo, the screen depth switcher described earlier in this chapter. To use an Fkey, you'll need to install it in one of the following three ways, all of which require software that is *not* provided with System 7:

- Attach the Fkey to the System file as you would a font using MasterJuggler or Suitcase II. You may also use QuicKeys or the shareware program Easy Keys by Kerry Clendinning. The latter program allows you to assign keystrokes to Fkeys, applications, and DAs.

- Use an Fkey installation utility such as Fkey Manager by Carlos Webber or the newer Fkey Lackey by Alex Chaffee. These utilities can be used to install Fkeys just as you install fonts using the Font/DA Mover. Though both programs are over two years old, they continue to work with System 7.

- Open the Fkey file in ResEdit 2.1. Then open the FKEY resource. Select the resource file in the FKEYs window and copy it. Now close the Fkey file and open the current System file. Open the System's FKEY resource and paste, as shown in Figure 6.63.

FIGURE 6.63

*U*sing ResEdit, you may
copy an Fkey resource
and paste it into the
System File.

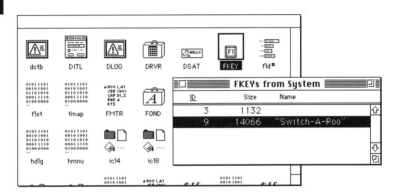

USING SYSTEM 7.1 WITH NON-ROMAN ALPHABETS

Under System 7.0 and System 7.0.1, you could equip your Mac with multiple language scripts. A language script (also referred to as a script) is a writing system that works with keyboard layouts to allow you to communicate in a language other than English. You could install language scripts as the primary or secondary language on your computer. In either case, the Roman language script—the language script that is included in your and my System software—would remain available. This would allow you to write in more than one language (provided that you are using an application that supported multiple language scripts).

All this remains true under System 7.1. The main difference is that System 7.1 makes it even easier to accommodate other language scripts, and allows for some language scripts that System 7.0 did not. System 7.0

could support single-byte language scripts and not double-byte language scripts. A single-byte language is one where all the characters of the language could be accommodated in one byte. As you recall, a byte is made up of eight bits. A bit can have two values, 0 or 1 (off or on). String two bits together and you can produce four combinations—00, 01, 10, and 11—or four values, two values for the first bit times two values for the second bit. So, string eight bits together, forming a byte, and you can produce 256 values (two times itself, eight times). For a language like English, in which less than one hundred values are needed so that each letter, number, and symbol of punctuation can be uniquely defined, 256 value is more than enough. But what about a language like Japanese, Korean, or Chinese, the last of which contains more than 40,000 characters? For these languages, a double-byte language script is used. A double-byte, or two bytes, equals 16 bits, which gives 256 times 256 or 65536 values. System 7.0 was not compatible with these double-byte language scripts, but System 7.1 is. Figure 6.64 shows a WordPerfect document written in Japanese.

This document was created on WordPerfect 2.2 for Japanese. The Mac that made it had the Japanese language script installed as the primary language and English as the secondary.

A *WordPerfect document written in Japanese*

System 7.1 uses a technology known as WorldScript. WorldScript is simply two extensions (WorldScript I and WorldScript II) that bring more uniformity to language scripts. Before, when a new Mac would come out, the System had to be reengineered so that it was compatible with other languages. This resulted in a considerable amount of time before users in non-Roman language-speaking countries could gain access to the new Macs. The language scripts would then be developed independently in each country, each with its own extension for handling the behavior of the script (like the keyboard layout of the manner in which the characters were addressed). This meant that if you wanted to use more than one language script on a Mac, then the two language scripts could run interference with one another. The WorldScript extensions eliminate the need of the separate extensions by providing a single system architecture that can be applied to different languages. WorldScript I handles all the Roman alphabet languages and Russian as well as other single-byte languages, such as Hebrew and Arabic, that are written in a manner not like English— both Hebrew and Arabic read right to left—and in which the characters of the language are context sensitive—Arabic letters are dependent on the letters that surround them in a word and will take different forms as the case may warrant. WorldScript II is for the double-byte languages.

To gain access to another language, you must install the specific language script, the proper WorldScript extension, and at least one font for that language. You may also want to install the supporting files, such as control panels and desk accessories, that are available for that language. Once AppleScript is available (see Chapter 11), you will be able to display AppleScript scripts in the primary language of your Mac, despite the language that the script was written in originally.

When two language scripts are available in the same system software, you may switch between them using the Keyboard menu that appears between the Help and Applications menu on the right side of the menu bar, as shown in Figure 6.65.

SELECTIVELY LOADING CONTROL PANELS

System 7 now allows you to disable control panel and system extensions by pressing the Shift key during startup. But this is hardly adequate when trying to determine extension conflicts or simply turn on and off specific extensions without having to sequester them to a special out-of-the-way folder.

FIGURE 6.65

When using a foreign language script, a special Keyboard menu appears between the Help and Application menus on the right side of the menu bar. Both WorldScript - extensions are present on this Mac.

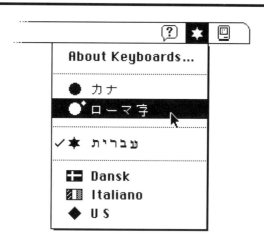

At least two utilities extensions are available that allow you to turn control panels and system extensions on and off at will. These are Extensions Manager by Ricardo Batista at Apple Computer and INIT Picker from Microseeds, both shown in Figure 6.66. Included on the disks that you can order with the coupon found at the back of this book, Extensions Manager creates special subfolders in the System folder where it stores disabled control panels and system extensions. Sold commercially, INIT Picker is the preferred program since it works more seamlessly, without the use of folders, and offers additional functionality. For example, you may change the order in which control panels and system extensions load, sort extensions alphabetically, and check for loading conflicts.

ORGANIZING YOUR APPLE MENU

Note that the Apple menu lists icon names in alphabetical order. Special characters are alphabetized as described in Chapter 3 (refer to Figure 3.9). Thus, you may reorder commands in the Apple menu by changing the name of icons in the Apple Menu Items folder. For example, you may insert a space before the name of an icon that you use often, such as the Chooser DA or the Control Panels alias, to send that command to the top of the menu. To create a boundary between commands, you create an alias (or other small file) and rename it "– – – – – – –." The resulting effect is demonstrated in Figure 6.67.

FIGURE 6.66

Extensions Manager (left) and InitPicker (right) both allow you to enable and disable control panels and system extensions selectively.

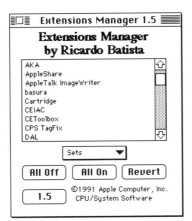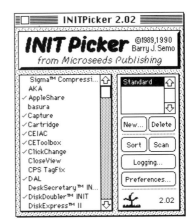

FIGURE 6.67

Add special characters to the beginning of DA and alias names to alter their locations in the Apple menu. Dummy files may be used to create boundaries which divide commands into logical groups.

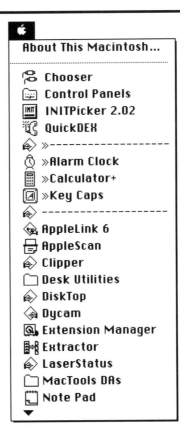

If that technique violates your aesthetic sensibilities, there is a better solution, but it costs money. Microseeds' HAM lets you reorder Apple menu commands as simply as dragging them inside a scrolling list, as shown in Figure 6.68.

One of HAM's additional functions is that it turns all folders in your Apple Menu Items folder into hierarchical submenus. Therefore, instead of displaying the Control Panels directory window, choosing the Control Panels command displays a submenu that lets you choose from individual control panels, as shown in Figure 6.69. Two additional utilities, NowMenus from Now Software and Hand-Off II from Connectix, also provide this capability.

FIGURE 6.68

The HAM control panel provides a scrolling list in which you may change the order of command names under the Apple menu.

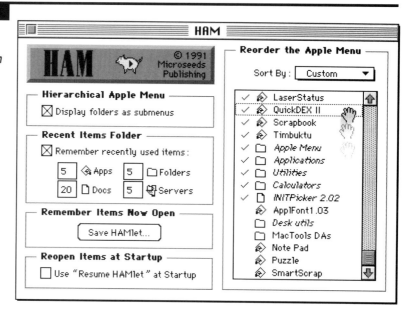

INSTALLING A DA IN AN APPLICATION

Under System 7.1, desk accessories can run independently, but they can also run from inside an application. Suppose, for example, that you use MacroMind Director, the most powerful multimedia program for the Mac. Included with Director is a little art work selection DA called Art Grabber. Unfortunately, this DA is not very useful outside the context of Director. Therefore, to avoid cluttering up your Apple menu inside other applications, you may want Art Grabber to be available only when Director is running in the foreground. To accomplish this, you must install Art Grabber *inside* Director using Font/DA Mover 4.1. Inside Font/DA Mover 4.1, you open the Art Grabber DA suitcase and then Option-click the right-hand Open... button to open the desired application. You copy the DA file into the application file, and you are done. It's that easy.

This technique can also be used to combine DAs and applications logically in order to reduce the number of commands displayed in the Apple menu. You may also use it to prevent other people who use your machine from accessing certain DAs that can be used to manipulate sensitive data.

FIGURE 6.69

*N*owMenus, HAM, and Hand-Off II allows you to access the contents of subfolders directly via hierarchical submenus.

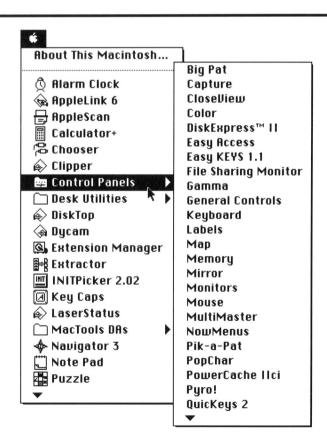

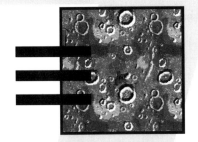

Customizing the
Finder Desktop—Aliases
and Other Techniques

T HE MAC IS viewed by many as a high-tech
toy. This opinion may have something to
do with the first Macintosh computer, which offered a small screen, no
expandability, only 128K of RAM, a slow engine, and a graphical interface that was great for the uninitiated but hampered the productivity of
experienced users.

A wide variety of Macintosh models are available these days. While
the least expensive of these computers continues to offer dinky screens
and no expandability, most of them are at least moderately fast and provide admirable memory capacity. Furthermore, the GUI has shaped up—
with the considerable help of System 7—to be remarkably flexible, and
conducive to the needs of both novice and experienced users alike. The
best of the Macintosh line is the Quadra 950, which offers built-in support for any Apple color monitor, 5 expansion slots with built-in networking, up to 128MB of RAM, space to accommodate an internal CD-ROM
or removable cartridge drive, and blindingly fast CPU speed. At roughly
$10,000 including a monitor, it's hardly my idea of a toy (unless, of
course, your Lamborghini is in the shop).

But, hey, so what if you own a powerful machine? That doesn't
mean you can't have fun with it! That doesn't mean it isn't an *insanely
great* toy!

In this chapter, I hope to show you just how mesmerizingly fun your
computer can be by extolling the virtues of desktop customization. Fix
up your Finder desktop. Endow it with a little bit of your personality. *Be
one with your computer!* Some of this information will be stuff you can find
in any book—how to use aliases, how to create custom icons, that kind
of thing. But some of it… well now, that's for me to know and you to
find out.

GETTING STARTED

In this section, I'll talk about the two methods that System 7 provides for customizing the Finder desktop. These include the Views control panel and the Make Alias command. Some might argue that the Labels control panel and Get Info comments belong in this discussion as well, but since they are more specifically oriented toward identifying files than altering their appearance, these features are relegated to the following chapter.

THE VIEWS CONTROL PANEL

The simplest and most direct method to customize your Finder desktop is to use the Views control panel, shown in Figure 7.1. Here, you may select the font and size used to represent icon names, set the distance between icons, and determine the information that appears in a list view.

FIGURE 7.1

The Views control panel provides a straightforward method for customizing the appearance of your Finder desktop.

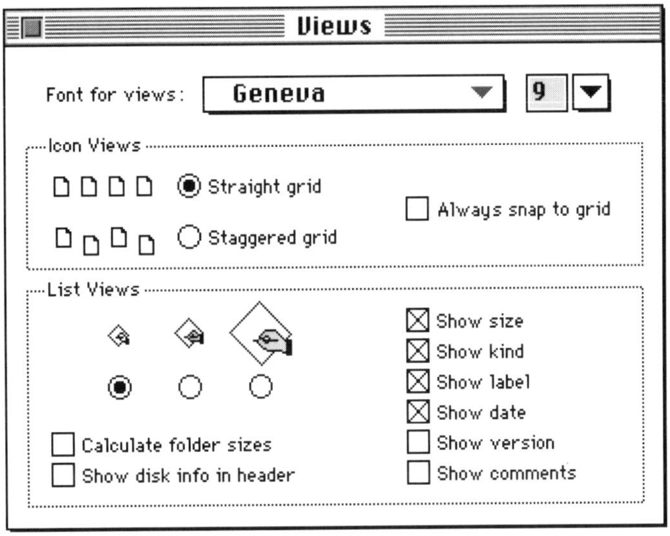

Name Views

Normally, icon names—whether displayed in an icon or list view—appear in 9-point Geneva, as shown in the first example of Figure 7.2. This has always been the case, ever since the first Mac system software. You may,

FIGURE 7.2

Icon names shown in 9-point Geneva (top) and 11-point New York (bottom).

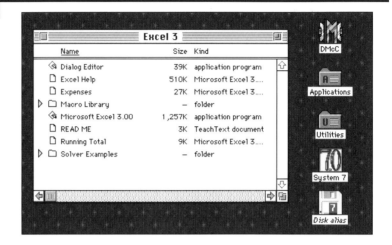

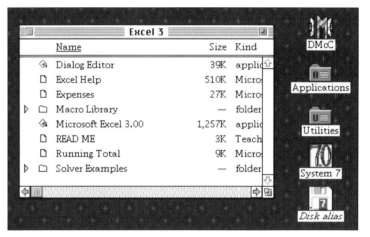

however, change the font and type size used by choosing new options from the "Font for views" pop-up menus at the top of the Views control panel. In the second example of Figure 7.2, the font has been changed to 11-point New York. Various type sizes between 9 and 24-point are permitted, including 9, 10, 11, 12, 14, 18, and 24. The larger sizes may prove particularly useful for users with vision problems.

Icon Views

The options in the "Icon Views" area toward the top of the Views window control how files react to being dragged in an icon view. You may activate the Finder's built-in grid by selecting the "Always snap to grid" check box. The grid then affects new and dragged icons; existing icons will not be relocated to align to the grid automatically.

Finder 7 provides two grids—straight and staggered—neither of which can be altered. Both grids interspace icons 64 pixels horizontally and 52 pixels vertically, as shown in Figure 7.3.

FIGURE 7.3

The result of using a straight (top) and staggered (bottom) grid. Note that icon names frequently overlap when using the straight grid.

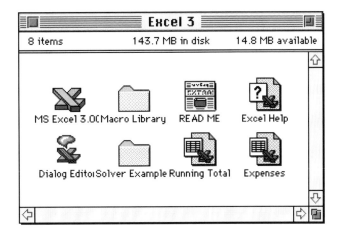

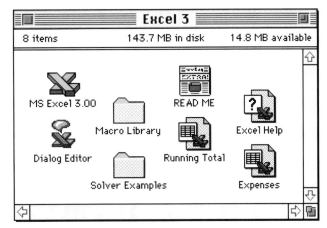

> If the grid is inactive (the "Always snap to grid" check
> box is *not* selected), press the ⌘ key when dragging an
> icon to force it to align to the current grid. If the grid is
> turned on, Command-dragging allows an icon to move
> independently of the grid.

List Views

The options in the "List Views" area at the bottom of the Views window
determine the appearance of icons and related information in a list view.
You select one of the three radio buttons in the "List Views" area to
specify the appearance of icons displayed on the far left side of a list view,
as shown in Figure 7.4. The left radio button is the default setting; the
middle and right radio buttons produce icons that are comparable in
size to those displayed in the small and standard icon views, respectively.

In a list view, the Size column posts the sizes of all files. By default,
however, folder sizes are not displayed, since the system software requires
a little time to calculate this information. You select the "Calculate folder
sizes" check box inside the Views window to calculate folder sizes, as
demonstrated in the second example of Figure 7.5. Folder size calculations may be made in the background so they don't interrupt other
operations you may wish to perform. Unless displaying folder sizes
noticeably slows the performance of your machine, I recommend that
you activate this option. (This option is dimmed when the "Show size"
check box is not selected.)

The next check box, "Show disk info in header," causes a second
line of information to appear in the header of any directory window displayed in list view, as shown in the final example of Figure 7.5. This line
tells the number of icons in the current folder, the amount of data on
the current disk, and the amount of room that remains free on the current disk. In past versions of the system software, this information was
visible only in an icon view (refer to Figure 7.3). By selecting this option,
you may avoid a lot of switching back and forth between views; all the information you need is available at a single glance.

FIGURE 7.4

A single list view as it appears when its icons are displayed at small (top), medium (middle), and large (bottom) sizes.

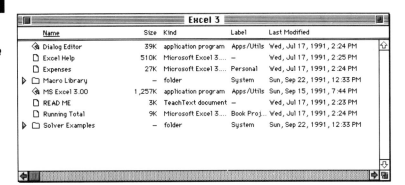

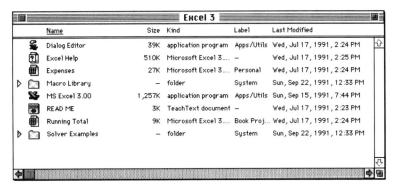

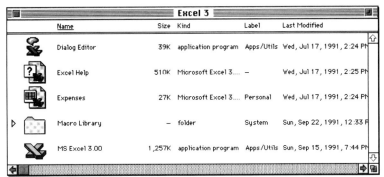

FIGURE 7.5

A single list view shown when "Calculate folder sizes" is turned off (top), when that same option is turned on (middle), and when "Show disk info in header" is turned on (bottom).

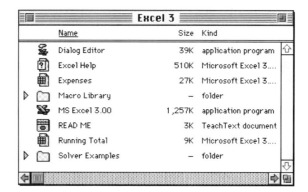

	Name	Size	Kind
	Dialog Editor	39K	application program
	Excel Help	510K	Microsoft Excel 3….
	Expenses	27K	Microsoft Excel 3….
▷	Macro Library	—	folder
	MS Excel 3.00	1,257K	application program
	READ ME	3K	TeachText document
	Running Total	9K	Microsoft Excel 3….
▷	Solver Examples	—	folder

Excel 3

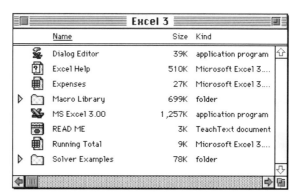

	Name	Size	Kind
	Dialog Editor	39K	application program
	Excel Help	510K	Microsoft Excel 3….
	Expenses	27K	Microsoft Excel 3….
▷	Macro Library	699K	folder
	MS Excel 3.00	1,257K	application program
	READ ME	3K	TeachText document
	Running Total	9K	Microsoft Excel 3….
▷	Solver Examples	78K	folder

Excel 3

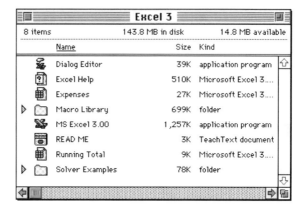

Excel 3

8 items   143.8 MB in disk   14.8 MB available

	Name	Size	Kind
	Dialog Editor	39K	application program
	Excel Help	510K	Microsoft Excel 3….
	Expenses	27K	Microsoft Excel 3….
▷	Macro Library	699K	folder
	MS Excel 3.00	1,257K	application program
	READ ME	3K	TeachText document
	Running Total	9K	Microsoft Excel 3….
▷	Solver Examples	78K	folder

The check boxes on the right side of the "List Views" area determine which columns are visible in a list view. The "Name" column is always displayed, but others may be turned on and off. Note that when you turn a column on, it will display in the View menu; when you turn it off, the command disappears. If you were to turn all of these options off, for example, the View menu would contain only three commands: by Small Icon, by Icon, and by Name.

The settings specified in the Views control panel are applied to all directory windows at the Finder level, as well as the Finder desktop.

CREATING AND USING ALIASES

Second on System 7's list of built-in customization features is the *alias,* which is an icon whose sole purpose is to act as a stand-in for another icon. Suppose you use PageMaker. When you installed the product, it was copied to a folder on your hard drive called *Aldus PageMaker,* which you then placed inside a folder called *Desktop Publishing,* which is located inside a folder called *Applications,* which can be accessed by opening your hard drive directory window.

Rather than go to all the work of digging out the PageMaker application icon every time you want to use the program, you can create an alias for it. You can position the alias anywhere you like; obvious choices include the desktop and the Apple Menu Items folder, as demonstrated in Figures 7.6 and 7.7 respectively. You can double-click the alias icon or choose its command from the Apple menu. The alias references the original application and opens it.

To automatically launch an application immediately after starting up your computer, you place the alias for an application inside the Startup Items folder. This is preferable to positioning the original application in the Startup Items folder, since many applications must be placed in separate folders of their own that contain supplementary and support files.

FIGURE 7.6

Application aliases can be arranged on the Finder desktop for speedy access...

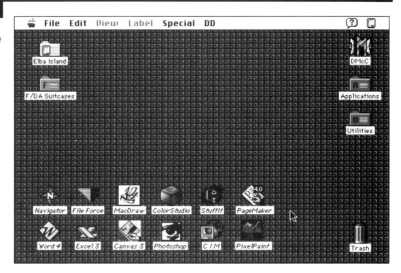

FIGURE 7.7

...or they may be positioned inside the Apple Menu Items folder so that they appear as commands under the Apple menu..

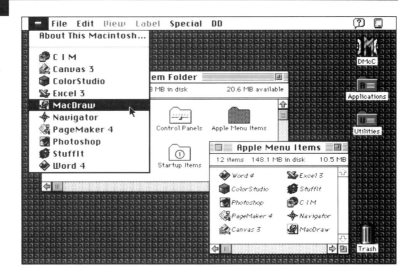

In addition to applications, an alias may be created for any file, folder, or disk. To create an alias, you select the original icon and choose the Make Alias command from the File menu. A duplicate of the icon with an italicized name will appear slightly offset from the original, as shown in the second example of Figure 7.8. This duplicate icon—which is the alias itself—is an independent file that consumes less than 3K of

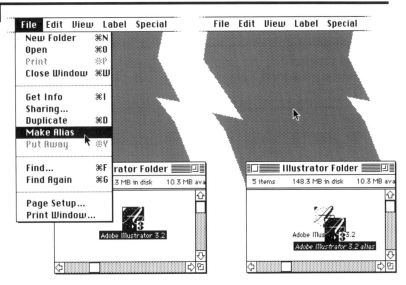

Choosing the Make Alias command (left) creates an alias of the original icon (right).

disk space, just enough to reference the location and the icon of the original file.

After you create an alias, you will want to do two things with it: 1) Move it to a new folder and 2) rename it. To prevent naming conflicts, the system software automatically appends the word *alias* to the end of the original icon name. However, there is no reason to leave this name intact once the alias has been relocated, since the icon is already distinguished from original icons by its italic name.

You may make as many aliases of a single file, folder, or disk as you like. To create multiple aliases of a single icon, you may apply the Make Alias command over and over again. Better yet, you can simply duplicate the first alias by Option-dragging it to other folders. No matter how you create them, all aliases will reference the same original file, folder, or disk, as demonstrated by Figure 7.9.

All aliases for a single icon—even duplicates of aliases—reference the original icon directly.

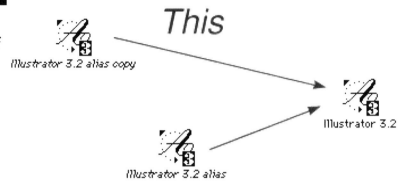

Illustrator 3.2 alias copy

This

Illustrator 3.2

Illustrator 3.2 alias

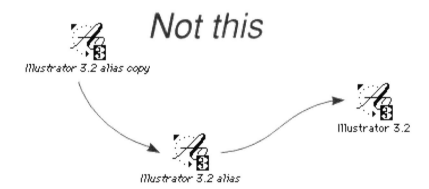

Not this

Illustrator 3.2 alias copy

Illustrator 3.2 alias

Illustrator 3.2

 **W**ARNING

Do *not* make an alias of an alias. The second alias will reference the first; if you ever delete the first alias, the second will be disconnected. Either make an alias of the original or make a duplicate of the first alias.

LEARNING FUNDAMENTAL CONCEPTS

That's basically all there is to using aliases. The rest is common sense, right? I mean, here's this one file, it represents another file. Simple stuff. But like many issues related to using System 7, there's a lot more to aliases than meets the eye. Does renaming or moving the original affect the alias? How do you create an alias of a file on a different disk? What operations can you perform on the alias that leave the original untouched? Suffice it to say, I couldn't stand here and claim that this is everything you need to know if I didn't try to tell you all about it.

THE TENACIOUS THREAD

First questions first: The "thread" that references an alias to its original file cannot be broken by moving or renaming an alias or its original icon. This is because, rather than referencing the path of the original icon—such as Hard Drive:Illustrator Folder:Adobe Illustrator 3.2—the alias references the original icon's file number, assigned automatically by the system software when the file is copied or created on disk.

For example, suppose that File A inside Folder A has been assigned the file number 25,000. This number is unique and may not be changed (although it may be viewed using a disk-editing utility such as FileEdit— part of MacTools Deluxe—or Symantec Tools). After creating an alias for File A, you rename the original file to File B and move it to Folder B. Now, you deliberately try to fool the alias by creating a second file, naming it File A, and placing it in Folder A so that its path is identical to the original File A. Despite your tomfoolery, double-clicking the File A alias icon will still launch the original icon, now called File B in Folder B, since it is the only file on disk with the file number 25,000.

Therefore, you may move and rename icons and their aliases without worry. The only way to break the link between alias and original is to throw away one of the two files. In fact, the alias of a deleted original is entirely useless. Such an alias cannot bring the original icon back from the dead, nor can it be linked to a different icon. It can only be deleted as well.

I P

If you're unsure of what original is referenced by what alias, select the alias and choose the Get Info command from the File menu. After the Info dialog box displays, you click the Find Original button as shown in Figure 7.10. A directory window will appear in front of all others that contains the selected original icon. If the original has been deleted, a message will appear saying that the original cannot be found.

FIGURE 7.10

Click the Find Original button in an Info dialog box to locate the original file referenced by a selected alias.

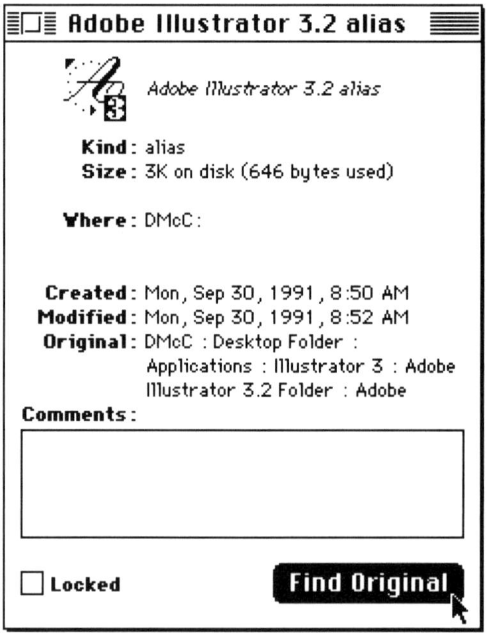

≡☐≣ **Adobe Illustrator 3.2 alias** ≣

Adobe Illustrator 3.2 alias

Kind: alias
Size: 3K on disk (646 bytes used)

Where: DMcC:

Created: Mon, Sep 30, 1991, 8:50 AM
Modified: Mon, Sep 30, 1991, 8:52 AM
Original: DMcC : Desktop Folder :
Applications : Illustrator 3 : Adobe
Illustrator 3.2 Folder : Adobe

Comments:

☐ **Locked**   **Find Original**

ALIASING DISKS AND THEIR FILES

Aliasing a disk or a shared folder can be especially useful if you store regularly used data on floppy disks, cartridges, or shared disks. You just select the disk or shared folder icon and choose the Make Alias command from the File menu as you would when creating an alias for any other icon. The alias will be created on the current startup drive. When you dismount the original disk, the alias remains on the startup drive. If you double-click the alias of an unmounted disk, a message like that shown in Figure 7.11 will display, requesting that you insert the aliased disk. Once inserted, a directory window will open to display the contents of the disk.

FIGURE 7.11

When you double-click an alias for a disk, the system software checks to see if the disk is available.

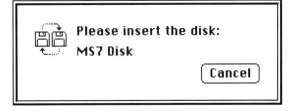

Please insert the disk:
MS7 Disk

Cancel

You may also create aliases for files and folders stored on remote disks. For example, I have a separate folder set up on my startup drive called *Off-World Applications* on which I keep aliases for seldom used applications that are stored on removable cartridges. If I choose, I can even assign a keyboard equivalent to the alias using QuicKeys or the like. Then when I press the key combination that launches the application, I don't even have to remember the cartridge upon which the original is stored. The system asks for the cartridge by name, I find it and insert it, and away I go. What could be simpler?

Normally, when you create an alias for a file or folder, the alias is created on the same disk as the original. However, when aliasing icons on remote disks, it is desirable to locate the alias on the startup drive. To ensure that an alias is created on the startup drive, you lock the disk before inserting it. Then when you choose the Make Alias command, the message shown in Figure 7.12 will appear, informing you that the current disk is locked and that an alias may only be created if it is located on the desktop of the current startup drive.

If it is not convenient to lock the disk before inserting it, you must first create the alias on the remote disk, then copy the alias to the startup disk, and finally delete the alias from the original disk. Though the intermediate alias is deleted, the link between startup alias and original remote icon remains intact.

You may use similar techniques when aliasing files and folders from a disk shared over a network. If your access privileges to a shared folder or disk prohibit you from making changes, it is as if the folder or disk were locked. When you choose the Make Alias command, the system software will inform you that you lack sufficient access privileges and that an alias may only be created if it is located on the desktop of the current startup drive. If your access privileges include making changes, the alias for a selected icon will be created on the shared disk. You will then have to copy the alias from the shared disk to your hard drive and delete the alias on the shared disk.

FIGURE 7.12

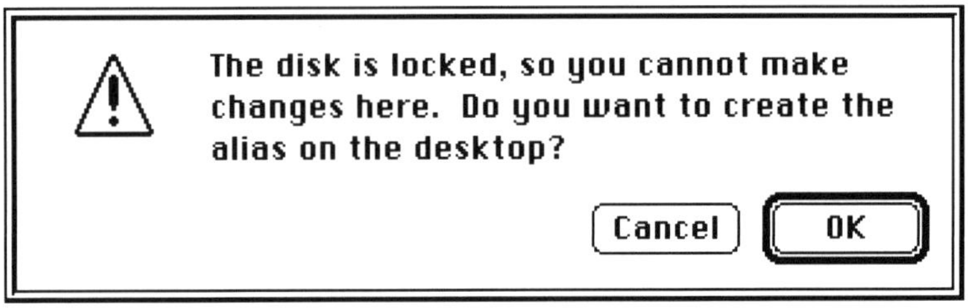

The alias for an icon on a locked disk may only be positioned on the desktop of the startup drive.

 The disk is locked, so you cannot make changes here. Do you want to create the alias on the desktop?

Cancel   OK

ALIAS VERSUS ORIGINAL

Much of the time, an operation enacted on an alias affects the original file, folder, or disk. But many operations will affect the alias specifically, leaving the original untouched. Operations that affect the original include the following:

- **Opening.** When you double-click an alias, you open the original file, folder, or disk.

- **Drag opening.** If you drag a compatible document onto an application alias, the original application will launch and load the dragged file. You may also drag a document alias onto an application original, or drag a document alias onto an application alias.

- **Opening from inside an application.** When you open an alias from inside a running application, the original file is opened. To my knowledge, only ResEdit allows you to open and edit aliases (by selecting the "Use Alias instead of original check box," as shown in Figure 7.13.

- **Application switching.** If you double-click an alias for an application that is running in the background, that application will be brought to the foreground, even if the application was previously hidden.

FIGURE 7.13

ResEdit is the only application that allows you to open an alias instead of an original file.

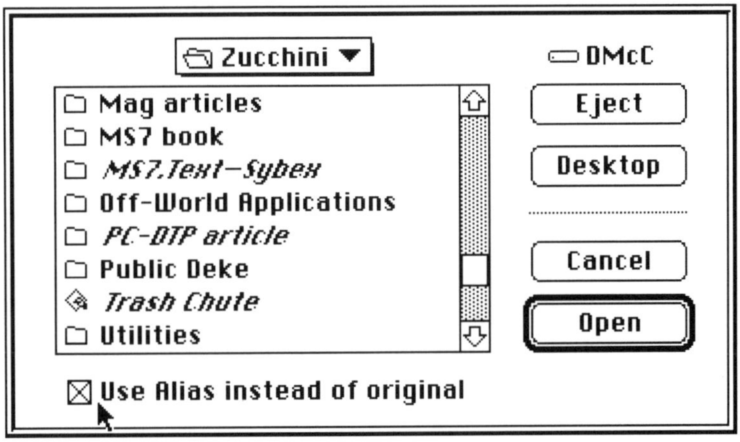

These operations affect the alias itself:

- **Moving.** When you move an alias to a different folder location, only the alias is moved.

- **Copying.** When you copy an alias from one location to another, or duplicate an alias inside the current folder, the alias itself is copied, resulting in a second alias of the original icon.

- **Renaming.** You may change the name of an alias without in any way affecting the original.

- **Labeling the alias.** If you apply a color from the Label menu to an alias, the alias is colored but the original is unchanged.

- **Customizing the alias icon.** If you paste a new icon into the Info dialog box, as I'll explain later in this chapter, the new icon takes effect for the alias only.

- **Deleting.** Throwing an alias in the Trash neither deletes nor dismounts the original icon. Only the alias itself is sent to the Trash folder.

- **Aliasing.** When you choose the Make Alias command for a selected alias, you alias the alias, which in turn aliases the original.

Probably the most valuable attribute of an alias is that you can throw it away without harming the original. If your machine is used by children or other persons unfamiliar with Macs or other computers, you may be better off allowing them to only use aliases. This way, if the person throws a file away, the original remains intact; all you'll have to do is create a new alias. (If only these things existed back when I worked for a service bureau—the hours of labor we might have saved!)

ALIASING UTILITIES

Aliases have made a big splash with programmers. So much, in fact, that a tidy variety of notable utilities have been created to help users create and organize aliases. Among these are AKA, FinderHack, MountAlias, Nom de Plume, Alias Stylist, and for those who use aliases to the extreme, Alias Assassin. Each of these works as following:

- **AKA.** While the version of this system extension I used (0.5) was a little buggy, Fred Monroe's AKA is a great idea. It allows you to simultaneously create and relocate an alias as simply as Control-dragging an original icon from one folder to another. Monroe claims an upgraded version is in the works. (Hey, he's a college student; give the guy a break.) AKA can be found over CompuServe and America Online bundled with Basura and Dropple Menu under the name Fred's Finder Hacks.

- **FinderHack.** Created by Donald Brown, this system extension is a combination trash/alias utility. When loaded, it creates a Futz menu to the right of the Special menu at the Finder level, as shown in Figure 7.14. After selecting an icon, you may choose a command from the Futz menu to move the icon to the Trash folder, delete the icon directly, make an alias of the icon at a specified location under a specified name, and create an alias automatically inside the Apple Menu Items folder. FinderHack is included on the disks which you can order with the coupon found at the back of this book.

FIGURE 7.14

FinderHack produces a Futz menu that allows you to delete or make an alias for a selected icon.

- **MountAlias.** Written by Jeff Miller, this control panel automatically creates an alias of every shared folder or disk you mount and stores these aliases in a specified folder. Once a shared folder has been mounted a first time manually, you can bypass the rigmarole as simply as double-clicking an alias. This utility is included on the disks which you can order with the coupon found at the back of this book.

- **Nom de Plume.** Like FinderHack, Nom de Plume allows you to create an alias of a selected icon and position it inside any of several folders. As shown in Figure 7.15, this self-running application by Bill Monk requires that you select icons via a dialog box. Unlike FinderHack, you may not name aliases; they are named automatically. But on the up side, you can create many aliases from a single dialog box. This and the following Bill Monk utilities may be found in the ZMac forum on CompuServe.

Nom de Plume enables you to create an alias and specify its location in the folder hierarchy.

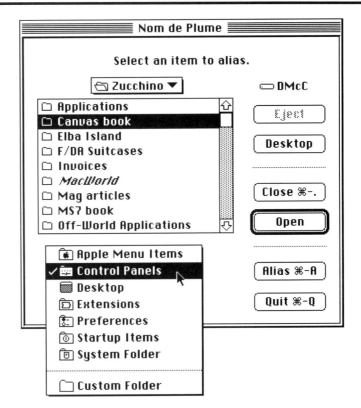

- **Alias Stylist.** Another utility by Bill Monk, Alias Stylist lets you change the type style used to represent alias names, from italic to bold, outline, expanded, and so on.

- **Alias Assassin.** Third in the Bill Monk series, this utility finds and deletes any alias that has lost its original, perfect for those of us who verge on alias-dependent. As you can see in Figure 7.16, Alias Assassin cleans up your disk, frees up idle disk space, and saves you the time that would otherwise be required to search and destroy aliases manually. (Now if there was only a similar utility for deleting old, unused preference files!)

FIGURE 7.16

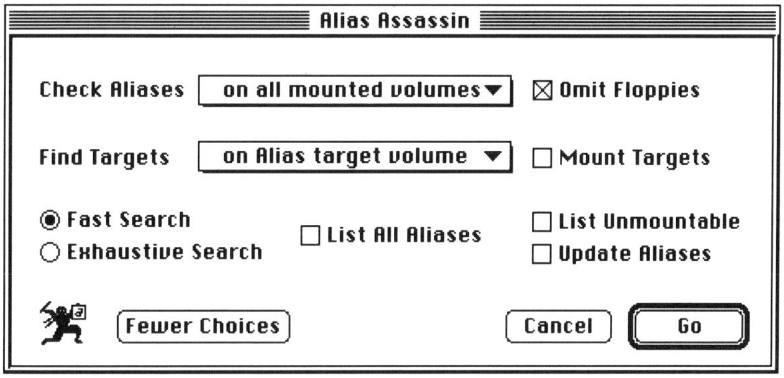

Alias Assassin finds and destroys unused alias files that are just taking up space on your disk by finding all aliases, matching them up with targets, and deleting aliases for which no targets can be found.

CHANGING ICONS

All right, I think that pretty near exhausts the topic of aliases. No doubt a truly clever person could think of more to discuss. But while we wait for such a person to come along, let's turn our communal attention to bigger and better things; namely, custom icons.

Normally, files and folders receive icons based on their file type. For example, except for the System Folder and its subfolders, all folders look the same. All screen fonts look the same, and so on. Applications, desk accessories, control panels, and system extensions may be assigned unique icons, but the files created by those utilities appear uniform. For example, all files created in Microsoft Word and saved in the "Normal" format use one icon, all Word files saved in the text-only format receive another.

In a nutshell, a file is assigned an icon based on both its creator code and its type code. Files with identical codes receive identical icons.

That's the normal world. Under System 7, however, you can create a custom icon for a single file, folder, or disk. This icon applies to the selected file, folder, or disk only; files with matching type and creator codes remain unaffected.

To change an icon, I advise the following steps. You will need a painting program. MacPaint will suffice if you use a built-in or other black-and-white monitor. However, you'll want a color bitmap-editing program if you use a gray-scale or color monitor. These include Studio/8, PixelPaint, Color MacCheese, Photoshop, Color Studio... there's tons of them.

1. Select the icon you want to edit.

2. Choose the Get Info command from the File menu.

3. Once the Info dialog box displays, select the icon in the upper left corner. A 32-by-32-pixel square will surround the icon, as shown in Figure 7.17. Choose the Copy command from the Edit menu (⌘-C) to transfer the icon to the Clipboard.

FIGURE 7.17

You may select and copy the icon of a file, folder, or disk in the Info dialog box.

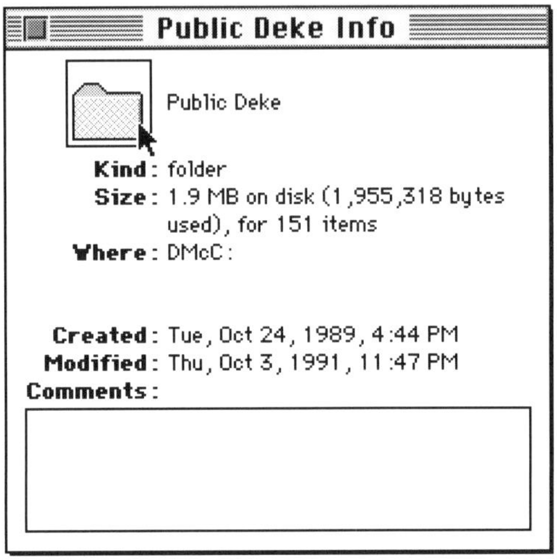

Public Deke Info

Public Deke

Kind: folder
Size: 1.9 MB on disk (1,955,318 bytes used), for 151 items
Where: DMcC:

Created: Tue, Oct 24, 1989, 4:44 PM
Modified: Thu, Oct 3, 1991, 11:47 PM
Comments:

4. If you haven't already done so, launch your painting program.

5. Create a new painting and paste the icon into it.

6. Edit the icon as desired. Be sure not to exceed the boundaries of the standard 32-by-32-pixel icon size. (If you do, your icon will be automatically shrunk when you apply it to the selected file.) A sample editing cycle is demonstrated in Figure 7.18.

7. Select the completed icon and copy it.

8. Return to the Finder. Select the icon in the upper-left corner of the Info dialog box and paste. Voila, your custom icon is complete!

T I P

The following ideas may help you achieve the best results when creating custom icons:

- **Select all 32 pixels.** When copying the finished icon to paste it back into the Info dialog box, you'll want to select a 32-by-32-pixel area regardless of the size of the icon. If you select an area smaller than 32 pixels horizontally or vertically, your icon will automatically be centered in the icon area, which may not be exactly what you want. For example, centering an icon vertically typically leaves too much room between the icon and its name when viewed at the Finder level. By selecting all 32 pixels horizontally and vertically,

FIGURE 7.18

Pasting (left), editing (middle), and completing (right) an icon in a color painting program at a magnified view size.

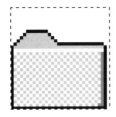

you assure that the icon fits inside the icon area exactly the way you want it to.

- **Use the System palette.** If you use a color monitor, your painting program can access any of 16 million colors (though it may not be able to display more than 256 colors in a single painting). The Finder, however, uses a fixed palette of no more than 256 colors, none of which may be changed. This palette is called the *System palette.* All color paint programs offer this palette. For the most predictable results, do not select colors outside the System palette, or they will be *dithered* (separated into patterns) to conform to the System palette when pasted at the Finder level. Dithered icons sometimes appear acceptable, but often look like… well, not very good.

- **Use grays and blue-grays.** This may sound like an odd tip, but you'll want to rely primarily on grays (including black and white) and gray-blues when creating color icons. The reason is that these colors are most receptive to additional colorization, such as that applied using a command from the Finder's Label menu. For example, an orange label applied to a gray icon looks a heck of a lot better than an orange label applied to a green icon (blech). Because of the arrangement of colors in the System palette, gray-blue colors are also receptive to colorization. Use other colors— reds, yellows, greens—sparingly to color special elements. To get a feel for how this works, examine the icons provided for the desk accessories and control panels that accompany System 7.

EXPLORING ADVANCED TOPICS

If you want to customize icons, the Get Info and Paste commands are all you need to know. But you want to create icons that look good in all situations—whether displayed on black-and-white or color monitors, or displayed at the standard or small icon view—you'll need to learn a little more. And that little extra knowledge requires a fair amount of extra effort.

After the following advanced icon discussion, I'll pursue other power-user subjects including how to rebuild the desktop, how to create 64-by-64-pixel desktop patterns, how to add keyboard equivalents to the Finder menus, and how to zap the PRAM.

ICON MASKING

If you are creating color icons, there may come a time when one of your pristine little paintings ends up looking drastically wrong when pasted into the Info dialog box. Areas that should be colored appear white. The first example in Figure 7.19 shows two versions of a single icon. The left version displays the icon as it appeared when completed in my painting program. The right version displays the icon as it appears when pasted into the Info dialog box. Assuming I selected the entire image before copying it from the painting program (which I did), what happened to half the colors in the icon?

The answer is *nothing*. All colors are intact, just as I created them. However, some colors are invisible because the *icon mask* has been

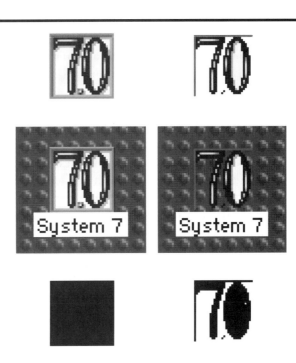

FIGURE 7.19

*E*nlarged versions of an icon as I created it and as it appears in the Info dialog box (top), the same icons against a pattern background (middle), and the masks associated with each icon (bottom).

created incorrectly. The mask determines which portions of an icon are opaque and which portions are transparent. To ensure the entire icon is opaque, the mask should look like the one shown in the lower-left corner of Figure 7.19. Instead, it looks like the one in the lower-right corner, which renders much of the icon invisible.

No doubt you'll want to know how to remedy this problem. For that information, skip to the next paragraph. But first, why doesn't the Finder just create the icon mask correctly in the first place? My icon fills the entire 32-by-32-pixel area, but many of your icons will not. Therefore, it would be silly for the Finder to create a 32-by-32-pixel mask for every icon it comes in contact with. Instead, the Finder masks only those areas that are enclosed by dark outlines. By "dark," I mean any color that is closer to black than it is to white on the color brightness scale. A mask may only contain black and white pixels, so if a color in an icon is even a tad too light, the Finder reads it as white and makes it transparent. Colors closer to black are read as black and made opaque. An area that is light but is entirely surrounded by a dark outline, such as the center of the *0* in Figure 7.19, is also made opaque.

To fix the problem, you'll need ResEdit 2.1 or later. To be safe, first make a copy of the file with the messed up icon. Then launch ResEdit and open the duplicate file. Double-click on the "icl8" resource, which represents the 8-bit (256-color), 32-by-32-pixel version of the icon. Your custom icon will display, exactly as you drew it, in the icl8 window. It will be labeled −16455, as shown in Figure 7.20. (All custom icons receive the resource number −16455 under System 7.1.)

Double-click the −16455 resource to display the Icon Family window, shown in Figure 7.21. Here you may edit the black-and-white version of an icon ("ICN#"), the 4-bit version of an icon ("icl4"), 16-by-16-pixel versions of the icon ("ics#," "ics8," and "ics4"), and the small and large icon masks (both labeled "Mask"). You select the larger "Mask" resource and modify it in the giant pixel-edit area in the center of the window. Your changes will be reflected in the demonstration area on the far right side of the window.

Once you alter the icon mask to your satisfaction, close the Icon Family window, choose Save from the File menu (⌘-S), and quit ResEdit.

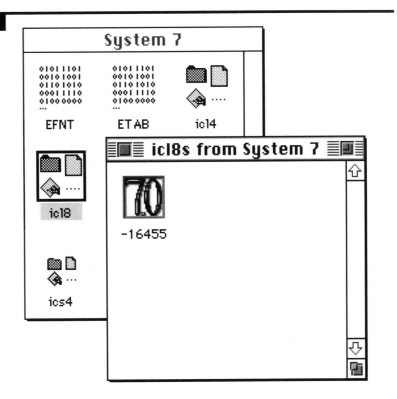

FIGURE 7.20

*The "icl8" resource,
which is shorthand for
"icon large 8-bit."*

THE INVISIBLE DESKTOP FILES

Hold onto your hats, because we're going to have to fly through the
remaining issues, beginning with the Desktop files. Previous versions of
the system software relied on a single Desktop file that contained information about all files with which the Finder came in contact. Specifically,
the file held icons, Info dialog box comments, and file path information.
The Desktop file was invisible, but could be viewed using Disktop and
other file management utilities.

In System 7, the Desktop file remains in use on any disk under
2MB, which includes all floppy disks. If a disk is larger than 2MB, the
Desktop file is broken up into two files—Desktop DB and Desktop DF,
and a Desktop folder. (Sometimes, a Desktop file is left over. If you see a
file called *Desktop* on your hard disk, you may delete it.) The Desktop
folder contains all icons that are displayed on the Finder desktop. The

FIGURE 7.21

The Icon Family window as it appears when the "ic18" (top) and "Mask" (bottom) resources are selected.

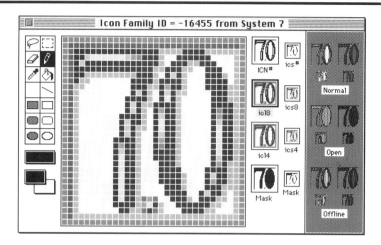

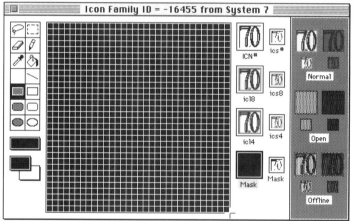

Desktop DB contains all file path information. The Desktop DF file references application icons, so that files and icons are combined accurately on screen.

As in System 6 and earlier, the Desktop file on a floppy disk is a resource file. The Desktop file may be opened and edited in ResEdit to customize the appearance of icons and make other adjustments. The Desktop DB and Desktop DF files, however, are data files. They may not be opened in ResEdit nor may they be altered by non-programmers. Therefore, the only way to revise the Desktop files on a hard drive is to rebuild them automatically.

There are a variety of reasons you might wish to rebuild the desktop. For one, desk accessories and other system utilities may not display their proper icons when first installed. Also, the Desktop files may become damaged, in which case you may be greeted by the "Disk has minor problems" or the more serious "Disk is damaged" error message. Although this problem is less prevalent under System 7 than it was under System 6, it can still happen.

To rebuild the Desktop file of a floppy disk, eject the disk, then reinsert it while pressing the ⌘ and Option keys. The message shown in Figure 7.22 will display, asking if you are sure you want to rebuild the disk's Desktop file. You click the OK button or press Return. Note that all comments entered into the Info dialog box for all files on the current disk will be deleted (despite what you may have read in other books on the subject).

Rebuilding the Desktop files on the current startup disk is a little trickier. To rebuild any Desktop file, you have to press the ⌘ and Option keys when a disk mounts. Since the startup disk cannot be dismounted, you may only rebuild the startup desktop when starting up your computer. Well, there is one other way, but it's risky. On rare occasions, you may end up crashing your computer or creating temporary SCSI chain problems. So I'll explain how it works, but don't say I didn't warn you if your computer blows up. (Okay, it's not *that* bad.)

1. Make sure at least one application is running in addition to the Finder.

2. At the Finder level, press ⌘-Option-Escape to force the Finder application to quit. A message will display, telling you that all of your changes will be lost. Click the Force Quit button to continue.

FIGURE 7.22

This message warns you that you are about to rebuild the Desktop file.

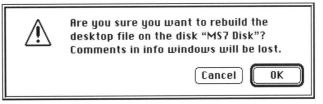

3. Under System 7, your Finder cannot remain quit, so it will restart again. (If you are going to encounter any problems, this is where they'll probably occur. If the Finder restarts successfully, you're in the clear.) Immediately after you click the Force Quit button, press and hold the ⌘ and Option keys.

4. A message will display, asking if you are sure you want to rebuild the disk's Desktop files. Click the OK button or press Return. A typical hard drive will take anywhere from two to five minutes to rebuild.

Desktop Patterns

By now, you know that you can edit the appearance of your desktop pattern using the General Controls control panel. But if you own a color monitor, there's two problems with this method. First, you're limited to the 256 colors in the System palette. Second, you're limited to an 8-by-8-pixel pattern. In fact, the System file allows you to create patterns that use any of 16 million colors and measure as large as 64-by-64 pixels. But how? Why, using ResEdit, of course.

If you're at all concerned about making a mistake, you should first make a copy of your System file. Next, you should launch ResEdit and open the duplicate System. The System file contains four pattern resources, "PAT," "PAT#," "ppat," and "ppt#." The "PAT#" and "ppt#" resources contain the default black-and-white and color patterns, respectively, displayed in the General Controls control panel. The "PAT" or "ppat" resource contains the black-and-white or color pattern currently being used.

You should open the "ppat" resource. The ppat window will contain a single resource, numbered 16. You double-click this resource to display a pixel-editing window, which is similar to the one provided for editing icons. You should choose the Pattern Size... command from the ppat menu on the right side of the menu bar. The Pattern Size dialog box shown in Figure 7.23 will appear. You can select a larger pattern size, and then click the Resize button or press Return. The pixel-editing area will enlarge. You should create the desired pattern, save your changes, and quit ResEdit. Finally, you should restart your machine to see your new background pattern.

FIGURE 7.23

Choose the Pattern Size... command from the ppat menu in ResEdit to change the size of the desktop pattern.

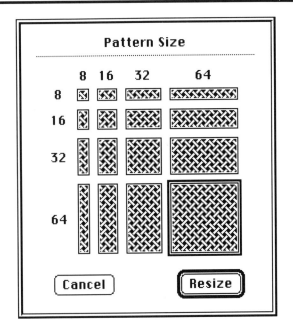

 I P

If you're a fan of desktop patterns, you'll drop everything you're doing and buy WallPaper, a control panel marketed by a company called Thought I Could. WallPaper provides tools for creating patterns as large as 128 by 128 pixels. You may personalize patterns, assign them special icons on disk, drag patterns around in the canvas area to make sure they mesh correctly... all in all, it's a perfect pattern editing tool; offhand, I can't imagine anything better. And for less than $60, the program includes a trove of pre-made patterns, many of which are nothing short of spectacular like the lunar landscape shown in Figure 7.24.

FIGURE 7.24

The WallPaper utility allows you to create full-color patterns as large as 128 by 128 pixels.

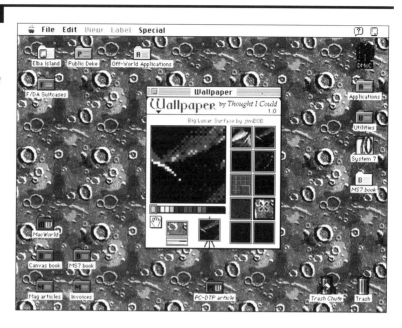

CREATING STARTUP SCREENS

When you startup your computer, a message displays welcoming you to the Macintosh computer. This is the *startup screen.* You can change the startup screen by creating a bitmapped file in the startup screen file format and saving under the name *StartupScreen* in the root directory of the System folder.

As of this writing, five programs support the startup screen format. These include PixelPaint 2.1, SuperPaint 3.0, UltraPaint 1.1, ColorIt 2.0, and Canvas 3.0. Any color image is acceptable. If the image contains more than the 256 colors provided by the System palette, the image will be dithered to fit. A sample startup screen is shown in Figure 7.25.

OTHER DESKTOP MODIFICATIONS

ResEdit allows you to make additional changes to your system software's graphic interface. If you open a copy of the System file using ResEdit, you'll find a number of user-editable items. The "ICON" resource, for example, contains the three warning icons that accompany Macintosh alert messages. Figure 7.26 shows how each of these might be edited. You may also colorize these icons by adding similarly numbered resources to the "cicn" resource.

A custom startup screen created using Canvas 3.0

Some common warning icons (top) and their possible substitutes (bottom) as altered inside ResEdit 2.1.

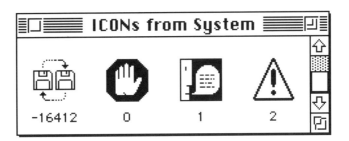

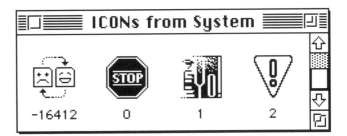

Other items that may be edited include cursors, dialog boxes, scroll bar patterns (number 17 inside the "PAT" resource), and so on. But if you're seriously interested in customizing your desktop and you have a few extra bucks lying around, you might want to purchase ClickChange from Dubl-Click Software. As you can see in Figure 7.27, this wonderful control panel provides color cursors, sounds that play at specific events such as ejecting a disk or shutting down your computer, color control like that provided with the old Kolor cdev, plus custom button, scroll bar, and window alternatives. You can make your system software resemble the Next, Microsoft Windows on the IBM PC, or any of a number of other computer interfaces. All in all, ClickChange provides an ideal alternative to personalize your Macintosh environment.

Provided on the disks which you can order with the coupon found at the back of this book is a system extension called Greg's Buttons that adds dimension to buttons, radio buttons, and check boxes throughout all dialog boxes viewed on a color or gray-scale monitor. Written by Greg Landweber, it also adds colored versions of the disk eject icon and the three warning icons, as shown in Figure 7.28.

FIGURE 7.27

ClickChange provides over a hundred replacements for the clock cursor alone, including a bouncing Helocar like the one from the recent Apple television ad.

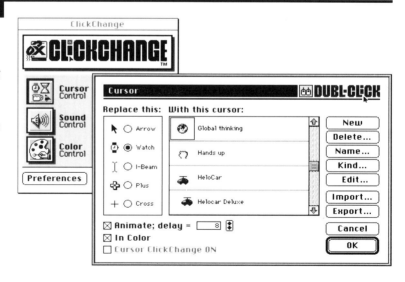

FIGURE 7.28

Included as part of Greg's Buttons are color versions of the icons from Figure 7.26.

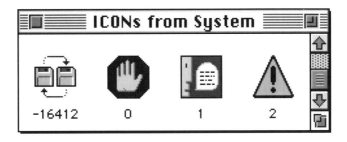

ADDING FINDER KEYBOARD EQUIVALENTS

Many of the commands available at the Finder level offer keyboard equivalents. But even more do not. Wouldn't it be nice to empty the Trash folder by pressing ⌘-T? Or restart your computer by pressing ⌘-R?

In Finder 6, you could easily add keyboard equivalents by manipulating the "MENU" resource in ResEdit. In Finder 7, this resource has been eliminated. In its place is the less friendly "fmnu" resource. While this resource can be edited—resource 1252 represents the File menu, 1253 represents the Edit menu, 1254 represents the View menu, and 1255 represents the Special menu (see Figure 7.29)— keyboard equivalents have to be added in a coded hex format, which requires more hacking than I am willing to tolerate.

FIGURE 7.29

Finder 7's Special menu as viewed in ResEdit. What ever happened to the friendly "MENU" resource?

```
 ▤▭▤   fmnu ID = 1255 from Finder ▤▤▤
  000000    0001 0009 0000 04E7    □□□□□□□□  ⇧
  000008    0000 0000 0753 7065    □□□□□Spe
  000010    6369 616C 636C 6561    cialclea
  000018    4006 0000 0843 6C65    @□□□□Cle
  000020    616E 2055 7000 656D    an Up□em
  000028    7074 8006 0000 0045    pt爱□□□□E
  000030    6D70 7479 2054 7261    mpty Tra
  000038    7368 C900 7878 7830    sh…□xxx0
  000040    0000 0000 012D 7365    □□□□□-se
  000048    6A65 1002 4500 0A45    je□□E□□E
  000050    6A65 6374 2044 6973    ject Dis
  000058    6B00 7365 7261 1002    k□sera□□
  000060    0000 0B45 7261 7365    □□□Erase
  000068    2044 6973 6BC9 7878     Disk…xx
  000070    7830 0000 0000 012D    x0□□□□□-
  000078    7265 7374 8100 0000    rest爱□□□
  000080    0752 6573 7461 7274    □Restart
  000088    7368 7574 8104 0000    shut爱□□□
  000090    0153                   □S
  000098
  0000A0                                     ⇩
```

An easier alternative to editing the "fmnu" resource is to create keyboard equivalents using a macro program such as QuicKeys or Tempo II. If neither of these are available to you, you might want to try out Adam Stein's Finder 7 Menus, which is provided on the disks which you can order with the coupon found at the back of this book. Using this application, you may open a copy of the Finder and access its menus. As demonstrated in Figure 7.30, you choose the command to which you want to assign a keyboard equivalent, enter the desired keystroke, and click OK. It's that easy. When you're finished, you can quit the application, drag the old Finder out of the System folder, drag the new Finder in, and reboot.

Note that Finder 7 Menus is a shareware application and you are expected to pay a registration fee if you expect to use this software.

FIGURE 7.30

Finder 7 Menus allows you to choose a Finder command and assign a keystroke.

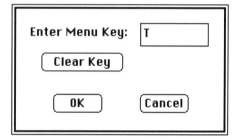

RAMMA ZAPPA PRAM

Many of the user settings I've discussed in this and the previous chapter are stored in the Macintosh *parameter RAM,* PRAM for short (pronounced pea-ram). This small amount of isolated memory, typically 256 bytes in size, is powered by the Mac's internal battery. This allows the machine to retain certain key bits of information at all times, even when it's turned off. For example, have you ever noticed how your Mac always knows the current time and date, even when the machine has been turned off for days at a time or a lightning storm has set every VCR in your house to blinking? Thank the PRAM, the Mac's only eternal source of editable information.

Most of the entries in the PRAM are set using control panels. These include the current time and date, desktop pattern, mouse tracking speed, sound and volume, screen depth setting, keyboard repeat and layout settings, highlight color, startup disk, and default application font (the font used to create screen information inside applications when no specific typeface is requested, normally 9-point Geneva).

The information in PRAM is read into standard RAM during your computer's startup sequence. If this information ever becomes damaged, or if you simply want to restore default settings to the General Controls, Mouse, Keyboard, Sound, Color, Monitor, and Startup Disk control panels, you may reset the PRAM by "zapping" it. Zapping erases all information from the PRAM—except, miraculously, the time—and restores original values from ROM.

Under System 6, zapping the PRAM was a simple matter of pressing ⌘-Control-Option and choosing the Control Panel command from the Apple menu. But now that the Control Panel has been replaced by a folder, Apple has introduced a much more bizarre procedure. For the best results, do the following:

1. Quit all applications except the Finder.

2. Press and *hold* the key combination: ⌘-Option-P-R. (If you're having problems, try this: Press both ⌘ and Option with your thumb, R with your first finger and P with your pinkie.)

3. Without releasing, choose the Restart command from the Special menu.

4. Keep holding those keys!

5. As always happens when you restart your computer, a chord will sound and the screen will momentarily turn black. The gray screen will appear, as if the machine is preparing to load the system software. Instead, however, a second chord will sound and the screen will turn black again, as if the computer were restarting again. That was the zap. You may now release the ⌘, Option, P, and R keys.

6. Following the second chord, the machine will start up as normal. When the Finder desktop displays, you'll notice that the background has changed to gray. You may also notice that your mouse is tracking at a different speed. Take a few moments to restore the settings in the General Controls, Mouse, Keyboard, Sound, Color, Monitor, and Startup Disk control panels. Begin using your machine as normal.

Organizing, Categorizing, and Locating Files on Your Hard Drive

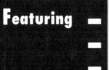
S TILL WITH ME, huh? Unbelievable! Given my attention span, I would have found something else to do long ago. However, in recognition of your patience—and I say this only to you people who have read every page; it doesn't count if you were referred here by the index—I reward you with this chapter. Well, all right… this chapter may not be a "reward" but it's good just the same.

In the following pages, I'll discuss how to organize files on your hard drive, including how to locate files, add labels and comments, and create stationery pads which act as templates for future files. I'll also look at how to use ResEdit and a few other utilities to make up for some of System 7's most obvious deficiencies.

GETTING STARTED

System 7 provides two methods for annotating an icon, whether it's a file, folder, or disk. The first method is the Label menu, which can be customized using the Labels control panel. The second method is the "Comments" options in an icon's Info dialog box.

THE LABELS CONTROL PANEL

At the Finder level, any icon can be assigned a color and a label from the Label menu (an updated version of the Color menu from System 6). The Label menu is available whether you use a color, gray-scale, or black-and-white monitor; however, you may assign only labels when using a black-and-white monitor.

The first example in Figure 8.1 shows the Label menu as it appears by default when displayed on a color or gray-scale monitor. If you use a black-and-white monitor, only the label names will display. To edit both label colors and their respective names, you open the Labels control panel. As you can see in the second example of the figure, the control panel offers option boxes for both colors and names. You can highlight a name and enter a new one up to 31 characters in length. You click on a color option to display the Apple Color Picker dialog box, as shown in Figure 8.2. You can select a new color and click the OK button to return to the Labels control panel. All changes will be reflected in the Label menu

FIGURE 8.1

The default colors and label names shown in the Label menu (left) and Labels control panel (right).

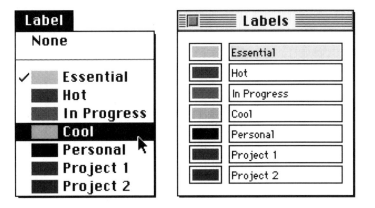

FIGURE 8.2

The Apple Color Picker dialog box permits you to select from 16 million colors available on the Macintosh computer. (The Finder, however, only allows 256 of these colors displayed at a time.)

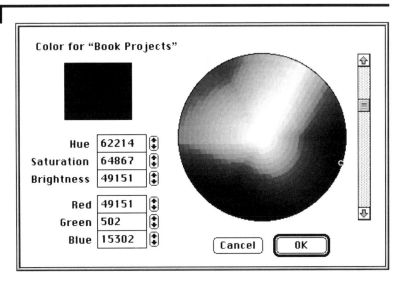

as you make changes to the control panel, as demonstrated in Figure 8.3. Existing labeled icons will also change to match the new labels.

The following explanation describes how to use the Apple Color Picker dialog box. If you are already familiar with basic color theory, skip to the *Get Info Comments* discussion. Otherwise, you should read on.

The Apple Color Picker allows you to edit a single color at a time according to one of two *color models*. The first is the *red-green-blue* model (or simply RGB) and the second is the *hue-saturation-brightness* model (or simply HSB).

FIGURE 8.3

*E*diting the colors and names in the Labels control panel (left) changes the commands in the Label menu (right) as well as the color of all existing labeled icons.

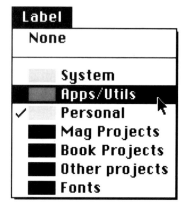

The RGB Color Model

When using the RGB model, colors are defined by mixing two or more *primary hues*. The amount of each hue mixed is called its *intensity*, as measured from 0 (no hue) to 65,535 (full intensity). The RGB model is also called the *additive primary model*, because a color becomes lighter as you add higher intensities of primary hues. All monitors and other projection devices—including televisions that use light to display colors—rely on the additive model.

The additive primary model consists of three hues—red, green, and blue—from which all colors in the visible spectrum may be derived. These primary hues can be mixed as follows:

- Mix equal intensities of red and green to make yellow. Subtract some red to produce chartreuse; subtract some green to produce orange.

- Mix equal intensities of green and blue to make cyan. Subtract some green to produce turquoise; subtract some blue to produce jade.

- Mix equal intensities of blue and red to make purple. Subtract some blue to produce magenta; subtract some red to produce violet.

- Mix equal intensities of red, green, and blue to make gray or white.

- Change all values to 0 to create black (or darkness).

The HSB Color Model

This HSB color model makes use of the properties of hue, saturation, and brightness. The *hue* of a color is measured on a color wheel representing the entire visible spectrum. The wheel is divided into 65,535 sections. Some of the most popular hues are found at the following numeric locations:

Red	0	Cyan	33,000
Orange	5500	Blue	44,000
Yellow	11,000	Violet	49,000
Chartreuse	16,500	Purple	54,500
Green	22,000	Magenta	60,000
Jade	27,500		

Saturation represents the purity of a color. A saturation of 0 is always gray; a saturation of 65,535 is required to produce the most vivid versions of each of the colors listed above. You can think of the saturation value as the difference between a black-and-white television and a color television. When the saturation value is low, all information about a color is expressed except the hue itself. Most natural colors require moderate saturation values. Highly saturated colors appear vivid.

Brightness is the lightness or darkness of a color. A brightness of 0 is always black; a brightness of 65,535 is used to achieve each of the colors listed above. For example, if the hue is red, a brightness value of 65,535 will produce bright red; 49,000 produces medium red; 32,500 produces dark red; and 16,000 makes a red so dark that it appears almost black.

Using the Apple Color Picker

To change a color using the RGB color model, you can enter values from 0 to 65,535 in the "Red," "Green," and "Blue" option boxes. Alternatively, you may click the up or down arrow icon next to each option box to raise or lower the corresponding value. You press Tab to advance from one option box to the next.

To change a color using the HSB model, you can alter the values in the "Hue," "Saturation," and "Brightness" option boxes, or you may reposition the *color-adjustment dot* inside the *color wheel* on the right-hand side of the dialog box. The color wheel works in association with the nearby scroll bar. The color wheel and scroll bar may be adjusted as follows:

- To change the hue, you move the color-adjustment dot around the perimeter of the wheel.

- To alter the saturation, you move the color-adjustment dot between the perimeter and center of the wheel. Colors along the perimeter have a saturation value of 65,535; the center color has a saturation value of 0.

- To change the brightness, you move the scroll box within the scroll bar. The top of the scroll bar equates to a brightness value of 65,535; the bottom equates to 0.

After you press the Tab key or complete an adjustment to the color wheel or scroll bar, the new color will display in the *new color box* above the option boxes. Directly below the new color box is the *original color box,* which shows the color as it appeared prior to the new changes, so that you may continuously compare the current color to the original setting. You click the OK button or press Return when you are satisfied with your color adjustment.

It is generally a good idea to let your monitor warm up at least 20 minutes before adjusting color in the Labels control panels. This gives screen colors a chance to "settle" and become less volatile.

GET INFO COMMENTS

Another way to label your icons is to add personal comments. You select an icon and choose the Get Info command from the File menu (⌘-I) to display the specialized Info window for that icon, as shown in Figure 8.4. You can enter any desired information or file-handling instructions in the "Comments" option box. A comment may be as long as 199 characters.

FIGURE 8.4

*U*se the "Comments" option box in an Info dialog box to annotate a select icon.

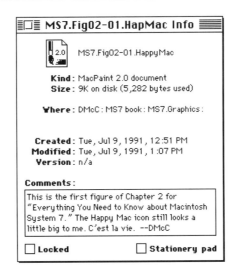

> While comments are copied with an icon when the icon is copied from one folder or disk to another, they are not entirely stable. They can be easily edited by other users. Worse yet, all comments are deleted when you or any other user rebuilds the Desktop file(s) for a disk or hard drive, as described in the previous chapter. If you want to create comments, a more reliable solution is presented near the end of this chapter in the *Exploring Advanced Topics* section.

Note that comments are *not* shared between original icons and their aliases.

LEARNING FUNDAMENTAL CONCEPTS

Labels and comments or not only useful for notating an icon, they may also be used to categorize icons on disk. For example, similarly labeled icons within a single folder may be organized into groups by choosing the by Label command from the View menu. Also, you may locate files on disk based on their labels or the contents of their comments. In fact, you can locate files according to just about any criteria, as you'll discover in the following pages.

BASIC FILE-FINDING TECHNIQUES

Prior to System 7, the Macintosh system software provided a simple—and lame—Find feature in the form of a desk accessory. The feature's slow speed and lack of medium- and high-end searching options forced many users to look outside their system software for commercial alternatives. Several extremely functional programs filled the void, most at a price.

The Find… command is one case in which Apple has taken the best of what was available in the commercial market and integrated it into System 7. This command is fast and flexible, offering the ability to search every file attribute that can be viewed from the Finder.

You choose the Find… command from the File menu (⌘-F) to display the Find dialog box shown in Figure 8.5. At first glance, this dialog box is remarkably straightforward. You can enter or paste up to 31 characters into the "Find" option box. You can click the Find button or press Return to search the contents of all mounted disks for the first icon that contains your entry. The Find… command is not case sensitive, so if you enter "Page," it might find "Page," "page," or "PAGE." The directory window that holds the found icon will be opened automatically with the found icon itself selected. If the found icon represents a folder or a file located on the Finder desktop, or a disk or shared folder, a message will display alerting you to the fact. You click OK or press Return to acknowledge the message and automatically select the found icon.

To continue your search using the same criteria, you choose the Find Again command from the File menu (⌘-G). The system software searches through the open directory window that contained the previously found icon and, if no matches are found, automatically closes the window and continues its search inside other folders.

TIP

> The Find Again command automatically closes a directory window opened by a previous invocation of the Find… or Find Again command. However, if the open folder contains multiple icons that match the current find criteria but you aren't interested in any of them, you may close the directory window manually (⌘-W) and then choose the Find Again command (⌘-G). This instructs the system software that you wish to skip the closed folder and move on to other portions of the disk.

FIGURE 8.5

You can search icon names using the Find dialog box.

```
╔══════════════ Find ══════════════╗
║                                   ║
║  Find: [That $5 bill I lost last Summer   ]
║                                   ║
║  ( More Choices )   ( Cancel ) (( Find ))
╚═══════════════════════════════════╝
```

The Find... and Find Again commands search through icon names in the following order:

1. The names of all icons on the desktop.

2. The contents of all open folders on the current startup disk.

3. The root directories of all folders on the desktop that belong to the startup disk.

4. The contents of all other folders on the startup disk.

5. All folders on all other mounted disks.

When no more matches can be found, your computer will sound a beep and the find operation will halt.

ADDITIONAL FILE-FINDING OPTIONS

To display additional file-finding options inside the Find dialog box, you should click the More Choices button. The dialog box will immediately expand, as shown in Figure 8.6. This dialog box contains a total of five options. The top three options control: 1) the icon attribute that you want to search, 2) a modifier that determines the degree to which attribute and find criteria must match, and 3) the name, value, or other criteria that you want to find. You can use the "Search" pop-up menu to specify the disks or icons to be searched. You select the "all at once" check box to display all matching icons simultaneously, rather than one at a time.

FIGURE 8.6

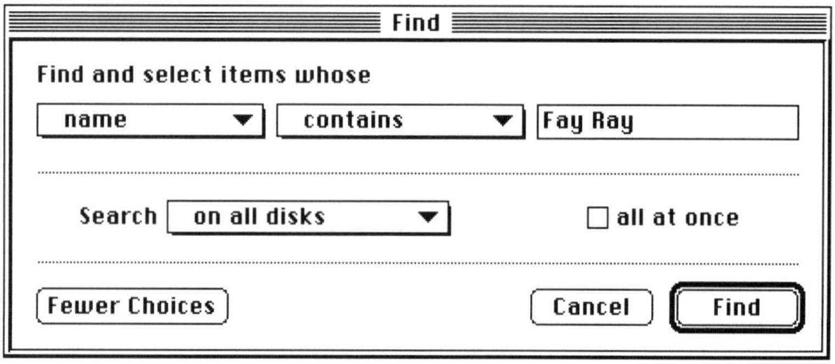

Click the More Choices button to expand the Find dialog box.

Find

Find and select items whose

| name ▼ | contains ▼ | Fay Ray |

Search [on all disks ▼]   ☐ all at once

[Fewer Choices]   [Cancel] [Find]

The first pop-up menu in the upper-left corner of the Find dialog box contains all file attributes that can be displayed at the Finder level. These include name, size, kind, label, date first created, date most recently modified, version number, comments, and whether or not the icon is locked. Each of these attributes as well as its specialized modifier and criteria options are displayed in Figure 8.7.

The nine attributes shown in Figure 8.7 may be used as follows:

- **Name.** You choose the "name" option to search icon names on all mounted disks. The default modifier option finds any icon name that contains the entry in the criteria option box. The modifier may also be configured so it finds only icon names that start with the criteria entry, end with the entry, exactly match the entry ("is" option), do not exactly match the entry ("is not"), or do not contain the entry.

FIGURE 8.7

The nine attributes that you can search from the Find dialog box along with corresponding modifier and criteria options.

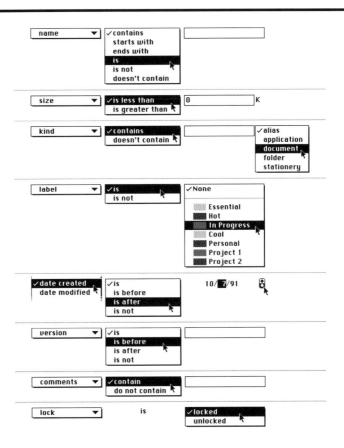

- **Size.** You choose the "size" option to search files according to their disk size in kilobytes. You may either search for icons that are smaller or larger than a specified size.

- **Kind.** You choose this option to search icons according to their kind. On one hand, you may enter a partial criteria and then find all files whose kind attribute either contains or does not contain the entry. For example, you might enter the criteria "suit" to locate (or eliminate) all suitcase files, including (or excluding) the System file. On the other hand, you can choose a predetermined criteria to search for aliases, applications, documents, folders, or stationery pads.

- **Label.** You use this option to search for icons that have or have not been assigned a specific color from the Label menu.

- **Date created.** To view the date an icon was created, you have to choose the Get Info command from the File menu (⌘-I). The date displayed in a directory window is the date an icon was last modified (as described in the next item). You may search for icons that were created on ("is"), before, or after a specified date. You may also search for icons that were not created on a specific date ("is not"). You click the month, date, or year and click the arrow icons or enter a new value to change the search criteria.

- **Date modified.** This option offers the same modifier and criteria options offered by "date created." This date represents the last time an icon was opened and saved or—in the case of a folder or disk—the last time the icon's contents were altered.

- **Version.** You use this option to search applications and other utilities that offer version numbers. Documents, folders, and disks offer no version information. (You may, however, add version information of your own using ResEdit, as described in the Exploring Advanced Topics section later in this chapter. You may then search this information as an alternative to searching comments.)

- **Comments.** If you haven't rebuilt your desktop lately, you can search information entered into the "Comments" option in the Info dialog box. Comments may be set to either contain or not contain your criteria entry.

- **Lock.** You use this option to search files for whether they're locked or unlocked.

It may seem extraneous, but the "lock" option is among the most useful functions offered by the Find dialog box. More often than not, I find locked files to be something of an irritant since they cannot be altered or thrown away. It's one thing when *I* lock a file; that means *I* don't want it deleted or altered. But it's quite another when the file is automatically installed as locked. If you want to automate the hunt-down-and-unlock process, you can create a simple macro that finds a locked file (⌘-F), pauses a moment to allow the operation to complete, opens the Info dialog box (⌘-I), deselects the "Locked" check box, closes the Info dialog box (⌘-W), and continues the search (⌘-F).

WHAT TO SEARCH

You use the "Search" pop-up menu to specify the disks, folders, or even files that you want to search. As shown in Figure 8.8, you may search any or all mounted disks. If a single directory window is open and active, you may search only that window by choosing the "inside <active directory window>" option. If no directory window is active, an "on the desktop" option appears instead. When selected, this option searches all mounted disks, not just those icons that are located on the desktop, thus duplicating the effect of the "on all disks" option. (Pretty silly, huh?) If you selected one or

---

FIGURE 8.8

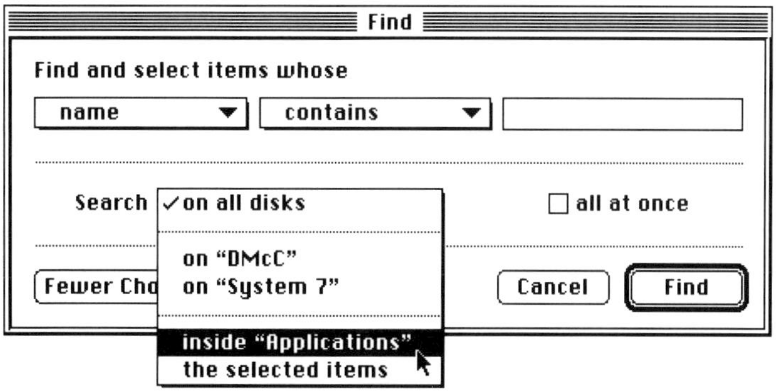

Choose an option from the "Search" pop-up menus to determine the files, folders, and disks that are searched.

more icons before displaying the Find dialog box, you may search the selected icons only by choosing "the selected items" option.

You should keep in mind that the contents of selected folders and disks are *not* searched when you choose "the selected items" option. Therefore, if you want to search the contents of a single folder only (and the folders within that folder), open that folder, make sure it's the active directory window, and choose the "inside <active directory window>" option from the "Search" pop-up menu.

You should note that the Find... and Find Again commands may not be used to search through the contents of any suitcase file, which includes the System file. Even if the System file is open, displaying its contents in the active directory window, the "Search" pop-up menu ignores it. As shown in Figure 8.9, the Find dialog box treats the System file as if it doesn't exist except as a standard file whose contents are not accessible to the Finder. You may, however, search fonts, sounds, keyboard layouts, and language scripts that are located in a standard folder.

Finally, you may select the "all at once" check box to show all matching icons that can be displayed in a single list view. In some cases, this eliminates the need for the Find Again command. But if more than one folder on the desktop contains entry matches, a message will appear telling you that you need to choose Find Again to find other matching icons.

FIGURE 8.9

The options in the Find dialog box do not recognize the contents of the System file or any other suitcase file.

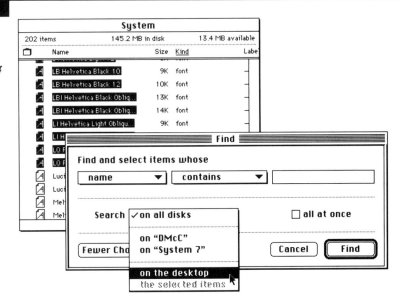

CREATING STATIONERY PADS

That's it for the Find… command. But before I begin *Exploring Advanced Topics,* I'd like to mention one more not-very-difficult method by which System 7 allows you to categorize documents. In addition to the alias, System 7 introduced a second new kind of file called the *stationery pad.* Designed to function as a template for future documents, a stationery pad can be opened to create an untitled document. In this way, you may create several documents that exploit the same basic layout or formula, while never running the risk of saving over the original layout or formula file.

If an application supports stationery pads, you can create a stationery pad from within the application when saving a file. Figure 8.10 shows a typical document destination dialog box that appears when you choose an application's Save command. Of the two icons in the lower-right corner of the dialog box, you should select the standard page icon to save the file normally, select the template icon (shown as selected in the figure) to save the file as a stationery pad.

If an application does *not* support stationery pads, as many don't, you can convert a document to a stationery pad at the Finder level. You select the document and choose the Get Info command from the File menu (⌘-I). Then select the "Stationery pad" check box in the lower-right corner of the Get Info dialog box, as shown in Figure 8.11. The icon in the upper-left corner will immediately change to the generic

FIGURE 8.10

If an application supports stationery pads, it may offer two page icons when saving a file. The left icon represents a standard document; the right icon represents a stationery pad.

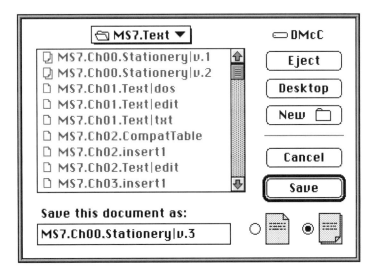

FIGURE 8.11

*U*se the Info dialog box
to convert a document to
a stationery pad at the
Finder level.

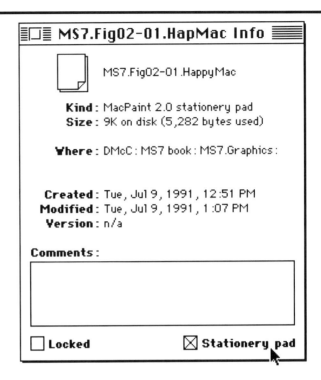

template icon. Under System 7, any document can be made into a
stationery pad. However, note that this rules out disks, folders, applications, and aliases.

USING STATIONERY PADS

It is amazing how few applications—even among those that purport to
be System 7-savvy—do not support the stationery pad feature. Some
programs, PageMaker and MacDraw Pro among them, provide their own
template features which, thus far, are not compatible with stationery
pads as implemented in System 7. In fact, as of this writing, I could only
find two stationery pad supporters: TeachText 7.0 and Excel 3.0. While
doubtless (or should I say hopefully?) others will join in, the pace has
been slow so far.

While it's no more than a slight inconvenience to convert a standard document to a stationery pad at the Finder level, using an existing
stationery pad is a different issue. When you open a stationery pad in a

program that does not support the feature, a message displays like the one shown in Figure 8.12, warning you that the file is a stationery pad but that your changes will be saved to the stationery pad itself, just as if it were a standard document (which it is, so far as the current application is concerned).

What's a would-be stationery pad user to do? Ultimately, you have two alternatives, one of which I'll explain now and one of which I'll present in the following tip. The sure-fire way to open a stationery pad without risking overwriting the file is to open it from the Finder. When you double-click a stationery pad at the Finder level, the dialog box shown in Figure 8.13 appears, requesting that you assign a name to the new file that will be created based on the stationery pad's contents. You click the Save In... button to save the file in a different folder and then click OK or press Return to save the new file in the current folder. Provided you don't save the new file with the same name as the original stationery pad, the contents of the stationery pad file are protected.

FIGURE 8.12

This alert message appears if you try to open a stationery pad inside an application that does not support stationery pads.

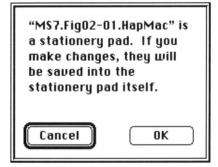

"MS7.Fig02-01.HapMac" is a stationery pad. If you make changes, they will be saved into the stationery pad itself.

Cancel   OK

FIGURE 8.13

You are given the opportunity to create a new file when opening a stationery pad from the Finder.

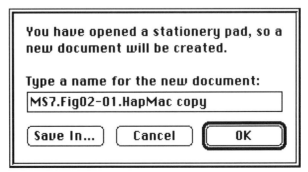

You have opened a stationery pad, so a new document will be created.

Type a name for the new document:

MS7.Fig02-01.HapMac copy

Save In...   Cancel   OK

Unfortunately, opening a stationery pad file from the Finder is not always convenient. It may require a lot of digging around through folders that is more easily accomplished from inside an application. If you want to open a stationery file inside a non-supportive application without running the risk of overwriting the file, lock it. That's right, just select the "Locked" check box in the Info dialog box. When you open the file, the message shown in Figure 8.12 will appear as usual. You can click OK without fear, make the desired changes and then choose the Save command. Rather than saving over the original stationery pad, a message will appear, telling you that the file is locked and cannot be overwritten. (Some applications transfer you directly to the document destination dialog box where you are expected to assign a new name and location to the file.) While a handful of programs will not open locked files, this technique is compatible with the overwhelming majority of applications.

EXPLORING ADVANCED TOPICS

When you think of advanced hard drive management issues, you might think of hardware-related stuff. Well, don't. For one thing, hardware is beyond the scope of this book. For another, if you're like me, you enjoy messing around with the innards of a computer about as much as you like fixing your car, which is never. Frankly, computer guts gross me out.

Having shared with you that deep, dark secret, I say we stick to software issues. For one, I'll discuss how to protect your files from being renamed, deleted, or modified, both by using the standard "Locked" option and by employing techniques that are more permanent by virtue of the fact that they're less accessible to other users. I'll also explain how to modify a file to include comments that can be viewed at the Finder level and will remain intact after rebuilding a disk's Desktop files. If none of this sounds like anything you're interested in, take comfort in the fact that these pages serve to fill out the book and make it look more impressive while it sits on your shelf and gets dusty. (Hey, I'm just trying to look on the bright side.)

LOCKING AND PROTECTING FILES

So far in this chapter, I've made several references to the "Locked" option inside the Info dialog box, but I have yet to properly introduce it. Just so you know, the "Locked" option serves the following purposes:

- **Protect a file's name.** When locked, a file may not be renamed.

- **Hamper a file's deletion.** A locked file may not be deleted by merely choosing the Empty Trash command from the Special menu. You must press Option and choose Empty Trash to delete a locked file, which can be enough of a deterrence to give a user second thoughts about permanently erasing an important document.

- **Protect a file's contents.** When a file is locked, it cannot be overwritten. Locking files may prove especially useful when you want to prevent a file from being edited while it is being shared with other users. (You should note that locking a file does not prevent users from copying the contents of a file or integrating them into a different file.)

All in all, however, locking a file is an unreliable method for ensuring the file's protection since all a user has to do to unprotect the file is choose Get Info and deselect the "Locked" option. The best way to protect a file is to modify its *Finder flags* using ResEdit (or some comparable utility).

Protecting an Icon's Name

You may have noticed that you can't rename many of the files included with System 7. For example, you should try to rename the Finder. Unless you duplicate the file to create a new copy of the Finder, it can't be done. Next, you should select the Finder and choose the Get Info command. You'll notice that the "Locked" option is *not* selected. How can this be?

Version 2.1.1 of ResEdit offers access to a special name locking bit (which can be set to on or off) included inside the header of every icon. To access this bit, you choose the Get File/Folder Info from ResEdit's File menu and then open the document whose name you want to protect. An Info window like that shown in Figure 8.14 will appear. You should note that there are three locking options: 1) "File Locked," performs the same function as the "Locked" option in the Info dialog box, which is available from the Finder; 2) "Resources Locked," protects resource information from being altered, which is unnecessary for most documents; and 3) "Locked" in the upper-right corner of the dialog box. The "Locked" option protects the name of the document only. You'll notice that when you select this option, the file name listed to the left of the option changes from editable to fixed. The name will also remain un-editable at the Finder level. (Experienced users should note that the "Locked" option corresponds to the old "System" bit.)

FIGURE 8.14

Inside the ResEdit 2.1.1 Info dialog box, select the "Locked" option to prevent the current file's name from being edited. (Your Info dialog box will look different if you're using ResEdit 2.1.)

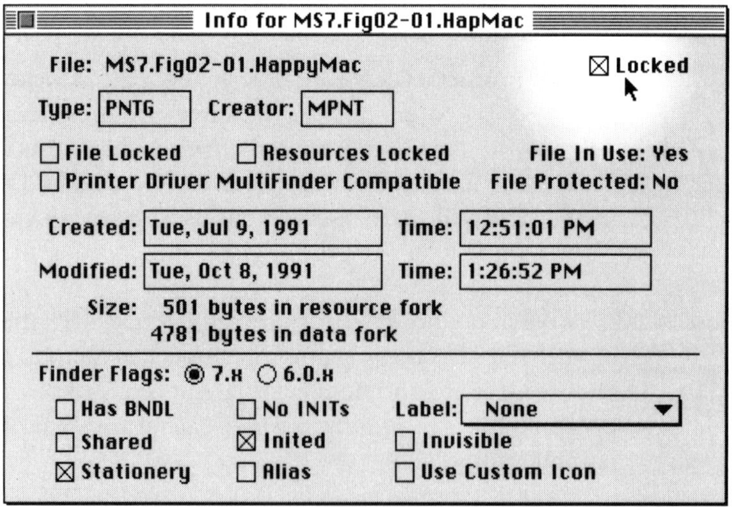

```
┌─────────────────────────────────────────────────────────────┐
│ ▉▉  ═══════════ Info for MS7.Fig02-01.HapMac ═══════════     │
├─────────────────────────────────────────────────────────────┤
│   File: MS7.Fig02-01.HappyMac              ⊠ Locked          │
│                                              ▶               │
│   Type: │PNTG│    Creator: │MPNT│                            │
│                                                              │
│   ☐ File Locked       ☐ Resources Locked    File In Use: Yes │
│   ☐ Printer Driver MultiFinder Compatible   File Protected: No│
│                                                              │
│   Created: │Tue, Jul 9, 1991│      Time: │12:51:01 PM│       │
│                                                              │
│   Modified: │Tue, Oct 8, 1991│     Time: │1:26:52 PM│        │
│      Size:   501 bytes in resource fork                      │
│              4781 bytes in data fork                         │
│   ─────────────────────────────────────────────────────     │
│   Finder Flags: ● 7.H  ○ 6.0.H                               │
│      ☐ Has BNDL    ☐ No INITs    Label: │ None        ▼│     │
│      ☐ Shared      ⊠ Inited      ☐ Invisible                 │
│      ⊠ Stationery  ☐ Alias       ☐ Use Custom Icon           │
└─────────────────────────────────────────────────────────────┘
```

Ensuring an Icon is not Deleted

There's really only one way to prevent a file from being deleted, and that's to make it invisible. After all, a file that can't be seen can't be dragged to the Trash folder. Like the "Locked" option described in the previous paragraph, the "Invisible" option is made available as a check box in the ResEdit Info dialog box, as shown in Figure 8.15. When you select this option, the icon can no longer be viewed from the Finder desktop.

The obvious problem with this solution is that a file that can't be seen from the Finder also cannot be seen from inside most applications. Therefore, making a MacPaint file invisible potentially prevents you from opening the file and displaying its contents. To overcome this difficulty, you'll need to use a file launching utility such as DiskTop from CE Software. Or better yet, you should assign the file a keyboard equivalent using a macro utility such as QuicKeys or Tempo, both of which can see invisible files. In this way, you can instruct users how to open a file without ever showing them where the heck it is.

FIGURE 8.15

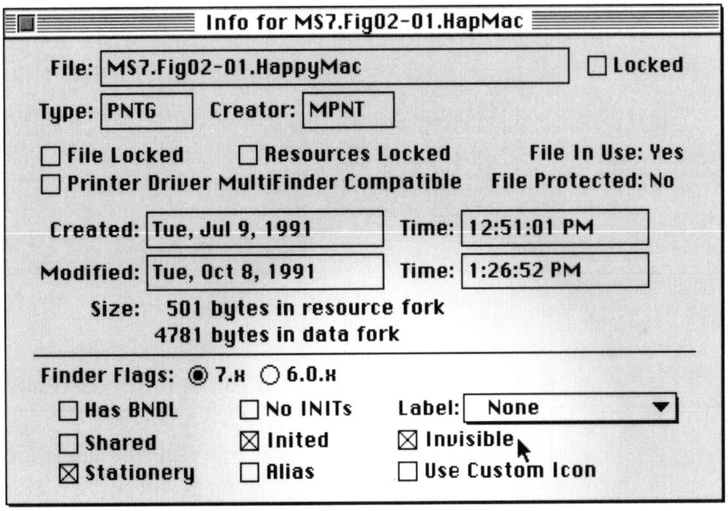

*S*elect the "Invisible" option to prevent a file from being deleted.

Info for MS7.Fig02-01.HapMac
File: MS7.Fig02-01.HappyMac   ☐ Locked
Type: PNTG   Creator: MPNT
☐ File Locked   ☐ Resources Locked   File In Use: Yes
☐ Printer Driver MultiFinder Compatible   File Protected: No
Created: Tue, Jul 9, 1991   Time: 12:51:01 PM
Modified: Tue, Oct 8, 1991   Time: 1:26:52 PM
Size: 501 bytes in resource fork
4781 bytes in data fork
Finder Flags: ⦿ 7.ᴙ ○ 6.0.ᴙ
☐ Has BNDL   ☐ No INITs   Label: None ▼
☐ Shared   ☒ Inited   ☒ Invisible
☒ Stationery   ☐ Alias   ☐ Use Custom Icon

Preventing a Document from Being Modified

This one's the hardest because it's darn near impossible. The only sure-fire way to protect a document from being modified—namely, its text and graphics—is to store the file as a special kind of uneditable Teach-Text document. While text in this format will not retain its formatting, and it can be fairly difficult to correctly align text and graphics, your document is fully protected. Neither text nor graphics may be modified, nor may they be copied for modification in some other piece of software.

Here's how it works:

1. Save the text that you want to protect as a text-only file. This is an option in almost every word-processor available for the Mac. Any graphics that have been imported into the file will be automatically deleted during this step.

2. Open the text-only file in TeachText. Add one non-breaking space (created by pressing Option-Spacebar) for each graphic that you wish to add to the document. Each non-breaking space character represents the top of an imported image.

3. For best results, insert a carriage return above each non-breaking space so that there is a blank line separating the graphic from the text above it. Insert several carriage returns beneath a non-breaking space to compensate for each graphic's height.

4. Save the TeachText file and close it. TeachText will open PICT images for viewing purposes, but it does not allow you to import or paste graphics. To perform this step, you'll need ResEdit and the Scrapbook desk accessory.

5. Launch the desired graphics application. Open each graphic file that you want to display inside the protected document (bitmapped images only), copy it, and paste it into the Scrapbook.

6. Launch ResEdit. Open the Scrapbook file inside the System Folder. Next, double-click on the file's PICT resource to open it. The PICTs window will display the contents of the Scrapbook, as shown in Figure 8.16. Scroll through the images and select the image that you want to appear first in the TeachText file. Choose the Copy command from the Edit menu (⌘-C).

7. Still inside ResEdit, open the TeachText file. The message shown in Figure 8.17 will appear, telling you that no resource fork currently exists for this file. Click the OK button to add a resource fork and open the file.

FIGURE 8.16

The contents of the Scrapbook as displayed inside ResEdit 2.1.

FIGURE 8.17

This message displays when you try to open a file in ResEdit that has no resource fork (as is the case for most standard documents).

8. Choose the Paste command from the Edit menu (⌘-V). A PICT resource will be created automatically. Open this resource to see the image you just pasted.

9. Bring the PICTs window for the Scrapbook window to the foreground to copy the image that you want to appear second in the TeachText file.

10. Bring the PICTs window for the TeachText file to the foreground and paste the second image.

11. Repeat steps 9 and 10 for the third, fourth, fifth, and so on images that you want to add to the TeachText document. When you have finished copying and pasting all graphics, close the Scrapbook file.

12. Select the first image in the PICT resource inside the TeachText file. Choose the Get Resource Info command from the Resource menu (⌘-I). The Resource Info dialog box will display, as shown in Figure 8.18. Enter 1000 into the "ID" option box and click the close box.

13. Select the second image and change its ID number to 1001, change the third image to ID number 1002, and so on, in sequential order.

14. Save your changes and close the TeachText file.

15. Switch back to the TeachText application and open the TeachText file. The images you added to the file inside ResEdit will appear at the locations where you added non-breaking space characters, as demonstrated in Figure 8.19.

16. Edit the text to make it jive better with the graphics. Note that the graphics have a tendency to disappear as you add text or change their locations. To force the document to

FIGURE 8.18

TeachText displays PICT images in numerical order, beginning at ID number 1000.

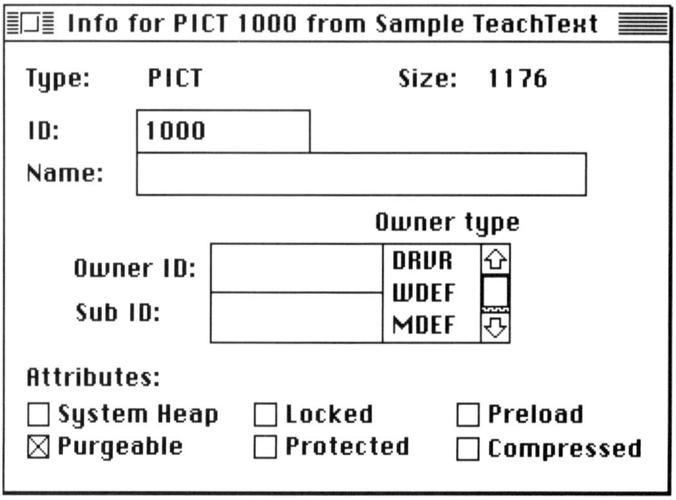

FIGURE 8.19

The top of each graphic added to a TeachText document aligns to a non-breaking space character.

refresh on screen, scroll the document or adjust the window size.

17. Now for the part you've been waiting for: How to prevent this document from being edited. Save your changes and close the file.

18. Return to ResEdit and choose the Get File/Folder Info... command from the File menu. Open the TeachText document.

19. Inside the Info dialog box, change the "Type" option from "TEXT" to "ttro" (all lowercase), as shown in Figure 8.20. Save your changes and close the dialog box.

20. Switch back to TeachText and open your file. Now try to edit it. A beep will sound for each time you click inside the window. If you hassle the program enough, a message will appear telling you that you cannot modify the file; you may only read and print it.

FIGURE 8.20

TeachText documents with the file type code "ttro" cannot be edited. To edit such a file in the future, simply change its type code back to "TEXT."

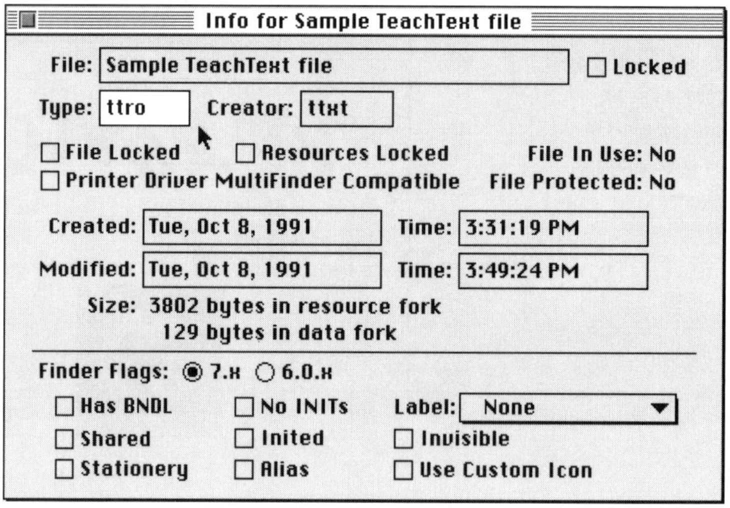

```
☰■☰☰☰☰☰   Info for Sample TeachText file   ☰☰☰☰☰☰

    File: Sample TeachText file              ☐ Locked

    Type: ttro      Creator: ttxt

    ☐ File Locked        ☐ Resources Locked      File In Use: No
    ☐ Printer Driver MultiFinder Compatible   File Protected: No

    Created: Tue, Oct 8, 1991        Time: 3:31:19 PM
    Modified: Tue, Oct 8, 1991       Time: 3:49:24 PM
         Size:  3802 bytes in resource fork
                129 bytes in data fork
    ─────────────────────────────────────────────────
    Finder Flags:  ◉ 7.x  ○ 6.0.x
         ☐ Has BNDL      ☐ No INITs     Label: None        ▼
         ☐ Shared        ☐ Inited       ☐ Invisible
         ☐ Stationery    ☐ Alias        ☐ Use Custom Icon
```

Certainly, none of these methods is foolproof. However, since all of these techniques involve the use of ResEdit or a similar file editing tool—hardly a staple of most user's libraries—you're probably pretty safe, far safer than if you had simply relied on the Finder's "Locked" option.

One last item: When using previous versions of the Macintosh system software, you used to be able to prevent a file from being copied by activating its NoCopy bit, also called the Bozo bit. Under System 7, this exact bit has been converted to the Stationery bit. Therefore, any file that was set to NoCopy under an older system will be read by System 7 as a stationery pad. Also, if you select the NoCopy bit using an old version of FileEdit, Symantec Tools, DiskTop, or the like, you will in fact be converting the file to a stationery pad. For most users, this will never be an issue. But if you moonlight as a hacker, it may be an interesting point to note.

CREATING PERMANENT COMMENTS

Under System 6, you could protect file comments from being deleted by using a utility such as Minor Repairs from FirstAid Software or FileSaver, part of Norton Utilities for the Macintosh. As of this writing, neither of the newest versions of these programs—Minor Changes 1.01 nor FileSaver 1.1—work with System 7 (though there is a utility by Maurice Volaski, called CommentKeeper, that does work with System 7). So how the heck are you supposed to make any *reasonable* use of file comments? What good are they if they're going to disappear any time the Desktop files are rebuilt?

If comments are unreliable, you have to look elsewhere. The elsewhere that makes the most sense is the version information. Like comments, version info can be searched using the Find... command and viewed using the Get Info command. Unlike comments, however, versions can be edited only inside ResEdit and become part of the file itself, not part of any Desktop file.

The other nice thing about versions is that there's two of them for every icon. Figure 8.21 shows where these two versions appear in the Info dialog box. Text stored in the "vers" number 1 resource shows up as standard "Version" information. Text stored in the "vers" number 2 resource displays directly beneath the file name.

To create version information for a file, do the following:

1. Open the file in ResEdit. In most cases, an alert message will display, telling you that you may only open the file by

FIGURE 8.21

*E*ach icon can contain two "vers" resources that can be displayed by choosing the Get Info command.

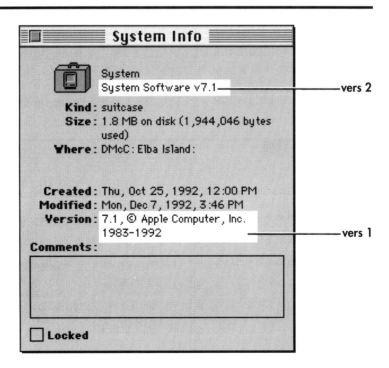

adding a resource fork to it, as shown back in Figure 8.17. Click OK to continue.

2. Now choose the Create New Resource command from the Resource menu (⌘-K). The Select New Type dialog box shown in Figure 8.22 will appear. Select the resource type "vers" from the scrolling list and click the OK button or press Return.

3. ResEdit automatically creates a "vers" resource and opens it to display the vers window shown in Figure 8.23. Add whatever information you want to appear in the Info dialog box at the Finder level into the "Long version string (visible in Get Info)" option box at the bottom of the window.

4. If you want to be able to search for this version information via the Find... command, you'll have to enter a number into the "Version number" options. Remember: the Find dialog box only offers options for finding versions that do or do not match a certain number or fall before or after an entered number.

5. Click the close box to close the vers window. To determine where the version information appears in the Info dialog box, choose the Get Resource Info command from the Resource menu (⌘-I). Enter 1 in the "ID" option to position the version text near the bottom of the Info dialog box; enter 2 to position the text near the top.

FIGURE 8.22

The Select New Type dialog box allows you to determine the resource type created inside ResEdit.

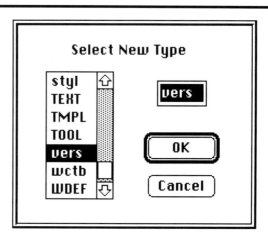

FIGURE 8.23

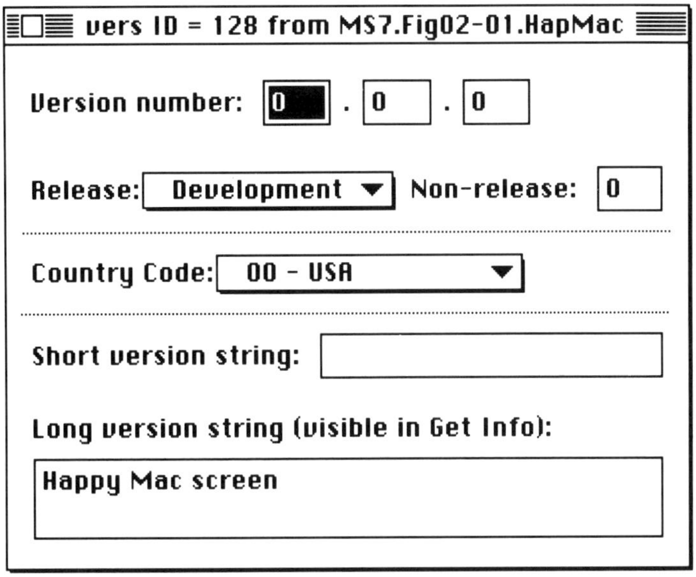

Enter the desired comments into the "Long version string" option at the bottom of the window.

▤☐▤ uers ID = 128 from MS7.Fig02-01.HapMac ▤

Uersion number: [0▮] . [0] . [0]

Release: [Development ▼]   **Non-release:** [0]

Country Code: [00 – USA   ▼]

Short version string: [   ]

Long version string (visible in Get Info):

[**Happy Mac screen**   ]

6. Click the close box. To create a second "vers" resource, choose the Create New Resource command (⌘-K) and repeat steps 3 through 5. Then save the file and quit ResEdit.

7. After returning to the Finder level, select the file and choose the Get Info command from the File menu (⌘-I). The new version information will display in the Info dialog box.

Sometimes changes made to a file inside ResEdit will not show up at the Finder level until you force the Finder desktop to update. To do this, go to the Finder level, press ⌘-Option-Escape, and click the Force Quit button. When the Finder relaunches, your changes will be made visible.

Expanding
and Managing
Application Memory

O WNING A COMPUTER is one long
▬▬ game of keeping up with the Joneses.
Many of us covet our neighbors' computers more urgently than any
possessions short of their homes, cars, or spouses. (Just in case you don't
recognize it, that's the *bright* side of computer lust.) The dark side is that
almost the instant you buy a computer, something better comes along,
or the price drops $1000, or some new application that you absolutely
require will only run on the newest, most top-of-the-line gadget.

It wouldn't be so bad if computer lust were based on vanity alone.
But so much of our computer desires are founded on the most practical
of practical issues: *performance.* The better your computer runs, the
faster you can work. The faster your computer runs, the more you can
accomplish. The more your computer runs, the better *you* are. It's the
mantra of a turning millennium, man.

I guess that's why we ogle at memory. First, it ages well. While you
sometimes need to add memory, you rarely have to replace it. Second, it
enhances performance. It increases the speed of your machine by providing additional space to perform calculations without having to load
and unload software. It also increases your personal capacity to perform
by allowing you to create larger documents, juggle multiple applications,
and use more complicated software.

RAM is one of the few items you can add to a Macintosh that increases your ability to perform any computer-oriented task; for the time
being, it's relatively inexpensive. How else can you dramatically increase
the performance of your current computer for less than the price of a
typical application?

So when you find yourself coming down with a severe case of computer lust, follow this simple prescription: Take 2MB of RAM and read
this chapter in the morning.

GETTING STARTED

System 7 requires at least 2MB of RAM to run. This is based on the assumption that your System file contains a moderate sampling of fonts and sounds and that you're using no commercial control panel or system extension such as QuicKeys or Adobe Type Manager. When loaded, a stripped-down System 7 consumes just over 1MB of RAM, leaving the remaining 1MB or so to run MacPaint, Microsoft Word, or some other smallish application.

With so little RAM, memory management is not much of an issue. However, you will sometimes need to adjust the manner in which RAM is used by your software, even if you plan on running only one application in addition to the Finder at a time.

APPLICATION MEMORY

The amount of RAM set aside for use by a program is called the *application memory.* You can adjust the amount of application memory assigned to a program before launching it using the Get Info command in the File menu (⌘-I). For example, suppose you are using Microsoft Word. Before launching the program, you select its icon at the Finder level and choose Get Info. The Info dialog box shown in Figure 9.1 will appear. A "Memory" option is available in the lower-right corner of the dialog box. The "Suggested size" value indicates the minimum amount of RAM the selected program was designed to use. You may not change this value. However, you may adjust the "Minimum size" and the "Preferred size" options, in which you may specify the least and most amount of RAM that an application can be assigned when it launches.

The "Preferred size" value is the amount of RAM that an application will launch with, given that you have that much RAM available on your Mac. If you have less RAM than the "Preferred size" requests, then the application will launch with as much as it can get. The only thing that limits this process is the "Minimum size" value. An application will *not* launch if there is less RAM available than the amount requested in the "Minimum size" option, and the warning in Figure 9.2 will display. The only time an application will launch with less RAM allocated to it

FIGURE 9.1

The Get Info command may be used to adjust the amount of application memory assigned to the selected program.

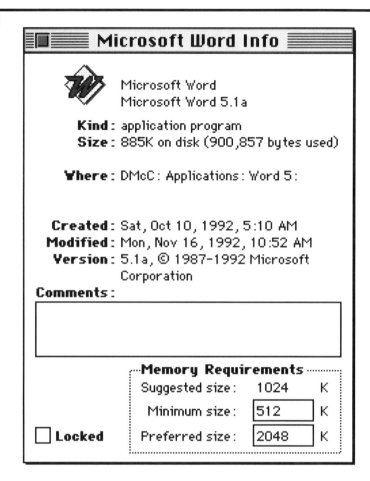

than entered into the "Preferred size" option, is if it is the last application to be launched before your RAM is filled to capacity. This can cause problems, as explained in the next section.

If possible, you will generally want to set the "Preferred size" option to an amount greater than or equal to the "Suggested size" value. In some cases, if available memory is scarce, you may sometimes set the "Minimum size" and "Preferred size" options to amounts smaller than the "Suggested size" value, although you should take care to restore the original application memory value after you finish using the program.

MAKING EFFICIENT USE OF LIMITED MEMORY

Changing the "Minimum size" and "Preferred size" values is a simple task. So the question for most users is not how to adjust application memory, but why. After all, you may have gone years without ever so much as noticing the amount of application memory allotted to a program. Why start fooling around with it now?

The reason is that System 7 provides a slightly more complicated operating environment than those offered by previous versions of the system software. Under System 7, you have no choice but to run multiple applications at a time. To use any program, you must run it and the Finder application simultaneously. Therefore, if you don't pay attention to memory allotment, you may very easily run into problems.

For example, suppose you want to run Microsoft Word, as is, on a 2MB machine. Every program is supplied with a default application RAM setting, entered into the "Minimum size" and "Preferred size" options. In the case of Microsoft Word, the default "Minimum size" value is 512K, half the "Suggested size" value, and the "Preferred size" value is 2048K, twice the "Suggested size" value (see Figure 9.2). But System 7 does not leave 2048K of RAM (or even 1024K, for that matter) on a 2MB machine. As a result, even though Word would like to open with the full 2048K, if you don't change the default values, it will use all the remaining RAM instead (provided more than 512K of RAM is available).

Your natural reaction may be to say, "Fine, go for it. Why the heck bug me about such a trivial issue?" After all, the program will launch successfully, confirming your suspicions that your Mac is a big whiner. But you are missing what is going on behind the scenes. If you were to switch to the Finder and choose the About This Macintosh… command from the Apple menu, you would see that your RAM has been divvied up like

FIGURE 9.2

When you launch an application with less RAM available than needed by the "Minimum size" value, the application cannot open.

Insufficient memory to open this application.

OK

Berlin after the second World War. As shown in Figure 9.3, two applications are currently running, leaving a "Largest Unused Block" value of zero K; in other words, there is no memory left. In filling the RAM to capacity, you have created a generally unstable working environment.

For example, to complete a particularly difficult operation, a program can request an extra supply of *temporary memory* from the system software. If no extra memory is available, your application will be forced to cancel the operation and display an out-of-memory error. If your application is unprepared for such an event, your computer may even crash.

But when using a relatively simple application like Microsoft Word, complex operations of this nature are uncommon. It's more likely that you'll want to perform an operation outside the range of Word's capabilities, such as adding up a handful of numbers or locating a special character. These operations may require the use of a desk accessory like Calculator or Key Caps. But if you try to open either DA, a message like the one shown in Figure 9.4 will appear, telling you that there isn't

---

FIGURE 9.3

*O*nce a program is launched to fill all available memory, zero K will be left to open other programs.

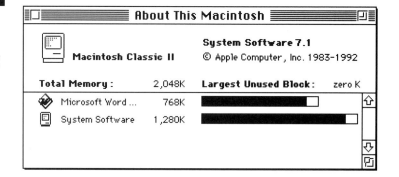

FIGURE 9.4

*W*hen your computer's RAM is filled to capacity, even small programs such as desk accessories cannot be opened.

The desk accessory "Key Caps" could not be opened, because there isn't enough memory available. Closing windows or quitting application programs can make more memory available.

OK

enough memory available. If you want to use Key Caps, you'll have to quit Microsoft Word first.

Filling all available RAM limits your mobility. Therefore, you should reduce the application RAM value to a size that will accommodate the program while leaving enough room to open additional utilities as you need them.

APPLICATION RAM RESTRICTIONS

Two last bits of information about application memory: First, you may *not* change the "Minimum size" or "Preferred size" options when an application is running. A dotted line will surround the "Minimum size" and "Preferred size" values to show that they are not available for adjustments. If you want to assign more or less RAM to a program, you must quit the program, change the "Preferred size" value, and then relaunch the program.

Second, you may adjust the amount of RAM assigned to an application *only*. A document, for example, may not be assigned a specific RAM value; rather, it is loaded into the application RAM made available to the current program. Extensions, control panels, and other system utilities are loaded into the portion of RAM allocated to the system software.

The odd folks out are desk accessories, which are assigned a combination of application RAM *and* system software RAM. Each desk accessory, regardless of complexity, is automatically assigned 20K of application RAM. Any additional memory required is provided by the system. For example, Figure 9.5 shows the About This Macintosh dialog box as it tracks the loading of a couple of desk accessories. In the first example, no DA is loaded and 256K of RAM remains available. In the second example, I open the Key Caps DA, which gets 20K of application RAM and another 15K from the system software, which leaves $256 - 20 - 15 = 221$K of free RAM. In the third example I open the much larger DiskTop DA. Another 20K of application RAM is doled out. But because of DiskTop's increased complexity, the system software is forced to grow by 101K. As a result, it's impossible to specify and difficult to predict how much memory a desk accessory will require.

FIGURE 9.5

The About This Macintosh dialog box shown when no DA is open (top), when Key Caps is open (middle), and when both Key Caps and Disktop are open (bottom).

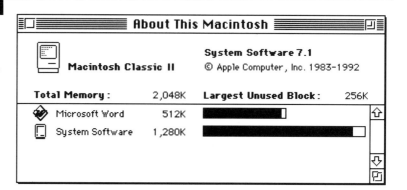

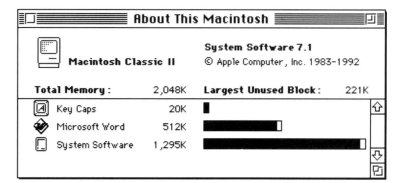

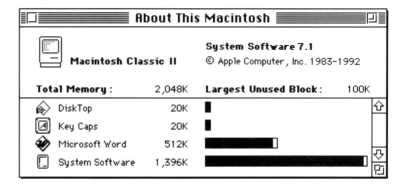

LEARNING FUNDAMENTAL CONCEPTS

Determining the amount of RAM to be used by an application is a matter of adjusting a single option. But adjusting the amount of memory available to the system software is a more complicated issue. Generally speaking, System 7 does most of the work for you. Unlike when using System 5 or System 6 in combination with MultiFinder, you *cannot* adjust the amount of application RAM assigned to the Finder under System 7. This task is handled automatically by the system software when your computer starts up. In addition, the portion of RAM assigned to the system software shrinks and grows automatically to compensate for various operations. For example, the system might grow to accommodate the opening of a desk accessory or control panel. It might also adjust to receive the contents of the Clipboard when swapping elements from one program to another.

Nevertheless, a small but essential portion of system memory control is left to you. System 7 provides a Memory control panel which allows you to determine the manner in which memory is recognized and utilized by the system software. Using the "Virtual Memory" option, you may even add to your supply of available RAM by appropriating free space from your hard drive. This option and others are discussed in the following pages.

One note about the Memory control panel: Its appearance changes depending on the machine you're using. If you're using a Macintosh Plus, SE, Classic, or Portable, the control panel offers a single option, as shown in Figure 9.6. These computers may not take advantage of virtual memory or 32-bit addressing (introduced later), so those options are not included. If you use a Mac II with an optional PMMU chip, or an SE/30, IIx, or IIcx, the Memory control panel gains a "Virtual Memory" option, as shown in Figure 9.7. If you use a II, SE/30, IIx, or IIcx in conjunction with the utility Mode32 (distributed free through Apple and included on the disks which you can order with the coupon found at the back of this

FIGURE 9.6

The Memory control panel as seen on most single-unit Macs and the Macintosh Portable.

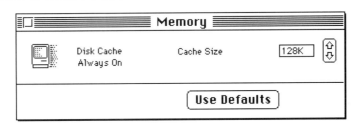

book), or if you use any of the newer high-end machines including the Classic II, LC, Performa 200, LC II, Performa 400, IIsi, IIci, Performa 600, IIvx, Quadra 700, Quadra 900, or Quadra 950, your Memory control panel will contain three options, as shown in Figure 9.8. Finally, if you use any of the PowerBook family (except for the PowerBook 100) equipped with System 7.1, a "RAM Disk" option will be added, as shown in Figure 9.9. (The PowerBook 100 also offers the "RAM Disk" option, but it lacks the "Virtual Memory" and "32-Bit Addressing" options.)

FIGURE 9.7

The same control panel as seen on a 68020 machine with a PMMU chip.

FIGURE 9.8

The Memory control panel available to machines that offer 32-bit clean ROMs, or are used in conjunction with Mode32.

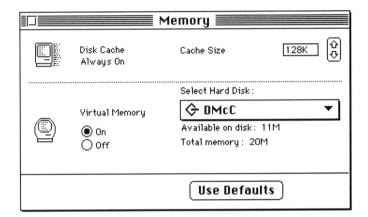

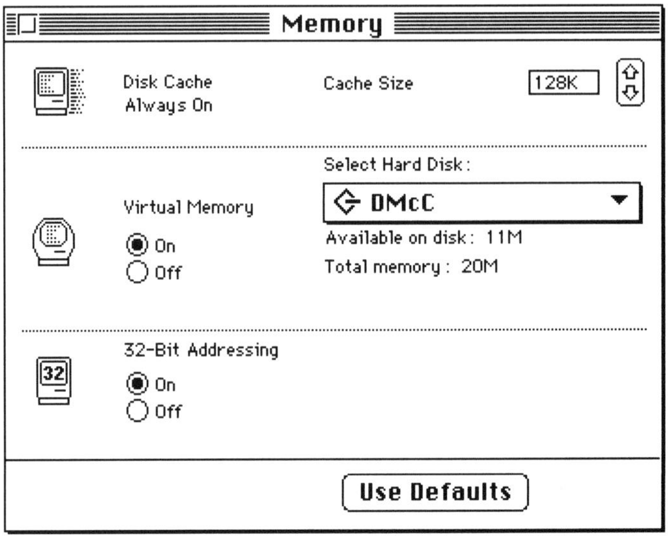

FIGURE 9.9

System 7.0 and System 7.1 each offer a "RAM Disk" option applicable to portable computers.

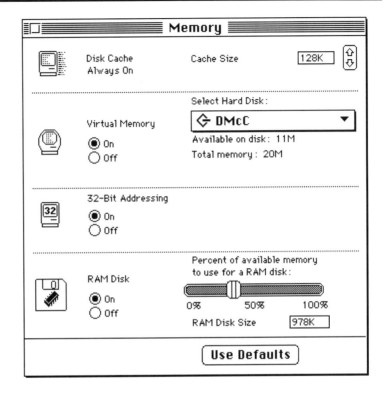

If you need a refresher, the capabilities of each Macintosh computer that supports System 7 are listed in Table 2.1 in Chapter 2.

All changes made inside the Memory control panel will take effect only after you reboot your computer. Click the Default button to restore the default settings in force when you first began using System 7.

DISK CACHE

One rule of thumb that's prerequisite to understanding the Memory control panel: Chips are fast; disks are slow. Data can be read from and written to RAM as much as 400 times faster than it can be read from or written to a hard disk. That's why when you launch an application, it is first copied from disk into RAM to enable the program to run at a reasonable speed. The slowest operations occur when portions of a program have to be loaded from disk, or when you save or open a document.

Disk cache is a portion of the system software RAM that helps to speed up disk-related operations. Whenever data is read from or written to disk, the data is *cached*—that is, stored for temporary retrieval—to this portion of RAM. The argument goes that what you accessed most recently, you'll soon need again. For example, suppose you've opened a particularly large document in PageMaker. The entire document cannot be loaded into RAM all at once, so only the two-page spread currently displayed on screen is copied to RAM; the rest is written to a temporary holding file on disk, called a *disk buffer*. When you change pages, the new two-page spread is written to RAM. The old pages are written to the disk buffer and backed up to the disk cache in RAM (provided enough space is available). Chances are good that you'll return to those two pages stored in the disk cache before going on to new pages. Perhaps you forgot to correct a typo or you need to take a second look at a graphic. When returning to the previous page spread, the pages can be retrieved from RAM much faster than from disk. In a nutshell, creating a document typically involves a lot of working and reworking. The disk cache speeds up the reworking experience.

By default, 32K of disk cache are assigned for every 1MB of RAM available to your machine. For example, if your Mac is equipped with 4MB of RAM, the disk cache will be set initially to 128K. However, you may adjust the disk cache anywhere from 32K to 128K per 1MB of RAM (and sometimes even higher) by clicking the up and down arrow icons to the right of the "Cache Size" option box. Increasing the amount of disk cache enables it to hold more data, thus increasing the likelihood that data required by the CPU will be available in RAM and won't have to be read from disk. However, increasing the disk cache also takes memory away from the amount of free RAM available to run applications. Therefore, you have to strike a balance between speedy retrieval and your desire to use multiple programs at one time.

Determining the right amount of disk cache is largely a matter of personal preference. As a rule of thumb, I advise that you start out using the default 32K of disk cache per 1MB of RAM. Try this setting out for a few days until you get a feel for the computer's speed and the number of applications you can use at a time. Then boost the disk cache to 64K per 1MB of RAM. If the increased setting provides noticeably faster performance without limiting your ability to run applications, leave it set this way, or perhaps even experiment with increasing the disk cache further. If you notice no speed improvement, or if you can't use as many applications at a time as you're used to using, reduce the disk cache incrementally until you find the most desirable setting.

Note that the "Disk Cache" option is almost identical to the "RAM Cache" option offered by the General control panel in previous versions of the system software. The only difference is that the "Disk Cache" option cannot be turned off. (The reason that the option has been renamed is that it was named incorrectly in the first place. Technically, *RAM cache* is a special bank of extremely fast RAM that caches data retrieved from standard, slower RAM.) Also note that in previous versions of the system software, there was a bug that slowed the performance of the disk cache when set above 512K. This problem was remedied in System 7.

VIRTUAL MEMORY

Virtual memory allows you to use free space on your hard drive to augment the amount of RAM available to your computer. For example, you can use 8MB of hard drive space to simulate 8MB of RAM. In fact, in conjunction with 32-bit addressing (discussed later), you can access up to 1,024MB— over a gigabyte—of virtual memory. If your Mac does not allow 32-bit addressing, as discussed at the beginning of the *Learning Fundamental Concepts* section, you can access up to 14MB of total memory minus 1MB for each NuBus card installed in your computer. (As luck would have it, most computers that lack 32-bit addressing also lack NuBus slots, so the NuBus card limitation is not an issue. The only exceptions are the Mac II, IIx, and IIcx, which can be made to support 32-bit addressing using Mode32.)

Virtual memory works as follows: Suppose your machine is equipped with 5MB of "real" RAM. You turn on the "Virtual Memory" option, then click the up arrow icon to boost the memory supply to 8MB, as shown in Figure 9.10. The *full amount* of the desired memory setting must be free on disk—in this case 8MB, not merely the 3MB difference between the real RAM and the desired memory. This holds true at all times, even if the desired memory is only 1MB more than you have in real RAM. If sufficient disk space is not available, a message will display reading "Not enough room on disk" and you will have to choose a different disk from the "Select Hard Disk" pop-up menu or free up some room on the current disk.

Upon closing the Memory control panel, the system software creates an invisible file on your hard drive called *VM Storage,* as demonstrated in

Figure 9.11. A piece of hardware called the *Paged Memory Management Unit* (or PMMU) notes the exact locations—bit for bit—of the VM Storage file on disk and *maps* them to specific bit locations in RAM.

When using virtual memory, data is swapped back and forth between the real RAM and the VM Storage file, a technique called *page swapping*. Most commonly, page swapping occurs when switching between open

FIGURE 9.10

*A*fter selecting the "On" radio button, click the up arrow icon to boost the amount of virtual memory supplied by the chosen hard drive.

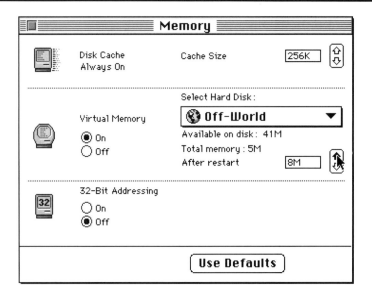

FIGURE 9.11

*T*he invisible VM Storage file viewed using the DiskTop desk accessory. Note that the VM Storage file is as large as the virtual memory setting.

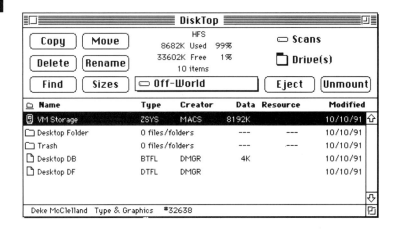

programs. For example, when switching between Photoshop and Page-Maker, the Photoshop program is copied from RAM onto your hard drive. The PageMaker file is then read from disk into RAM.

Page swapping takes less time than loading a program from disk since the data is merely mapped from one location to another rather than read and interpreted. However, it is slower than simply storing and retrieving data in RAM. As the discrepancy between real RAM and virtual memory grows, page swapping becomes more frequent, thus slowing your performance. Virtual memory can prove especially slow when page swapping is required to complete an operation within a single application. To avoid this problem, you will probably want to avoid using more than twice as much virtual memory as you have real RAM. Of course, this is only a guideline. You may need to use more or less virtual memory depending on the number of applications you wish to run and the complexity of your documents. Ultimately, if you find yourself doing less working than listening to the hard drive whir around, you'll want to lower the virtual memory setting or, better yet, purchase some additional RAM and deactivate virtual memory altogether.

TIP

System 7 does not allow you to use a removable cartridge as a virtual memory storage device. If it did and you were to remove the cartridge while in the process of using it to supply virtual memory, the results could be catastrophic—machine crashes, rebooting problems, dogs living with cats... it'd be a regular Pandora's box. But hey, you're an adult. If you left your cartridge the heck alone, you wouldn't have any problems. So if you think you can control yourself, there's a utility included on the disks which you can order with the coupon found at the back of this book called VM-Eject that alters the Memory control panel so its recognizes removable cartridges. Then insert a newly formatted 45MB cartridge and away you go. But remember, never, *never* eject the removable cartridge without first turning off virtual memory and restarting your computer!

EXPLORING ADVANCED TOPICS

The final option in the Memory control panel, "32-Bit Addressing," is easy to use but difficult to understand. For this reason, I'll cover it in the context of an advanced discussion. Following that, I'll throw in a few tips on viewing running applications and memory settings using the About This Macintosh… command in the Apple menu.

*3*2-BIT ADDRESSING

When active, 32-bit addressing (not to be confused with 32-bit Quick-Draw or 32-bit video) allows you to use more RAM. An *address* is a serial number (expressed as a *binary number*, that is, it contains only 1s and 0s) that identifies a unique byte of RAM. Normally, your computer relies on *24-bit addressing*, in which serial numbers are 24 digits long, permitting 2^{24} = 16,777,216 permutations. Each permutation represents a unique byte, which translates to 16MB of RAM. Unfortunately, the upper 8MB of RAM are sectioned off into a no-man's-land of RAM called *high memory* which, for the most part, goes ignored. Thus, you are left with only 8MB of RAM to run your system software and all applications.

If your Mac is equipped with no more than 8MB of RAM, 24-bit addressing is sufficient and is available to all models of Macintosh computers. (Due to hardware limitations, the Mac Plus, SE, and Classic can be equipped with no more than 4MB of RAM.) However, if you install 4MB SIMMs (*single in-line memory modules*, which are the small rectangular boards on which RAM chips are distributed), your Mac will be equipped with at least 17MB of RAM, most of which is wasted under 24-bit addressing. To break the 8MB barrier, System 7.1 permits *32-bit addressing*, which permits 2^{32} = 4,294,967,296 permutations. Thus, in theory, a machine using 32-bit addressing is capable of recognizing 4 billion bytes (4 gigabytes) of RAM, more memory than an elephant! Again, not all of this memory is accessible. Only the first gigabyte can be used to run the system software and applications. And since no Mac except the Quadra 900 and Quadra 950 presently provides more than 8 SIMM slots and there is no SIMM larger than 16MB—and even 16MB SIMMs are more rumor than reality—you can't install more than 128MB of RAM on most machines. Therefore, virtual memory is required to break the 128MB barrier (and God knows, we're all dying to do that).

Pretty technical stuff, huh? All you really need to know is that you must turn on the "32-Bit Addressing" option to upgrade your machine beyond 8MB of RAM. If you own a SE/30, II, IIx, or IIcx, you can use Mode32 (included on the disks which you can order with the coupon found at the back of this book) to make your machine *32-bit clean*; that is, compatible with 32-bit addressing.

Also note that many applications that are still in circulation are not 32-bit clean. These applications may use the last 8 digits of serial number space for their own purposes or they may delete these digits entirely. In any case, such applications will not run reliably when 32-bit addressing is turned on. (Just because a program is old doesn't mean that it's not 32-bit clean. Many older programs were designed as 32-bit clean, even though the system software wasn't yet ready to support 32-bit addressing. If you suspect that a program is not 32-bit clean, call the vendor to confirm.)

I P

> **If you don't own a 32-bit clean machine or much of your software is not 32-bit clean, you may use the control panel Maxima from Connectix to access additional memory under 24-bit addressing. Provided that you have more than 8MB of RAM installed on your Mac, Maxima allows you to use 6MB of high memory and reserves the remaining 2MB of high memory as a *RAM disk*. This boosts your available memory to 14MB—without relying on virtual memory—and enables you to store a small amount of system software or other data on the RAM disk. (By the way, a RAM disk is a memory partition in which you can save files and folders just as you can on a standard disk, except that the RAM disk operates much more quickly.)**

THE ABOUT THIS MACINTOSH DIALOG BOX

After such a technical discussion, I figure you need a break. So even though this is still the normally stuffy *Exploring Advanced Topics* section, the rest of this chapter is devoted to some pretty easy stuff. (Psst, don't let the beginners know about this section; they'd ruin everything!)

Once you finish making adjustments to the Memory control panel, restart your computer to make the changes take effect. From that point on, you can choose the About This Macintosh... command from the Apple menu to see how your RAM is being used. Figure 9.12 shows the About This Macintosh dialog box, which contains the following information:

- **Macintosh Model.** The upper-left corner of the dialog box features an icon representing your computer, and names the current computer model.

- **System Software.** The upper-right corner shows the system software version number. If this number is less than 7.0, you've gone and bought the wrong book.

- **Built-in Memory.** If virtual memory is turned on, a "Built-in Memory" item will list the amount of real RAM installed in your machine. If virtual memory in turned off, the "Total Memory" item will appear in its place.

- **Total Memory.** This item show all the memory available for use on this machine. If virtual memory is turned on, the

---

FIGURE 9.12

The About This Macintosh dialog box as it appears when virtual memory is turned on.

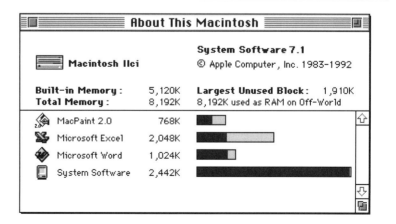

size and location of the VM Storage will be listed to the right of this item.

- **Largest Unused Block.** This item shows the largest contiguous area of RAM available to launch an application. If the RAM has become fragmented, this item will not represent the total amount of memory. Read the *Learning Fundamental Concepts* section of Chapter 4 for a complete discussion on memory fragmentation.

- **Running Applications.** Each running application, including the system software, is displayed in alphabetical order in the scrolling list in the bottom half of the About This Macintosh dialog box. The amount of application RAM used by each program is displayed as a long rectangle. Inside the rectangle, a dark bar shows the amount of memory inside the application RAM that is currently being used.

If you are only using 24-bit addressing on a machine with over 8MB of real RAM installed, the "Total Memory" item will show all installed RAM, but your system software will appear to take up the overwhelming majority of it, as demonstrated in the first example of Figure 9.13. After you turn on the "32-Bit Addressing" option, the system software will appear to shrink to its normal size, freeing RAM space to run additional applications. In reality, of course, it is merely recognizing memory that it could not previously address.

By default, the scrolling list in the About This Macintosh dialog box is large enough to display four running applications including the system software. However, provided you have installed sufficient RAM, it's no trick to run more than four applications at a time. Under System 7, you may resize the About This Macintosh by dragging its size box, as shown in Figure 9.14.

FIGURE 9.13

When using over 8MB of RAM, the system software will appear to consume an enormous portion of the total memory when 24-bit addressing is in effect (top). The system software appears to shrink to normal size when 32-bit addressing is activated (bottom).

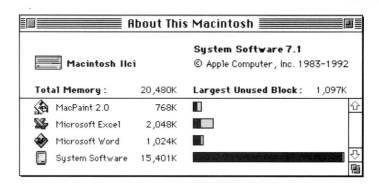

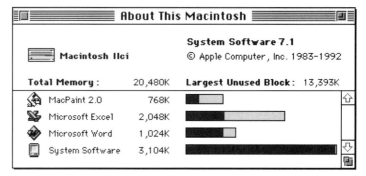

FIGURE 9.14

Drag the size box in the lower-right corner of the About This Macintosh dialog box to display more than four running applications at a time.

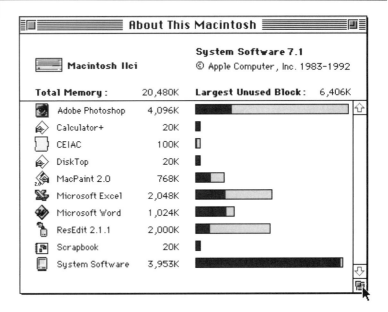

It's nice to be able to monitor the exact amount of
RAM reserved by each application. But it would be even
nicer to see exactly how much of the reserved RAM is being
used and exactly how much remains free. The dark horizontal
bar to the right of each application in the About This
Macintosh dialog box gives you a feel for this information,
but there are times when a numerical value would be more
helpful. Well, you're in luck. As shown in Figure 9.15,
numerical values accurate to within 1K can be displayed
using System 7's built-in help function. Choose the Show
Balloons command from the Help menu. Then position
your cursor over the desired application bar. The help
balloon will itemize the purpose of the bar, and list the space
reserved and the space used by the corresponding
application.

FIGURE 9.15

*C*hoose the Show
Balloons command from
the Help menu to display
the exact amount of
memory reserved for and
used by an application. In
this case, Photoshop has
reserved 4MB of
application RAM, but is
only using 1,207K of it.
This leaves almost 3MB of
application RAM to load
additional documents.

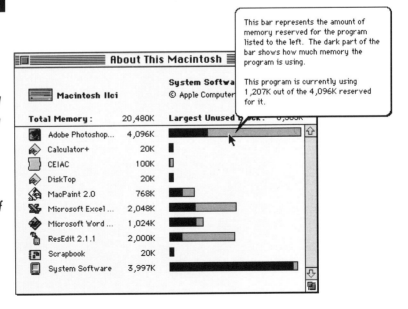

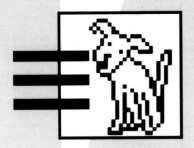

Inside the
System 7–
Savvy Application

I F YOU RAN the Compatibility Checker ▬ before installing System 7, you were no doubt alarmed to see how many of your recent software acquisitions were branded "Mostly compatible," "Must upgrade," or "Not available" (the last indicating that the Checker has not been made aware of a program's existence). The problem with these pronouncements is that they're estimates at best. Even the upgraded Compatibility Checker 2.0 is based not on actual tests conducted by Apple, but on information provided by individual software vendors. At best, the advice provided by the Compatibility Checker is incomplete; on occasion, it's just plain wrong.

If you took the Checker's verdicts with a grain of salt and set about using the new system software as normal, you may have found that the majority of your applications—whether upgraded or not—at least run under System 7. Of course, there are exceptions. Popular utilities such as Adobe Type Manager 1.0, QuicKeys 2.0, and SuitCase II 1.2 are among the long list of old-version control panels and system extensions that simply will not work with System 7 and truly *must* be upgraded. Only a few full-blown applications refuse to launch.

Why should you care? Ideally, you want an application to do more than just run. After all, it did *that* under System 6. The best applications support specific functions that are new to System 7. Some notable programs that are System 7-savvy include:

- **Accountant, Inc. 2.2.** Accounting program from Softsync/BLOC.

- **Adobe Illustrator 3.2.** PostScript drawing program from Adobe Systems.

- **Canvas 3.0.** QuickDraw drawing program from Deneba.

- **Claris Resolve 1.0.** Spreadsheet program from Claris.

- **ColorStudio 1.5.** Image-editing application from Letraset.

- **FileMaker Pro 2.0.** File management program from Claris.

- **Fourth Dimension 2.2.** Database management program from ACIUS.

- **FreeHand 3.1.** PostScript drawing program from Aldus.

- **GreatWorks 1.0.** Integrated software from Symantec.

- **HyperCard 2.1.** Hypertext program from Claris.

- **Lotus 1-2-3/Mac 1.0.** Spreadsheet program from Lotus.

- **MacWrite Pro 1.0.** Word processor from Claris.

- **MacProject 2.5.** Project-management software from Claris.

- **Microsoft Excel 4.0.** Spreadsheet program from Microsoft.

- **Microsoft Word 5.0.** Word processor from Microsoft.

- **PageMaker 5.0.** Page-layout application from Aldus.

- **Photoshop 2.5.** Image-editing application from Adobe Systems.

- **PixelPaint Professional 2.0.** Color paint program from SuperMac.

- **QuarkXPress 3.2.** Page-layout application from Quark.

- **Quicken 3.0.** Financial management program from Intuit.

- **Supercard 1.6.** Hypertext program from Aldus.
- **WordPerfect 2.1.** Word processor from WordPerfect.

An application that works reliably under System 7 is said to be *System 7-compatible*. However, an application that takes full advantage of new system software capabilities is deemed *System 7-savvy* (or the less flashy *System 7-friendly*). To be System 7-savvy, an application must provide *all* of the following:

- **Balloon help.** You should be able to choose the Show Balloons command from the Help menu or use Helium (included on the disks that you can order with the coupon found at the back of this book) to display pop-up information about tools, commands, and options.
- **TrueType.** A System 7-savvy application not only displays and prints TrueType fonts, but allows you to scale a character from 1 to 32,000 points in single point increments.
- **Publish and subscribe.** The most versatile of System 7's inside-application features is the *Edition Manager*, which allows you to store "live" documents to disk and share them with other applications. I'll discuss this feature in depth later in this chapter.
- **Apple events.** System 7-savvy applications can talk to each other and share features using the new *Inter-Application Communication* protocol. IAC is the subject of Chapter 11.
- **32-bit addressing.** A savvy application is 32-bit clean. When using the Memory control panel's "32-Bit Addressing" option (described in the previous chapter), an application should run without problems.

Those are the five official criteria. However, when purchasing an application, you'll want to dig a little deeper. Does it open stationery pads as untitled documents and can it save stationery pads to disk? Can it perform time-consuming operations in the background, allowing you to make more efficient use of your time by working in other foreground applications? Can it be shared over a network (as discussed in Chapter 12), and can it read and write data stored on shared volumes? To be perfectly honest, I've seen few applications that satisfy all of these requirements, though more are coming out every day. However, all criteria should be considered important for your enjoying an application and fully exploiting the capabilities of System 7.

GETTING STARTED

In this section, I'll discuss the document selection and document destination dialog boxes. Both are generic dialog box types provided with System 7 for use inside any application. But since it is the job of each application to implement these dialog boxes, you will find that their appearances vary from one application to another. However, with the exception of the New Folder button and stationery pad options, all applications provide the options discussed in the following pages.

OPENING A DOCUMENT

Every application is filled with its share of unique commands and features. However, some routines are shared between virtually all Macintosh applications. The opening and saving of documents is a good example. When you choose the Open... command from an application's File menu (⌘-O), the *document selection dialog box* appears, requesting that you locate and select the existing document that you wish to open. As you can see in Figure 10.1, the document selection dialog box provides a *scrolling icon list* that contains the names of all subfolders in the current folder as well as all files that can be opened in the current application. A small icon to the left of each name indicates whether it represents a document, stationery pad, edition file (as described in the *Learning Fundamental Concepts* section), or folder. Alias names will appear italicized.

The scrolling list may be used as follows:

- **Select an icon.** You select a file or folder by clicking on its name.

- **Select by key entry.** To quickly locate a specific icon name, you can enter the first few letters of the icons name from the keyboard. The first icon name that begins with these

FIGURE 10.1

The document selection dialog box allows you to open or import a document into the current application. You should note that this dialog box may vary in appearance from one application to the next.

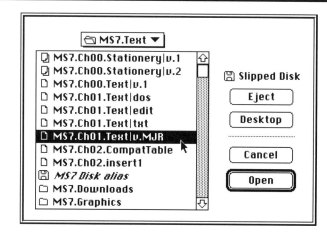

letters will be selected in alphabetical order. (Any typing performed in the document selection dialog does not appear on screen.)

- **Scroll through the list.** You press the ↑ key to select the icon directly above the currently selected icon. You press the ↓ key to select the next icon down. You press and hold either key to scroll up or down the icon list one name at a time. You press the PageUp or PageDown key to scroll up or down several names at a time. Press the Home key to scroll all the way to the top of the list; press the End key to scroll all the way to the bottom.

- **Open an icon.** You open a file or folder by double-clicking its name or by selecting it and pressing the Return key.

- **Open a folder.** If a folder name is selected, you press ⌘-↓ to open that folder and display its contents.

- **Close a folder.** To close the current folder and display the contents of its parent folder (that is, the folder that contains the current folder), you press ⌘-↑. You may also close the current folder by clicking on the disk icon above the Eject button.

Above the scrolling icon list is a *folder bar,* which allows you to open any parent folder. You can drag from the folder bar to display a pop-up menu, as illustrated in Figure 10.2. The name of the current folder will appear first, followed by the name of the folder that contains the current folder, and so on. You choose the desired folder as you would a command; the contents of that folder will display in the scrolling list.

To the right of the scrolling list is the name of the current hard drive, floppy disk, or shared volume. Below the disk name are four buttons. Under System 7, each button has a keyboard equivalent, indicated in parentheses:

- **Eject (⌘-E).** Ejects the current disk from the disk drive. The disk will remain mounted, allowing you to access it later. You should be careful when you eject cartridges and shared folders because these can be difficult to retrieve. If the current disk is a hard drive, the Eject button will appear dimmed.

- **Desktop (⌘-D).** Exits the current folder and displays the contents of the Desktop Folder in the scrolling list. The Desktop Folder is an invisible folder that contains all files and folders displayed on the Finder desktop.

- **Cancel (⌘-Period).** Cancels the Open... operation and returns to the application desktop.

FIGURE 10.2

You drag from the folder bar to display the contents of parent folders.

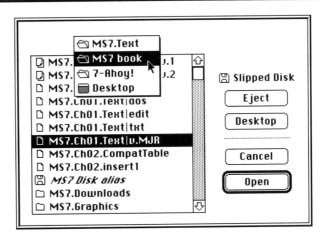

- **Open (⌘-O).** Opens the select file or folder icon. The fact that the Open button is surrounded by a heavy outline shows that it can also be activated by pressing the Return or Enter key.

I P

If you are familiar with previous versions of the Macintosh system software, you will notice that the Desktop button appears in place of the old Drive button. However, while the Drive button may be gone, its functionality remains. Under System 7, you can switch from one drive to another from the keyboard. You press ⌘-→ to display the root directory of the next mounted disk. You press ⌘-← to display the contents of the previous mounted disk.

SAVING A DOCUMENT

When you choose the Save (⌘-S) or Save As... command from an application's File menu, the *document destination dialog box* appears, as shown in Figure 10.3. This dialog box requires that you name the

FIGURE 10.3

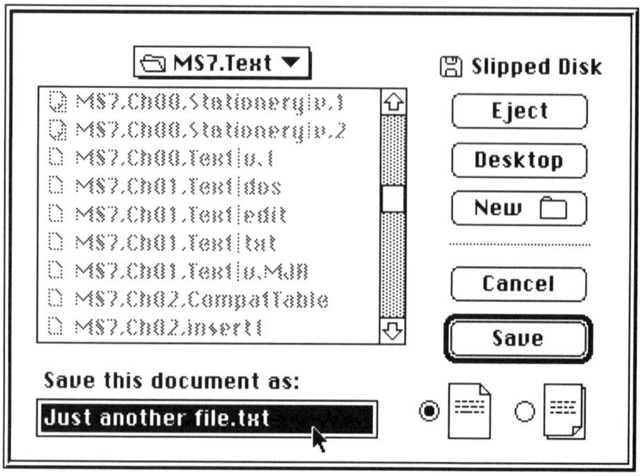

The document destination dialog box allows you to save or export a document to disk. In this example, the dialog box is shown as it appears when the "Save" option box is active.

⌐ MS7.Text ▼

☑ MS7.Ch00.Stationery|v.1
☑ MS7.Ch00.Stationery|v.2
▢ MS7.Ch00.Text|v.1
▢ MS7.Ch01.Text|dos
▢ MS7.Ch01.Text|edit
▢ MS7.Ch01.Text|txt
▢ MS7.Ch01.Text|v.MJB
▢ MS7.Ch02.CompatTable
▢ MS7.Ch02.insert1

💾 Slipped Disk

[Eject]
[Desktop]
[New 📁]

[Cancel]
[Save]

Save this document as:
[Just another file.txt]

current document and determine its location. As you can see in the document selection dialog box, a scrolling icon list shows the names of all files and subfolders in the current folder. File names appear dimmed because they may not be selected. Folder names appear black so that they may be selected and opened.

When you first display the document destination dialog box, the "Save" option box in the lower-left corner is active. You can enter a file name (up to 32 characters) under which you want to store the current document.

If you click on the scroll bar or anywhere inside the scrolling list, you activate the scrolling list and deactivate the "Save" option box. A heavy line surrounds the active scrolling list, as shown in Figure 10.4. Text entered from the keyboard now has no effect on the current document name; rather, it scrolls the display of existing file names, as when you enter characters in the document selection dialog box. When a folder name is selected, you may press ⌘-↓ to open that folder. You press ⌘-↑ to close the current folder and display the contents of the parent folder. You may also use the PageUp, PageDown, Home, and End keys to scroll through icon names in the active list.

FIGURE 10.4

The document destination dialog box as it appears when the scrolling list is active.

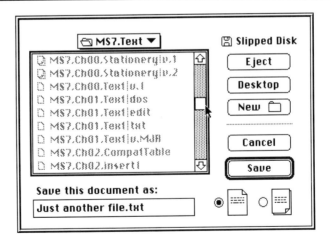

> **You press the Tab key to toggle back and forth between the activation of the "Save" option box and the scrolling icon list.**

The folder bar allows you to ascend the folder hierarchy just as it does in the document selection dialog box. The Eject, Desktop, and Cancel buttons also work identically to their document-selection counterparts. They even react to the same keyboard equivalents. The two unique document-destination buttons work as follows:

- **New Folder (⌘-N).** Creates a new subfolder in the current folder. Upon clicking the New Folder button, you are asked to name the prospective folder, as shown in Figure 10.5. If you find that many or even most of your applications are missing this button, don't be alarmed. It's merely another indication of a lack of System 7-savvy.

- **Save (⌘-S).** Saves the current document under the name specified in the "Save" option box. If no name has been entered, the Save button appears dimmed. If a folder icon is selected in the scrolling list, the Save button temporarily changes to an Open button (which is the reason that the button also reacts to pressing ⌘-O, even when labeled "Save"). The fact that the Save button is surrounded by a heavy outline shows that it can also be activated by pressing the Return or Enter key.

FIGURE 10.5

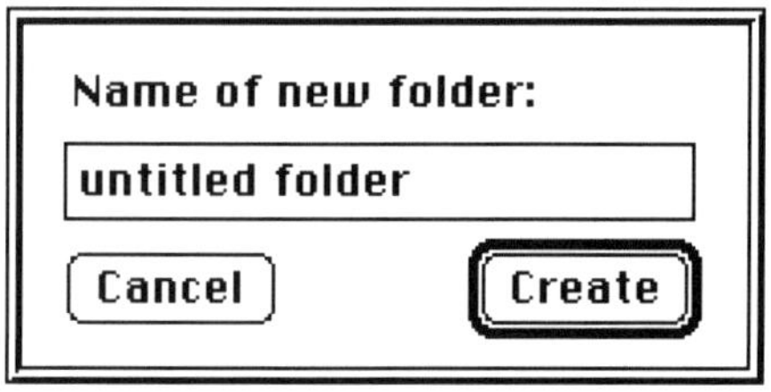

System 7-savvy applications now include a button that lets you create and name a new folder before saving a document.

Name of new folder:

untitled folder

Cancel   Create

The two icons in the lower-right corner of the dialog box allow you to save a document as a standard document file or as a stationery pad that will open in an untitled window. (Stationery pads are covered in Chapter 8.)

If you try to save a document under a name already taken by an existing document, stationery pad, edition file, or alias in the current folder, the message shown in Figure 10.6 will appear, asking whether you want to replace the existing file. You click the Replace button to over-write the existing file; click Cancel or press Return to cancel the save operation and return to the document destination dialog box. (You may not save over an existing folder.)

FIGURE 10.6

A Macintosh application will warn you before it saves over an existing file.

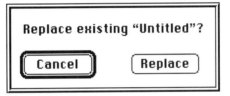

If you close a document or quit an application without saving the most recent changes made to the current file, the message shown in Figure 10.7 will appear, warning you that you are about to toast some hard work. To save your changes, you click the Save button or press Return. To close the file without saving, you click the Don't Save button. You click Cancel or press ⌘-Period to return to the document window without closing the file or saving it. Canceling is especially useful if you want to use the Save As... command to change the name or location of a file.

FIGURE 10.7

You are also warned if you try to close a document without saving the most recent changes.

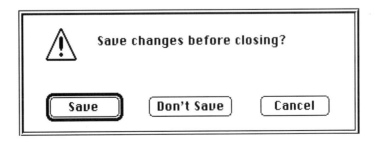

LEARNING FUNDAMENTAL CONCEPTS

System 7's most powerful addition to the capabilities of a savvy application is the *Edition Manager,* which permits you to save a detail in one document, import the detail into another document, and automatically update the imported detail any time you make changes to the original. By using this feature, you may create "live" links between documents so that a single update to, say, a year-end sales spreadsheet is automatically reflected in the yearly earnings bar chart, the annual growth line chart, the departmental share pie chart, and all three charts as featured in the annual report. So now when someone hands you a last-minute addition that affects 19 different documents and asks, "This won't be a problem, will it?" you won't have to go through the lengthy process of explaining how it is in fact a *huge* problem as you watch his or her eyes glaze over. You can put on a brave face and announce, "Not for *me* it isn't," knowing all the while that you're looking at 15 minutes of work, tops. It's another example of computers finally operating as you always dreamed they would.

MEET THE EDITION MANAGER

When the Mac first made its big splash in the Year of our Orwell, 1984, one of its most desirable features was the Clipboard. Although it's taken largely for granted nowadays, the Clipboard allowed users to copy a selected word or graphic from one document and paste it into another. Any character, word, paragraph, image, or combination of the four could be duplicated, traded between applications, or stored in the Scrapbook for later use.

One big problem with the Clipboard is that it provides no link between the original text or graphic and the duplicate. Updating the original does not update the duplicate. The Edition Manager remedies this problem by allowing you to export text and graphic to an *edition file* on disk, import the file into another document in the same or a different application, and update the imported edition every time the original is updated.

Another problem with the Clipboard is that you can't share its contents over a network. Oh sure, you can copy an element, paste it into the Scrapbook, and copy the Scrapbook to a shared folder, from which another user can copy the Scrapbook to his or her System Folder, open the Scrapbook file, copy the element, and paste it. However, that's more work than simply sharing the document from which the original element was copied! What I'm saying here—for those of you who are more confused than when you started this paragraph—is that you cannot simply copy an element and share your Clipboard for other users to access.

Again, the Edition Manager triumphs in this area. After exporting text and/or graphics to an edition file, the file may be shared over a network and imported into an open document by any networked user. If you make a change to the original edition and update it on disk, all imported versions of the edition will update automatically across all machines that share the edition file. Documents that are currently closed but linked to the edition file will update when they are opened. Imagine a writer, a designer, and a layout person simultaneously working on stages of a single magazine page over three different networked machines. The layout person integrates last-minute editorial changes from the writer and juggles art and photo submissions from the designer as they occur with no lag time whatsoever. An imported line of text at the top of the page might even carry written instructions from the designer that update periodically. The possibilities are endless.

PUBLISH AND SUBSCRIBE

Any understanding of the Clipboard hinges on a familiarity with three fundamental operations: *cut, copy,* and *paste.* To cut an element is to remove it from the document and store it in the Clipboard; to copy an element is to store a duplicate of the element in the Clipboard; and to paste an element is to retrieve a copy of the contents of the Clipboard and store it in the current document. All three operations correspond to commands in the Edit menu.

Likewise, to use Edition Manager, you must understand how to *publish* and how to *subscribe.* To publish a selection, you export it to disk in the form of an edition file. To subscribe to an edition file, you import the contents of the file into the current document.

Like cut, copy, and paste, the publish and subscribe operations correspond to commands under the Edit menu. Unfortunately, these commands are not implemented as consistently as their Clipboard counterparts from one application to another. Generally, you will find three primary Edition Manager commands in any System 7-savvy program. These are Create Publisher..., Subscribe To..., and Publisher/Subscriber Options....

Publishing an Edition File

To publish a portion of a document, you first select the text and graphic elements that you want to export to disk. Next, you choose the Create Publisher... command from the Edit menu to display the *edition destination dialog box,* that is shown in Figure 10.8. The selected elements will appear in the "Preview" area on the left side of the dialog box, allowing you to confirm the items you intend to publish. You enter a name for the edition file into the "Name of new edition" option box. You use the Eject, Desktop, New Folder, and Cancel commands as described for the document destination dialog box earlier in this chapter. You click the Publish button or press Return to save the edition file to disk.

An edition file is typically stored in the PICT format, but some applications allow you to publish edition files in the TIFF, EPS, text-only, and RTF formats as well. No doubt additional formats will gain support in the future.

An element saved to disk as an edition file is called a *publisher.* A light gray border may surround the publisher to distinguish it from other elements in the current document. Depending on the current application, you may be able to display or hide this border using a Show/Hide Borders command.

FIGURE 10.8

You choose the Create Publisher... command (left) to display the edition destination dialog box (right), which allows you to create a new edition file (bottom).

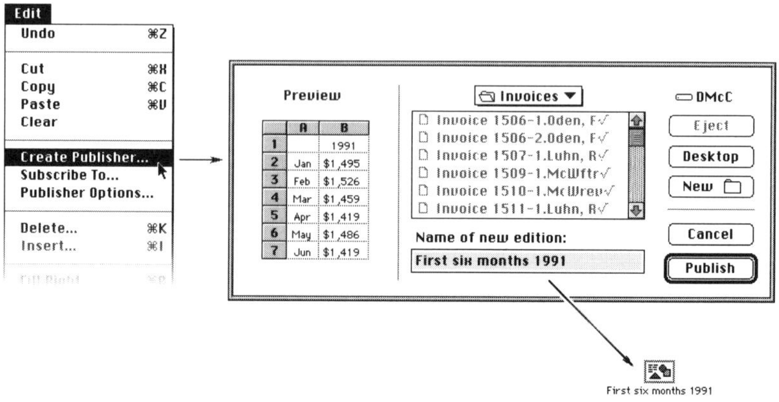

First six months 1991

> After publishing one or more edition files, be sure to save the current document to disk using the Save command. In many applications, creating a publisher is not enough to ensure its existence on disk. If you don't save the current document, the edition file will be abandoned.

Subscribing to an Edition File

To subscribe to an existing edition file stored on disk, you choose the Subscribe To... command from the Edit menu. The *edition selection dialog box* will appear, as shown in Figure 10.9. You locate and select the edition file to which you want to subscribe by using the scrolling list, folder bar, and the Eject and Desktop buttons (the document selection dialog box was described earlier in this chapter). The contents of the selected edition file will appear in the "Preview" area on the left side of the dialog box. You click the Subscribe button or press ⌘–S or Return to import the selected edition into the current document.

An imported edition element is called a *subscriber.* A dark gray border may surround the subscriber to distinguish it from other elements in the current document. Depending on the current application, you may be able to display or hide this border using a Show/Hide Borders command.

FIGURE 10.9

You choose the Subscribe To... command (left) to display the edition selection dialog box (right).

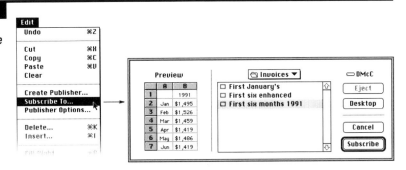

Edition File Options

The third edition file command allows you to set options pertaining to the selected edition element. If you have selected a publisher, you may choose the Publisher Options... command to display the *publisher options* dialog box shown in Figure 10.10. This dialog box contains the following options:

- **Publisher to.** You use this pop-up menu to determine the location of the publisher element's edition file on disk. You may not alter the path of the file; you may only look at it.

- **Send Editions.** You use these options to specify when the edition file on disk is updated. When "On Save" is selected, the edition file updates every time you save the current document to disk. If you select "Manually," the edition file updates only when you click the Send Edition Now button. A line of text appears below the radio button, displaying the last time the edition file was updated. If the "Manually" option is selected, a second line of text tells when the publisher element was last manipulated.

- **Cancel Publisher.** You click this button to destroy the link between publisher and edition file. An alert message will appear, confirming that you want to remove the publisher; (convert the publisher into a standard element). The edition file remains on disk, but the link between the edition file and the current document is erased.

When you click the Cancel Publisher, Cancel, or OK buttons, you exit the publisher options dialog box.

FIGURE 10.10

*Y*ou choose the Publisher Options... command (left) to display the publisher options dialog box (right).

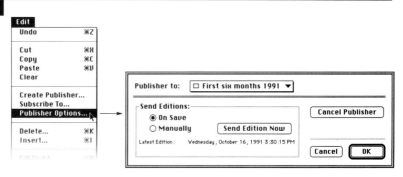

If you select a subscriber, the Publisher Options... command changes to a Subscriber Options... command. You choose this command to display the *subscriber options* dialog box shown in Figure 10.11.

- **Subscriber to.** You use this pop-up menu to determine the location of the subscriber element's edition file on disk. You may not alter the path of the file; you may only look at it.

- **Get Editions.** You use these options to tell the current application when to update the selected subscriber. If "Automatically" is selected, the subscriber updates any time a change is made to its corresponding edition file. If the edition file is changed while the current document is closed, the subscriber will update the next time the document is opened. If you select "Manually," the subscriber updates only when you click the Get Edition Now button. A line of text appears below the radio buttons, displaying the last time the edition file was saved to disk. If the "Manually" option is selected, a second line of text tells when the subscriber was last updated.

- **Cancel Subscriber.** You click this button to destroy the link between subscriber and edition file. An alert message will appear, confirming that you want to remove the subscriber; (convert the subscriber into a standard element). The edition file remains on disk, but the link between the edition file and the current document is erased.

- **Open Publisher.** You click this button to open the document that contains the publisher used to create the edition file

FIGURE 10.11

You choose the Subscriber Options... command (left) to display the subscriber options dialog box (right).

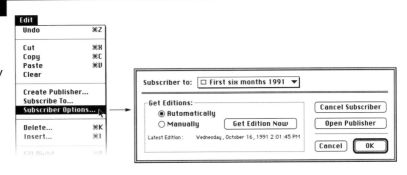

for the selected subscriber. If necessary, the application used to create the document will launch; if not, it will switch to the foreground. The document is then opened and scrolled to the location of the publisher, which will appear selected.

By clicking the Cancel Subscriber, Open Publisher, Cancel, or OK buttons, you exit the subscriber options dialog box.

> **In many applications, you may quickly access the publisher options dialog box by double-clicking a publisher element. Likewise, you may display the subscriber options dialog box by double-clicking a subscriber. To open the document that contains a subscriber's publisher, you press the Option key while double-clicking a subscriber element. (These shortcuts do not work in all applications.)**

*M*AKING CHANGES TO AN EDITION

Typically, you may perform only limited alterations to a subscriber inside the subscribing document. Some examples include the following:

- **Move the subscriber.** Any application that supports the Edition Manager will let you reposition a subscriber on the page.

- **Reformat text.** If the application permits formatting, you will probably be allowed to change the font, type size, and style of all text in the subscriber.

- **Resize the subscriber.** You drag the corner handle of a subscriber to stretch it or reduce it in size. You shift-drag a corner handle to resize the subscriber proportionally.

- **Crop the subscriber.** A word processor or desktop publishing program may let you crop a subscriber to hide portions of the element.

More serious alterations—such as coloring an image, adding lines to a drawing, or fixing typographical errors in text—must be performed on the original publisher element. This document may be opened from inside a subscribing document by clicking the Open Publisher button in the subscriber options dialog box.

At the Finder level, you may open a publisher document as follows: Double-click the edition file that you want to edit. A window will appear, displaying the contents of the edition file, as shown in Figure 10.12. At the bottom of the window are listed the format or formats used to save the current edition file and an Open Publisher button which, when clicked, opens the original document that contains the publisher.

The publisher cannot be opened if the original document that contains the publisher has been removed or deleted. Deleting an original document, however, does not cause the deletion of an edition file.

FIGURE 10.12

You double-click an edition file at the Finder level to display its contents and access the Open Publisher button.

First six months 1991

	A	B
1		1991
2	Jan	$1,495
3	Feb	$1,526
4	Mar	$1,459
5	Apr	$1,419
6	May	$1,486
7	Jun	$1,419

TEXT BIFF RTF ...   **Open Publisher**

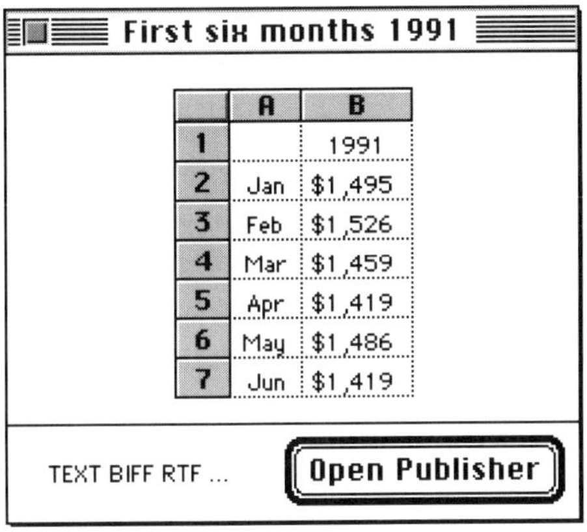

EXPLORING ADVANCED TOPICS

That's it so far as Apple's contribution to the world of System 7-savviness is concerned. But that doesn't have to be where it ends. If you're willing to invest a few of your hard-earned nickels in a couple of application enhancing utilities, you'll find your money well invested. My recommendations for the best savviness boosters are Traffic Controller from Tactic Software, Super Boomerang from Now Software, and Shortcut from

Aladdin Systems. The first program enhances your ability to use and maintain edition files. The second and third improve the speed at which you can locate and open files by adding options to any navigation dialog box. All three programs are discussed in the following pages.

MONITORING EDITION TRAFFIC

Traffic Controller includes a system extension to monitor the creation and alteration of edition files as well as a program for organizing them. When first launched, you may instruct the Traffic Controller program to search for each and every edition file contained on one or more hard drives. If any disks are aliased on the selected hard drive, they will be searched as well. Next, Traffic Controller displays a window showing three columns, one for documents that contain publishers, one for linked edition files, and a third column for documents that contain subscribers. On-screen lines connect publishers to their edition files and edition files to their subscribers.

You can find out more information about a single publisher, edition file, or subscriber by displaying the Thread window that is shown in Figure 10.13. Here you may view an entire "family" of linked documents; that is, you can view all documents related to a single publisher, edition

---

FIGURE 10.13

The Thread window allows you to view a family of linked documents, delete stray edition files, or resolve discrepancies between linked documents.

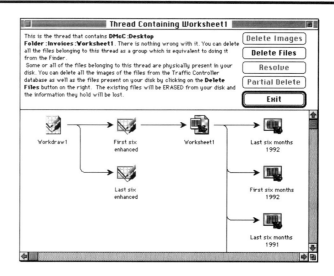

file, or subscriber. If an edition file has been orphaned due to the deletion of its publisher or through the duplication of the edition file at the Finder level, the Thread window provides options that may be used to delete the orphan or relink it to a former publisher.

If you need to figure out whether an edition file is likely to be compatible with a prospective subscriber, you may use the Traffic Controller program to display detailed information about a selected file. As you can see in Figure 10.14, the Information window shows a preview of the edition followed by its path. Below this is a list of file formats supported by the current edition file. To be strictly compatible, a subscribing application needs to support at least one of the formats contained in the edition file. If you're interested in retaining text formatting, as when importing

FIGURE 10.14

The Information window shows all file formats contained in the current edition file.

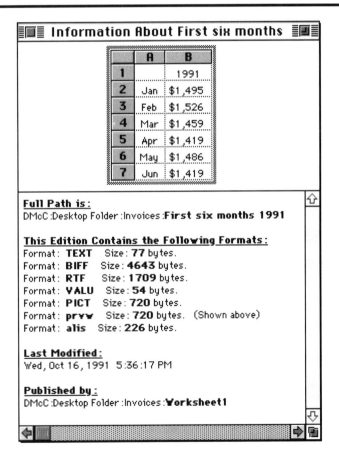

text into a word processor or desktop publishing program, check to see that an edition file offers RTF (rich text format) or some similar formatting code.

Traffic Controller also lets you track multiple versions of a single edition file saved at different times. This can be extremely useful if you need to document the creation of an in-house newsletter or other publication. If a previous version of an edition file is preferable to the most recent version, you may unlink the new one and relink the old one. Finally, you may time- and date-stamp edition files and print catalogs of linked files contained on a specified disk.

NAVIGATING THROUGH FOLDERS

When traveling the byways of the hierarchical file system, nothing beats a navigation utility like Super Boomerang or Shortcut. Distributed as a control panel, Super Boomerang adds a menu along the top of all navigation dialog boxes, which include the document selection, document destination, edition selection, and edition destination dialog boxes. As shown in Figure 10.15, this menu tracks the location of recently visited folders and files. To expedite the location of frequently used files and folders, you may instruct Super Boomerang to remember certain icons

---

FIGURE 10.15

Super Boomerang adds a menu across the top of dialog boxes, allowing you to navigate through folders more quickly.

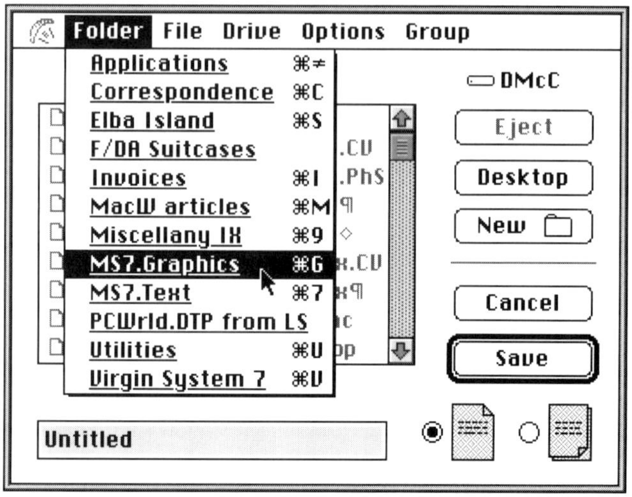

permanently. You may also assign keystrokes that open files or take you directly to specified folders. A "Rebound" feature automatically advances the scrolling file list to the last document opened.

All in all, Super Boomerang is my idea of the perfect navigational aid. But if you're a heavy-duty StuffIt user or you're simply looking for something a little less expensive, you might prefer the competing control panel, Shortcut. While it lacks Super Boomerang's straightforward menu bar and it doesn't allow you to assign keystrokes to files and folders, there's a lot to like about Shortcut. It provides a Fast Find... command for locating files and folders without having to return to the Finder, as demonstrated in Figure 10.16. It allows you to display information about a file and even change its type and creator codes. You can also send a file to the Trash folder, empty the Trash, or even "shred" a file, which deletes it entirely so it cannot be recovered. Finally, you may examine the contents of StuffIt files, as well as unstuff and stuff documents on the fly.

Depending on your preferences, either Super Boomerang or Shortcut should be considered a must addition to any power user's library.

FIGURE 10.16

Shortcut adds a Fast Find... command to any navigation dialog box (left) which allows you to search files, folders, and the contents of StuffIt files (right).

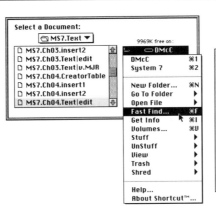

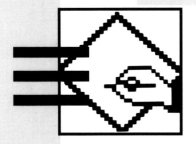

Inter-Application Communication—the Future of the MacProgram Integration

MACHINES MAKE YOUR life easier by replicating tasks. Take a lawn mower, for example. The mower engine rotates the cutting blade at a consistent speed and angle, clipping each blade of grass at the same length as the blade that precedes it. The result is a uniform lawn that looks for all the world like wall-to-wall carpeting. Compare that to the prospect of cutting your lawn manually using a scythe and you may perhaps gain a greater appreciation for the immense wonders of suburbia.

By contrast, computers help you to perform tasks by replicating data, whether that data comprises numbers, text, graphics, or all three. If you want to use a single graphic to illustrate two different documents, you don't have to draw it twice. Having drawn it once, you can paste it onto as many pages as you wish. And if others want to use that same graphic in their documents, you can share the graphic without any sacrifice to the appearance or integrity of the original.

In the previous chapter, I introduced the idea of replicating and sharing data using Clipboard commands and Edition Manager functions. Both features allow you to share data created in one document with another document, application, or user. However, copying and publishing represent only the tip of the sharing iceberg. In these last two chapters, I'll concentrate on two additional and ultimately more versatile sharing techniques supported by System 7. In this chapter, you'll learn how to share data stored in RAM, called *Inter-Application Communication* (or IAC as it is known to the acronymologists). In Chapter 12, I'll explain how you may share data stored on disk, a technique called *file sharing*.

Look who's talking, Version 7

Inter-Application Communication is too pompous to sound like anything more than an inflated and intentionally incomprehensible excuse for a new acronym. However, it's actually a straightforward concept. IAC provides an environment in which programs may communicate with each other and share not only data, but also capabilities.

For example, suppose you're conducting a seminar in Pittsburg. At the end of every day's class, you are required to modem attendance lists and performance evaluations to your employer's home base in San Jose. On top of it all, your employer is notoriously cheap, allotting you a painfully tight traveling budget. Rather than complain, you've managed a solution that cuts down on long-distance charges, which is one of your biggest expenses. Prior to connecting with the home office, you instruct your communications software—say, MicroPhone II 4.0 II—to compress the files, thus reducing your long-distance charges by about 50%. However, though powerful in a variety of areas, MicroPhone II provides no compression capabilities. Instead, the software has to rely on a dedicated compression utility—say StuffIt Deluxe 3.0—as follows: MicroPhone automatically launches the StuffIt Deluxe application, and instructs StuffIt to read the file from disk, compress it into a single document, and store it back to disk. MicroPhone II then quits StuffIt Deluxe, calls the home office, uploads the compressed document, and hangs up. By virtue of the fact that MicroPhone II can communicate with and request capabilities from StuffIt Deluxe, the software has saved you time, effort, and money.

Getting started

Before I lead you any farther down the garden path, let me warn you that there's very little hands-on experience to be gained from reading this chapter. System 7 provides options that control program-to-program communication over a network; you can send a few rinky-dink commands back and forth between System 7-savvy programs. For now, unfortunately, the benefits of IAC are more theoretical than real.

However, even a beginner—and who of us *isn't* a beginner when it comes to this topic?—can benefit by knowing what the future of Macintosh software will bring. So read on if you're interested, skip it if you're not, come back later if you aren't ready. This chapter won't be going anywhere without you.

THE INNER WORKINGS OF IAC

In the broadest sense, IAC is any form of communication and data swapping that occurs between two documents or applications. The following capabilities are the four levels of IAC that may one day be supported and exploited by all System 7-savvy applications:

- **Clipboard functions.** Although the term Inter-Application Communication didn't exist seven years ago, the Clipboard did. It was the first and it remains the most prevalent way in which documents can share information.

- **The Edition Manager.** Described in the previous chapter, the Edition Manager allows you to create "live" links between documents. One document publishes an edition file and a second document subscribes to it. Each time the publisher is altered, the subscriber is updated to reflect the changes.

- **Apple events.** Every application creates its own little world. It offers unique commands, tools, and options, performs unique operations, and handles data in its own special way. But when applications start talking to each other, they can't all speak in different tongues. *Apple events,* introduced with System 7, standardizes the translation of data between programs by providing a handful of routines that may be sent and retrieved between commercial applications and the Finder.

- **Scripted events.** Using Apple events, you can communicate through one program to another. But to get the most out of the multitasking environment, you need to be able to communicate with applications directly using a *scripting language.* Imagine being able to set up strings of operations that involve multiple applications. Whether or not these applications can communicate with each other, you could create scripted routines that act as translators and even control the actions of various applications from a centralized location, such as the Finder. Because scripting verges on programming, it will be of most interest to advanced users. But it will also permit programmers to set up customized workstations that can be exploited by any user regardless of experience. For the personal user, bulletin boards will no doubt carry libraries of scripted utilities that call up isolated features from the Finder and other applications.

The Clipboard and the Editions Manager are covered in the previous chapter. Apple events is the subject of this and the *Learning Fundamental Concepts* sections of this chapter. If you're feeling very adventurous, you can read the *Exploring Advanced Topics* section for an overview of scripted events.

PROGRAM LINKING

To share data, two programs must support Apple events and they must be permitted to communicate. This communication, called *program linking,* is always permitted between two programs that are running on the same Macintosh computer under System 7. However, when running programs on different machines connected via a network (as discussed in Chapter 12), communication can be turned on and off. (Note that if you're working on a stand-alone Mac that is *not* connected to other computers, this isn't an issue, in which case you may want to skip this section and move on to *Learning Fundamental Concepts.*)

For example, suppose you're using Microsoft Excel while other users on different Macs are sharing data stored on your hard drive. Do you want them to be able to access the data that you're currently manipulating in Excel? Do you want them to be able to borrow some of Excel's capabilities to augment their programs, thus slowing Excel's performance on your machine? Your answers to these questions depend on your circumstances. If the data you're currently manipulating is classified, then the answer is no and you'll want to turn program linking off. If you and an associate are working on a project simultaneously and you need to be able to share data back and forth, the answer is yes and you'll want to turn program linking on.

By default, program linking is turned off. To turn it on, you open the Sharing Setup control panel and then click the Start button in the "Program Linking" area at the bottom of the Sharing Setup window, as shown in Figure 11.1. The Start button will toggle to a Stop button and the message inside the "Status" box will change to read, "Program linking is on. Click Stop to prevent other users from linking to your shared programs."

Click the close box to close the Sharing Setup control panel. The "Program Linking" option will remain on, even if you restart your machine, until the next time you turn the option off.

The "Program Linking" option as it appears when turned off (top) and when turned on (bottom).

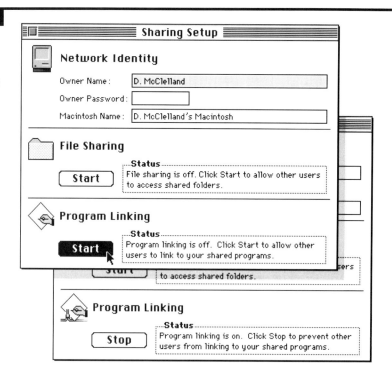

Selective Program Linking

Once "Program Linking" has been initiated, remote users may access data and capabilities from any program on your machine. However, you may prefer to relegate which applications are allowed to communicate and which are not on a program by program basis. For example, suppose you plan on using Microsoft Excel heavily throughout the day, but you won't be relying as heavily on Claris Resolve. To prevent slow downs, you can turn off program linking for Excel only, while leaving Resolve's capabilities to be accessed by remote users. The following text explains how to deactivate and activate program linking for specific applications.

After activating the "Program Linking" option in the Sharing Setup control panel, you may selectively allow and disallow applications to be accessed by remote users. Select the desired application icon and choose the Sharing… command from the File menu. A window similar to the one shown in Figure 11.2 will appear. A single option is offered in the form of the "Allow remote program linking" check box. By default, the option is checked allowing the selected application to talk with other applications over a network. Deselect the option to discontinue communication with the selected application only.

Note that turning on and off program linking, whether for a single program or for an entire machine, affects only whether or not remote users can access *your* applications. It does *not* affect whether or not you may access programs on other machines. For example, even though you turned off program linking for Microsoft Excel, you may still use Excel to gather data and capabilities from a program on another computer.

The Sharing… command may not be applied to desk accessories, control panels, or system extensions since data from these types of utilities may not be shared. Furthermore, program linking for a selected

---

FIGURE 11.2

Use the "Allow remote program linking" option to activate and deactivate program linking for a single application.

application may be turned on and off only if: 1) the program is *not* running and 2) the "Program Linking" option in the Sharing Setup control panel has been activated. If program linking has not yet been initiated for the current machine when you try to apply the Sharing... command to an application, the message shown in Figure 11.3 will appear, preventing you from adjusting the setting of the current application until machine-wide program sharing is turned on.

You can also control which users can share data and capabilities from applications on your machine. This and other information on controlling the degree of access allowed to remote users is the subject of the following chapter.

FIGURE 11.3

This message appears if you choose the Sharing... command before initiating program linking for the current machine.

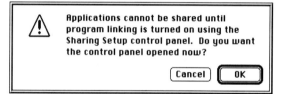

Learning Fundamental Concepts

Once you've established program linking (if necessary), how do you use it? The answer to this question varies from one application to another. At this stage in the game, there aren't enough programs supporting IAC to put together any kind of universal guidelines. Instead, I'll discuss some broad IAC characteristics. I'll also demonstrate how IAC can be put to work using HyperCard 2.1 in combination with a savvy application, such as the spreadsheet program Claris Resolve (both sold separately).

Apple Events

Apple events include four categories of messages, called *events,* that may be transmitted between applications, including the Finder. Each category serves as a hallmark of System 7-savviness. For example, if a product supports required events, but not core events (both defined below), it is just barely System 7-savvy. It will be able to receive messages from the Finder, but it won't be able to communicate with other applications on any meaningful level. The applications that will share information most adequately will support at least the first three of the four events categories described below.

Note that the following discussions are not intended to serve as a guide to actually implementing Apple events. This is the job of your specific application. Rather, these introductions are designed to help you understand how the events work and to recognize the capabilities offered by any software you may intend to purchase for use with System 7. Also, a lack of support for Apple events does not in any way prevent a program from running under System 7. It merely prevents the program from communicating with System 7-savvy applications.

Required events   *Required events* include four simple messages that must be recognized by any savvy application:

- **Open Application.** When received, this event causes an application to launch, just as if you had double-clicked the application icon at the Finder level. This event also initializes an application's event support, allowing it to receive and interpret additional events.

- **Open Documents.** This event instructs an application to open a specified document. If an application can open more than one document at a time, the event may request that multiple documents be opened.

- **Print Documents.** This event causes an application to print one or more specified documents without opening them or displaying windows for them. The standard print dialog box will appear, once for each document, to request the number of pages you wish to print.

- **Quit Application.** The receiving program closes all windows, quits, and returns the user to the Finder or to the most recent application displayed on screen. If the most recent changes to an open document have not been saved, a standard "Save changes?" message will appear to warn the user.

When you select a document at the Finder level and choose the Print command from the File menu (⌘-P), you are taking advantage of all four required events. The Open Application event launches the program that was used to create the document; the Open Documents and Print Documents events tell the application to open the selected document and then print it; and when the print operation is complete, the Quit Application event quits the program and returns to the Finder level.

Core events
Core events are a collection of messages that Apple recommends that all System 7-savvy applications support. Unlike the required events, they are not mandatory, but they will enable an application to communicate with a broad range of fellow applications, including those that perform entirely different functions. For example, for a word processor to trade data with a spreadsheet program, both programs need to support core events.

Functional-area events
When two applications offer similar sets of features, they should share support for a collection of *functional-area events*. For example, suppose that you have one program the enables you to edit text, another that checks the spelling of text, and another that examines the use of grammar. All three of these programs fall into the broader category of text-processing applications. To effectively exchange data and share capabilities, all three programs should offer a uniform set of functional-area events that ensure the exchange of formatting attributes, special characters, hyphenation breaks, header and footer identification, footnote markers, and so on.

Custom events
If a single vendor decides to create events to use throughout its own line of applications, these are called *custom events*. By definition, all custom events are registered with Apple. However, whether or not they are published in the *Apple Events Registry* for inclusion with other programs or kept a secret for the proprietary use throughout a vendor's program line is up to the vendor. For example, support for a custom event may be shared by the Claris programs HyperCard, MacProject, and Resolve, but unknown to similar applications from competing vendors such as Microsoft or Aldus.

EVENT SUPPORT

Core events, functional-area events, and custom events are constantly growing in number. Some have been designed by Apple, but many have been suggested by key software vendors. A complete list of these events and the functions they perform is included in a publication distributed to all Macintosh software developers called the *Apple Event Registry*. It is up to each individual development team in charge of creating an application to select which events it will implement and which it will ignore. Therefore, when purchasing a program, it is probably a good idea to ask the vendor for a list of the specific applications with which the program is known to be able to trade data.

For example, HyperCard 2.1 is able the send core events to any System 7-savvy application. To select an application with which you want to communicate from inside HyperCard, first choose the Message command from the Go menu (⌘-M) to display the message window. Then enter the string *answer program* " " into the window and press Return. The Link dialog box shown in Figure 11.4 will appear. If you are working on a network, select the desired computer from the "Macintosh" scrolling list on the left side of the dialog box. All savvy applications that are currently running on that computer will display in the "Programs" list on the right. Select the desired application and click the OK button or press Return.

FIGURE 11.4

*E*nter the string shown in the message window (top) and press the Return key to display the Link dialog box (bottom).

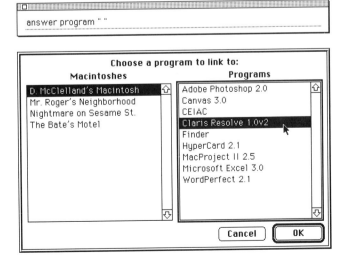

HyperCard puts the selected program name into the variable "it." If you enter the string *put it* into the message window and press Return, the full application name including network path will display.

To send a message to the application, you may enter the string *send [event] to program it* where [event] stands for the HyperCard command equivalent of the event name. For example, suppose you are running Claris Resolve, which is System 7-savvy. When you launch the program, Resolve automatically creates a new window. The following exercise will close that window from inside HyperCard 2.1 and then quit the Resolve application:

1. Bring the HyperCard application to the foreground.

2. Choose the Message command from the Go menu (⌘-M), enter the string *answer program " "*, and press Return. The Link dialog box will display.

3. Select the Claris Resolve application from the "Programs" list, as shown in Figure 11.4, and press Return. This places the network path to Claris Resolve into the "it" variable.

4. Enter the string *send close to the program it* and press Return. You will see the new Resolve window close in the background.

5. Now change the string slightly to *send quit to the program it* and press Return. You will see the Resolve application quit. To confirm, check the Application menu. Notice that the Resolve application is no longer running.

Wow, pretty exciting, huh? Perhaps not, but it does give you a general idea of how Apple events can be put to work on a user level.

EXPLORING ADVANCED TOPICS

If you tried out the previous exercise, you created a *user script.* In other words, you controlled your environment directly using Apple events. Via IAC, System 7 provides the vocabulary for a user to juggle programs and initiate operations using scripts, but it provides no user interface. In the previous exercise, you used HyperCard as an interface. Unfortunately, HyperCard lacks a sufficient number of commands to produce sophisticated results. Also, you cannot use HyperCard to send custom events without a special SendAppleEvent XCMD available to developers.

What's needed is a full-fledged scripting shell. The following are two ideas that are either in the works or presently available.

APPLESCRIPT

Apple has proposed a scripting language called AppleScript which will take advantage of something called the Open Scripting Architecture. AppleScript will enable users to create scripts that manage the Finder desktop and perform multistep operations without a lot of mousing around. Unfortunately, it is not due out until sometime in the dim future.

FRONTIER

In the meantime, a general-purpose scripting program is available now in the form of Frontier from UserLand Software. At its most fundamental level, Frontier is a language application, complete with a compiler, much like Think Pascal. To the nonprogrammer, its organization may prove daunting enough to scare off all but the most intrepid users. However, in a matter of a few hours, I was able to take advantage of a number of Frontier's unique capabilities.

For example, Frontier allows you to edit the Frontier application itself to fit your specific needs. Clicking a Menu Bar button brings up a window of custom menu options. You insert the menus you want to display in the Frontier menu bar and create and script commands that appear inside those menus. As shown in Figure 11.5, command scripts may be remarkably simple. The script used to launch ResEdit, for example, requires only two lines of straightforward code, one that launches the application and another that brings the ResEdit application to the foreground (which in most cases in unnecessary). Figure 11.6 shows the menu created using the options shown in Figure 11.5.

Frontier's scripting window relies on an outlining metaphor. Commands in the Menu Bar window, for example, may be dragged up or down to alter their placement in the menu. You may also demote a command to make it appear in a submenu, or promote a command to form a new menu item.

FIGURE 11.5

Frontier allows you to edit its menu bar by scripting special commands.

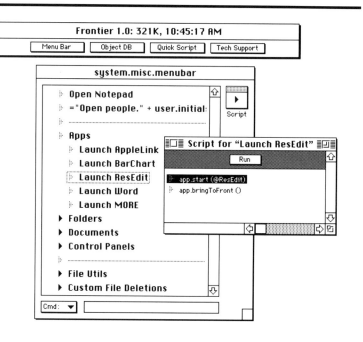

FIGURE 11.6

The result of the command entries shown in the previous figure.

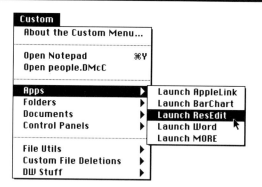

To create your own scripting routine, you add a new "object" to Frontier's scripting database. For example, to create a new application launcher, you may simply enter the string *app.start (@Resolve)* into the Script window (much like the highlighted string shown in Figure 11.5). However, you need to tell Frontier what the term *Resolve* means by creating a new object. As shown in Figure 11.7, an application object

FIGURE 11.7

Frontier allows you to define new scripting routines using the object database.

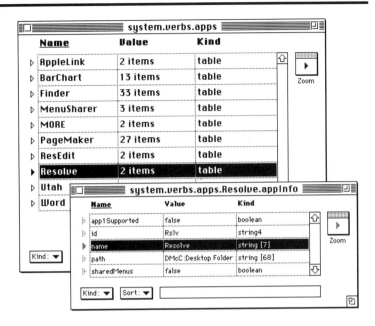

comprises a name, such as *Resolve,* a creator code, in this case *Rslv,* and the path of the application on disk.

Frontier will provide a menu sharing feature that allows you to add menus and commands to any application that supports the feature. The program also comes with a collection of desktop scripts than can be run independently without the use of Frontier. In fact, the Open Folder application included on the disk at the back of this book is an example of a desktop script.

All in all, Frontier appears positioned to make the kind of splash the Macintosh community hasn't witnessed since HyperCard. Truly, it's a remarkable application, something like a programming software, macro utility, and ResEdit all wrapped into one. However, like IAC itself, the success of Frontier will pivot on the support that other vendors provide for the product. And that test may be a long time coming.

SCRIPTING WITH MACROS

Most of us aren't programmers. For this reason, two macros utilities are quickly shaping up to offer users an opportunity to send and receive

Apple events via keystrokes. QuicKeys 2.1 and Tempo II Plus 2.1 will both offer support for Apple events. Since both are provided as control panels, and Apple events cannot be received by keystrokes, both programs come with a broadcaster/receiver utility. The utility that accompanies QuicKeys, CE/IAC, will to be able to share events with *any* control panel or extension. But because of its historic provision of more sophisticated abilities, Tempo is likely to be the more stalwart communicator. For example, you'll be able to send an Apple event to Tempo that tells it to begin recording, run programs or even other macros, and then save the recording to disk. In fact, an Apple event will be able to play or record any macro just as a user would. Tempo will also be able to work in tandem with Frontier: A Frontier script may be used to call a Tempo macro or vice versa. And if an application lacks support for IAC, as is currently the case for most programs, Tempo may serve as an interpreter, performing operations and accessing features that are not available to Frontier.

For now, it's all a big pipe dream. However, I for one have a great deal of faith in IAC. With its potential to link both applications and users together, it seems very likely that its success will determine the future of Macintosh program integration.

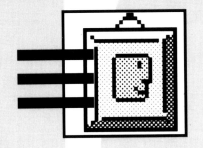

Sharing
Data over
a Network

A LOT HAS BEEN written about the enormous advantages of the System 7 Finder. Aliases, hierarchical folder display, the Apple Menu Items folder, custom icons, and so on are all new to Finder 7. Don't get me wrong, the new Finder is great, but for my money, the most substantial improvement to the new Macintosh system software is built-in *file sharing*. This should come as good news to network users who still rely on Shiva's problematic MacTOPS. Now, for the price of a couple of PhoneNET cables and some telephone wire, you can hook two Macs together and share the contents of your hard drives. You can also share the same printer, share applications, share a backup device… your mother never *dreamed* you'd learn to share so well!

Best of all, it's easy. In fact, it's so easy and so cheap that if you have more than two Macintosh computers within 50 feet of each other, you might as well cable them together to form a *network*. If you're already working on a network, skip to the *Getting Started* section later in this chapter to learn how to use System 7's built-in networking features. If you're not, here are a few reasons to connect:

- **Transferring documents.** Without a network, you transfer files from one computer to another by copying them to a floppy disk and manually handing or flinging that floppy disk to another user, a process euphemistically termed "sneaker net." When computers are networked, files can be transferred by mounting a shared folder from someone else's hard drive and drag-copying the contents to your machine. It saves time, cuts down on wear and tear to your disk drive, and eliminates floppy-related injuries. (When hurled, those disks are as lethal as ninja stars!)

- **Electronic mail.** Using electronic mail, you can communicate with other users in other rooms without leaving your chair. Programs like CE Software's QuickMail and Microsoft Mail can be had cheaply and they allow users to exchange messages without yelling at each other. For large networks, Pacer Software's PacerForum organizes in-house discussions into topics. It also allows users to open attached files directly (rather than first copying them to the local hard disk).

- **PostScript printing.** A network is essential if you own a PostScript laser printer—including the old-model LaserWriter and LaserWriter Plus, the newer line of second-generation LaserWriters (the Personal NT, II NT, II NTX, IIf, and IIg), and the assorted Macintosh-compatible printers from Hewlett Packard, Texas Instruments, AST, QMS, and others. Why? First, laser printers are expensive, so you don't want to be purchasing one for every machine in the office. Second, they're the simplest to share of Mac-related hardware. Since 1985, you've been able to network a PostScript laser printer between multiple Macs without using any special software. You just need to select the LaserWriter printer driver using the Chooser desk accessory and away you go. (Non-PostScript printers, like the LaserWriter IISC, the Personal LaserWriter SC, and Personal LaserWriter LS cannot be shared.)

- **Network backup.** Networked computers are easier to back up than their independent counterparts. For example, after connecting a SyQuest removable cartridge drive or tape backup system to one computer on a network, you can share the drive with other machines, allowing all users on the network to copy their work to the drive at the end of the day. When combined with an automated backup utility like Dantz Development's Retrospect, you can eliminate lost data entirely.

- **Sharing other hardware.** Hard drives and PostScript printers aren't the only peripherals that can be shared. By installing a LocalTalk Option board, for example, you can share an ImageWriter II. Network modems such as Shiva's NetModem are designed to satisfy the needs of multiple users. You may also use Solutions International's FaxGate Plus to share access to fax modems such as DoveFax or OrchidFax. Other fax modems, including Computer Friends' LightFax 9624 and Cypress Research's FaxPro, include their own client/server software.

- **Communicate with the uncivilized.** All models of Macintosh computers can be networked together. Even early models that require old system software, like the 128K, 512E, and the Lisa (for crying out loud), can be networked with System 7 Macs. The Apple IIGS may be networked to a Macintosh, as can the Apple IIe with a LocalTalk interface board. You may also communicate with DOS machines by installing Farallon's PhoneNet Card PC. In fact, it's easier to connect an IBM PC to a Mac than it is to connect it to another PC! Combined with Insignia Solutions' Universal SoftPC or SoftAT, you can even run DOS software and open DOS files.

BUILDING A NETWORK

Now that you know why you should be using a network, let's talk about how. System 7 supports three kinds of networks, all of which are compatible with *AppleTalk,* which is the Mac's local area network (LAN) hardware. AppleTalk is built around a specialized AppleTalk chip that is part of every Macintosh.

LocalTalk

The simplest networking solution is *LocalTalk.* You plug a LocalTalk connector box into the printer port of each computer that you want to network. A connector must also be attached to each AppleTalk printer. Each connector provides two jacks for LocalTalk cables, one in and one out (although it doesn't matter which you use as which). Attach a cable from one connector to another to network two machines. Continue attaching cables to network other machines. Note: Do *not* attach the first and last hardware devices in a network to create a closed loop. For the best results, you'll want to attach *terminating resistors* to the empty jacks in the first and last connector boxes.

LocalTalk's first drawback is its price, which can run anywhere from $75 for the connector box and a 6-foot cable to $125 for a lone 75-foot extension cable. Under such conditions, third-party equivalents are bound to pop up. Farallon's PhoneNET connectors are the original low-cost substitute for LocalTalk, providing a substantial savings in that they allow you to connect machines using standard 4-conductor phone wire. (The household 2-conductor wire won't work.) PhoneNET also allows you to extend the range of the network from the LocalTalk maximum of 1000 feet to 3000 feet. Mixed networks using LocalTalk, PhoneNET, and PhoneNET clones are perfectly acceptable. (Farallon even sells a Local-Talk to PhoneNET adaptor cable.)

LocalTalk supports up to 32 devices, including computers and printers. And while System 7's built-in networking capabilities won't allow more than 10 computers to share data at a time, the remaining computers can access connected AppleTalk printers. But due to speed problems, LocalTalk is generally only acceptable for creating small networks involving three to five machines. A LocalTalk network transfers data at 230 *kilobits* (230,000 bits, or about 29K) per second, roughly 24 times as fast as a 9600-bit-per-second modem. This may sound fast, but when 10 users are sending and receiving data over the same wires, operations can slow to a crawl. And when a network involves more than 10 users, you simply *have* to find new solutions.

EtherTalk

To speed up transmission, you can upgrade your LocalTalk system to *EtherTalk,* which is the implementation of the Mac's built-in AppleTalk protocol to conform with a faster *Ethernet* network. Ethernet connectors support speeds up to 10 *megabits* (10 million bits, or 1,250K) per second, over 40 times as fast as LocalTalk. Named for the ancient concept of an astronomical fabric that binds the stars, Ethernet is the most popular network option for UNIX and VAX machines and is popular for PC networking as well. However, upgrading your Macs for use with Ethernet demands an astronomical fee. A $500 card must be added to each machine on the network. Ethernet also requires heavy coaxial cabling in place of LocalTalk's twisted-pair cables or phone wire.

For the ultimate in computer integration, you can create an *internet,* which is a large network made up of smaller networks. The technique is particularly useful if you want to use System 7's built-in networking software to communicate with more than 10 machines. Say you have 20 machines, for example. You might create two networks of 10 machines each, one of which is a LocalTalk network and the other of which relies on Ethernet, and then combine the two networks using a *router* such as Shiva's FastPath 5 (about $2500). Routers prevent random signals from one network from entering the other, thus slimming down network traffic. To make it clear to users which network is which, you can separate computers into *zones* using the Network control panel (discussed later in this chapter).

TokenTalk

Ethernet shares one problem with its LocalTalk counterpart: *contention.* Any Mac on an Ethernet or LocalTalk network can be sending out messages at the same time as any other computer on the network. The result is that two messages bound in different directions may collide, resulting in their annihilation. After a certain period of time, both computers decide that their signals have been lost in space, and send out new messages, wasting communication time. Increasing the number of computers on your network increases the potential for contention. Given sufficient activity, the numbers of signals swell to create a sort of electronic gridlock, with messages bashing into each other more often than they get through.

A *token-ring* network is a closed network (the first and last devices are connected) in which only one machine is permitted to speak at a time. The others must wait for their turn to speak; in the meantime, they listen. A sequence of bits called a *token* is passed from one device to the next to identify the speaker. Typical token-ring networks transfer data at 4 megabits per second, slower than an Ethernet network (although, because all signals get through, a token-ring network may test out faster than Ethernet). But some newer-model token-rings solutions can transfer data as fast as 16 megabits per second.

AppleTalk protocol that conforms to token-ring hardware is called *TokenTalk.*

Getting Started

Now that you know more than you ever wanted to know about the different networking options available for the Mac, it's time to begin discussing System 7's built-in networking software. In this section, I'll explain how a beginning user can access networked disks and folders supplied by other machines. This discussion assumes that file sharing has already been established by more experienced users on your network. The *Learning Fundamental Concepts* section explains how you can share files of your own and specify to what extent the shared files may be manipulated. Finally, the *Exploring Advanced Topics* section explains how to organize users and groups, assign computers to internet zones. I'll also take a look at Timbuktu, the networking alternative from Farallon.

A SYSTEM 6 MACHINE ON A SYSTEM 7 NETWORK

A machine with only 1MB of RAM cannot use System 7. A machine with 2MB of RAM under System 7 provides about the same amount of free memory with which to run applications as a machine with 1MB of RAM under System 6. The point I'm trying to make here is that just about any machine will require a memory upgrade to compensate for the installation of System 7.

In the short run, therefore, it's hard to justify the expense of upgrading a fleet of machines to make them compatible with System 7. While you may eventually have to upgrade all machines to keep pace with future software enhancements, you may well want to continue running some low-memory machines under System 6 for another year or so.

Although System 6 provides no file-sharing functions of its own, System 7 will accommodate networked machines running under System 6. For example, you can print files over a network using System 6 and you can access files shared by System 7 machines. The opposite is *not* true, however: It is currently impossible to share files from System 6 to System 7.

Before you begin using System 6 on a System 7 network, you must prepare the System 6 machine by installing the updated LaserWriter driver and copying the AppleShare Chooser extension to the System Folder. Each of these procedures is explained in the following sections.

Installing the Printer Drivers

Two printer files are essential to outputting documents from a PostScript laser printer or imagesetting device. These are the Laser Prep and Laser-Writer files. The Laser Prep file serves as a dictionary of terms used to translate the Mac's abbreviated printing code into true PostScript. It must be available in the printer's RAM before you can print any document. The LaserWriter file is a printer driver that checks the printer's RAM to make sure the Laser Prep file is available. If it cannot find the Laser Prep file, the driver downloads it automatically. The driver then consults the Laser Prep dictionary to perform the code translation.

Every time a new version of the system software is released, new versions of the Laser Prep and LaserWriter files accompany it. This is good news for improved printing technology and bad news for compatibility. A new version of the LaserWriter driver can never use an old version of the Laser Prep file. If a System 7 LaserWriter driver finds the System 6 Laser Prep file hanging out in the printer's RAM, it thinks, *What the heck is this? I can't use this!* It then displays the message shown in Figure 12.1. You click the OK button to automatically reboot the printer and download a new version of the Laser Prep file. Click Cancel to abandon the print operation.

This may not seem like much of a problem at first, but wait until you have to put up with it a few times. The rebooting process is slow and it monopolizes your machine in the process. Also, it's extremely irritating (one of those things that makes you mutter, "Dang, I *hate* computers!" and other bits of sacrilege).

FIGURE 12.1

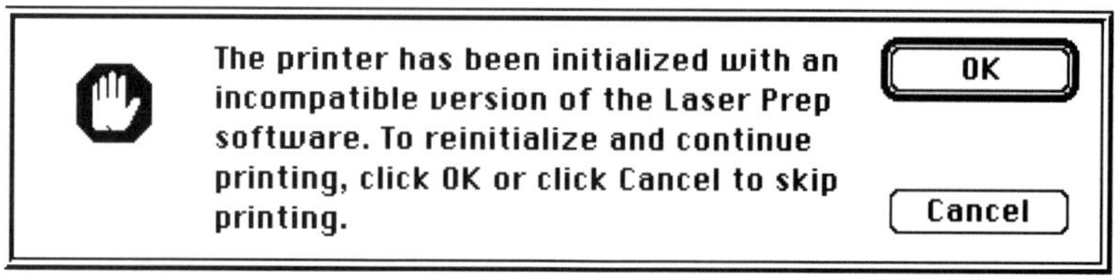

This error message displays when using System 6 and System 7 Laser Prep files on the same network.

The printer has been initialized with an incompatible version of the Laser Prep software. To reinitialize and continue printing, click OK or click Cancel to skip printing.

[OK]

[Cancel]

Luckily, this problem can be entirely eliminated by installing the LaserWriter file—which includes built-in LaserPrep—on your old System 6 machine. Here's how you do it:

1. Insert the *Printing* disk that accompanies your System 7 software package. The contents of the disk will appear on the desktop as shown in Figure 12.2.

2. Double-click the Installer icon in the upper-left corner of the Printing directory window to launch the Installer utility.

3. Once the splash screen appears, as shown in Figure 12.3, read the instructions and press the Return key to continue.

4. The Easy Install dialog box will next appear, similar to the one shown back in Figure 2.4 (Chapter 2). Click the Install button or press Return to install the new printer drivers.

5. When the installation is finished, click the Quit button to return to the Finder and dismount the *Printing* disk (drag it to the trash).

Was that easy or what? Dang, computers are great.

FIGURE 12.2

Launch the Installer utility on the Printing disk to install new printer drivers on the System 6 machine.

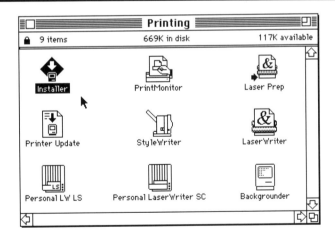

FIGURE 12.3

The splash screen explains how the Installer utility works.

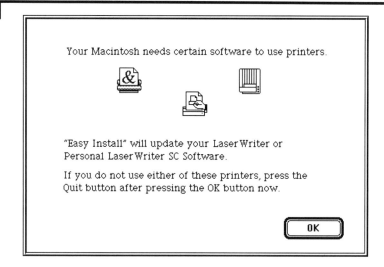

Installing AppleShare

Okay, now for part two. The AppleShare driver is your link to shared data. It can be installed very simply by drag-copying it into the System Folder as follows:

1. Insert the *Utilities 1* disk that accompanies your original System 6 software package. (Do *not* use the AppleShare driver included with System 7. Though it will work, it will also cause a variety of problems.) Double-click the system folder to open it. The contents of the System Folder will appear on the desktop as shown in Figure 12.4.

2. Drag the AppleShare file from the System Folder directory window onto the System Folder on the startup disk. The AppleShare file will copy to the new destination.

3. When the copy procedure completes, dismount the *Utilities 1* disk.

4. Restart your computer to load the AppleShare driver into memory.

AppleShare is a Chooser extension. But unlike most Chooser extensions, it must load into RAM to operate correctly. Therefore, if you are

Copy the AppleShare driver from the Tidbits disk to the System Folder on the System 6 machine.

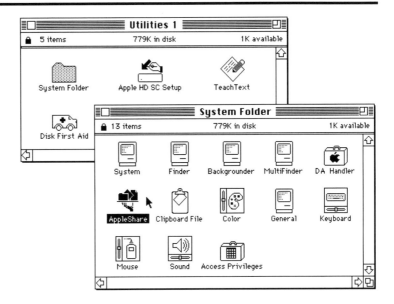

using an init manager such as INIT Picker, be sure to activate the Apple-Share file before restarting your machine.

Choosing a Server

When you share files, you are called a *server.* When you access files from the hard drives of networked computers, you are a *client.* You can even be both a client and a server at the same time by sharing a folder from your hard drive and accessing a folder from someone else's hard drive.

To access shared files, whether from a machine equipped with System 6 or a machine that uses System 7, you must select a server using the Chooser desk accessory. From there, you log on either as a registered user or as a guest and select the share folders that you would like to use. Though generally straightforward, the log-on procedure is lengthy, as described below:

1. Open the Chooser. Choose the Chooser command from the Apple menu. The Chooser dialog box will display, as shown in Figure 12.5.

FIGURE 12.5

Select the AppleShare icon, then select a server computer from the Chooser dialog box.

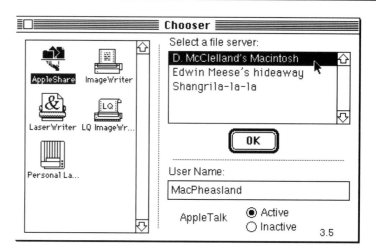

2. **Select the AppleShare driver.** Select the AppleShare icon from the scrolling list of icons on the left side of the dialog box.

3. **Select a file server and click OK.** The "Select a file server" scrolling list will appear in the upper right corner, offering the names of all computer's that are currently sharing files. Select the desired computer name and click the OK button or press Return.

4. **Enter user name and password.** The *client option dialog box* will appear next, as shown in Figure 12.6. Here, you may choose to log on as a registered user or as a network guest. When a server specifies the folders and disks that are to be shared, she or he may opt to assign certain security measures, called *access privileges,* to the shared data. If you are known to the server, you may be listed in the server's *client base* (sometimes called *users and groups*). Generally, you will know whether or not this is the case because you will have been assigned a network name and a password by your network administrator. To try it out, select the "Registered User" radio button. The "Name" option box automatically contains the user name assigned to the current computer. Most likely, you will want to leave this option as is. If you

FIGURE 12.6

The client option dialog box allows you to log on as a guest or as a registered user.

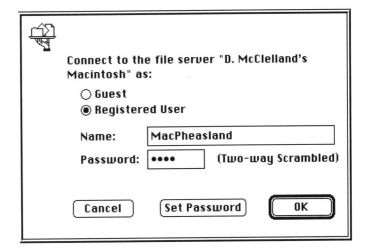

have been assigned a password, enter it into the "Password" option box. It will appear as a series of bullets to prevent others from seeing it. If you make a mistake, backspace the entire password and try again.

5a. Password problem. Click the OK button to continue. If you entered your password incorrectly, a message will display asking you to reenter it. If this continues to be a problem, consult with your network administrator or the server to find out what your password is or to get it changed.

5b. User name problem. If the server's client base does not contain your network name, the message shown in Figure 12.7 will appear, asking you to reenter your name. Again, you may want to contact your network administrator or talk to the server directly. If neither options are available, return to the client option dialog box and select the "Guest" radio button. You don't need a name or a password to be a guest, but your access privileges may be more limited.

6. Select shared volumes. Once you have successfully exited the client option dialog box, you will be greeted by the *shared items dialog box* shown in Figure 12.8. A scrolling list of all shared folders and disks available from the current server

FIGURE 12.7

Messages will appear if either your computer name (shown here) or password is not registered with the server's client base.

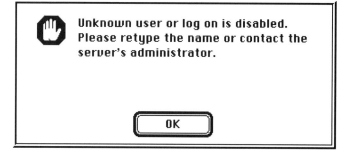

> Unknown user or log on is disabled. Please retype the name or contact the server's administrator.
>
> [OK]

FIGURE 12.8

The shared items dialog box permits you to select the volumes that you want to use, as well as instruct AppleShare to mount volumes automatically during startup.

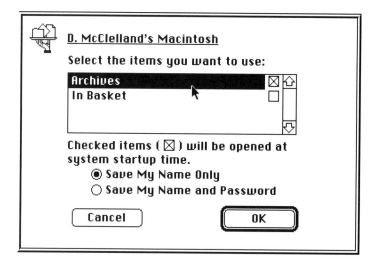

> D. McClelland's Macintosh
>
> Select the items you want to use:
>
> ☒ Archives
> ☐ In Basket
>
> Checked items (☒) will be opened at system startup time.
> ◉ Save My Name Only
> ○ Save My Name and Password
>
> [Cancel]   [OK]

appears near the top of the dialog box. Select the desired folder or disk—known generically as a *volume*—by clicking on it. Shift-click to select multiple volumes.

7. Specify volumes to be mounted automatically. If you desire that a volume be mounted automatically every time you start up your computer, select the check box to the right of the volume name. Two radio buttons will appear below the list. Select "Save My Name Only" to instruct AppleShare to automatically transmit your computer name when mounting the volume; you will be presented with the client option dialog box during the startup procedure so that you may

enter your password manually. If this is too much effort or
you simply aren't that concerned about security, select the
"Save My Name and Password" radio button to instruct
AppleShare to mount the volume without bothering you.

8. **Exit to the Finder.** Click the OK button or press Return to
exit the shared items dialog box and return to the Finder.
The selected volumes will appear on your Finder desktop.

If you'll refer back to Figure 12.6, you'll see that I skipped an option, the Set Password button, which lets you change your password if the
server's client base permits. If you are prohibited from changing your
password, a message will display when you click the Set Password button
that prevents you from continuing. However, if yours is a laid-back working environment, clicking the Set Password button brings up the dialog
box shown in the first example of Figure 12.9. Here, you are asked to
enter your existing password and then enter a new, more desirable
password. To confirm your choice, you will be asked to reenter the new
password after you click the OK button.

For safety's sake, you may want to write your password down and
stick it in your purse or wallet. If security is an issue, avoid using obvious
passwords like your initials or your birth date. A completely random password referenced to a macro keyboard equivalent is often the best choice.

FIGURE 12.9

*Click the Set Password
button in the client option
dialog box to enter a new
password (top). After you
click OK, a message will
ask you to confirm your
new password by
repeating it (bottom).*

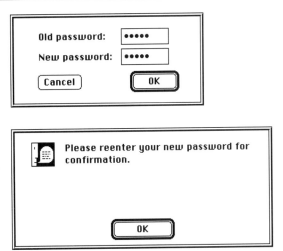

Old password: •••••
New password: •••••

Cancel   OK

Please reenter your new password for
confirmation.

OK

USING ACCESSED VOLUMES

Once you have mounted a volume on your desktop, you can use it much like a standard disk or folder. However, as you work, it is a good idea to keep the following points in mind:

Get Info

Using the Get Info command from the File menu (⌘-I), you can add comments to a shared volume or assign the volume a new icon just as you can a standard folder or disk (provided you are allowed to modify the volume). While this new comment or icon may not immediately affect the appearance of the shared disk or folder on the server's machine, it will affect its appearance to all clients who mount the volume from this point on, and it will change the volume's appearance on the server's machine after the server restarts his or her computer.

One other note: If the name of the volume is longer than 8 characters, try clicking on the volume name in the Info dialog box. As illustrated in Figure 12.10, the name will appear truncated. This "short name," as it is called, represents the name that the volume is assigned on non-Macintosh computers, including the IBM PC. An exclamation point precedes the short name to show that it looks different on a PC than it does on a Mac. The exclamation point is followed by the first seven characters of the name, a period, and the next three characters. The rest of the volume name is abandoned. Also note that spaces are replaced with underlines, since spaces are not allowed in DOS file names.

FIGURE 12.10

Click the volume name in the Info dialog box (left) to view the short name that appears on DOS machines (right).

Small Icons

When accessing shared volumes, you may begin to see several tiny icons that you haven't seen previously when using the Mac. Each of these icons, all of which are displayed in Figure 12.11, have specific meanings:

- **Activity arrows.** The activity arrows flash in the far left corner of the menu bar to indicate that data is being transferred to or from your computer. If your computer is running particularly slow and the activity icon is flashing, you know it's due to network activity. Otherwise, the slowness is due to the speed limitations of your computer or that of the application you're using.

- **Can't see folders.** One or more of three icons may display beneath the title bar of a volume directory window. A folder with a slash through it indicates that the server forbids you to see any folders in the current volume, or the contents of those folders. Only documents contained in the root directory can be seen.

- **Can't see files.** The icon of a page with a slash through it indicates that the server forbids you to see any files in the current volume, whether they may be applications, system utilities, documents, stationery pads, or aliases. You are allowed to see folders only (particularly useful for a private "in basket" in which you may send messages and files to the server, but you may not view what other users have sent).

FIGURE 12.11

The activity icon that displays in the far left corner of the menu bar (top), as well as the can't see folders icon (left), the can't see files icon (middle), and the can't make changes icon (right) which appear at the top of directory windows.

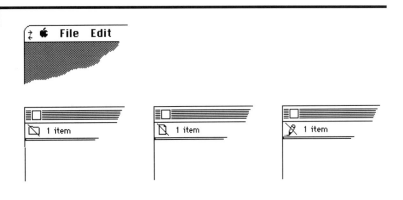

- **Can't make changes.** The icon of a pencil with a slash through it indicates that you are not allowed to modify the current volume. In fact, the volume will act exactly like a locked disk. While you can copy files and folders from a locked volume, you cannot save files to it, create new folders, modify the volume icon, or add comments.

The Quick Mount

If you use a volume on a regular basis and you want to avoid the hassle of accessing the volume via the Chooser every time you want to use it, create an alias for that volume by choosing the Make Alias command from the File menu. From that point on, merely double-click the alias to mount the volume. The client option dialog box from Figure 12.6 will appear. Enter your password and away you go.

> If even this is too much work, try out the MountAlias control panel by Jeff Miller which is included on the disks offered on the coupon found at the back of this book. This ingenious little utility will automatically create an alias for every volume that you mount. You specify the folder in which the aliases are saved and select the naming scheme. MountAlias does the rest for you.

Server Closing Down

While working on a shared volume, you may be suddenly interrupted by the message shown in Figure 12.12. The message tells you that a volume is about to dismount (or has already dismounted, as in the case of a server machine crash). You have so many minutes to finish using the volume—copy files and save changes. There is nothing you can do to stop a dismount of this kind, except perhaps to beg the server (the actual person using the serving machine, that is) to let you use the volume for a little while longer. If the server acquiesces, a message like the one shown in Figure 12.13 will appear, informing you that the volume will remain available.

FIGURE 12.12

This message appears when a volume is about to dismount automatically due to server cutoff or machine crash.

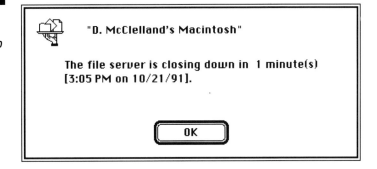

> "D. McClelland's Macintosh"
>
> The file server is closing down in 1 minute(s) [3:05 PM on 10/21/91].
>
> OK

FIGURE 12.13

This message is like a reprieve from the governor; you can use the volume a little while longer.

> "D. McClelland's Macintosh"
>
> The file server is no longer closing down.
>
> OK

Dismounting a Volume

You may dismount a volume of your own free will by dragging it to the Trash icon and releasing, as when dismounting a disk. You may also select the volume and choose the Put Away command from the File menu (⌘-Y).

LEARNING FUNDAMENTAL CONCEPTS

So, you want to become a file server. With file serving comes power. You can determine who sees what, who can make changes, and who is tormented by a lack of volume availability. You can even change access privileges while a volume is being shared, cut people off randomly in the middle of using a volume, and throw their files in the Trash as they work on them. All of this may sound like a big joke—I know it makes *me* chuckle—but an irresponsible server can wreak havoc on a network. Therefore, you must exercise care and thought when altering sharing options. Before you perform an alteration that affects a client, particularly if that client is logged on to one of your volumes, you may want to consult with that person to see how he or she will be affected.

So much for the ethics lesson; let's get on with the options themselves.

(PS: If you're using System 6, you can't be a server. You can only share volumes provided by other servers as described in the previous pages. The privileges of being a server are yet another reason to upgrade to System 7.)

BECOMING A SERVER

Serving a folder or disk is a four-step process:

1. **Server identity.** Identify yourself using Sharing Setup control panel.

2. **File sharing.** Activate the "File Sharing" option.

3. **Sharing folders and disks.** Permit individual folders and disks (other than floppy disks) to be shared using the Sharing… command from the File menu.

4. **Extending access privileges.** Specify the extent to which named clients and guests can view and manipulate the current folder or disk using the options in the middle of the access privileges dialog box.

That's really all there is to it. If these steps are enough to get you started, you might want to experiment before going farther. If you prefer to find out more information before continuing, each step is explained in depth in the following pages.

Server Identity

Open the Sharing Setup control panel to begin the volume serving process. The top of the Sharing Setup window is devoted to the "Network

Identity" options with which you identify yourself as a server. Name your-self and your machine by entering information into the "Owner Name," "Owner Password," and "Macintosh Name" option boxes. Your owner name (or *server name*) and owner password (*server password*) allow you to log on to your computer from a different machine and make changes to the manner in which folders and disks are served. In fact, as machine owner, you can serve up your entire hard drive even if no part of it is cur-rently being shared. (File sharing, however, must be active.) Although not required, you will most likely want to use the same name as a server that you use as a client. However, your server password should be unique. Other servers can access and even assign your client password; a separate server password prevents other users from altering your server settings and accessing protected information of a personal or private nature.

The server password may be up to eight characters long. Like the "Password" option in the client option dialog box, the "Owner Password" option box is case sensitive (capital and lowercase letters are considered to be different characters). Again, avoid obvious passwords (such as the one shown in Figure 12.14). After the password is entered, the characters

FIGURE 12.14

After you enter a server password (top) and tab to the next option, bullets replace the password characters so other users cannot view them (bottom).

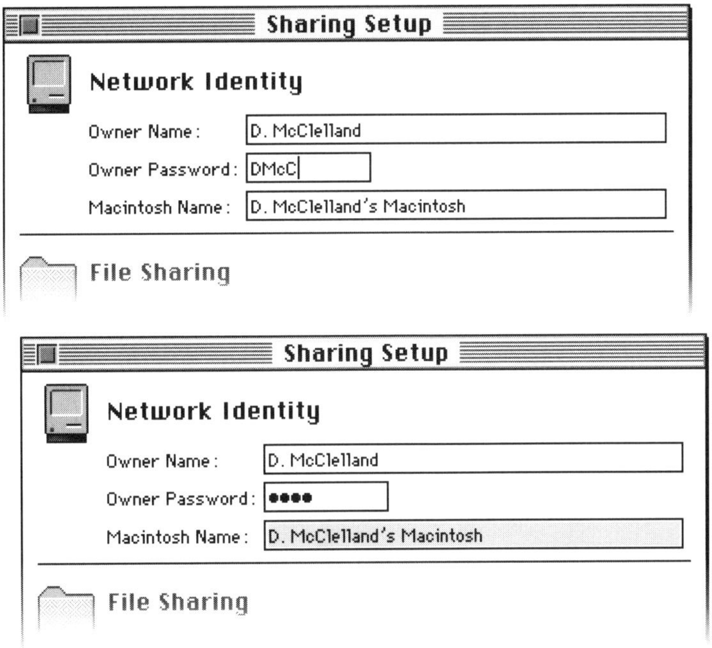

in the "Owner Password" option box change to bullets. Note: You can *never* again display your server password, so remember it or write it down and store it in a safe place.

> **While the Sharing Setup window will not display your current server password, it allows anyone using your computer to alter it by entering new characters into the "Owner Password" option box. Unfortunately, Apple provides no way for you to lock this option. However, because the Sharing Setup control panel contains no init data that has to load into RAM during startup (many control panels do), you may move it to an obscure location without affecting the performance of your computer. You may even rename the control panel so that someone using your computer cannot search for the file by name using the Find… command. If security is job number one, you can copy the file to a floppy disk and delete it from your hard drive altogether. When you want to make changes to Sharing Setup options, you can insert the disk and use the control panel. In the meantime, you may keep it hidden.**

File Sharing

To serve data, your machine must be made available in the "Select a file server" scrolling list in a networked user's Chooser window (refer to Figure 12.5). You accomplish this by activating the "File Sharing" option in the Sharing Setup control panel. By default, file sharing is turned off. To turn it on, click the Start button in the "File Sharing" area in the middle of the Sharing Setup window. The Start button will toggle to a Cancel button and the message inside the "Status" box will change to read, "File sharing is starting up," as shown in Figure 12.15. After a few moments,

FIGURE 12.15

The "File Sharing" option as it appears when in the process of starting up (top) and when turned on (bottom).

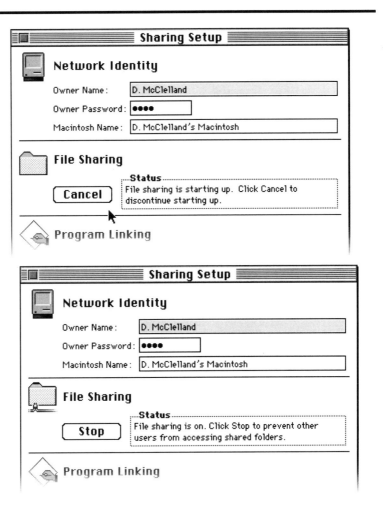

the Cancel button will change to a Stop button and the message will change to read, "File sharing is on."

Click the close box to close the Sharing Setup control panel. The "File Sharing" option will remain on, even if you restart your machine, until the next time you turn the option off.

In order to share a removable cartridge, the cartridge must be inserted prior to activating the File Sharing option. The flip side of this is that if a cartridge is mounted at the time of sharing startup, you will *not* be allowed to dismount it. Dragging the cartridge icon to the Trash will produce a message that says the cartridge cannot be put away because it is being shared (even if you are specifically sharing no item on the cartridge). Therefore, if you don't care about sharing a cartridge and you're more interested in being able to swap cartridges in and out of the drive, do *not* turn on file sharing while a cartridge is mounted. First dismount it, then turn on file sharing, and remount the cartridge. If file sharing is always turned on, make sure no cartridge is in your drive at the time of startup. Note that this is not a problem for floppy disks, since floppies cannot be shared.

Sharing Folders and Disks

Once file sharing is active, you may indicate the specific folders and disks that you want to share. Select a desired folder or disk icon and choose the Sharing... command from the File menu. An *access privileges dialog box* like the one shown in Figure 12.16 will appear. Select the "Share this item and its contents" check box to make this folder available to other users. It will now appear in the scrolling list near the top of the shared items dialog box (refer to Figure 12.8) when another user logs on as a client to your machine.

Extending Access Privileges

The fourth step in sharing a folder or disk is to assign *access privileges,* which determine what networked clients can and cannot see and do to the contents of you hard drive. For the most part, access privileges are controlled using the nine check boxes in the middle of the access

FIGURE 12.16

Select a folder and choose Sharing... from the File menu to display the access privileges dialog box.

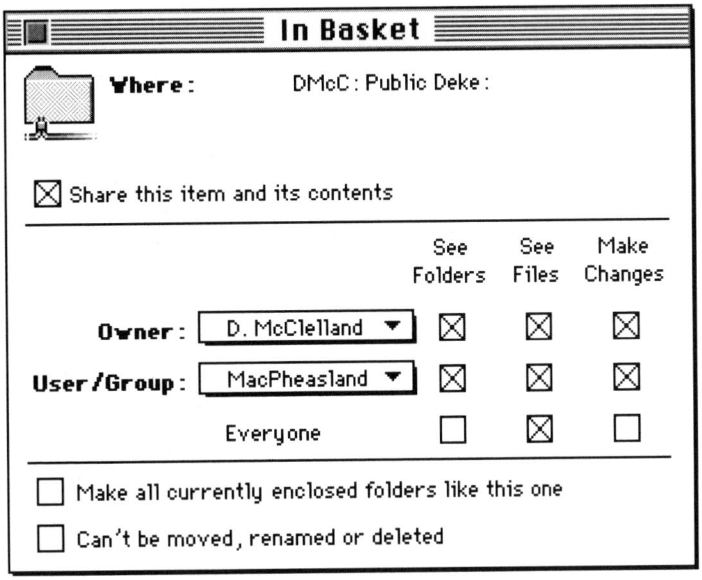

privileges dialog box. These options are grouped into three columns:

- **See Folders.** When a check box in this column is selected, the corresponding user can see all folders in the current volume. If you deselect the option, the user cannot see any folders in the current volume, or the contents of those folders. Only documents contained in the root directory will be visible.

- **See Files.** When a check box in this column is selected, the corresponding user can see all files—applications, system utilities, documents, stationery pads, or aliases—in the current volume. If you deselect the option, the user may see what appear to be empty folders only. This option is particularly useful for creating a private "in basket" in which a client may send messages and files to you without being able to see what other users have sent.

- **Make Changes.** When a check box in this column is selected, the corresponding user may save files to the current volume, create new folders, and so on. If you deselect the option, the volume is treated as locked. The user can copy files from the volume, but that's it.

These three privilege columns match up with three categories of clients, arranged into rows:

- **Owner.** Choose an option from the "Owner" pop-up menu to determine the *owner* of the current volume; that is, the user who can change volume privileges from a remote location. By selecting the current volume and choosing the Sharing... command from the File menu, you as the server can always change the access privileges. But when using a different machine on the network, only the owner may make such changes. By default, ownership is assigned to you, but you may choose another user or group from your client base (as shown in Figure 12.17) or choose the "<Any User>" option to allow all clients to change access privileges. (To establish a client base, read the *Exploring Advanced Topics* section later in this chapter.) When the owner chooses the Sharing... command from another machine, the access privileges dialog box will appear as

FIGURE 12.17

Choose an option from the "Owner" pop-up menu to grant a user or group of users the ability to change privileges from a different machine on the network.

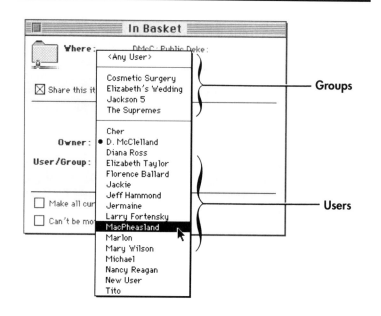

shown in Figure 12.18. The only difference is that the "Owner" and "User/Group" pop-up menus are substituted with option boxes, in which the owner must enter a new owner or user name that exactly matches an entry in the server's client base. By contrast, a normal client who is not granted ownership privileges sees the dialog box shown in Figure 12.19 when she or he chooses the Sharing...

FIGURE 12.18

The access privileges dialog box as it appears when accessed by an owner from a different machine on the network.

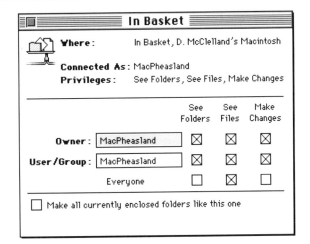

FIGURE 12.19

When accessed by a non-owner on the network, all options are dimmed in the access privileges dialog box. The client can view the settings, but not make changes.

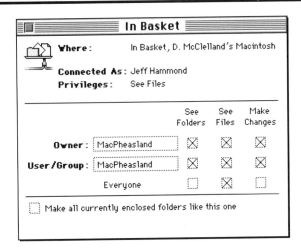

command for a mounted volume. Note that all options are dimmed in the client's dialog box.

- **User/Group.** You may subdivide clients into two categories: 1) those that you grant special privileges and 2) everybody else. Choose an option from the "User/Group" pop-up menu to determine which users or group of users from your client base are assigned special privileges. Then use the check boxes to determine what those privileges are.

- **Everyone.** The last row of check boxes stands for all clients that are not represented as an owner or privileged user or group. This includes users who log on as guests. Use the check boxes to determine what privileges all users are allowed.

Generally speaking, you will want to assign the owner at least as many privileges as the privileged users, who should be assigned at least as many privileges as everyone else. I'll discuss some common variations in the *Child Volumes* section, which follows.

Two additional check boxes are available at the bottom of the access privileges dialog box:

- **Make all currently enclosed folders like this one.** As I'll explain in the next section, the folders inside the current volume, which are called *child volumes,* may be assigned their own unique access privileges. To bring the children into line and make them all match the parent, select this check box.

- **Can't be moved, renamed or deleted.** When checked, this option prevents the current volume from being changed by any user, including yourself. You will not be able to move the folder to a new location, rename it, throw it away, change its icon, or add comments in the Info dialog box. (If a disk is selected, this option will not be available since hard drive, removable cartridges, and other shared disks can never be moved, renamed, or trashed.)

Click the close box to close the access privileges dialog box. All settings will remain in force, even if you restart your machine, until the next time you or the volume owner again change the access privileges.

CHILD VOLUMES

Figure 12.20 shows how shared folders look at the Finder level. In the figure, the folder named *Temporary* is not shared, so it looks like a standard folder. The folder named *In Basket* is shared, but no one is currently using it. The folder named *Archives* is being shared and is currently mounted on a client's machine.

Figure 12.20 also shows the contents of one of the shared folders. Inside this folder are two child folders. The thin black strip across the top of each folder shows that they are children and that they are owned by the server. Using the Sharing... command from the File menu, you may change the access privileges assigned to child folders just as you have for the parent folder. The access privileges dialog box shown in Figure 12.21 belongs to a child folder. Note that this dialog box is almost identical to the one shown in Figure 12.16, except that the "Share this item and its contents" check box has disappeared, having been replaced by the "Same as enclosing folder" check box. To make changes to the settings in this dialog box, you must deselect the "Same as enclosing folder" check box, thus making a clean break from the parent folder.

FIGURE 12.20

*F*olders shown as they appear when not shared (left), shared but not in use (center), and both shared and in use (right). Also shown are two child folders (bottom).

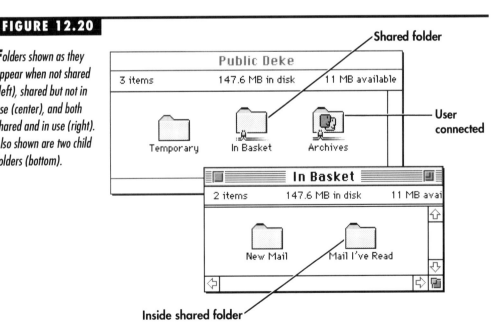

FIGURE 12.21

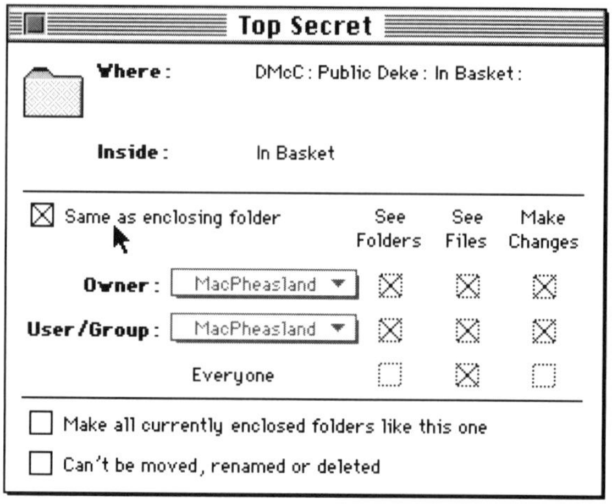

Deselect the "Same as enclosing folder" check box to assign different access privileges to the child folder than those assigned to the parent.

Child folders are assigned different types of icons on a client's desktop to demonstrate the privileges associated with the folder. For example, if the client has been deemed the folder's owner, a black strip displays across the top of the folder, as shown in the first example of Figure 12.22. If the client is not the owner, but she or he can see either files or folders, the folder appears without any special markings. If the client cannot see either files or folders but can save files inside the folder, a belt surrounds the folder icon and a down-point arrow displays above it, as shown in the third example of Figure 12.22. If the client cannot make changes or see any file or folder, the folder is totally inaccessible to the client, so the down-pointing arrow disappears.

*M*ONITORING CLIENT ACTIVITY

To see which clients are currently using your volumes, open the File Sharing Monitor control panel. As shown in Figure 12.23, this control panel contains two scrolling lists, one of parent volumes shared from the current machine ("Shared Items") and one of the clients who are using them ("Connected Users"). The "File Sharing Activity" thermometer demonstrates the percentage of your computer's total processing ability that is being devoted to clients. Generally, you shouldn't allow the thermometer to get past the halfway mark.

FIGURE 12.22

Four ways in which a child folder may be altered to achieve varying effects. Key options are highlighted in black.

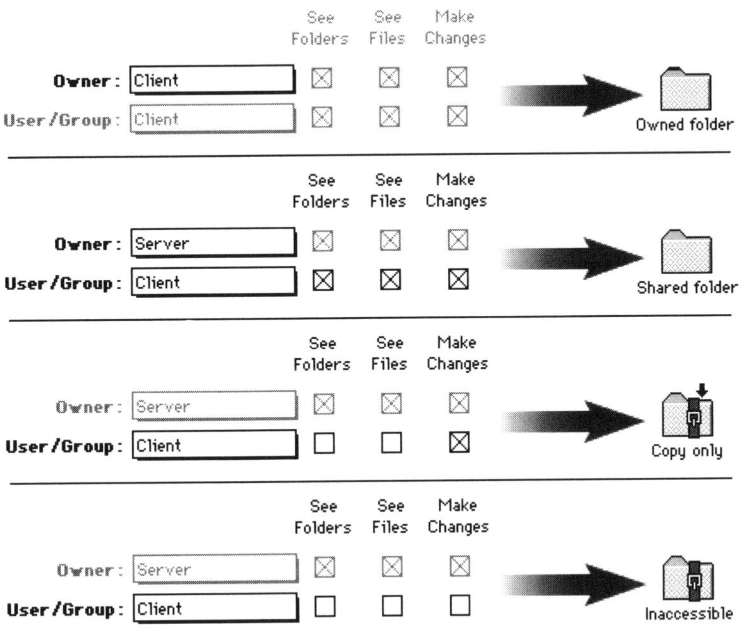

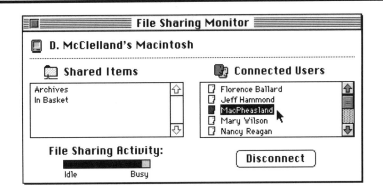

FIGURE 12.23

The File Sharing Monitor control panel shows all shared volumes, all logged-on clients, and a thermometer that measures the amount of CPU attention that is being spent on the clients.

File Sharing Monitor

D. McClelland's Macintosh

Shared Items
- Archives
- In Basket

Connected Users
- Florence Ballard
- Jeff Hammond
- MacPheasland
- Mary Wilson
- Nancy Reagan

File Sharing Activity:

Idle   Busy

[Disconnect]

If the thermometer gets too full, or your machine is simply running too darn slow, you may select one or more clients from the "Connect Users" list and cut them off by clicking the Disconnect button. A message will appear, asking you how many minutes you want to give the clients to collect their things before you boot them off the volume. The client will get a message similar to the one shown back in Figure 12.12.

My recommendation: Warn clients manually about five minutes before cutting them off. Then when the time comes, enter 0 in response to this message and press Return to cut clients off instantaneously. If you enter a larger number, like 1 or 5, you have to sit there with your machine tied up for that period of time. System 7 cannot disconnect clients in the background.

Note that disconnecting clients does not disallow them from relogging on the second they get a chance. If a client keeps pestering you, you can alter his or her client privileges using the Users & Groups control panel to make a more lasting impression. This technique is described in the *Exploring Advanced Topics* section.

DEACTIVATING FILE SHARING

To deactivate file sharing, open the Sharing Setup control panel and click the Stop button in the "File Sharing" area. Note that this does not affect current clients, it just prevents new clients from logging on.

EXPLORING ADVANCED TOPICS

I'll wrap up this chapter and, in fact, this book by discussing how you as a network administrator can go about setting up an effective network. I'll start by explaining how to create a client base using the Users & Groups control panel. I'll then examine the Network control panel. And finally, I'll take a look at Farallon's extraordinary Timbuktu 4.0 which allows you to control the operation of a remote machine over a network.

ESTABLISHING A CLIENT BASE

You don't have to be a rocket scientist to set up a client base. In fact, compared with issues I've discussed in the previous *Exploring Advanced Topics* sections of this book, it's a snap. Then why am I including this discussion in the advanced section? Because *nothing* about file sharing is difficult; it's *all* easy. Well, pretty easy anyway. Oh, heck, read on and find out for yourself.

Open the User & Groups control panel to display a Users & Groups directory window, similar the one shown in Figure 12.24. This window represents every single user in your client base. If this is the first time you've opened the Users & Groups control panel, you'll probably see only two icons: one labeled <Guest> and another that is labeled with your current server name.

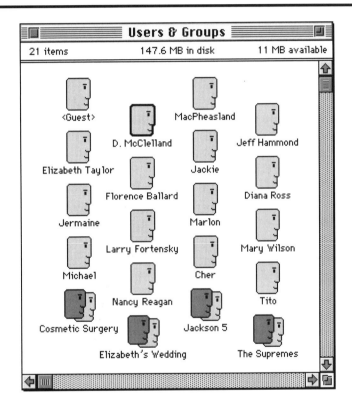

FIGURE 12.24

The Users & Groups window contains an icon for each and every user in your client base.

Adding a New Client

To create a new client, choose the New User command from the File menu (⌘-N). A new head icon (aren't they stupid looking?) will appear in the Users & Groups window with the name *New User*. Change the name to match the name of one of the users on your network. Create more users as needed.

These names that you create in the Users & Groups directory window are the same names that will appear in the "User/Group" pop-up menu in the access privileges dialog box (see Figure 12.16). But because the dialog box only permits you to choose one "User/Group" option for each volume, you will need to assemble clients into *user groups* to more adequately categorize their needs and their privileges.

Creating User Groups

To create a new user group, choose the New Group command from the File menu. One of those heinously ugly double-headed icons will appear (like the ones shown along the bottom of the window in Figure 12.24) bearing the name *New Group*. Again, name the icon something more appropriate. Groups are like folders. Drag a user icon onto the group icon to add the corresponding client to the user group. But rather than being moved into the group, the user icon is copied into the group. This allows you to add a single user to multiple groups, as demonstrated in Figure 12.25. At any time, you may double-click a group icon to open the group and look at its contents. User icons appear as picture frames to show that they're copies of the original user icons.

FIGURE 12.25

A single client may belong to multiple user groups.

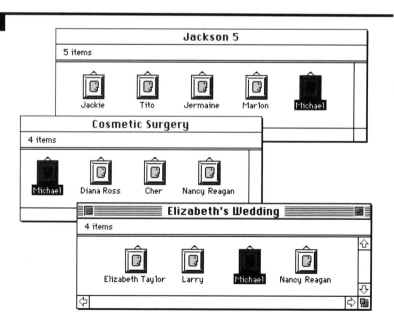

Note that a group may not be added to a group, nor may any two user or group icons be assigned the same name.

Assigning Client Privileges

Just as you may specify the access privileges associated with a shared volume, you may adjust the privileges associated with a single client. Double-click a user icon, either in the Users & Groups directory window or inside an open group window, to display the *client privileges dialog box* shown in Figure 12.26. This dialog box contains the following options:

- **User Password.** Here you may enter an 8-character password for the current client. The characters will change to bullets after the password is entered.

FIGURE 12.26

Use the client privileges dialog box to specify access privileges for a single client.

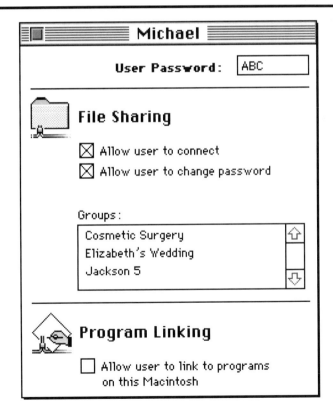

- **Allow user to connect.** Use this check box to determine whether or not a specific client is allowed to log on to your machine.

- **Allow user to change password.** If you don't want clients changing their own passwords, deselect this check box. Otherwise, leave it selected.

- **Allow user to link to programs on this Macintosh.** This check box determines whether a client's applications are allowed to communicate with your applications, as described in Chapter 11.

The "Groups" scrolling list displays the names of all groups to which the current client belongs.

TIP

> This may come off as being something of a mean tip, but clients can sometimes be a problem over a network. If you cut off a client by deselecting the "Allow user to connect" check box, that client can still access your computer as a guest. To prevent this from happening, double-click the <Guest> icon and deselect the "Allow guest to connect" check box for this dialog box as well.

ASSIGNING CONNECTIONS AND ZONES

If your network is one of several networks linked together to form an internet, you'll need to use the Network control panel to select an Apple-Talk connection and assign zones. Otherwise, you can skip to the next discussion.

Open the Network control panel to display a simple window containing connection icons, as shown in Figure 12.27. If yours is a Local-Talk network, select the "LocalTalk" icon. If you're working on an Ethernet or token-ring network, select the "EtherTalk" or "TokenTalk" icon.

The Network control panel also allows you to assign the current computer to a specific zone. After selecting a connection icon, double-click the icon to display the *zone assignment dialog box* shown in Figure 12.28. Select a zone name from the scrolling list to assign the current Macintosh to that zone. Then click the OK button or press Return.

Zones will display in a scrolling list in the bottom-left corner of the Chooser window.

FIGURE 12.27

The Network control panel allows you to select the current AppleTalk connection when working on an Ethernet or token-ring network.

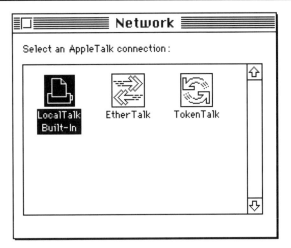

FIGURE 12.28

Use the zone assignment dialog box to assign the current computer to an existing zone.

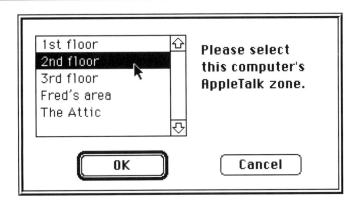

TIMBUKTU

If you really want to be the network boss, you'll want to purchase Timbuktu from Farallon. Newly upgraded for use with System 7, this utility allows you to access another machine remotely, display the contents of its screen in a window on your monitor (called observing), and even control the operation of the machine. To use Timbuktu, individual copies of the software must be purchased for each machine from which and on which you intend to operate the product. For it to be at all useful, you'll need at least two copies. You then set up at least one machine to supply "Guest Access," as shown in Figure 12.29, causing it to act as the host. This allows a second Mac to log on to the first and access functions. Just as with System 7's built-in networking software, access privileges can be assigned, some of which are available to all users and some of which require passwords.

When accessing another machine, whether observing or controlling it, Timbuktu offers a window into the other computer's screen, as demonstrated in Figure 12.30. The window will update automatically to reflect changes made to the original machine's desktop. The window may be sent to the background when not in use, just like any other application.

Timbuktu is easy to use, although most users don't realize the immediate benefits of using it. Several benefits include:

- **Training.** Training a new employee by looking over his or her shoulder or vice versa is frequently an unsatisfactory experience. By permitting two machines to observe each

---

FIGURE 12.29

The Timbuktu desk accessory window allows you to activate "Guest Access," set up access privileges, and access another Timbuktu user's machine.

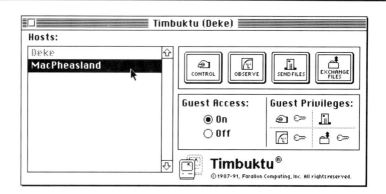

FIGURE 12.30

The screen from my SE/30 as it appears when displayed on my Mac IIci in "Control" mode. So long as my cursor is inside the window, I can control the operation of the SE/30. When I move the cursor out of the window, I control operations on my IIci.

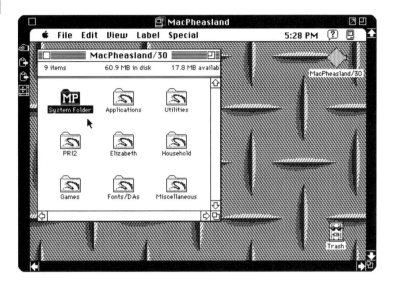

other, you can perform operations on your machine that can be viewed on the trainees machine. You can then request the trainee to duplicate your actions and watch his or her progress remotely.

- **Sharing Clipboards.** By using Timbuktu, you can copy an element from a document on a colleague's computer, transfer the Clipboard to your machine, and paste the element into a document on your machine.

- **Sharing a project.** You and a co-worker can make changes to a single project simultaneously by granting control privileges to one user while the other user acts as host.

- **Long document printing.** Books and other long documents can take hours to print, especially when outputting to a high-end imagesetter such as a Linotronic or Varityper. By using Timbuktu, you can set up the print job on a remote machine and monitor its progress.

- **Complex data processing.** Complex mathematical operations—whether performed using a spreadsheet, scientific application, or in response to a three-dimensional rendering program—can tie up your machine for literally hours.

Using the "Control" option, you can initiate the calculation on a remote machine and periodically see how it's progressing without interrupting your ability to perform operations on your Mac.

- **Security.** By setting up, say, four machines as hosts and one machine with a large-screen monitor as observer, you can display the contents of the other four screens on a single computer, enabling a security specialist to observe all operations performed on remote machines. Taken to its limit, this may sound like an Orwellian nightmare; still, it can prove useful for monitoring the manipulation of highly sensitive data.

Timbuktu enhances the capabilities of a single machine by adding the processing capabilities of other machines to its repertoire.

QuickTime

SYSTEM 7.1 INCLUDES QuickTime 1.5, a
system extension that enables you to in-
tegrate *QuickTime movies* into applications, provided that these applications
are QuickTime compatible. The "movies" are actually assembled sequen-
ces of digitized video images and sounds that are created in one of the
QuickTime movie applications and saved in the QuickTime format.
Microsoft Word 5.1, for example, now allows you to paste a QuickTime
movie into a file just as you would paste a picture into a file. Can you imagine, a letter to the grandparents that contains actual footage of
junior's first steps instead of just photographs? And what about those
sounds that the little duffer is uttering? That is something an ordinary letter can never capture. Such a file would, of course, have to be played
back to the intended audience on another computer equipped with the
QuickTime extension, and not merely read.

QUICKTIME COMPRESSION

QuickTime provides software compressors designed to reduce the size of
bitmapped—and only bitmapped—photo, animation, and video files.
This means that object-oriented artwork is not compressed under Quick-
Time, but this is not much of a limitation. Photoshop 2.0.1, for example,
incorporates the QuickTime JPEG (Joint Photographic Experts Group)
photo compressor for condensing the size of images saved in the PICT
format. JPEG can compress an image up to $1/100$ of its original size by
removing unnecessary data from the image, such as detail that the
human eye cannot see without the aid of magnification. Thus, JPEG
works best for images with little perceivable detail and smooth transitions
between the colors in the image. The old photograph in Figure A.1 was
scanned and saved in the regular PICT format. The scan was then
opened in Photoshop 2.0.1 and was saved three times in the PICT format
with the JPEG compression, once in each of the quality settings that
Photoshop supports—from left to right: high, medium, and low quality.

FIGURE A.1

A scan of a photograph compressed with JPEG.

The quality setting for the JPEG compression also has an effect on the amount of reduction. For example, in Figure A.2, the left image was saved in the PICT format with JPEG compression set for the highest quality. It compressed to roughly ¾ of the size of the original. The image on the right was compressed under the lowest quality setting and saved to a size of roughly 1/30 of that of the original; its final size is more than twenty times smaller than that of the left image. Granted, the one on the right is not going to win any awards—oh, and I suppose that the one on the left ain't blue ribbon material either—but it is rather remarkable for its size.

The animation compressor, introduced by Apple for computer-generated animation, and the video compressor, also Apple's, both provide spatial compression to each image, in a frame-by-frame manner, similar to what JPEG does for photo images. Both also allow you to control the color depth associated with the compression. You can also control the quality of the compression for each frame. So, within the same movie, you can save one scene, consisting of frames of low detail, at a lower quality compression than another scene, consisting of frames that have a lot of detail. Both of these factors have an effect on the amount of compression.

FIGURE A.2

The left image retained most of its original quality, gaining only a moderate saving in file size. The right image's quality was sacrificed, increasing the compression.

Some QuickTime editing utilities including SuperMac's ScreenPlay, allow you view, edit, and compress QuickTime movies. Figure A.3 shows the results of three different animation compression settings on one of the two (already compressed) QuickTime movies included with System 7.1. The three images in the figure are stills copied from the compressed movies. ScreenPlay allows you to specify the compression quality of the entire movie using a slider bar with a scale from zero to four (where a setting of zero will basically ensure that your Mac will crash any time you try to play the movie back after the compression). I compressed the movie entitled "7.MooV" three different times, each time at a different quality setting. The first time I compressed the movie, I set the slider bar to the maximum quality setting of four. This resulted in a movie that was larger and of slightly lesser quality than the original, as shown in the left image of Figure A.3. This means that the original was compressed at a quality setting lower than ScreenPlay's setting of four. Since ScreenPlay does not fully decompress a movie (restore the original data intact), the quality was not restored when I tried to compress the movie, "7.MooV," at a higher quality setting and I only succeeded in enlarging the file (and reducing the quality!). I then compressed the movie at a quality setting of two, as shown in the middle image of Figure A.3. This resulted in a saving of about 20K. Finally, I compressed the movie at a quality setting of just above zero (0.06 to be exact), as shown in the right image of Figure A.3. The file reduced to roughly 1/10 of the size of the original, but at the expense of quality. As you can see, the fish has lost most of its character and looks very little like the original.

Provided that you have the necessary hardware, other applications, including Adobe's Premier or DiVA's VideoShop, allow you to capture, edit, and play your own movies. Though enticing, this QuickTime option is easier said than done. Necessary hardware includes a video-capture board connected to a video-input device, such as a VCR camcorder, and

FIGURE A.3

The animation compressor allows you to compress animated movies; the quality setting dictates the file's final size.

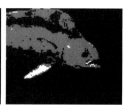

ample storage room, such as a SyQuest or optical cartridge device. Compressing an animated or video sequence takes roughly five times longer than it takes to play the sequence.

QUICKTIME AND SYSTEM 7.1

As far as System 7.1 goes, your access to the world of QuickTime is rather limited. System 7.1 provides the QuickTime extension, which—as I have said—allows you to use QuickTime movies and the QuickTime compression in applications, but does not, in itself, allow you to produce Quick-Time movies. System 7.1 does provide you with two QuickTime movies and a revised version of Scrapbook that lets you play movies. Below are instructions on installing the QuickTime extension and using the Quick-Time movies included with System 7.1. (The following steps assume that you have the QuickTime disk or the equivalent disk images.)

INSTALLING QUICKTIME

1. Insert the disk labeled QuickTime.

2. Double-click on the icon to reveal the contents (as shown in Figure A.4).

FIGURE A.4

The contents of the QuickTime disk

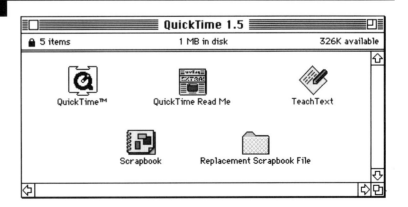

3. Select the QuickTime extension, the Scrapbook DA, and the Replacement Scrapbook File folder and drag them onto your System Folder icon.

4. A message will display asking you if it's okay to place the contents inside special places in the System Folder. Click OK. Then a message will ask if you want to replace your old Scrapbook DA (Figure A.5). Click OK to replace it. This does not replace the contents of the Scrapbook, it only replaces the old DA with the new DA that supports QuickTime.

5. After your Mac has finished copying the files, you will see a message, as shown in Figure A.6. Click OK to exit the message. Next, double-click to open your System Folder.

FIGURE A.5

This warning displays when you replace your old Scrapbook with the new QuickTime Scrapbook included with System 7.1.

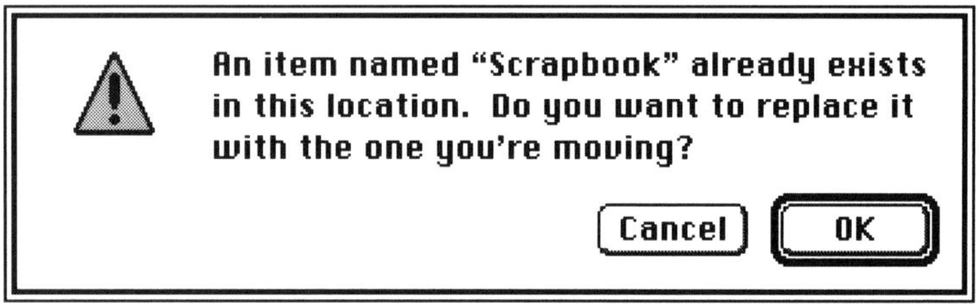

An item named "Scrapbook" already exists in this location. Do you want to replace it with the one you're moving?

Cancel   OK

FIGURE A.6

After your Mac has finished copying files into your System Folder, this message informs you of the placement of all the files.

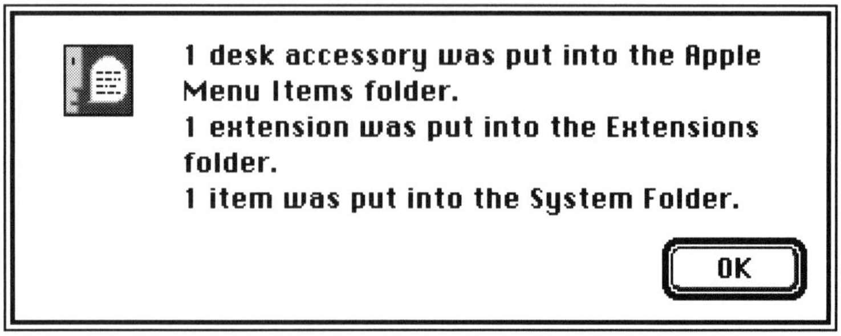

1 desk accessory was put into the Apple Menu Items folder.
1 extension was put into the Extensions folder.
1 item was put into the System Folder.

OK

6. Create a new folder (call it "old Scrapbook," for example) and drag the old Scrapbook File there, so that you can retain the contents of the old Scrapbook without interfering with the new Scrapbook File that you have copied. The new one is in the Replacement Scrapbook File folder.

7. Open the Replacement Scrapbook File folder to display the contents, as shown in Figure A.7. The new Scrapbook File is in this folder so that you can copy the folder to your System Folder without replacing your old Scrapbook File.

FIGURE A.7

The contents of the Replacement Scrapbook File folder

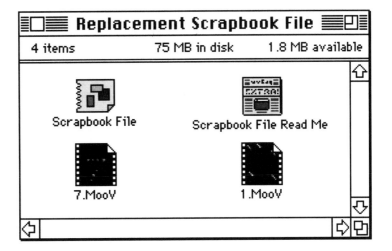

8. Select the Scrapbook File and the two movies, "1.MooV" and "7.MooV," and drag them into the System Folder directory. Then, close the Replacement Scrapbook File folder and your System Folder. (You can throw the Replacement Scrapbook in the trash if you want to.)

9. Choose the Scrapbook DA from the Apple menu and restart your computer.

10. Click on the slider bar to move the indicator forward so that the page reads 2/9. This will take a couple of seconds since the Scrapbook is loading the data from the movie 7.MooV into the second page. Figure A.8 shows the second page of the Scrapbook DA after 7.MooV has been loaded.

FIGURE A.8

Once installed, your new Scrapbook DA will contain the movie, "7.MooV," on the second page. Under System 7.1, Scrapbook allows you to play and edit any movies you have placed into it.

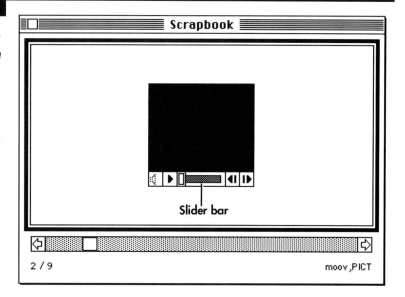

11. Click on the slider bar again to move the indicator forward so that the page reads 3/9. This will take a couple of seconds since the Scrapbook is loading the data from the movie 1.MooV into the third page. Figure A.9 shows the third page of the Scrapbook DA after 1.MooV has been loaded.

FIGURE A.9

Once installed, your new Scrapbook DA will contain the movie, "1.MooV," on the third page.

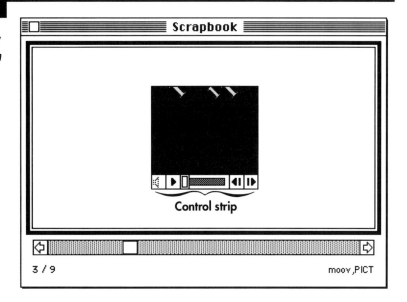

VIEWING QUICKTIME 1.5

Now you can view either of the movies. Notice, in Figure A.9, that there is a control strip along the bottom of the movie. These buttons allow you to play the movie and control the sound. The two movies included with System 7.1 do not include sound, so the first button (the one that looks like a speaker) is dimmed. When you come across a movie that has sound, the button will allow you to access a pop-up volume control, as shown in Figure A.10.

The second button is the play button. Press it and the movie will play from the current frame to the end. You don't have to start at the first frame every time. As the movie plays, the indicator advances along the slider bar in the center of the control strip. By clicking anywhere on the slider bar except on the indicator itself, you can go directly to the frame that corresponds with that position. Thus, clicking on the right-most part of the slider bar advances you to the last frame of the movie, while clicking on the very center of the bar moves you to the frame that

Clicking and holding on the volume button displays the pop-up volume control slider bar.

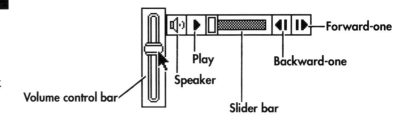

Forward-one

Play

Backward-one

Speaker

Volume control bar

Slider bar

falls in the middle of the movie. If you click and hold on the indicator, you can then move the mouse back and forth to cue through the movie. When you cue the movie in this manner, the movie does not play smoothly because you are moving the indicator faster than the QuickTime extension can interpret and display individual frames. This is especially true if you drag the indicator to the left.

The last two buttons play the movie backward or forward one frame at a time. As a hidden feature of these buttons, press the Control key as you click and hold on either of them. The buttons are then replaced by a small slider bar, as shown in Figure A.11. This smaller slider bar allows you to play the movie in either direction at different speeds. It performs much the same as does dragging the indicator on the center slider bar,

The small slider bar replaces the forward-one and backward-one buttons when you hold the Control key while clicking and holding on the buttons.

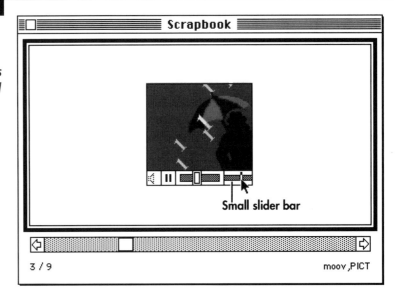

Scrapbook

Small slider bar

3 / 9

moov,PICT

while giving you a smoother play. Drag the small indicator just to the right of center, and the movie will play at the slowest rate allowed, sort of like a 45 RPM record played at 33 RPM. If you play the entire "1.MooV" movie at this rate, then it lasts for about sixteen seconds (verses the normal time of four seconds from beginning to end). If you move the small indicator all the way to the right, you play the movie at a rate that is better than twice normal. Moving the small indicator to the left of center plays the movie backwards. Move it just to the right of center for the best play. You can vary the rate of play by moving the small indicator while viewing the movie. Move the small indicator over the white gap in the center of the slider bar to stop the movie.

You can also use the right and left arrow buttons in the control bar along with the Option key. Option-click the left arrow to move to the first frame; option-click the right arrow to move to the last frame. The ← and → keys on the keyboard also let you move between frames. Press once on either key to move frame-by-frame or press and hold on either key to play the movie in that direction. Press Option and the ← key to jump to the first frame or press Option-→ to advance to the last frame.

WHAT GOOD IS IT?

If you don't have any applications that support QuickTime, outside of the new Scrapbook DA that comes with System 7.1, then all you can do is play the two movies, "1.MooV" and "7.MooV," over and over again. You may think that loading the QuickTime extension onto your hard drive is a waste of time and disk space. But keep in mind that with more and more software manufacturers incorporating support for QuickTime into the newer versions of their software, you are bound to get a program that requires QuickTime. Admittedly, making your own QuickTime movies is quite a bit of work. But what about the movies that you can find on bulletin boards? You will need disk space to download them, but with a program like Aladdin's Popcorn—which is included on the disks you can order with the coupon found at the back of this book—you can cut the movies down to size by keeping only the parts that you really need. Some games use QuickTime: To play "Who Killed Sam Rupert," a murder-mystery game, you must have the QuickTime extension loaded. Furthermore, the compression abilities that QuickTime provides are worth more than their weight in megabytes. Photoshop 2.0.1 is only one of the many graphics programs that uses QuickTime compression. Color It, with a price of around $300, also supports QuickTime. The 50 to 1 compression ratio that the QuickTime JPEG module provides, makes it possible to store a fair-size video library on an average hard drive.

On the other hand, if you don't need the QuickTime extension and you have tired of viewing your two movies over and over, you may not want to keep QuickTime loaded on your Mac. It takes up space that you may be able to put to better use. Altogether, the QuickTime extension and the two movies consume a little less than a megabyte of disk space and the QuickTime extension uses more than 300K of RAM when you boot up your Mac. Of course, if you do remove the QuickTime extension, be sure that you keep a backup copy of it on floppy disk. You may not want it now, but later you could very easily find it to be just the ticket.

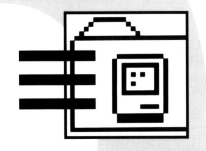

At Ease

SYSTEM 7.1 PROVIDES an alternative to ■ the Finder called At Ease. It is oriented towards more inexperienced users since only a minimal amount of instruction on how to use it is necessary. At Ease can act as a security system of sorts, allowing access to only those files that you have chosen to place at its disposal. More than that, you can restrict access to the Finder to those who know the password you've entered.

The Finder is *always* in operation and At Ease is layered on top of it. If At Ease is turned off (via the At Ease control panel, described later in this appendix), then you can only use the Finder. If At Ease is turned on, then it runs "on top" of the Finder; however, you still can go to the Finder level and see your old familiar desktop.

At Ease is divided into two "panels" that look much like a larger version of the Finder's folder icon, as shown in Figure B.1. The two panels, the Applications panel and the Documents panel, each contain at least one "page." Each application or document available in At Ease has a button with the appropriate icon on it. Each page can hold up to twenty buttons and new pages are added as needed. The arrows in the lower-left and/or right corners allow you to move between the pages of the panels; you can also use the ← and → keys on the keyboard to move around. Move between the two panels by clicking on the desired panel or by pressing the Tab key.

Single-click a button to open a particular application or document. You can open multiple applications and documents as you can in the System 7.1 Finder. You can then move between the open items by using the Applications menu as you would in the Finder.

FIGURE B.1

At Ease consists of the Applications panel made up of pages of buttons for all the applications you have loaded into At Ease, and the Documents panel which contains the same for the documents or files you are using in those applications.

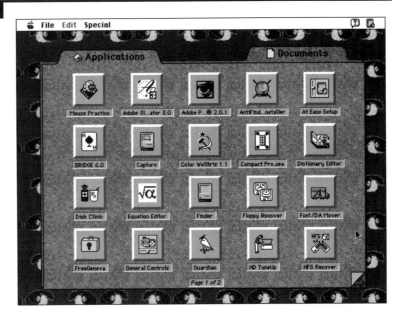

INSTALLING AT EASE

Before you install At Ease, check the Control Panels folder in the System Folder to see if At Ease has already been installed. If you are upgrading to System 7.1, then you will probably have to install At Ease. If At Ease is already installed on your computer, then skip ahead to *Customizing At Ease*, later in this appendix.

The following steps assume that you have the At Ease Installer disk or the equivalent disk images. My upgrade package included only one 1.44MB disk for the At Ease installation. The accompanying documentation referred to two 800K disks for At Ease. It does not matter which format you have; the following steps apply to both.

1. Insert the disk labeled At Ease Installer (or At Ease Install 1 if you have two disks).

2. Double-click on the icon to reveal the contents (as shown in Figure B.2).

The contents of the At Ease Installer disk

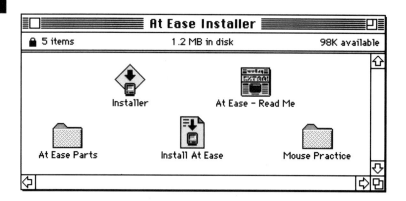

3. Double-click on the Installer icon to open the Installer utility.

4. Once the Welcome to the At Ease Installer screen is displayed, as shown in Figure B.3, read it and click OK or press the Return key to continue.

The first screen to appear explains how options in the upcoming Installer utility work.

Welcome to the At Ease Installer

This program installs the At Ease system software extension in your System Folder.

At Ease

The Installer also creates a new folder on your hard disk called "Mouse Practice," containing the program "Mouse Practice," which teaches novice users basic mouse skills.

Mouse Practice

When you have finished installing At Ease, please run the "At Ease Setup" control panel to turn At Ease on.

At Ease Setup

OK

5. The Easy Install dialog box will display, as shown in Figure B.4. Check that the disk named at the bottom of the dotted rectangle is the hard drive onto which you want to install At Ease (it should be the startup disk—the one with the System on it). If it is not, then click the Switch Disk button until the correct disk name appears.

6. Listed inside the dotted rectangle are the applications that the Easy Install is ready to place onto the chosen hard drive. If you want to subtract from the list, click the Customize button and select the desired installation options from the scrolling list in the Customize dialog box.

7. Click the Install button, instructing the Installer utility to begin the installation process. Follow the instructions on your screen. If you have two At Ease Install disks, then you'll have to swap disks as instructed on the screen.

8. When installation is complete, click the Quit button to exit the Installer, and eject your At Ease Installer disk. Then, restart your computer.

FIGURE B.4

The Easy Install dialog box allows you to install At Ease automatically.

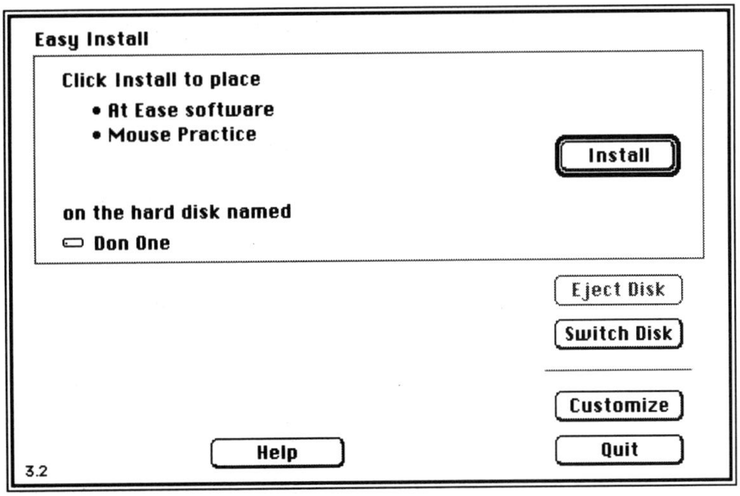

Easy Install

Click Install to place
  • At Ease software
  • Mouse Practice

[Install]

on the hard disk named
▭ Don One

[Eject Disk]
[Switch Disk]

[Customize]
[Help]   [Quit]

3.2

INSTALLING AT EASE ON A NETWORK

You may install At Ease on a network. First you will have to place At Ease on a file server and then install it individually on each computer. The following steps assume that you have the At Ease Installer disk (or disks as the case may be) or the equivalent disk images.

1. Create a new folder on the file server by choosing the New Folder command from the File menu at the desktop and give it a name.

2. Insert the disk labeled At Ease Installer (or At Ease Install 1).

3. Drag the At Ease Install disk icon onto the newly created folder. If you have two disks, then you will have to insert the other disk and drag its icon onto the new folder icon after the first disk is completed.

4. Open the new folder. Inside, another folder named At Ease Install should appear. If you used two disks, then two folders should appear named At Ease Install 1 and At Ease Install 2.

5. Open the At Ease Install folder (or the At Ease Install 1 folder) and drag the Installer icon and the At Ease Install icon outside of the At Ease Install folder and onto the new folder that you created.

6. Go to any computer that has the appropriate access privileges and is connected to the file server.

7. Double-click on the Installer icon to open the Installer utility.

8. Once the Welcome to the At Ease Installer screen is displayed, as shown in Figure B.3, read it and click on OK or press the Return key to continue.

9. The Easy Install dialog box will display, as shown in Figure B.4. Check that the disk named at the bottom of the dotted rectangle is the hard drive onto which you want to install At Ease (your startup disk). If it is not, then click the Switch Disk button until the correct disk name appears.

10. Listed inside the dotted rectangle are the applications that the Easy Install is ready to place onto the chosen hard drive. If you want to subtract from the list, click the Customize button and select the desired installation options from the scrolling list in the Customize dialog box.

11. Click the Install button, instructing the Installer utility to begin the installation process. If you have two At Ease Install disks, then you'll have to swap disks as instructed on the screen.

12. When installation is complete, click the Quit button to exit the Installer. Then, restart your computer.

If At Ease has been installed successfully, it will have added four items to your Mac: the At Ease application to the System Folder, the At Ease Setup control panel to the Control Panels folder, the At Ease Items folder, and the Control Panel Handler extension to the Extensions folder. Also, if you installed At Ease by the Easy Install method, then Mouse Practice was also installed in the root directory of your hard disk. You can throw it out now or you can read about it first in *Mouse Practice*, at the end of this appendix, and then throw it out if you like.

REMOVING AT EASE

Removing At Ease would seem to be the last thing that you need to learn, but, since you need the At Ease Installer disk(s) to properly remove At Ease, this is a good time to remind you to hang on to the Installer disk(s). With that in mind, removing At Ease is similar to installing it.

1. Open the At Ease Setup control panel (located in the Control Panels folder in the System Folder), and select the "Off" radio button. Then close the At Ease Setup control panel.

2. Insert the disk labeled At Ease Installer (or At Ease Install 1 if you have two disks).

3. Double-click on the icon to reveal the contents (as shown in Figure B.2).

4. Double-click on the Installer icon to open the Installer utility.

5. Once the Welcome to the At Ease Installer screen in displayed, as shown in Figure B.3, read it and click OK or press the Return key to continue.

6. The Easy Install dialog box will display, as shown in Figure B.4. Check that the disk named at the bottom of the dotted rectangle is the hard drive on which At Ease is installed. If it is not, then click the Switch Disk button until the correct disk name appears.

7. Click the Customize button.

8. Select At Ease from the scrolling list.

9. Hold down the Option key to change the Install button into the Remove button, as shown in Figure B.5.

10. Click the Remove button to instruct the Installer utility to remove At Ease from your hard drive.

FIGURE B.5

At Ease was selected from the scrolling list and the Option key is pressed so that the Insert button became the Remove button.

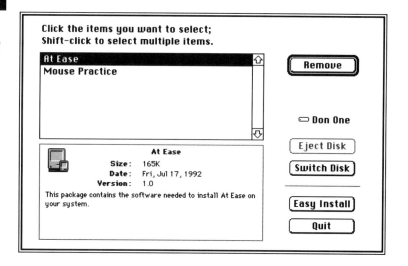

CUSTOMIZING AT EASE

You now are ready to pick and choose the applications and files that will be available through At Ease. The installation process put the At Ease Setup control panel icon in your Control Panels folder. Double-click on the At Ease Setup control panel icon to display the At Ease Setup dialog box, as shown in Figure B.6. Here you can turn At Ease off or on, select applications and files for At Ease, decide how new files are saved, and setup a password if needed.

First, you must turn on At Ease with the At Ease control panel. This allows you access to the three buttons on the control panel and your computer will start up with At Ease when it is restarted. Turning At Ease on and off requires you to restart your computer (but don't restart it yet!). But any other changes you make to the At Ease Setup control panel, via the buttons discussed below, take effect immediately.

FIGURE B.6

The At Ease Setup control panel contains three buttons. (They are dimmed when the Off radio button is selected.)

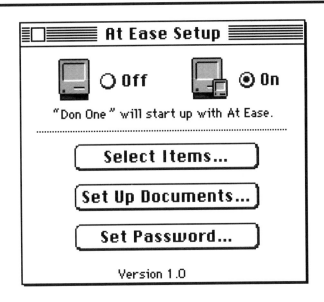

THE SELECT ITEMS... BUTTON

Click the first button, Select Items..., to display the box shown in Figure B.7. The top scrolling list displays the folders, applications, and files found in the folder named in the pop-up menu above the scrolling list. The bottom scrolling list displays all the applications and files available to At Ease. When you first open this box, the bottom At Ease scrolling list will be empty (unless you used Easy Install for At Ease, in which case the scrolling list will contain Mouse Practice alias). At Ease does not use folders as the Finder does. To add applications and files to At Ease individually, click on your choice from the top scrolling list to highlight it, then click on the Add button. An alias of the application or file will appear in the bottom scrolling list. You can expedite the process by holding down the Shift key while clicking on the desired applications or files. As you have seen many times in this book, Shift-clicking on a scrolling list allows you to select multiple items at once.

FIGURE B.7

This box displays after you click the Select Items... button on the At Ease control panel.

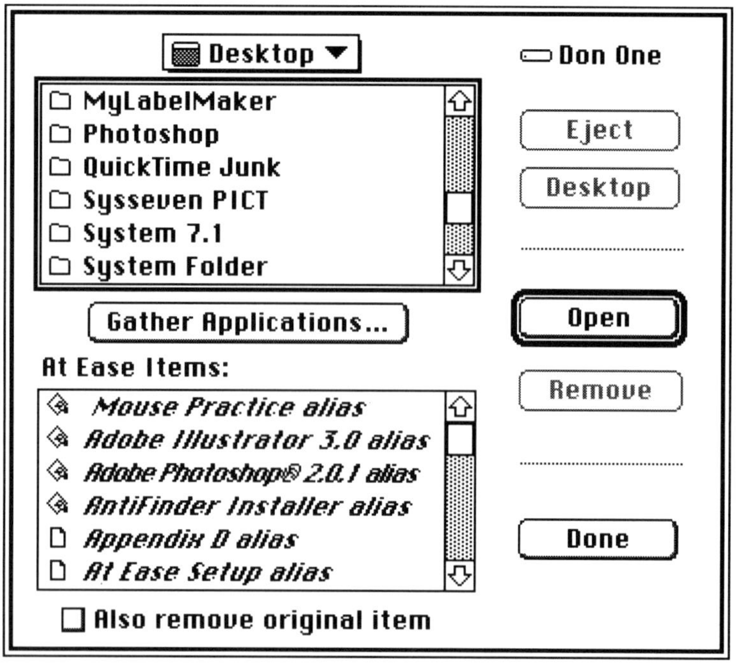

Desktop ▼   ⊂⊃ Don One

☐ MyLabelMaker   Eject
☐ Photoshop
☐ QuickTime Junk   Desktop
☐ Sysseven PICT
☐ System 7.1
☐ System Folder

Gather Applications...   Open

At Ease Items:
⬦ *Mouse Practice alias*   Remove
⬦ *Adobe Illustrator 3.0 alias*
⬦ *Adobe Photoshop® 2.0.1 alias*
⬦ *AntiFinder Installer alias*
☐ *Appendix D alias*   Done
☐ *At Ease Setup alias*

☐ Also remove original item

If you want most or all of your applications available to At Ease, then click on the Gather Applications… button. A message will display telling you how many applications were found. You can either click the Add button to add aliases of all applications or you can click Cancel. The Gather Applications… button will only consider applications on your hard drive and not the files created by those applications. You will have to add them separately. To remove a selection, click on the item to highlight it, then click on the Remove button. When you are finished adding or removing, click on Done.

Remember, all you have done so far is add or remove aliases of applications or files from At Ease. It is possible to remove not only the alias but also the original item when you click on the Remove button. To do this, click on the Also remove original item check box. Now when you remove an alias from the At Ease scrolling list, you will also remove the original. A message will display to warn you that you are permanently removing the original from you hard drive. This featured is best suited for removing the items that are intended for use in and only in At Ease.

It is possible to add items to At Ease by a different method. When At Ease installs, it places a folder—the At Ease Items folder—in the System Folder. You can create an alias of an application or document (by choosing the Make Alias command from the File menu at the Finder level) and drag it to the At Ease Items folder. The alias will appear in the At Ease Items scrolling list the next time you open the At Ease Setup control panel and a button will appear on an At Ease panel, just as any other application or documents added to At Ease. You can also add an application or document, without creating an alias, to At Ease by this method. At Ease will create a button for the item and it will appear in the At Ease Items scrolling list.

Actually, I should expand on that last comment. I found it odd that I could add original applications and documents to the At Ease Items folder, especially when the At Ease manual referred to At Ease using aliases only. I decided to see if I could add the original of something important. Now, I really do not think this is anything anyone is going to do in the normal proceedings of using a Mac, but, in the interest of extremism, I dragged my Finder (that's right, the one in the System Folder) onto the At Ease Items folder. The folder accepted it without any complaints or warnings and displayed it along with all the aliases available to At Ease. This perplexed me since I know that the Finder should not be in the At Ease Items folder, but At Ease did not seem to know. The point is, even though At Ease will accept the original files of anything in the Desktop folder, only add aliases to the At Ease Items folder. At Ease is an alternative to the Finder, but it is, nevertheless, dependent upon the Finder and the roles cannot be reversed.

THE SETUP DOCUMENTS... BUTTON

Click on the second button in Figure B.6, Set Up Documents..., to display the Set Up Documents dialog box, as shown in Figure B.8. Here you have the options to allow files that are created in At Ease to be saved to the hard drive, to make the user provide a floppy disk for the files, neither, or both.

At Ease installs with the "Add a button to At Ease" option activated. This means that any file created and then saved in an application accessed through At Ease will show up as a button on the Documents panel of At Ease. The file is saved to the hard drive and an alias is created for the At Ease Items folder. Once At Ease has added a button to the Documents panel for a saved file, the file can be accessed by users of At Ease.

FIGURE B.8

The Set Up Documents dialog box allows you to decide whether files created in At Ease are saved to the hard drive or to a floppy disk.

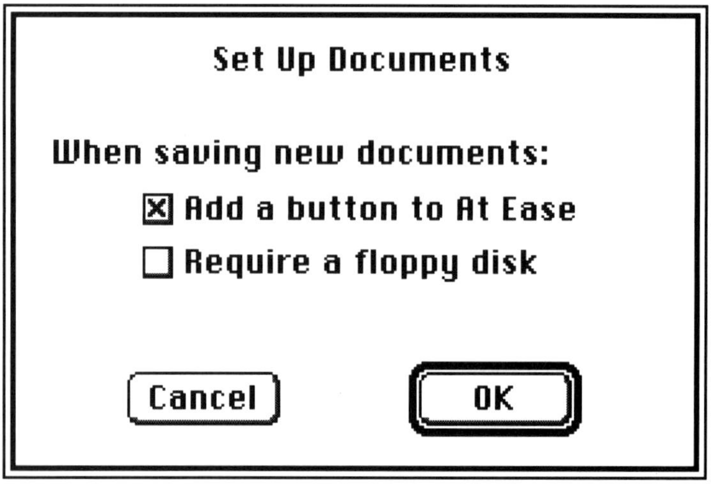

Set Up Documents

When saving new documents:

- ☒ **Add a button to At Ease**
- ☐ **Require a floppy disk**

[Cancel]   [OK]

Unless the application that created the file allows you to delete files, the file is then a permanent part of At Ease until it is removed by using the Select Items dialog box. If you have only one person using At Ease, then this option is probably fine. Alternatively, you can trash the file directly from the At Ease Items folder at the Finder level.

When the "Add a button to At Ease" option is activated, any items saved or newly loaded to your Mac at the Finder level will also get a button in At Ease. If you do not want this, then deactivate it when you are working at the Finder level.

On the other hand, if you have multiple users on At Ease, you might want At Ease to insist that each user saves any files created while working in At Ease to floppy disk. Your hard drive won't become cluttered with other people's files and files will remain the property of the authors. To do this, click on the Add a box to At Ease button to deactivate it and click on the Require a floppy disk box.

If neither option is selected, then a file saved while working At Ease is saved to the hard drive but no alias is created. It may seem as though the file could only be accessed at the Finder. This is not the case, since the file can usually be reopened in the application that created it. For example, if neither of the options in the Set Up Documents dialog box is selected and you created and saved a file in Microsoft Word while working in At Ease, then even though At Ease does not create a button for the file on the Documents panel, Word would still allow you to open the file (or any other readable file for that matter) at a later date. In other words, having neither option selected does not protect any files that you may have wanted secured if At Ease contains an application that can open the files.

The final possible combination, both options selected, means that all files must be saved to disk *and* a button is created for each file. At Ease will list an alias of the file in the bottom scrolling list of the box (the one that displays after clicking on the Select Items... button in the At Ease Setup control panel), even though the hard drive will show no record of the file. Instead, the original file is saved on the floppy disk. So, if you click the button for that file—which subsequently appears on the Documents panel of At Ease—then you will have to have available the floppy disk to which the file was saved.

THE SET PASSWORD... BUTTON

Click on the Set Password... button (see Figure B.6) to display the Set Password dialog box, as shown in Figure B.9. Here you can choose a password (with up to fifteen characters) and a clue (with up to fifty characters) for the password. If you choose a password, then any time an At Ease user tries to go to the Finder or open any application not listed in the At Ease Applications panel, the Password dialog box will appear (along with the clue, if you have chosen one) asking the user to enter the password, as shown in Figure B.10.

FIGURE B.9

The Set Password dialog box allows you to enter a password and a clue for the password.

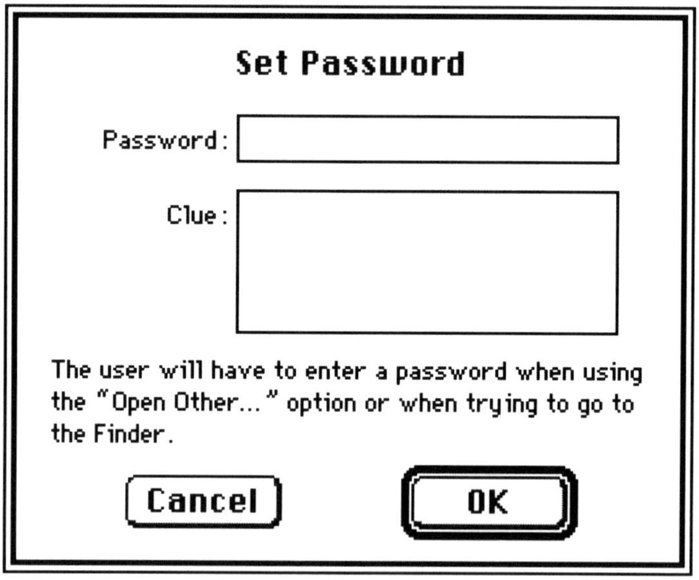

Set Password

Password: [   ]

Clue: [   ]

The user will have to enter a password when using the "Open Other..." option or when trying to go to the Finder.

[Cancel]   [OK]

The Password dialog box will continue to ask for the correct password until the correct password is given or until the Cancel button is clicked. So, in other words, you have unlimited tries to type in the correct password. This is helpful if you do not quite remember your password.

FIGURE B.10

If a password has been chosen, then the Password dialog box will display when necessary.

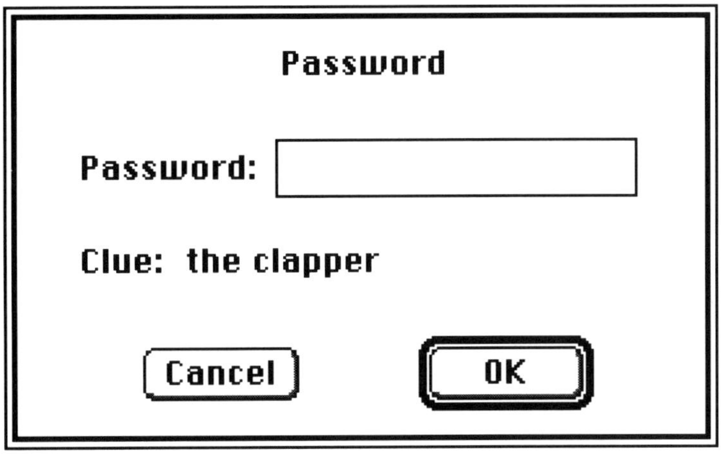

Password

Password: [   ]

Clue: the clapper

[Cancel]   [OK]

TIP

If you are going to be customizing At Ease on a regular basis, I recommend that you add an alias of the At Ease Setup control panel to your At Ease Items folder. This way, you can access the Setup control panel from within At Ease.

If you completely forget the password and need to go to the Finder, then you will have to restart your Mac with a startup disk that contains a System Folder. The Disk Tools disk that comes with System 7.1 is one such disk. As I said in Chapter 2, when you turn on your computer, the CPU looks for the startup disk in the floppy drive before it checks the hard drive. Thus, if you turn your computer on with the Disk Tools disk (or any other suitable startup disk), then your computer will display the Finder and not At Ease. You can then either throw out the At Ease Preferences file (found in the Preferences folder in the System Folder) or, more easily, change the password in the At Ease Setup control panel. If you throw out the At Ease Preferences file, then At Ease will start up with the default settings of adding a button to saved files and no password, and you will have to make changes to the At Ease Setup control panel after you have restarted your computer without the external startup disk.

If you do not have a copy of the Disk Tools disk, then you can easily copy someone else's System file and Finder onto a single disk (your local software dealer can help you out if you know of no other Mac owners, which is probably not the case), and restart your computer using that disk. Since you can bypass the password so easily, At Ease does not really serve as a good security system.

THE AT EASE DESKTOP

At Ease contains six menus: the Apple, File, Edit, Special, Help, and Applications. The Apple menu contains all the same entries as does the Finder's Apple menu except for the Control Panels folder. To remove or add applications to the At Ease Apple menu, you must add them to the Finder's Apple menu. At Ease will not ask for the password if you select an application from the Apple menu. As far as the control panels go, you can add any of them to At Ease as you would any other application. A button will appear for each control panel you add. You can even add the At Ease Setup control panel, but the password will be required if you have recorded one.

The File menu contains the Open Other... and Go To Finder commands, while the Finder's File menu contains the Go To At Ease command. The Open Other... command allows you to open applications and documents that do not appear in At Ease. The Go To Finder command allows you to do just that: go to the Finder. Both of these commands are protected by the password. An alternative method of getting to the Finder is to add an alias to the At Ease Setup. A button will appear and you will have to know the password just like for the Go to Finder command.

The Edit menu contains the same commands as the Finder's Edit menu except for Show Clipboard. It is not possible to add an alias of Clipboard to At Ease (I could not find out why this is not possible), but, if you want to have the Clipboard available at the At Ease level, you can place an alias of the Clipboard in the Apple Menu Items folder.

The commands in the Special, Help, and Applications menus function similarly to their counterparts at the Finder level. One thing to note is that once you go to the Finder from At Ease, the Finder's Application menu will list At Ease as an open application and you can go back to At Ease by selecting it from the Applications menu. If you do this, then the Applications menu in the At Ease level will list the Finder and you will be able to access it without the password. To ensure that this does not happen, you should move between the two via the respective commands in the File menus.

Overall, At Ease is very straightforward and is probably a good solution if you have inexperienced computer users sharing your Mac. It does, after all, present an uncluttered desktop where applications and documents are available in a what-you-see-is-what-you-get format. With children, for example, you could add all their games and educational applications to At Ease while protecting everything else on the Finder (though, I would not rely too heavily on the password-security even with children). As far as using At Ease over a network as a general replacement for the Finder, it seems a little silly and potentially risky. Someone could bypass the password-security with a startup disk and change the password.

*M*OUSE PRACTICE

If you installed At Ease by the Easy Install method, then you also installed an application called Mouse Practice. Mouse Practice is intended to help beginner mouse-users become comfortable with positioning the cursor and clicking and dragging objects with the mouse. It is geared towards children, especially those who cannot read. If you have small children who need a friendly introduction to the ways of a mouse, then you might want to look at it. But if you're looking to train adults, you can safely throw it out. Most adults will find Mouse Practice a drag (no pun intended); their needs can be better served by simply sitting down at Macs and experimenting with mice at their own paces.

Application
Creator
Codes

THE FOLLOWING IS a list of four-character creator codes that accompany every document created on a Macintosh computer. Each character code corresponds to a single application and is registered with Apple to ensure uniqueness. For example, a document that has been assigned the creator code "8BIM" was created using Adobe Photoshop.

Creator Code	Application	Creator Code	Application
+327	MacDFT Config	aca5	Family Builder
1ade	First Aid HFS	ACE2	A.M.E. INIT
1AID	First Aid HFS	ACE™	A.M.E. INIT #2
1SHT	1 Shot Opener	AcPC	Access PC
3DW	3D Works	ACTA	ActaAdvantage
4D03	4th DIMENSION	ADBb	Programmer's Key
4D93	FileForce	ADBM	Dbase Mac
4DDB	4D SQL Server	ADBS	Adobe Separator
4DSS	4D Calc	ADIS	American Discovery
4wrt	4D Write	ADJ3	_DATE
5ROi	FormatterFive INIT	ADrk	After Dark
8BIM	Adobe Photoshop	AdSv	SaveGuard
60&B	XP60+B	AICi	Slimeline INIT
?MAC	Portable Profiler	aLAT	AdminLAT
{−:J	MS Flight Simulator	ALCH	Alchemy
μ•A8	MacPlot Configure	ALD3	PageMaker
Aard	INITPicker	ALD4	PageMaker
Aask	Aask	ALGR	Algebra
aCa2	Fontographer	ALSP	PrePrint
aca4	Fontastic Plus	AOqc	America Online

Creator Code	Application	Creator Code	Application
APSC	AppleScan	AVT6	MacMainFrame 3287
APSC	Scanner	AVTC	Avatar Control Panel
aQD2	QuickColor	AvTR	MacMainFrame Client
ARKV	Archive	AvtR	MacMainFrame Graphics
ARKV	SmartImage	avTR	MacMainFrame Work.
ARST	SmartRestore	AΣop	Algebra Shop
ART3	Adobe Illustrator	BAKG	Queue INIT
ARTZ	Adobe Illustrator	BAKG	QueueWatcher
ASAT	Alisa	BAUd	LASER Award Maker
ASav	AutoSave II	BBN	Statistics Workshop
ASEP	Adobe Separator	BECK	~Mobius CDEV
atcp	AdminTCP	bFAX	BackFAX
ATMC	ATM	bjbc	Installer
ATR	Type Reunion	bMRN	Super Boomerang
ATRX	Audiotrax	BnFl	Blockers and Finders
AvaT	MacMainFrame Checker	BRAS	FAXGATE
AvT0	Gateway Client Driver	BSDt	Stepping Out II
Avt0	Token Ring Driver	BSWA	The Bank Street Writer
AvT1	Coax Gateway Server	BTHE	BigThesaurus
Avt1	SDLC Driver	BTRE	InterBase
AVT2	CUT Driver	Capt	Capture
AvT2	Token Ring Gateway Serv.	CCAD	Claris CAD
AVT4	DFT Driver	CCGT	Claris CGT
AvT5	SDLC Gateway Server	CCL	Macintosh Common Lisp

Creator Code	Application	Creator Code	Application
CCL2	Macintosh Common Lisp	CEMU	MockTerminal Utility
CCMa	Carbon Copy	CEQA	QM Administrator
CCRO	HostPrint	CEQS	QM Server
CD22	Fast Forms	CEST	MacBanner
CD30	Fast Forms Filler	CEtb	CEToolbox
CDCL	SILVERRUN-ERM	CEVC	Vaccine
CDDF	SILVERRUN-DFD	cfbj	Installer
CDEX	SILVERRUN-ERX	CGAT	CommGATE
CDFD	SILVERRUN-DFD	CGRF	CricketGraph
CDME	SILVERRUN-SRL	CHAZ	TrueType INIT
CDML	SILVERRUN-LDM	CLCK	Clicktracks
CdMn	Talking Moose	CLRZ	Colorizer
CDMR	SILVERRUN-RDM	clss	ClearVue/Classic
CDP0	SILVERRUN-ERX->RDM	Clue	STATUS*Profiler
CDsk	ColorDesk	CLY4	DeskPicture
CEBN	MacBILLBOARD	CMCC	Calendar Creator
CECM	CalendarMaker	CMCΔ	Color MacCheese
CEDA	QM Remote	cmri	MIDI Manager
CEEZ	EZ-Menu	CONN	Connect
CEFF	FolderShare	CP4D	4D Compiler
CEIM	IconMover	CPa1	3+File
CELM	QuickMail INIT	CPMS	KeyPlan
CELN	QuicKeys	CPSp	MacTools Partition INIT
CEMM	QM Menu	CrCr	ClickPaste

Creator Code	Application
CRDW	Cricket Draw
CRiK	C-Server
CRPR	CA Cricket Presents
CS1	CS-1
CSF	Comic Strip Factory
CSFX	QuickImage24
CSII	ColorSpace
CSii	QuickImage24
CSRV	C-Server Manager
CTV1	Mac II Video Card Util.
CUST	Customizer
CWMW	ConcertWare
CyGF	GatorInstaller
D2CI	Disinfectant INIT
D2CT	Disinfectant
D2SP	MacSpin
DAb2	DAtabase Builder
DAD2	Canvas
DART	DART
DATB	DATa
DbTk	DoubleTalk
DCAc	MacIRMA CUT
DCAG	MacIRMA PCLK Graphics
DCAh	MacIRMA API

Creator Code	Application
DCAI	MacIRMA Entry Emulator
DCAj	MacIRMAtrac Diagnostics
DCAk	MacIRMAtrac
DCAL	MacIRMA DAL
DCAm	MacIRMA Workstation
DCAq	MacIRMA Graphics Workstation
DCAs	MacIRMA SNA
DCAt	MacIRMA PrDriver
DCat	MacIRMATalk
dCpy	Disk Copy
DDAP	DiskDoubler App
DDIN	DiskDoubler INIT
DECA	MasterColor
DECB	NetCopy
DECC	DECnet Control
DECI	DECnet/Mac
DECK	DECK
DECN	NCP
DECO	Mail for Macintosh
DEXP	DiskExpress I
DExp	DiskExpress II
DFB0	MicroPhone II
DFCT	Disinfectant

Creator Code	Application
DGRH	DeltaGraph
DIDR	Digital Darkroom
DIMR	Dimmer
DkTP	DiskTop.Extras
DLP1	DiskLock
DLP6	FolderLock
DMgr	DriveManager
DMOV	Font/DA Mover
DnPg	DynoPage
dPro	MacDraw Pro
DPVW	DiskPaper Reader
Dr.W	STATUS* Mac
Drog	Easy Color Paint
DROV	DrawOver
DSIG	Comment
DskD	DiskDup+
Dskt	Time Drive
DSwI	Font/DA Juggler
DvCm	MARATHON COMM
DVDT	MacLink Plus/Translators
DVOI	MacLink Plus/Wang OIS
DVPC	MacLinkPlus/PC
DVSP	Port Control
DVVS	MacLink Plus/Wang VS

Creator Code	Application
DYNO	Dynodex
DZT4	Diskfit
DZT6	Network DiskFit
EAGP	Dollars and $ense
ebEM	MacProteus Front Panel
EECO	Direct Mail Application
EGH2	Cheque
ejct	800k Eject INIT
EMCD	Metro CD INIT
emCP	E-Machines
emg1	Thunder 7
Empw	Empower II
ENCC	Encore
ERIK	Mavis Beacon Teaches Typing
EVRX	Abaton Scanner Driver
EXCU	Exposure Pro Customizer
EXOD	eXodus
EXPL	Exposure Pro Personalizer
EXPR	Exposure Pro
EZTP	~Font Porter
F2Oi	F2MO INIT
F2Ri	F2RC INIT
F5Hi	FormatterFive INIT

Creator Code	Application	Creator Code	Application
FAFX	AppleFax	FSBA	AutoStart
fBL.	FolderBolt Admin.	FSBK	Fastback II
fBLT	FolderBolt	FSCS	ColorStudio
FCsc	StarCommand	FSPE	ImageStudio
fgs1	Shiva Modems	FSR1	IDEAcomm Utilities
FHA2	Aldus FreeHand	fsWF	Findswell
FHA3	Aldus FreeHand	FWRT	FullWrite Professional
FHrm	Font Harmony	FΣop	Math Shop Spotlight
FiDi	File Director	G*NS	SuperLaserSpool
FIL2	Microsoft File	GANt	MacSchedulePLUS
FILE	Microsoft File	GAnt	MacSchedule
FIv2	Full Impact	Gasp	Server Control
FLI	DaynaFile	GBox	GatorKeeper
FMK4	FileMaker II	gbox	GatorBoxTFTP
FMKR	FileMaker Plus	gc24	8•24 GC
FMPR	FileMaker Pro	GdCd	GuardCard Configure
Fmt1	FormatterOne	GDG2	Template Printer
Fmt2	FormatterTwo	GEOL	AppleLink
Fmt5	FormatterFive	GLAS	Full Impact
FNTC	eXodus	GLCK	SuperMatch INIT
FOSY	Forms Designer	Glxy	Galaxy
FOX+	FoxBASE+	GMK4	Grammatik Mac
Fram	FrameMaker	GNTC	Genetics Model
FRed	FontStudio	GRAV	Gravity Model

Creator Code	Application	Creator Code	Application
GRPW	GROUPwriter	iALZ	INIT Analyzer
GSQu	Geometric Supposer Quad.	IBGa	InterBridge Manager
GSTr	Geometric Supposer Tria.	IBXA	InBox+ Admin
GVCI	Teleport	IBXI	In-Box cdev
HCSV	HayesConnect Server	IBXI	In-Box INIT
HCVT	Runtime Converter	IBXM	TOPS InBox Server
HDFF	Hammer Install	IBXS	InBox Setup
HDPi	HDP	ICc8	Multi-Driver
Heap	HeapFixer	iDa!	IDEAcomm Printer
HELX	Double Helix	iFtk	Install FlashTalk
Hill	Screen Locker	iMGR	INIT Manager
Hint	NodeHint	INBX	In-Box
HISC	Mac-to-Mac	Info	PhoneNET Liaison
HLXE	Double Helix Engine	InOu	In/Out
HLXM	Double Helix Client	inpl	Inter•Poll
HLXN	Double Helix Server	INTU	Quicken
HMDM	HayesConnect	InUs	SCSIInUse
HNIK	Double Helix Utility	IOSv	In/Out Server
HOff	HAND-Off	ItgD	STATUS*Installer
HOTD	Hot Dog Stand	itrn	IDEAlink
HPOi	HPMO INIT	JAïN	Rival
HPPL	LCINIT	jBox	Jukebox
HUPD	Update Collection	jbx!	heirDA
I$Rc	ScreenRecorder	jbxç	AlarmsClock

Creator Code	Application	Creator Code	Application
JETA	MasterPaint	KUCI	Speed Beep
JP3D	Graph 3D	LANI	Sentinel
JPJF	Backmatic	LcOp	READ-IT! O.C.R.
JXFK	FinderKeys	LHGC	SUM Shield INIT
JXNM	NowMenus	Lkup	LookUp
JΣop	Math Shop Jr.	LMov	Layout Mover
KaAR	Memory Manager INIT	LONP	SUM Partition INIT
KAHL	THINK C	LSTP	LetraStudio
KCFD	SmartForm Designer	LWFU	LaserWriter Font Utility
KCFM	SmartForm Assistant	M240	Mac240
KIFI	AtOnce Import/Export	MACA	MacWrite
KISE	EtherPort SE	MacL	SmartFormat
KISS	AtOnce!	MacX	MacX
Kmc2	Art Importer	MADM	Mail Network Administrator
KMKM	KidsMath	MAJW	MediaMaker
KML9	NightWatch ShutDown	Marh	Mariah
KML]	MacSafe	MART	Modern Artist
KMLA	NightWatch Administrator	maxa	Maxima
KMLC	NightWatch Professor	maxb	MacsBug
KMLM	The Connection	MBBL	Money Building Blocks
KTCP	TCPort	MCFL	MacFlow
KTLK	FastPath Manager II	MCIT	MacInteriors
KTMV	MacVision Image Processing	MClk	SuperClock!
KTSW	KidsTime	McNt	MaxNotes

Creator Code	Application	Creator Code	Application
McSk	Vantage Opener	MMDR	MacroMind Director
MD20	MacDraft	mMKR	MailMaker
MDC2	LEXIS/NEXIS	MMsi	DataPak
MDFT	MacDraft	MMss	Meeting Maker Startup
MDPL	MacDraw II	MNET	CONNECT
MDRW	MacDraw	MNGR	Manager
MDsk	MultiDisk	mngr	Manager CDEV
MDSP	ModelShop	MoAK	Sumo INIT
MEMR	Ready Set Go!	mOCR	TYPIST
MER	MacIRMA Graphics Instructor	MODi	CannonMO INIT
MET1	Metamorphosis	MONY	WealthBuilder
MFIM	On Cue	MOR2	MORE
MFIT	Data Models	MORE	MORE
MIDA	Studio Vision	MPAP	MarcoPolo
MIDJ	EZVision	mpCd	MacPassword
mime	MacroMaker	mpCu	MacPassword Customizer
MIRR	MacTools Mirror	MPNT	MacPaint
MixA	SampleCell Editor	MPRJ	MacProject
MLTM	QM Forms	MPRX	MacProject II
MMak	Master List	MPRZ	MacProject II
MMAP	KidsMath	MPS	MPW
MMDA	MacroMind Accelerator	MrBK	HDBackup
MMdp	MacroMind Player	MRec	MacRecorder Driver
		MRJN	DesignStudio

Creator Code	Application
MRT2	ExpressTape
MSAd	Mail Network Admin.
MSBA	Microsoft BASIC
MSBB	Microsoft BASIC
MSBk	Mail Backup Utility
MSDi	Mail Dial-In Host
MSFS	DOS Mounter
MSGw	MS Mail Gateway Driver
MsGW	MS Mail Gateway Driver
MSMa	MS Mail Workstation Driver
MsMa	MS Mail Workstation
MSMt	Mail Tools
MSNP	MacSnoop
MSSa	Schedule+
MSSU	Microsoft Excel Setup
MSSv	MS Mail Server
MsSv	MS Mail Server
MsTl	Mail Tools
MSWD	Microsoft Word
MSWT	Microsoft Write
MT5i	MitekSQ INIT
mtcp	MacTCP
mtga	Apple-Digital
MTK1	Hard Disk Installer

Creator Code	Application
MTPC	Master Tracks Pro 4
Mtva	Aapps DigiVideo
MtvC	DigiVideo Color App
MULP	MarkUp
MUSS	Notewriter II
MW$.	QuickLock
MWII	MacWrite II
MWPR	MacWrite Pro
MWS3	Macintosh Workstation
mXNS	3+Mail CP
MYMC	Managing Your Money
MΣop	Math Shop
NAMR	The Namer
NBMZ	NumberMaze
NETB	PCSession Prep
NETu	Netutil
NISI	Nisus
NLdr	ConnectivityLoader
nmd0	NetModem
nmd2	NetSerial
nmd4	TeleBridge
nmd6	EtherGate
NMDF	NumberMaze Decimals & Fractions
NMgr	ConnectivityManager

Creator Code	Application	Creator Code	Application
NMUN	Number Munchers	ORTh	Sans Faute
NoO2	ORACLE Settings	OTNM	OutNumbered!
NSPU	Profiler	PBAP	PictureBase
NSrv	NameServer	PCB4	MacTools Backup
NTMP	NetAtlas	pcdv	Control-1
Ntrm	Netway 3270A	pchr	PatchBay
Ntrm	Netway 3270A/G	PCLI	PacerLink
NUTS	FileMaker	PCLJ	Redirector
NVSI	Mobius	PCLS	AT Driver
NwCU	CompleteUndelete	PCLS	TELNET Driver
NWin	StartUp Manager	PCLS	VDISK driver
nX^n	WriteNow	PCXT	SoftPC
ODMN	ODMS Client	PCXT	SoftPC EGA/AT
ODMS	ODMS Design Station	PFRD	Public Folder
ODMU	ODMS Server	PHNX	Dreams
OKYT	Okyto	PIT	PackIt III
OM$$	Omnis	PIXL	PixelPaint Professional
OMEG	Mathematica	PIXR	PixelPaint
ONLC	OL Startup	PIXZ	PixelPaint Professional
Optm	OPTIMA/32	PJMM	THINK Pascal
OPTZ	MacTools Optimizer	PLIR	RecvInit
ORAC	~OracleInit	PLP1	Persuasion
Orcl	Oracle	PLP2	Persuasion
ORGN	The Oregon Trail	PMAC	PhotoMac

Creator Code	Application	Creator Code	Application
PMAN	Queue Monitor	PTKT	Pantone Color Toolkit
pMgr	Personal*STATUS	puAB	Address Book Plus
PNC1	Norton Utilities	PVMO	PV Installer
PNC2	FileSaver	PVOi	PVINIT SMO
POFV	Point of View	PVSQ	PV Installer
POoi	DataPak M.O.	PVsq	PV INITSQ
PPcp	PassProof	PVXX	PV Installer
PPcp	PassProof cdev	PWIC	POWERicons
PPIN	PassProof Startup	PWRI	MindWrite
PPNT	PowerPoint	PYRO	Pyro!
PPul	PassProof User Log	Q100	DataStream
pQD1	Radius/GX	Q100	TapeDriver
prse	Prodigy	qbak	Tape Backup 40SC
PRSM	Prism	qcad	QuickCAD
PRTC	OmniPage	QCON	DAtabase Converter
PRZM	DataPrism	QED1	QUED-M
PSAP	Apple CD-ROM	QKKI	Tangent.INIT
PSI2	Microsoft Works	QKxi	Extension Manager
PSIP	Microsoft Works	Qky2	QuicKeys 2
PSMC	Forum	qmnt	Quick Mount
PSPT	Apple File Exchange	QSHT	Q-Sheet A/V
PT21	TPD INIT	QTAL	DAtabase Personalizer
PtBU	MacProteus Batteries	QVSt	QuickView Studio
pTEK	STATUS*Mac	R&R	IDEAcomm Mac

Creator Code	Application	Creator Code	Application
R2V2	Adobe Streamline	RPHO	PhotoRMan
Racc	Accelerator	RQA1	Accelerator
RADg	Radius Theatrics	Rqœ•	Color Pivot Resolutions
RAPP	RenderApp	RRHO	SecondSight
RATS	Manager	RRmt	RetrospectINIT
RATs	Manager	Rsan	RadiusMath
RC i	RicohCart INIT	RSCU	MacTools Rescue
RDR3	Talking Reader Rabbit	Rsdi	Classic/SE Display
RDUS	ImpressIT	RSED	ResEdit
Redx	Redux	Rslv	Claris Resolve
REGI	Reggie	RTLt	Live List
REND	RenderWorks	rTV	Radius Grabber
RFG2	FrameGrabber 324	RunF	RadiusWare
RFG3	ColorBoard 364 F.G.	RunH	Soft Pivot
Rfpd	Plus Display	RUNT	SuperCard
rGma	Precision Color	RVEC	VectRMan
RINI	!RManINIT	RWAR	MultiMaster
RMAZ	Reading Maze	Rxvr	Retrospect
RMG1	MediaGrabber	Rxvs	Retro.SCSI
RMgr	AppleTalk Tuner	SA4D	DigiSystem INIT
RO i	RicohMO INIT	sa30	Sound Accelerator
ROP	ClearVue/SE	sade	Sade
Rops	RasterOps Monitors	SAFE	MacSafe II Admin.
Rö40	RocketWare	SASH	A/UX Startup

Creator Code	Application
SBLR	Hard disk Deadbolt
Scav	Disk First Aid
SCde	Coach Pro
SCEZ	Smartcom
scfd	Finder Sounds
ScII	Suitcase II
SCOM	Smartcom II
ScoT	Personality!
SCPG	Personal Press
SCS!	SCSIProbe
scsi	Apple HD SC Setup
Sd2a	Sound Designer II
Sd2b	Audiomedia
Sd2c	Sound Designer II
Sd2d	Sound Designer II SC
SERM	AntiToxin
sFIX	MIDI Port Fix
SFLT	StrataFlight
SFX!	SoundEdit
shOT	Screenshot
SHOW	ImageWorks
shv0	Shiva Config
SHWP	ShowPlace
SILH	Silhouette

Creator Code	Application
SiLn	Silverlining
SIT!	StuffIt Deluxe
SI∞D	Infini-D
SLDD	Silver INIT
SMGA	Accelerator
SMJr	SAM Intercept Jr.
SMOi	Sony MO INIT
smon	SuperView
sMst	SoundMaster
SMSY	LaserFrame INIT
SNAP	ColorSnap 32+
snmg	Internet Manager
SOFT	NetSwitch
SOLC	Curator
SP3D	Super3D
spcd	SpeedCard
Spin	Globe
SPNT	SuperPaint
SPOT	MacTOPS Filing
SPSV	EasyShare INIT
SPWE	Spellswell
SQ5i	SyQuest INIT
SqQQ	SyQuest INIT
SqQq	SmartFormat Syquest

Creator Code	Application	Creator Code	Application
SRSE	MediaTracks	Tapi	APIDriver
SSDD	Silverscan	tCat	C•A•T III
SSIW	WordPerfect	tcjm	VideoSync
SSLA	MacMoney	TD02	SNA.3278
ST/1	Studio/1	TD10	MacNetway 3287
ST/8	Studio/8	TDDP	Netway1000
ST32	Studio/32	TDDR	Tri-Data API
STAT	StatView II	TDNT	MacNetway 3270
STAT	StatViewSE+Graphics	tdsc	Tape Disk
Stat	LW Status	Term	MacTerminal
STEP	Explorer	Th!U	Thunder 7 Utility
STHL	Vision	TIFM	TrueForm Setup
STO1	SUM Tools	TMCP	TurboMouse
Strx	Astrix	TMKR	Notification Toolbox
SupA	SuperANOVA	Tmon	TMON
SVFS	ifXFS	TMP2	Tempo II PLUS
svgb	SuperView II	Top	Start TOPS
SWMM	Success with Writing	Top4	FlashTalk INIT
SWVL	Swivel 3D	Tops	SoftTalk
T$2c	Timbuktu	Tops	Tops
T$r2	Timbuktu/Remote	tops	Tops DA
TAA2	TAA	Topz	TOPS
Tahi	TahitiMO INIT	Tprt	APIPrinter
TANK	ThinkTank	TPTC	tpdrvr

Creator Code	Application	Creator Code	Application
TPTP	TYPISTINIT	Uppr	DAtabase Upgrader
TRAF	TrafficWatch	VC3D	VersaCAD 3D
TRBS	Turbosynth	VCAD	VersacadII
TRFM	TrueForm Fill Out	VCCN	AntiToxin INIT
TRPZ	Trapeze	VEXI	Vantage External
TRX!	TRAX	VGDt	Clinic
tsi^	LapLink INIT	VGDt	SAM Virus Clinic
TSLP	PLICDR	VGrd	SAM Intercept
TSPL	Spool	view	SuperView
TSSB	NCP	VIPO	V.I.P.
TSSC	Net Control	VIRy	Virex
TSSI	TSSNet	Vis3	StrataVision 3d
TSSM	NetMail	VMEM	Virtual
TSSN	NetCopy	VPUB	Ventura Publisher
ttxt	TeachText	VTXP	VTXpress
TuMo	TurboMouse	wade	RasterOps Monitors
TWII	TrafficWatch II	Ware	FileGuard
TYAL	Adobe TypeAlign	WDGT	Widgets
UGff	Flowfazer	WILD	HyperCard
uins	EtherPort	Wjb?	Virex INIT
uLAT	LAT	WK11	White Knight
ULTR	UltraPaint	WMUN	Word Munchers
Undl	CompleteUndelete	WNGZ	Wingz
unis	Installer	WORD	Microsoft Word

Creator Code	Application	Creator Code	Application
WPC2	WordPerfect	WYSI	WYSIWYG Menus
Wsql	Quickletter	WΣop	Math Shop Spotlight
Wsti	Amazing Paint	XCEL	Microsoft Excel
Wtch	Watch	XFMT	eXodus
WVTX	MacInTax	XLDE	MS Excel Dialog Editor
WWST	Wagon train 1848	xstv	SuperVideo

Featured
Products
and Vendors

THROUGHOUT THIS BOOK, I have discussed utilities and other products that will augment your ability to use System 7 and exploit the power of your Macintosh computer. The following list of products includes vendors, addresses, phone numbers, and acquisition information. If a product is sold commercially, its price is listed. Products shown as *freeware* or *shareware* are typically available from bulletin board systems such as CompuServe or America Online. Freeware can be used without paying a fee. The only stipulations are that you can't modify the software, claim any rights to it, or distribute it commercially without express permission from the author. Shareware products are given away under the condition that you pay a registration fee if you intend to keep the software longer than the specified trial period. Shareware is sometimes called "honorware" since you are on your honor to pay the fee; the FBI won't be keeping an eye on you and the author has no recourse if you don't own up. However, at the risk of sounding like a nag, I consider every one of the products listed on the next few pages to be worth the price. For one-tenth of what you'd expect to pay for commercial software, you get technical support and upgrade information. You know if you can afford it or not, so do the right thing.

Products marked by an asterisk (*) are included on the disks that you can order with the coupon found at the back of this book.

AccessPC 1.1
Insignia Solutions
526 Clyde Ave.
Mountain View, CA 94043
(800) 848-7677, (415) 694-7600
$99.95

After Dark 2.0v
Berkeley Systems
2095 Rose St.
Berkeley, CA 94709
(510) 540-5535
$49.95

AKA
Fred Monroe
909 Church St., # C
Ann Arbor, MI 48104
Freeware

Alias Assassin
MonkWorks
3404 Waverly Dr.
Birmingham, AL 35209
Freeware available from Zmac

Alias Stylist
MonkWorks
3404 Waverly Dr.
Birmingham, AL 35209
Freeware available from Zmac

AntiFinder
Marcio Luis Teixeira
1601 W. Swallow, #B-9
Fort Collins, CO 80526
Shareware ($3)*

ATF Classic Type
Kingsley/ATF Type Corporation
2559-2 E. Broadway
Tucson, AZ 85716
(800) 289-8973, (602) 325-5884
$165

Basura
Fred Monroe
909 Church St., # C
Ann Arbor, MI 48104
Freeware

Bitstream TrueType Font Packs
Bitstream
215 First St.
Cambridge, MA 02142
(800) 522-3668, (617) 497-6222
$89 each

Calc+
Abbott Systems
62 Mountain Rd.
Pleasantville, NY 10570
(800) 552-9157, (914) 747-4171
$79

CalculatorZ
(Calculator Construction Set) 2.09
Dubl-Click Software
9316 Dearing Ave.
Chatsworth, CA 91311
(818) 700-9525
$99.95

CanOpener 1.1
Abbott Systems
62 Mountain Rd.
Pleasantville, NY 10570
(800) 552-9157, (914) 747-4171
$125

Capture 4.0
Mainstay, Inc.
5311-B Derry Avenue
Agoura Hills, CA 91301
(818) 991-6540
$129.95

CE/IAC 1.0
(included with QuicKeys)
CE Software
1801 Industrial Circle
West Des Moines, IA 50265
(515) 224-1995
$149

Claris Resolve 1.0
Claris Corporation
440 Clyde Ave.
Mountain View, CA 94043
(408) 987-7000
$399

ClickChange 1.05
Dubl-Click Software
9316 Dearing Ave.
Chatsworth, CA 91311
(818) 700-9525
$89.95

Compact Pro 1.31
Cyclos
551 Clipper St.
San Francisco, CA 94114
(415) 821-1448
Shareware ($25)*

Complete Undelete
Microcom, Inc.
3700 Lyckan Parkway, Suite B
Durham, NC 27707
(919) 490-1277
$79.95

CompuServe Information Manager 1.5
CompuServe
5000 Arlington Centre Blvd.
Columbus, OH 43220
(800) 848-8199, (614) 457-8600
$39.95

CompuServe Navigator 3.0.4
CompuServe
5000 Arlington Centre Blvd.
Columbus, OH 43220
(800) 848-8199, (614) 457-8600
$99.95

CrashBarrier
Casady & Greene
22734 Portola Dr.
Salinas, CA 93908
(408) 484-9228
$79.95

Desktop Selection of TrueType Fonts
Linotype-Hell Company
425 Oser Ave.
Hauppage, NY 11788
(800) 633-1900, (516) 434-2000
$185

Desktop TrueType Series
Agfa Compugraphic
90 Industrial Way
Wilmington, MA 01887
(800) 424-8973
starting at $99 each

DiskDoubler 3.7
Salient Software
124 University Avenue, #103
Palo Alto, CA 94301
(415) 321-5375
$79.95

DiskExpress II
ALSoft, Inc.
PO Box 927
Spring, TX 77383
(713) 353-4090
$89.95

DiskTop 4.01
CE Software
1801 Industrial Circle
West Des Moines, IA 50265
(515) 224-1995
$99.95

Dropple Menu
Fred Monroe
909 Church St., # C
Ann Arbor, MI 48104
Freeware

Finder 7 Menus
Insanely Great Software
126 Calvert Ave.
East Edison, NJ 08820
(908) 549-0590
Shareware ($10)*

Fkey Extender 1.0
Ian Hendry
10100 Torre Ave. #177
Cupertino, CA 95014
Freeware*

Fluent Laser Fonts Library
Casady & Greene
22734 Portola Dr.
Salinas, CA 93908
(408) 484-9228
$179.95

Fontek Library TrueType Typefaces
Letraset USA
40 Eisenhower Dr.
Paramus, NJ 07653
(800) 634-3463, (201) 845-6100
$39.95 each

FontMonger 1.0
Ares Software Corp.
561 Pilgrim Dr., Suite D
Foster City, CA 94404
(415) 578-9090
$99.95

Fontographer 3.3
Altsys Corporation
269 W. Renner Rd.
Richardson, TX 75080
(214) 680-2060
$495

FontStudio 2.0
Letraset USA
40 Eisenhower Dr.
Paramus, NJ 07653
(800) 634-3463, (201) 845-6100
$595

FreeGeneva
Bryan Ressler
4660 Persimmon Pl.
San Jose, CA 95129
Freeware*

Frontier 1.0
UserLand Software
490 California Ave.
Palo Alto, CA 94306
(415) 325-5700, (800) 845-1772
$179

Greg's Buttons
Greg Landweber
10 Wallingford Drive
Princeton, NJ 08540
Shareware ($10)

Hand-Off II 2.2.1
Connectix Corporation
125 Constitution Dr.
Menlo Park, CA 94025
(800) 950-5880
$99

Hierarchical Apple Menu (HAM) 1.0
Microseeds Publishing, Inc.
5801 Benjamin Circle Dr., Suite 103
Tampa, FL 33634
(813) 882-8635
$99

HyperCard Development Kit 2.1
Claris Corporation
440 Clyde Ave.
Mountain View, CA 94043
(408) 987-7000
$199

Image Club Typeface Library
Image Club Graphics
1902 11th St. S.E., Suite 5
Calgary, Alberta T2G 3G2, Canada
(800) 661-9410, (403) 262-8008
$25 each

Imprint Display Font Series
Monotype Typography
53 W. Jackson Blvd., Suite 504
Chicago, IL 60604
(800) 666-6897, (312) 855-1440
$29.95 each

In/Out
CE Software
1801 Industrial Circle
West Des Moines, IA 50265
(515) 224-1995
5-user pack—$199.95

InitPicker 2.02
Microseeds Publishing, Inc.
5801 Benjamin Circle Dr., Suite 103
Tampa, FL 33634
(813) 882-8635
$69

JumpStart
Insanely Great Software
126 Calvert Ave.
East Edison, NJ 08820
(908) 549-0590
Shareware ($14.99)

Just Click
Tactic Software Corp.
11925 SW 128th St.
Miami, FL 33186
(800) 344-4818, (305) 378-4110
Freeware

MacProject 2.5
Claris Corporation
440 Clyde Ave.
Mountain View, CA 94043
(408) 987-7000
$499

MacRecorder
Farallon Computing, Inc.
2000 Powell St., Suite 600
Emeryville, CA 94608
(510) 596-9000
$249

MacTools Deluxe 1.2
Central Point Software
15220 NW Greenbrier Parkway, #200
Beaverton, OR 97006
(800) 445-2110, (503) 690-8088
$129

MasterJuggler 1.57
ALSoft, Inc.
PO Box 927
Spring, TX 77383
(713) 353-4090
$49

Maxima 2.0.1
Connectix Corporation
125 Constitution Dr.
Menlo Park, CA 94025
(800) 950-5880
$129

Metamorphosis Pro 2.03
Altsys Corporation
269 W. Renner Rd.
Richardson, TX 75080
(214) 680-2060
$149

Microphone II 4.0
Software Ventures, Inc.
2907 Claremont Avenue
Berkeley, CA 94705
(510) 644-3232
$295

More After Dark
Berkeley Systems
2095 Rose St.
Berkeley, CA 94709
(510) 540-5535
$39.95

Mount Alias
Jeff Miller
20525 Mariani Ave., MS: 81EQ
Cupertino, CA 95014
Freeware*

Multi-Clip 2.1.7
Olduvai Corporation
7520 Red Rd., Suite A
South Miami, FL 33143
(305) 665-4665
$149

Multiple Master Typefaces
Adobe Systems Inc.
1585 Charleston Rd.
Mountain View, CA 94039
(415) 961-4400
Myriad—$370; Minon—$470

Nom de Plume
MonkWorks
3404 Waverly Dr.
Birmingham, AL 35209
Freeware available from Zmac

Norton Utilities for the Macintosh
Symantec Corporation
10201 Torre Avenue
Cupertino, CA 95014
(408) 253-9600
$129

Now Utilities
Now Software
520 SW Harrison, Suite 435
Portland, OR 97201
(503) 274-2800
$129

PacerForum 1.0
Pacer Software
7911 Herschel Ave., Suite 402
La Jolla, CA 92037
(619) 454-0565
$549

PhoneNET Card PC—LocalTalk
Farallon Computing, Inc.
2000 Powell St., Suite 600
Emeryville, CA 94608
(510) 596-9000
$295

PhoneNET Connectors
Farallon Computing, Inc.
2000 Powell St., Suite 600
Emeryville, CA 94608
(510) 596-9000
$59.95, 10-pack $395

PixelFlipper 1.3.3
Chris Sanchez
630 Barr Drive
Ames, IA 50010
(515) 233-6207
Shareware ($10)*

PwrSwitcher
David Lamkins
25 Sutcliffe Ave
Canton, MA 02021
Freeware

Pyro 4.0.1
Fifth Generation Systems
10049 N. Reiger Road
Baton Rouge, LA 70809
(504) 291-7221
$39.95

QuickDEX II 2.3
Casady & Greene
22734 Portola Dr.
Salinas, CA 93908
(408) 484-9228
$60

QuicKeys2 2.1
CE Software
1801 Industrial Circle
West Des Moines, IA 50265
(515) 224-1995
$149

QuickMail 2.5
CE Software
1801 Industrial Circle
West Des Moines, IA 50265
(515) 224-1995
5-user pack—$399

QuickTools
Advanced Software
1095 E. Duane Ave.
Sunnyvale, CA 94086
(408) 733-0745
$79.95

SCSI Probe 3.3
Robert Polic & Mike Puckett
3873 S. Park Place
Auburn, CA 95603
Freeware*

Shortcut 1.5
Aladdin Systems, Inc.
165 Westridge Dr.
Watsonville, CA 95076
(408) 761-6200
$79.95

SmartScrap and the Clipper II
Solutions International
30 Commerce St.
Wiliston, VT 05495
(802) 658-5506
$89.95

SoftAT
Insignia Solutions
526 Clyde Ave.
Mountain View, CA 94043
(800) 848-7677, (415) 694-7600
$499

SoftNode
Insignia Solutions
526 Clyde Ave.
Mountain View, CA 94043
(800) 848-7677, (415) 694-7600
$175

SoundEdit 2.05
Farallon Computing, Inc.
2000 Powell St., Suite 600
Emeryville, CA 94608
(510) 596-9000
$195

StuffIt Deluxe 3.0
Aladdin Systems, Inc.
165 Westridge Dr.
Watsonville, CA 95076
(408) 761-6200
$119.95

StuffIt SpaceMaker 1.0
Aladdin Systems, Inc.
165 Westridge Dr.
Watsonville, CA 95076
(408) 761-6200
$59.95

Suitcase II 1.2.11
Fifth Generation Systems
10049 N. Reiger Road
Baton Rouge, LA 70809
(504) 291-7221
$79

SuperBoomerang
(part of Now Utilities)
Now Software
520 SW Harrison, Suite 435
Portland, OR 97201
(503) 274-2800
$129

SuperClock
Steve Christensen
1514 Mt. Diablo
Milpitas, CA 95035
Freeware*

SuperQuickDEX
Casady & Greene
22734 Portola Dr.
Salinas, CA 93908
(408) 484-9228
$89.95

Switch-A-Roo
(part of ScreenGems)
Microseeds Publishing, Inc.
5801 Benjamin Circle Dr., Suite 103
Tampa, FL 33634
(813) 882-8635
$79

Symantec Utilities for the Macintosh (SUM)
Symantec Corporation
10201 Torre Ave.
Cupertino, CA 95014
(408) 253-9600
$149

System Picker
Kevin Aitken
20990 Valley Green Dr. #635
Cupertino, CA 95014
(408) 974-5899
Freeware*

Tempo II 2.1
Affinity MicroSystems Ltd.
1050 Walnut Street
Boulder, CO 80302
(303) 442-4840
$169.95

Tiles 1.0
CE Software
1801 Industrial Circle
West Des Moines, IA 50265
(515) 224-1995
$99.95

Timbuktu 4.01
Farallon Computing, Inc.
2000 Powell St., Suite 600
Emeryville, CA 94608
(510) 596-9000
$195, 10-pack $995

Traffic Controller Personal 1.0
Tactic Software Corp.
11925 SW 128th St.
Miami, FL 33186
(800) 344-4818, (305) 378-4110
$129

TrashMan 2.11
Dan Walkowski
212 E. Gregory #102
Champaign, IL 61820
Freeware

TrueType Starter Set
Casady & Greene
22734 Portola Dr.
Salinas, CA 93908
(408) 484-9228
$99.95

Universal SoftPC
Insignia Solutions
526 Clyde Ave.
Mountain View, CA 94043
(800) 848-7677, (415) 694-7600
$325

VirusBlockade II 2.0
Shulman Software Co.
364-$1/2$ Patterson Drive, Suite 300
Morgantown, WV 26505
(304) 598-2090
Shareware ($30)

VirusDetective 5.0
Shulman Software Co.
364-$1/2$ Patterson Drive, Suite 300
Morgantown, WV 26505
(304) 598-2090
Shareware ($40)*

Wallpaper
Thought I Could
107 University Place, Suite 4D
New York, NY 10003
(212) 673-9724
$59.99

White Knight 11.12
FreeSoft Company
105 McKinley Rd.
Beaver Falls, PA 15010
(412) 846-2700
$139

INDEX

This index contains certain typographical conventions to assist you in finding information. **Boldface** page numbers are references to definitions, commands, control panels, dialog boxes, and major discussions of topics. *Italics* indicate page numbers that reference figures.

A

B

background applications, **86**

background processing
    advantages, 105
    application compatibility, 340
    cautions, 109–110
    printing, 106–109, 184
    types of tasks for, 106–109

backups, importance of, 29

Balloon Help, **11–12**, 340

balloons, hiding or showing, 51

Basura utility, 71, 467

Batista, Ricardo, Extensions Manager,
    242, *243*

battery
    conserving, 225–226
    and parameter RAM (PRAM), 282–284

Battery desk accessory, *180*, 180–181

"The Battery desk accessory runs only on
    battery-powered Macintosh systems"
    message, *180*, 180

BBS (bulletin board services), 23. *See also*
    CompuServe

beeps. *See* sounds

Before You Install disk, 27–28

Berkeley Systems, After Dark, 233–234,
    234, 466, 471

Bernoulli removable hard drives, 29

Bézier curves, *127*, 127

Bitstream, 467

blessing (of System Folders), 31

blinking menus, 209

Bock, Jeff, Switch program, 91

bomb messages, **99**

Bookman font, 117, *118*

Bozo bit, 310

Brightness control panel, **197–198**, *198*

brightness of color, **289**, 290

Brown, Donald, FinderHack, 265

buffers, 326

built-in memory, 332

bulletin board services (BBS), 23

burn-in, **233**

buttons, described, *10*, 11

bytes, 240

C

caching, 326

Calc+ (Abbott Systems), 182, *183*, 467

Calculator Construction Set, CalculatorZ,
    467

Calculator desk accessory, *181*, 181–182

CalculatorZ (Calculator Construction
    Set), 467

Cancel (⌘-Period) command, **343**

Cancel button, *10*, 11

canceling, publisher-edition links, 352

CanOpener (Abbott Systems), 193, *194*,
    467

Canvas, 278

Capture (Mainstay), 232–233, 238, 467

cartridges
    erasing/formatting, 51
    removable, 329, 400

Casady & Greene
    CrashBarrier, 468
    Fluent Laser Fonts Library, 469
    QuickDEX II, 194–196, *195*, 472
    Super QuickDEX, 196, 473
    TrueType Starter Set, 474

cdevs (Control Panel devices), 20, 27, 29,
    164, 167

CE/IAC utility, 376, 467

Central Point Software, MacTools Deluxe,
    70, 259, 470

cents symbol (¢), 185

CE Software. *See also* QuicKeys macro
    utility
    DiskTop, *96*, 96, 193–194, *195*, 305,
        468, 472
    In/Out, 470
    QuickMail, 379, 472

E

N

SYBEX

FREE BROCHURE!

Complete this form today, and we'll send you a full-color brochure of Sybex bestsellers.

Please supply the name of the Sybex book purchased.

_____

How would you rate it?

_____ Excellent   _____ Very Good   _____ Average   _____ Poor

Why did you select this particular book?

_____ Recommended to me by a friend

_____ Recommended to me by store personnel

_____ Saw an advertisement in _____

_____ Author's reputation

_____ Saw in Sybex catalog

_____ Required textbook

_____ Sybex reputation

_____ Read book review in _____

_____ In-store display

_____ Other _____

Where did you buy it?

_____ Bookstore

_____ Computer Store or Software Store

_____ Catalog (name: _____)

_____ Direct from Sybex

_____ Other: _____

Did you buy this book with your personal funds?

_____ Yes   _____ No

About how many computer books do you buy each year?

_____ 1-3   _____ 3-5   _____ 5-7   _____ 7-9   _____ 10+

About how many Sybex books do you own?

_____ 1-3   _____ 3-5   _____ 5-7   _____ 7-9   _____ 10+

Please indicate your level of experience with the software covered in this book:

_____ Beginner   _____ Intermediate   _____ Advanced

Which types of software packages do you use regularly?

_____ Accounting   _____ Databases   _____ Networks

_____ Amiga   _____ Desktop Publishing   _____ Operating Systems

_____ Apple/Mac   _____ File Utilities   _____ Spreadsheets

_____ CAD   _____ Money Management   _____ Word Processing

_____ Communications   _____ Languages   _____ Other _____
                                                                          (please specify)

Which of the following best describes your job title?

_____ Administrative/Secretarial   _____ President/CEO

_____ Director   _____ Manager/Supervisor

_____ Engineer/Technician   _____ Other _____
                                                    (please specify)

Comments on the weaknesses/strengths of this book: _____

_____

_____

_____

_____

Name _____

Street _____

City/State/Zip _____

Phone _____

PLEASE FOLD, SEAL, AND MAIL TO SYBEX

SYBEX INC.
Department M
2021 CHALLENGER DR.
ALAMEDA, CALIFORNIA USA
94501

SYBEX

SEAL

About the Author

Deke McClelland is a Macintosh expert with over 20 titles to his credit, including the bestselling *Encyclopedia Macintosh*, from SYBEX. He is a regular contributor to MacWorld, and his articles have also appeared in *PC World*, *Publish*, and *Before & After*.

(Continued from inside front cover)

System 7 Quick Reference Table

USING SOFTWARE

Open selected file or application icon	⌘-O or ⌘-↓
Open selected icon and close current folder	⌘-Option-O or ⌘-Option-↓
Open a file with a specific application	drag file icon onto application icon
Switch to background application	click background item
Switch to background and hide current application	Option-click background item
Display publisher options dialog box	double-click publisher element
Display subscriber options dialog box	double-click subscriber element
Open original subscriber document	Option-double-click subscriber
Print current document	⌘-P
Quit current application	⌘-Q
Force quit current application	⌘-Option-Escape

USING SYSTEM UTILITIES

Chooser, select different driver icon	↓, →, ↑, or ←
Close View, turn on/off	⌘-Option-O
Close View, magnify outlined area	⌘-Option-X
Easy Access, turn on mouse keys	⌘-Shift-Clear
Easy Access, click with mouse keys	5 on keypad
Easy Access, move cursor	1, 4, 7, 8, 9, 6, 3, or 2 on keypad